Springer Proceedings in Business and Economics

Springer Proceedings in Business and Economics brings the most current research presented at conferences and workshops to a global readership. The series features volumes (in electronic and print formats) of selected contributions from conferences in all areas of economics, business, management, and finance. In addition to an overall evaluation by the publisher of the topical interest, scientific quality, and timeliness of each volume, each contribution is refereed to standards comparable to those of leading journals, resulting in authoritative contributions to the respective fields. Springer's production and distribution infrastructure ensures rapid publication and wide circulation of the latest developments in the most compelling and promising areas of research today.

The editorial development of volumes may be managed using Springer Nature's innovative EquinOCS, a proven online conference proceedings submission, management and review system. This system is designed to ensure an efficient timeline for your publication, making Springer Proceedings in Business and Economics the premier series to publish your workshop or conference volume.

This book series is indexed in SCOPUS.

Richard C. Geibel · Shalva Machavariani
Editors

Digital Management to Shape the Future

Proceedings of the 3rd International Scientific-Practical Conference (ISPC 2023)

Springer

Editors
Richard C. Geibel
IU International University
and E-Commerce Institute
Cologne, Germany

Shalva Machavariani
East European University
Tbilisi, Georgia

ISSN 2198-7246 ISSN 2198-7254 (electronic)
Springer Proceedings in Business and Economics
ISBN 978-3-031-66519-6 ISBN 978-3-031-66517-2 (eBook)
https://doi.org/10.1007/978-3-031-66517-2

This Springer imprint is published by the registered company Springer Nature Switzerland AG
The registered company address is: Gewerbestrasse 11, 6330 Cham, Switzerland

Preface

Three annual international conferences with a focus on digital management have already taken place. The latest "**International Scientific Practical Conference (ISPC) 2023**" focused on the topic of "**Digital Management to Shape the Future**" and took place on *24 and 25 November 2023* as a hybrid event in Tbilisi, Georgia. The East European University (EEU) organized together with the E-Commerce Institute (ECI) a very successful conference with great effort, at which 27 presentations were given in three parallel streams by 41 authors from the four continents of Africa, America, Asia, and Europe.

Our thanks go to the EEU organization team. These include, in particular, Teona Shugliashvili, who is currently doing her doctorate at LMU in Munich, and Tatia Gherkenashvili, who works as a coordinator at the EEU.

We are delighted that, after EEU and ECI, the American **Adelphi University** in Garden City, New York, USA, has become another cooperation partner of the ISPC.

The upcoming **ISPC 2024** will focus on the current topic of "**Digital Management and Artificial Intelligence**". It will take place on *10 and 11 October 2024* in Cologne, Germany, and will be hosted by **IU International University** at its beautiful premises in the Gerling Quarter (*ispc2024.com*). We are particularly pleased that IU, Germany's largest university with more than 130.000 students, has also become a partner university of the ISPC conference series.

We are looking forward to a lively participation at the **4th ISPC** and a further growth of the conference series with an increasing internationalization.

Richard C. Geibel
Professor at IU International University
Professor h.c. at East European University
Managing Director at E-Commerce Institute
Cologne, Germany

Shalva Machavariani
Vice-Rector for Scientific Affairs
East European University
Tbilisi, Georgia

MaryAnne M. Hyland
Dean Robert B. Willumstad School of Business
Adelphi University
Garden City, NY, USA

Contents

Study of Innovative Approach for Implementing Personnel-Fit Organizational Culture at Universities (Case of Georgia) and the Role of Digitalization

Tatia Gherkenashvili and Shalva Machavariani

Abstract In the current rapidly changing era the management of organizations including universities must intensively strive to find innovative ways for professional development of their employees (as organizations' key resource) to reach their potential. On the basis of the researches conducted in previous years one of the main path fort the personnel development is considered to be the implementation of an appropriate environment (Organizational Culture) at organizations in which person is best fitted. According to the Global Competitiveness Report, Georgia has an inappropriate indicators in the pillars such as: training of personnel with higher education corresponding to modern requirements, the country's innovative capabilities, the outflow of qualified personnel from organizations, technologies, research and development, and other strategic directions. One of the basic reasons of which is considered the imperfect organizational culture at universities, as on the basis of studies conducted in the world's leading universities there has always been a close linkage with the organizational culture as a factor determining the organizational performance. The purpose of this study is to develop an innovative approach for the establishment of an acceptable organizational environment at higher educational institutions of Georgia, considering the job specifications of University employees. For bringing the study purpose into the light the paper analyses the Quantitative (Google Form electronic Self-Assessment questionnaire) and Qualitative researches (in-depth Structured interview) carried out (in 2021–2023) with the local (Georgian) as well as International Universities (Czech Republic) personnel (Academic &Administrative) focused on revealing dominant Organizational culture OC (derived from CVF);

T. Gherkenashvili (✉)
East European University, Tbilisi, Georgia
e-mail: t.gherkenashvili@eeu.edu.ge

S. Machavariani
East European University, Tbilisi, Georgia
e-mail: s.machavariani@eeu.edu.ge

T. Gherkenashvili
East European University, I. Enukidze Str. 6, 0159 Tbilisi, Georgia

R. C. Geibel and S. Machavariani (eds.), *Digital Management to Shape the Future*,
Springer Proceedings in Business and Economics,
https://doi.org/10.1007/978-3-031-66517-2_1

also determining the attitude of university executives on creative environment (in particular, what kind of environment should exist for the university employees to increase their productivity) and finding out the OC indicators necessary to implement personnel oriented environment which serves as a guarantee of enhancing their potential that will be gradually reflected in the University performance. Paper also indicates the role of digitalization in the research process.

Keywords University Personnel-fit Organizational culture · Innovative approach · Google form electronic self-assessment questionnaire · In-depth structured interview

1 Introduction

The full use of the creative potential of the university staff is a prerequisite for the development of the higher education system, as it contributes to the training of qualified personnel, the expansion of innovative capabilities of universities, the increase in the effectiveness of scientific and research activities, the awareness raising and competitiveness of universities, the formation of high intellectual potential in society, which is ultimately important for the progress of the country.

In general, one of the effective means of using human resources with the maximum efficiency is through the proper formation of the organizational environment, which does not require spending such finances which may be problematic for the country. It is for this reason that the study of the organizational culture of universities and the development of recommendations for the formation of an effective organizational environment is a very relevant issue.

According to the Global Competitiveness Report of the World Economic Forum, significant attention should be paid in Georgia to: Innovation capability, Ease of finding skilled employees, Research Institutions prominence, Growth of innovative companies, Patent applications and other related factors.

It is worth noting that in this regard, the countries (USA, United Kingdom, Singapore, Japan, Germany, Netherlands, Switzerland, Denmark, France) where the universities are in leading positions in the world are leading. According to the conducted studies, one of the determining factors of the performance of their universities is the organizational culture (Coman & Bonciu, 2016).

At the university level, culture can be defined as the University stakeholders' values and beliefs, based on tradition and communicated verbally and nonverbally (Bartell, 2003; Deal & Kennedy, 1982). Values and beliefs are thought to greatly influence decision-making processes at universities (Bartell, 2003; Tierney, 1988) and shape individual and organizational behaviors.

The study of the organizational culture has risen in importance in the analysis of the universities because it is interested in the adaptation of its culture to the values and the behaviour of its members, for maintaining healthy state of mind and foster permanent improvement (Folch & Ion, 2009).

University culture basically comes from three sources; the beliefs, values, and assumptions of founders of organizations and the learning experiences of group members as their organizations evolve. Values, beliefs and assumptions can be thought greatly influence decision making processes at universities and shape individuals and organizational behaviors. There are many different ways how university culture can be assessed (Antić & Cerić, 2008). For example, Sporn (1996) differentiates two types of university organizational cultures: strong and weak. Strong university culture is characterized by shared values, strong norms of behavior and willingness of faculty to obey these norms. In contrast, weak culture is characterized by disagreement about main values, absence of norms and violation of written and unwritten norms of behavior at university (Antić & Cerić, 2008). A strong culture is one that not only tolerates debate and discussion of diverse and alternative views and strategies but rather actively encourages them for the sake of improvement of the quality of decision making and problem solutions (Bartell, 2003). According to Schein (1984), the strength or amount of culture can be defined in terms of the homogeneity and stability of group membership and the length and intensity of shared experience of the group. If a stable group has had a long, varied, intense history it will have a strong and highly differentiated culture. By the same idea, if a group has had a constantly shifting membership or has been together only for a short time and has not faced any difficult issues, it will, by definition, have a weak culture. By this definition, one could understand, a strong culture and a congruent culture is more effective than a weak and an incongruent or disconnected culture that is to say a strong culture is associated with organizational excellence (Cameron & Ettington, 1988).

In 1938, a universal list of the definition of culture was published, which consisted of 79 characteristics and 637 sub-characteristics of culture (Tharp, 2010). More than a hundred definitions of the term were subsequently created (Al Suwaidi, 2008). Today, Out of them the most commonly used one is: "Culture can be defined as a set of beliefs and behaviors that characterize a wide range of characteristics in an organization" (Hofstede et al., 1990). Organizational culture has never been more important to businesses and individuals than it is today. According to Peter Drucker: "Culture eats strategy for lunch". No strategy of the organization can be successful unless the culture necessary for its development is shared in the organization.

The purpose of the research presented in this paper is to develop an innovative approach to selecting the appropriate organizational environment for the university.

2 Importance of Innovation and Creativity and Their Essence

An organization is formed in order to make profit, for which it's required to focus on innovation. According to the data of OECD and Eurostat (2018) "overcoming current and future environmental, economic, and social challenges requires innovative ideas and innovative approaches, therefore policymakers consider innovation as an integrated and necessary part of policy."

Based on all of the above mentioned, world-class universities of the twenty-first century must necessarily be focused on innovation, since it is innovation that distinguishes a successful university from other universities in the world today.

Accordingly, in order to join the world's leading universities' ranking to maintain competitiveness and subsequent positioning under the conditions of globalization, huge rate of increasing idea and knowledge it is crucial to establish an environment that will boost innovativeness.

Definitions on innovation in the literature are different. Some of them is quite general, and others define it as idea implementation for creating product or service.

According to West and Farr (1990), Innovation is equated with novelty, which is a prerequisite for change.

Based on some definitions, creativity focuses on the thought process and intellectual activity to generate new solutions to problem solving. Others point out that "it is an individual's characteristic and intellectual abilities, directed to the creation of new products with different characteristics" (Arad et al., 1997).

Woodman et al. (1993) define it as "the procedure or process of creating a new value, needed product, service or idea by individuals working together in a complex social system" (p. 293).

According to Martins and Terblanche (2003) "Creativity, innovation and inventiveness are the keys to the success of today's knowledge-oriented organization". Plsek (1997, in Pesut, 2013) names 5 factors, emphasizing the importance of creativity and innovativeness at the organization:

1. Organization's long-term financial productivity is related to innovation;
2. customers demand innovation;
3. competitors become better at taking into account the experience of past innovations;
4. New technologies encourage innovation.

On the basis of Schein—"In order to be successful and adaptable to the environment, businesses must create a culture that fosters creativity and innovation" (Schein, 2004).

Anderson and Markides (2006) state that In order to gain an advantage among competitors, it is necessary to develop different strategies, such as 'thinking outside the box', but the difficulty is that creating a new, creative and different business model, service or product that goes beyond the framework and breaks the rules of the game is a difficult process to achieve.

According to the 4th Ed. of OSLO Manual—"*The Measurement of Scientific, Technological and Innovative Activities*": The term 'innovation' may refer to both the activity and its outcome. The general definition of innovation is as follows: "Innovation is a new or improved product or process that is significantly different from the organization's existing products and processes."

Due to the importance of innovation for the success of organization, many studies have been conducted for determining its key indicators (Crossan & Apaydin, 2010). Generally they could be grouped as individual, organizational, environmental levels. At the organizational level, the existing literature addresses size, organizational design, strategy, leadership, human resource practices, financial support, and organizational culture (Damanpour, 1987, 1991; Mumford, 2000).

Empirical research has confirmed the existence of a significant relationship between culture and innovation (Büschgens et al., 2013; Chang & Lee, 2007; Lau & Ngo, 2004; Lin et al., 2013; Miron et al., 2004; Naranjo-Valencia et al., 2012). What is not clear in the literature is what kind of culture enhances or inhibits innovation.

Four cultural values (creativity, autonomy, risk-taking and teamwork) are revealed that promote innovation (Naranjo-Valencia, 2010).

Innovation is based on coming up with new and creative ideas (Mumford, 2000). It is achieved through a combination of creativity and implementation of such ideas. Therefore, entrepreneurship requires creative people to support such processes, not only those who develop ideas, but also those who are involved in the processes of selecting, evaluating and implementing ideas (Jamrog et al., 2006; McLean, 2005). Therefore, an innovative culture on the one hand should not only encourage employees to think creatively and experiment (Shattow, 1996), but also must support in looking for new ways for problem solving and fulfill own ideas in spite of the fact that value of the results might not be clear (Miron et al., 2004).

Freedom that manifests itself in autonomy, power, and decision-making (Isaksen & Ekvall, 2010; Martin, 2002) is one of the most common elements associated with innovative culture. A free and autonomous environment increases the intrinsic motivation of employees, which is considered a key factor contributing to organizational creativity. (Amabile, 1998; McLean, 2005).

3 Competing Values Framework (CVF) and Research Methodology

In 1983, Kim Cameron and Rohrbaugh (Quinn & Rohrbaugh, 1983) studied the concept of organizational effectiveness and created a framework of competing values (see Fig. 1), which divided organizational culture into four categories: clan, adhocratic, market, and hierarchical (Davenport, 2015).

Kim Cameron and Robert Quinn in 2006 explained four types of culture as follows: Clan culture can be associated with small family businesses where loyalty to each

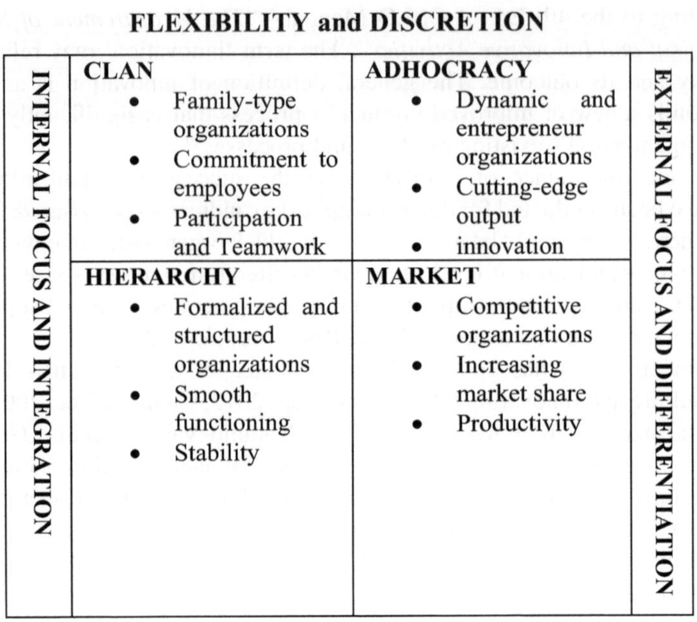

Fig. 1 Competing Values Framework (CVF) (*Source* Own graphic based on: Cameron & Quinn, 1999)

other is important. An adhocratic culture, which can be associated with small startups, is a dynamic, creative and entrepreneurial culture that emphasizes the value of creative innovation and encourages employees to take risks. A market culture, as most businesses competing to attract and satisfy customers may have, emphasizes productivity and is results-oriented. The hierarchical culture more 'bureaucratic' public sector institutions may have is stable and controlled by rules and policies.

The Competing Values Framework determines two major dimensions and four main clusters. The first dimension differentiates between organizational focus; internal versus external, while the second one indicates the preference about structure; stability and control versus flexibility and discretion. These two dimensions form four quadrants, each representing a different set of organizational culture indicators. Each quadrant is given a distinguishing label that denotes its most notable cultural characteristic; clan, adhocracy, market and hierarchy cultures (Cameron & Quinn, 1999).

The object of the conducted research is the administrative and academic personnel of higher educational institutions in Georgia and for comparison, studies have been conducted in the Czech Republic, and the subject of the research is to determine the personnel-fit types of organizational culture.

Empirical research was conducted in Georgia (Tbilisi State University, Technical University of Georgia, Institute of Public Affairs of Georgia, East European University, Black Sea International University, Ilia State University, Batumi Shota Rustaveli

State University, Kutaisi State University, as well as the University of Finance and Administration and the Masaryk Institute of Advanced Studies at Czech Technical University in Prague) in academic and administrative staff at existing private and State Universities with **combined quantitative and qualitative research methods**. In particular, the "questionnaire" design (stemmed from Organizational Culture Assessment Inventory-OCAI (Cameron & Quinn, 1999).was used in the quantitative research (an electronic Google Form self-assessment questionnaire for revealing the dominant organizational culture, which was sent to the respondents by e-mail and which included ranked questions for research on demographic characteristics and organizational culture.

The questionnaire consisted of 16 questions, from which the respondents were asked on a five-point Likert scale. An acceptable answer for them should be marked on the scale, of which 1 = completely disagree; 2 = disagree; 3 = agree more or less; 4 = agree; 5 = completely agree, and the qualitative research was conducted using the in-depth structured face-to-face interview method.

4 Results of Conducted Studies

Quantitative Data Statistical Analyses. Data obtained from quantitative research were processed by calculating the sum of variables (Sum), and counting the number of variable values (Count) or other. Using Ms Excel. We got a pivot table that shows the number of women and men, as well as their total, in each type of position (Academic or Administrative personnel) and Affiliation (Private or State University) and their inclination to specific organizational culture type.

Quantitative Research Results. The study sample consisted of 211 subjects. Each subject was an academic and administrative personnel of above mentioned Georgian (185 subjects) and for comparison, studies have been conducted in the Czech Republic (26 subjects) Private and State Universities.

Firstly the self-assessment questionnaire adapted and translated into Georgian language was sent to randomly selected Georgian Universities' personnel via e-mail. Afterwards an English language quelstionnaire was sent to the Visegrad Fund Project coordinator for the its dissemination in the Czech Republic Public and Private Universities' personnel.

Georgian Universities:

Answers to Demographic questions

- Totally 185 respondents from Georgian universities filled out the questionnaire, out of which 73 (39.5%) respondents were from private universities, and 112 (60.5%) from State universities;
- 104 (56.2%) of the respondents are academic personnel, and 81 (43.8%) are administrative personnel.

- In terms of gender distribution, 123 (66.5%) women and 62 (33.5%) men participated in the study.

Answers to reveal dominant organizational culture (see Table 1)

- Private Universities incline to Market Culture; State Universities incline to Adhocratic Culture.
- Private Universities' Academic personnel prefer Market and adhocratic cultures and administrative personnel prefer Market and Clan culture.
- State Universities' academic personnel prefer Clan and Adhocratic Cultures and administrative personnel prefer Hierarchy and Clan Cultures.

Czech Republic Universities

Answers to Demographic questions

- Totally 26 respondents from Czech Republic universities filled out the questionnaire, out of which 13 (50%) respondents were representatives of private universities, and 13 (50%) from State universities.
- 20 (76.9%) of the respondents were academic personnel, and 6 (23.1%) are administrative personnel.
- In terms of gender distribution, 16 (61.5%) women and 10 (38.5%) men participated in the study.

Answers to reveal dominant organizational culture (see Table 2)

- Private Universities' Academic personnel prefer Market and Adhocratic Cultures and Administrative personnel prefer Hierarchy and Market cultures.
- State Universities Academic personnel prefer market and Adhocratic cultures and Administrative personnel prefer Hierarchy and Market culture.

According to the data obtained by the conducted studies, the recommended subcultures for the Georgian Public and Private Universities will definitely ensure the work

Table 1 Dominant organizational culture at Georgian universities

	Hierarchy	Market	Clan	Adhocracy
Total sum	41	53	39	52
Private universities	10	28	18	17
Public universities	31	25	21	35

Table 2 Dominant organizational culture at Czech Republic universities

	Hierarchy	Market	Clan	Adhocracy
Total sum	12	6	3	5
Private universities	4	4	2	3
Public universities	8	2	1	2

efficiency of university employers. While comparison same data with Czech Republic Universities 50% of coincidence has revealed.

4.1 Qualitative Research Results and Its Analyses (Case of Georgia)

Qualitative research (in-depth structured interview) was conducted with an executives of higher educational institutions in Georgia.

Executives of Tbilisi State University (TSU), GeorgianTechnical University (GTU), Georgian Institute of Public Affairs (GIPA) and East European University (EEU) were interviewed Out of them were: Rector—1, Vce-rector—4, Dean—3, Head of scientific department—3, Academic personnel—5. Totally 16 interviews were conducted.

Based on the interview results:

- 100% of respondents believe that it is necessary to create an acceptable organizational environment for better use of human resources in higher educational institutions of the country;
- 69% of respondents believe that the issue of creating an acceptable organizational environment for the better use of human resources in the country's higher educational institutions is being given some attention, 25% think that no attention is being paid and 6% believe that this issue is being completely resolved;
- To the question, "What is the cause of the situation?" 39% of the respondents name financial opportunities, 31%—the existing practice, and the smallest 4%—another reason;
- 88% of the respondents give a positive answer, and 12% give a negative answer to the question, "Does different groups of employees in universities, depending on the nature of their work, need to work in a matching organizational environment?";
- To the next question, "Do the administrative and academic staff of the university have qualitatively different activities?" 94% answer that they do, and 6% believe that they do not;
- On the next question, "Does the administrative staff of the university need strictly written rules and procedures?" 94% of the respondents believe that it is necessary, while 6% think that it is not;
- And to the question, do the administrative staff carry out mainly creative works?" 94% of the respondents answered that they do not, and 6% gave a positive answer;
- 69% of respondents believe that the academic staff of the university does not need strictly written rules and procedures, while 31% think that the opposite is necessary;
- 100% of the respondents give a negative answer to the next question, "Does the academic staff perform mostly routine work?";
- To the next question, "Does the academic staff perform mainly creative work?" 87.5% believe that they do, and 12.5% give a negative answer;

- To the question, "How should the working environment for administrative staff be introduced?" 100% of the respondents' answer: "In accordance with the rules and requirements written by the statute";
- To the question, "How should the work environment for academic staff be introduced?" 64% of the respondents answered that the specifics of the service and the flexible conditions needed for group work should be taken into account. And according to 36%, the specifics of the service and the flexible conditions necessary for individual work are important;
- To the question, "What kind of obstacles have to be overcome in order to create a proper working environment for administrative staff?" 70% of the respondents mention financial barriers, and 30% indicate organizational barriers;
- To the question, "What kind of obstacles can be overcome in order to establish a proper working environment for the academic staff?" "47% of the respondents answered that the financial barrier; In the opinion of 31%, it is important to create a creative environment, and in the opinion of 22%, the selection of staff on professional grounds should be taken into account;
- In response to the question, "Should the organizational culture in the form of subcultures characteristic of an acceptable environment for employees be written in the development strategy of the university?" 56% of the respondents give a positive answer, and 44% give a negative answer;
- The absolute majority of the respondents—100% agree that it is very important to select the type of organizational culture for successful research activities;
- To the next question, "besides the financial factor, what should be paid special attention to for a successful scientific activity?" 52% of the respondents answer academic freedom, 27%—creative environment and 21%—appropriate management style.

Interviewed experts jointly indicated that Universities require:

- relevant organizational environment;
- establishing subcultures at the University;
- different organizational environment for academic and administrative personnel due to the fact that Academic staff perform creative work and administrative staff technical one;
- Creating a different organizational environment for research.

5 Conclusion and Recommendations

As a result of studying the scientific literature published in various countries and acquainting with the experience of the world's leading universities, we can conclude:

- Universities need to accurately define both the university culture and the subcultures of academic and administrative subdivisions;
- The effectiveness of academic and administrative staff activities and achieving synergy largely depends on the selected subcultures.

According to the results of the quantitative and qualitative studies conducted in the state and private universities of Georgia:

- State Universities' academic personnel prefer Clan and Adhocratic Cultures and administrative personnel prefer Hierarchy and Clan Cultures;
- Private Universities' Academic personnel prefer Market and adhocratic cultures and Administrative personnel prefer Market and Clan culture.

Suggesting two subcultures to the academic and administrative personnel is justified. As its possible to distribute personnel in accordance with the specification of their activities. It's also possible to use only one of the abovementioned subcultures. In this case its recommended to employ personnel considering not only their education and qualification but also their preference to the specific subculture.

Since the modern organization is considered to be quasi-organic formation this topic should be discussed in holistic way, which means that in order to boost Georgian Universities effectiveness firstly, higher education system of the country where the universities operate must be at the relevant level, meaning that all principles and prerequisites (see Fig. 2) of higher education innovative development must be more or less satisfied.

The next phase is the university executives' readiness to take actions and build innovative environment for which on the basis of conducted research and discussed content analyses the followings are needed:

To elaborate relevant strategy, structure, management fitted to university academic and administrative personnel, supportive mechanisms (rewards and recognition, time, information technologies and creative employees); financial support, open communication, innovative organizational environment and etc. It would be highly recommended to conduct study with the university students and reveal their organizational culture preference.

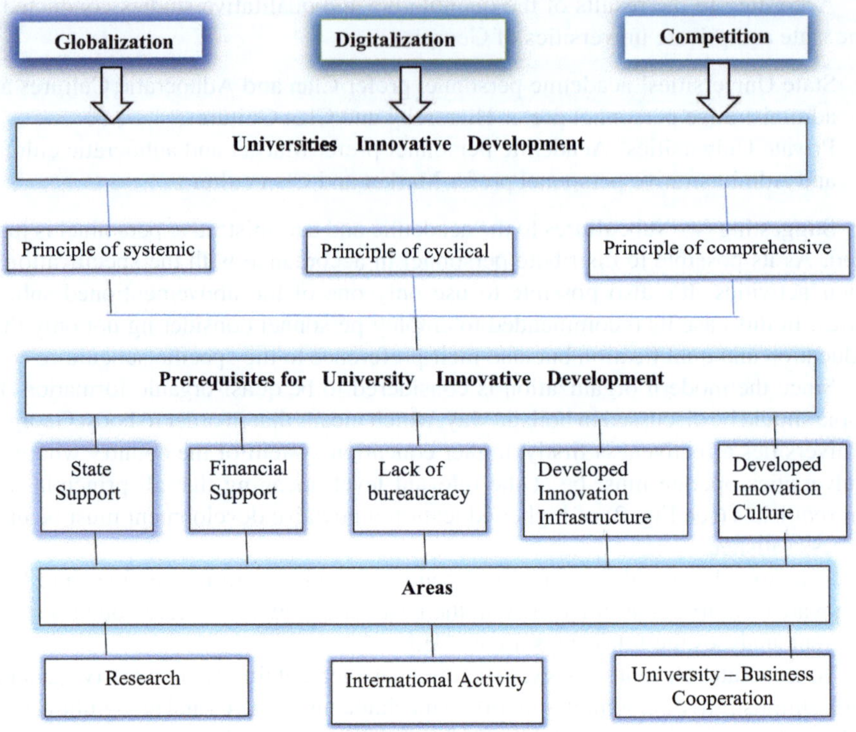

Fig. 2 Principles and prerequisites of higher education innovative development (*Source* Shaposhnykov et al., 2022)

References

Al Suwaidi, M. (2008). *When an Arab executive says "YES": Identifying different collectivistic values that influence the Arabian decision making process*. University of Pennsylvania Scholarly Common. http://repository.upenn.edu/cgi/viewcontent.cgi?article=1018&context=od_theses_msod

Amabile, T. (1998). How to kill creativity. *Harvard Business Review, 76*(5), 76–87.

Anderson, J., & Markides, C. (2006). Creativity is not enough: ICT enabled strategic innovation. *European Journal of Innovation Management, 9*(2), 129–148.

Antić, M., & Cerić, A. (2008). Organizational culture of faculty of civil engineering, University of Zagreb. In *8th International Conference: Organization, Technology and Management in Construction*.

Arad, S., Hanson, M. A., & Schneider, R. J. (1997). A framework for the study of relationships between organizational characteristics and organizational innovation. *The Journal of Creative Behavior, 31*(1), 42–58.

Bartell, M. (2003). Internationalization of universities: A university culture-based framework. *Higher Education, 45*, 43–70.

Büschgens, T., Bausch, A., & Balkin, D. (2013). Organizational culture and innovation: A meta-analytic review. *Journal of Product Innovation Management, 30*(4), 1–19. https://doi.org/10.1111/jpim.12021
Cameron, K. S., & Ettington, D. R. (1988). *The conceptual foundation of organizational culture.* University of Michigan.
Cameron, K. S., & Quinn, R. E. (1999). *Diagnosing and changing organizational culture based on the Competing Values Framework.* Addison-Wesley Publishing Company, Inc.
Chang, S.-C., & Lee, M.-S. (2007). The effects of organizational culture and knowledge management mechanisms on organizational innovation: An empirical study in Taiwan. *The Business Review, 7*(1), 295–301.
Coman, A., & Bonciu, C. (2016). Organizational culture in higher education: Learning from the best. *European Journal of Social Sciences Education and Research, 3*(1), 135–145. https://doi.org/10.26417/ejser.v6i1.p135-145
Crossan, M., & Apaydin, M. (2010). A multi-dimensional framework of organizational innovation: A systematic review of the literature. *Journal of Management Studies, 47*(6), 1154–1191. https://doi.org/10.1111/j.1467-6486.2009.00880.x
Damanpour, F. (1987). The adoption of technological, administrative, and ancillary innovations: Impact of organizational factors. *Journal of Management, 13*, 675–688.
Damanpour, F. (1991). Organizational innovation: A meta-analysis of effects of determinants and moderators. *Academy of Management Journal, 34*, 555–590.
Davenport, T. O. (2015). How HR plays its role in leadership development. *Strategic HR Review, 14*, 89–93. https://doi.org/10.1108/SHR-04-2015-0033
Deal, T.E., & Kennedy, A.A. (1982) *Corporate Cultures*: The rites and rituals of corporate life.
Folch, M. T., & Ion, G. (2009). Analysing the organizational culture of universities: Two models. *Higher Education in Europe, 34*(1), 143–154.
Hofstede, G., Neuijen, B., Ohayv, D. D., & Sanders, G. (1990). Measuring organizational culture: A qualitative and quantitative study across twenty cases. *Administrative Science Quarterly, 35*(2), 286–316.
Isaksen, S., & Ekvall, G. (2010). Managing for innovation: The two faces of tension in creative climates. *Creativity and Innovation Management, 19*(2), 73–88. https://doi.org/10.1111/j.1467-8691.2010.00558.x
Jamrog, J., Vickers, M., & Bear, D. (2006). Building and sustaining a culture that supports innovation. *Human Resource Planning, 29*(3), 9–19.
Lau, C.-M., & Ngo, H.-Y. (2004). The HR system, organizational culture, and product innovation. *International Business Review, 13*(6), 685–703.
Lin, H.-E., McDonough, E., Lin, S.-J., & Lin, C. (2013). Managing the exploitation/exploration paradox: The role of a learning capability and innovation ambidexterity. *Journal of Product Innovation Management, 30*(2), 262–278. https://doi.org/10.1111/j.1540-5885.2012.00998.x
Martin, J. (2002). *Organizational culture: Mapping the terrain.* Sage.
Martins, E. C., & Terblanche, F. (2003). Building organizational culture that stipulates creativity and innovation. *European Journal of Innovation Management, 6*(1), 64–74.
McLean, L. D. (2005). Organizational culture's influence on creativity and innovation: A review of the literature and implications for human resource development. *Advances in Developing Human Resources, 7*(2), 226–246.
Miron, E., Erez, M., & Naveh, E. (2004). Do personal characteristics and cultural values that promote innovation, quality, and efficiency compete or complement each other? *Journal of Organizational Behavior, 25*, 175–199.
Mumford, M. (2000). Managing creative people: Strategies and tactics for innovation. *Human Resource Management Review, 10*(3), 313–351.
Naranjo-Valencia, J. (2010). La cultura organizacional como determinante de la innovaci6n de producto (Un estudio empírico (Tesis doctoral inédita)). Universidad de Murcia.

Naranjo-Valencia, J., Jimènez-Jimènez, D., & Sanz-Valle, R. (2012). Es la cultura organizativa un determinante de la innovación en la empresa?. *Cuadernos de Economía y Dirección de la Empresa, 15*, 63–72.
OECD and Eurostat. (2018). *The measurement of scientific, technological and innovation activities Oslo manual 2018 guidelines for collecting, reporting and using data on innovation* (4th ed., p. 20). OECD Publishing
Quinn, R. E., & Rohrbaugh, J. (1983). A spatial model of effectiveness criteria: Towards a competing values approach to organizational analysis. *Management Science, 29*, 363–377. https://doi.org/10.1287/mnsc.29.3.363
Shaposhnykov, K., Filyppova, S., Lagodiienko, V., Krylov, D., & Svinarova, H. (2022). Universities innovative development under the globalization conditions. *Revista Tempos e Espaços em Educação, 15*(34), e17608. https://doi.org/10.20952/revtee.v15i34.17608
Shattow, M. (1996). Out of the blue. *Electric Perspectives, 21*(3), 44–54.
Schein, E. H. (1984). Coming to a new awareness of organizational culture. *Sloan Management Review, 25*(2), 3–16.
Schein, E. H. (2004). *Organizational culture and leadership*. Jossey-Bass.
Sporn, B. (1996). Managing university culture: An analysis of the relationship between institutional culture and management approaches. *Higher Education, 32*, 41–61.
Tharp, B. M. (2010). *Four organizational culture types, hawoth organizational culture*. White Paper. http://www.haworth.com/en-us/Knowledge/Workplace-Library/Documents/Four-Organizational-Culture-Types.
Tierney, W.G. (1988). Organizational culture in higher education: Defining the essentials. 126, Addison Wesley Publishing Company, Reading.
Times Higher Education World University Rankings: Best universities in the World 2022. https://www.timeshighereducation.com/student/best-universities/best-universities-world
Times Higher Education World University Rankings: 2022–2023.
West, M. A., & Farr, J. L. (1990). Innovation at work. In M. A. West & J. L. Farr (Eds.), *Innovation and creativity at work: Psychological and organizational strategies* (pp. 3–13). Wiley.
Woodman, R. W., Sawyer, J. E., & Griffin, R. W. (1993). Toward a theory of organizational creativity. *Academy of Management Review, 18*(2), 293–321.

Aspects of Using Distance Learning Platforms in Digital Education

Inga Gabisonia, Marine Khubua, and Maia Aghaia

Abstract Due to the challenges of the modern world, it is necessary for educational institutions to make their space as digital as possible. This circumstance serves the purpose of increasing access to quality education in specific circumstances. The purpose of the research of our paper is: creating the model of a digital school of online learning in order to prepare entrants on the bases of appropriate and flexible educational mission of a higher educational institution. This initiative will be beneficial for universities and it will serve the interest of the state as it is about the issue of providing quality education to citizens living in conflict zones, ethnic minorities, immigrants and foreign students. Our challenge is to create a curriculum and platform for a sustainable digital school, based on the study of the existing practices of digital transformation of the best international universities and schools; also issues of effective use and management of IT, student-centered, challenge-based teaching, competitiveness, digital education quality assessment issues. As distance learning tools we have used the well-tested distance learning system "Moodle" and educational and informational system "Studlab" at the university, which is a software product created by the Informatics Department of Sukhumi State University, as well as the website of Sukhumi State University. As research methods, we have selected desk research, observation, secondary research, questionnaires, which we have created and sent via Google and Microsoft applications. The research results have shown: (1) The number of engagement in digital school is low due to inadequate knowledge of modern technologies. (2) Professors and teachers have shown a great desire to acquire and develop digital skills in order to provide quality education to the entrants. (3) Employers, lecturers, and applicants have expressed interesting ideas and requirements for IT competencies and skills.

I. Gabisonia (✉) · M. Khubua · M. Aghaia
Sokhumi State University, Tbilisi, Georgia
e-mail: i.gabisonia@sou.edu.ge

M. Khubua
e-mail: m.khubua@sou.edu.ge

M. Aghaia
e-mail: m.aghaia@sou.edu.ge

R. C. Geibel and S. Machavariani (eds.), *Digital Management to Shape the Future*,
Springer Proceedings in Business and Economics,
https://doi.org/10.1007/978-3-031-66517-2_2

Keywords Distance learning · Digital school · Online teaching · Competence

1 Introduction

In this article We research Aspects of Using Distance Learning Platforms in Digital Education. Distance learning is online learning via the Internet. The World Wide Web allows you to exchange information instantly, create necessary databases, gather all required and necessary information and make them available to everyone around the world. Distance learning is an independent form of learning in which information technology plays a vital and crucial role. The popularity of distance learning is increasing day by day due to many reasons, such as: it provides a wide range of audience reach, anyone can study remotely, regardless of their location. Through distance learning any kind of training and teaching is conducted online via the Internet. It has many advantages as it saves time and financial resources, there is no need of transportation fare and accommodation, etc. And, most importantly, training can be combined with any other activities.

It is noteworthy to highlight that distance learning and e-learning are different concepts. Electronic learning (e-learning) is the use of new approaches in learning, among which the main idea is using of information technology (IT) and the Internet. If we consider distance learning, it is a broader concept that includes various forms and types. Its main difference is training literally "at a distance." All these forms of training are also used to obtain additional professional education.

2 Theory

Distance learning is a new term of our time, but it originated with the advent of postal communication. High Internet speeds have made it possible to take remote learning opportunities to a new level. Changes and advancements increased the need for new technologies and accordingly a new concept "E- learning" has appeared (Burden et al., 2019; He et al., 2014; Zakharov et al., 2022). Remote learning focuses on using the most modern programs. Today, training programs that can be mastered online are gradually replacing full-time and part-time forms of education. More and more educational organizations around the world are introducing online learning for the convenience of their students. The distance format allows you to structure the educational process more flexibly and suitably. Typically, educational programs are developed in accordance with professional standards and qualification requirements (Irimias et al., 2022).

Learners and students who have passed the enrollment procedure are formed into separate groups according to their specialties Bateson (1972). Training is conducted online and interactively via the Internet. In order to complete the training one needs a personal computer (or other computer device) with Internet access. Learners and students are provided with a key to the educational portal and access to its resources: materials for familiarization, video trainings and webinars, interactive tests and assignments. Distance learning is not difficult (Uvarov, 2019). The program interface is intuitive, educational portal interface is quite simple and aimed at a wide range of users. In order to be involved in distance learning any modern person needs to be aware of some technical issues and have basic computer skills: use programs such as MS Office, email and be able to type on a keyboard. Additionally, self-organization and time management skills, communication skills, the ability to listen, competent formulation of thoughts orally and in writing, and logical sequence of thinking will be useful. Distance learning is suitable for most people with a wide variety of characters and personalities. Passionate and creative people with a high level of motivation and a desire to learn as much as possible find it entertaining. There are also students who do not really like to study. Note that they also find the e-learning process quite exciting—the new form of delivery greatly diversifies even traditional programs. It's a fact that distance learning is different from regular one. It follows its own rules, but it works and is really worthy of being used everywhere (Bacos & Grove, 2019).

It is not arguable that today online learning is a unique opportunity to independently acquire profound knowledge and improve professional competencies by using the latest information technologies. Distance learning is ideal for active and creative individuals, working people, young mothers, as well as those who live for various reasons far from large cities. If the student applies for advanced training, it is assumed that the student already has secondary vocational or higher education, for which advanced training is necessary. For retraining, it is assumed that the student has a basic secondary vocational or higher education. In this case, the learning process during retraining focuses only on professional disciplines Aesaert et al. (2015), Gavaldon and McGarr (2019).

An electronic course is a convenient, inexpensive and, most importantly, fast way of learning, based on educational text materials, multimedia and interactive applications (their availability depends on the course program) Pramila-Savukoski (n.d.), Pramila-Savukoski et al. (2023). The entire process is subject to the curriculum; upon completion of training, a final certification is carried out and a diploma of the established form or a certificate of advanced training is issued, confirming the receipt of additional qualifications. There is no need to come for enrollment and it is one of the main advantages of distance learning. There is no need to come to the sessions to take the final exams as well. The educational process is conducted entirely online on the educational portal. All organizational issues can be resolved through telephone conversations, correspondence by e-mail, instant messengers or postal service. For e-learning one only needs a computer or tablet device and Internet access. It may be necessary to install a number of standard programs necessary for training (for example, the MS Office, etc. upon recommendation). E-Learning is based on electronic content (Angelova, 2020; Uvarov, 2019). The content refers to digital textbooks and recorded lectures. These are texts and diagrams, photographs, images, and videos. Currently, educational simulators and the possibility of creating virtual reality at the level of information technology are being widely introduced. Classes are held on the basis of an educational portal, where one is assigned a personal password and one is able to find everything they need. One simply can open the necessary documents, study, save some stuff in their computer or print if necessary. Classes can be either individual or joint. In the first case, it is one's independent work, completing assignments according to study materials. Any learner can download video lectures or view it on the educational portal in one's personal account or YouTube. In this particular case permanent Internet connection is not required as it has already been mentioned all materials can be downloaded and saved in one's computer device, and, if necessary, printed. There is no doubt that self-training is considered as the main component of distance learning programs. Independent work is required to obtain practical skills, deepen and consolidate knowledge and information, as well as to develop the most important professional competencies. Everyone is given the opportunity to study lecture material, recommended literature—textbooks, digitized in the course database. Also, one can watch educational films, videos and listen to audio recordings of lectures. Recordings of previously held webinars and video conferences serve as interesting and educational material for self-study.

The second type of classes are online events (webinars, conferences) based on pre-generated lists of participants, when students and teachers gather at the same time in one virtual place and discuss certain issues together. Such classes are very close to real classrooms: you can see and hear the teacher, communicate with colleagues, only all actions take place on the monitor of your computer in real time (Brown & Poortman, 2018). A stable Internet connection is required when participating in webinars and taking test tasks. A webinar is a live video conference with a presentation by one or more speakers. The webinar is accompanied by a chat, questions are asked to the speaker, and discussions are held. Webinars are prepared in advance; the organizers notify students about the time of the webinar and issue an access code to it by email. All educational material on the training portal is divided into blocks. Testing, as a rule, is expected at the end of each such block (from 3 to 10 questions). Upon completion of the training, the student is asked to take an extended test (final certification). If the student answers incorrectly, the system recommends him/her to re-study certain material and one is given another attempt to pass the test.

Practical training can be carried out via distance learning. When performing practical work, it is possible to use any available sources of information, but direct copying of texts (except for quoting) and plagiarism are not allowed. If any are detected by the verification systems of the educational portal, the written exam will not be considered passed. For such purposes, for example, the Turnitin system is used. Distance retraining is ideal for working people. They will not need to go on vacation during the sessions; they can study without interrupting their working and significantly changing usual lifestyle. Flexible free schedule is one of the main advantages as well. Distance learning is also a great opportunity for young mothers as they can study with their babies on their lap. Geographical boundaries are not limited, i.e. even being in the most remote outback, one can get an education in a prestigious educational organization. The main thing one need is Internet access. Distance courses and training programs are developed on the basis of professional standards and qualification requirements. All educational materials are updated as changes occur and new trends and information emerge. It is much faster to update electronic learning materials than to republish a printed publication (textbook, monograph, etc.). Each innovation (in legislation, science, and practice) can be quickly reflected in the materials of the distance program. New technologies inherent in distance learning contribute to the elimination of illiteracy in provincial areas, which is still relevant for our country Paudel (2021). Thus, distance education provides free access to up-to-date information and knowledge. It allows one quickly obtain a new profession and find employment in any field. Enrollment in distance learning is possible via e-mail. A description of the training program, curriculum, as well as information about instructors are provided. Anyone is able to submit an application in electronic form. The final certification is carried out online in the form of testing; personal presence is not required.

Many institutions would like to organize online schools due to current challenges in education field (Brown & Poortman, 2018; Irimias et al., 2022). In order to start online school it is essential to have a well-developed business plan as it determines key factors such as start-up costs, sources of income, market solvency and the potential profitability of the project. The costs of running a school include teacher fees, technical infrastructure support, website and learning platform support, and advertising costs. For example, you can create a full-fledged educational project based on an online platform, where there is a personal account for students, analytics in one place and the ability to work with calculations (Bacos & Grove, 2019; Zakharov et al., 2022). A business plan also describes aspects of creating and developing a business, including goals, strategy, structure, and organization. Additionally, the business plan can contain information about services, products, potential markets, financial forecasts or action plans. It helps entrepreneurs determine how successful their company can be, how much time and resources it will take to launch it. Without a good business plan, a company will face financial difficulties or failure. It allows one to determine a promotion and marketing strategy and find out one's target audience. During the research phase, it is important to understand the advantages and disadvantages of online school. It will definitely attract the right audience. There is need for carrying out market research. After doing some market research, a strategy for promoting the project should be developed. For this purpose, promotion channels such as social networks, contextual advertising, SEO, etc. should be selected.

A financial plan is an important and vital step as well. Here they determine what expenses the company expects, how much it will take to develop and promote one's online school. Many provide information about the income they plan to receive after launch. It is important to estimate how many students one need to get started and how long it will take. Finally, after entrepreneurs have conducted market research, identified goals and objectives, developed a promotion strategy and drawn up a financial plan, they can move on to an action plan. The steps here will depend on the plans for implementing the business plan. It is best to make a specific plan for creating courses and training programs. Next, one need to include website and software development, information about promoting an online school or attracting students.

Online courses is the most common type of distance education now. Most edtech projects are built in course format. They use different approaches, tools, methods, types of lessons. For example, this could be mass accessible training without limits on the number of participants, group, paired or individual lessons. Some experts or schools use recorded lessons, others use webinars.

Positive aspects:

- Accessibility: Anyone with internet access can take them. Students do not need to travel to the other side of the city, coordinate time with the teacher, or arrange their schedule.
- Flexibility: The electronic format allows students to complete lessons at their own pace. You can study at any time in a convenient place.
- Varied content: usually courses consist of a series of video lectures, materials, tests, and interactive classes that are conducted on an online platform.
- Prices: This format is usually cheaper than full-time programs, and some courses are free.
- Internationalization: being in a small city, you can take lessons from top experts from anywhere on the map.

Negative aspects:

- Limited interaction: Early classes may lack feedback and communication with teachers and other students, making it difficult to ask questions or evaluate your progress.
- Low completion rate: This is the downside of flexibility—staying motivated and completing the course is much more difficult.
- Validation: Although some educational programs provide certificates, they may not be recognized by employers or educational institutions. Students can easily cheat when taking tests on exams, which is why not everyone trusts such courses.

Use an LMS or online platform through which students access resources, participate in webinars, and complete interactive tests and assignments livari et al. (2020), Maya-Jariego et al. (2023), Mishra et al. (2020). You can combine this with traditional classes—lectures or seminars. Develop multimedia materials, such as video lessons, podcasts, interactive simulations with online access Papagiannidis et al. (2020).

Provide opportunities for independent learning. You can include self-study units in your educational product, such as online tutorials or exercises. This will allow students to work at their own pace and receive more personalized support and feedback.

Plan offline events. The main complaint about the remote format is the lack of communication and exchange of experience between participants. If the basis of the course is online, then live meetings can be a good addition.

Implement an analytics system to track student progress: this helps improve content, increase engagement, and personalize the process.

Self-study is one of the main components of distance education, since students themselves are responsible for moving towards the goal and organizing the process. For this method, developers need to prepare learning materials, exercises, homework, tests, videos and other content. To organize work, learning platforms are used, for example, Skillspace. You can upload lessons, audio, simulators, quizzes here.

Students in your online school can watch, pause, or rewind the videos multiple times, which can help them better understand the material.

Self-learning helps develop critical thinking and problem-solving skills as students come to their own conclusions—the role of teachers or supervisors is supportive. This method encourages the development of a sense of independence, which can be useful in both personal and professional contexts.

Cooperative learning—This method involves interaction in pairs or groups as one of the main tools for achieving educational goals. Students exchange ideas, knowledge, experience, and help each other. Collaborative work can take many forms, from structured group activities and discussions to more open-ended project-based learning.

An additional positive effect of the technique is the development of interpersonal communication skills, increased motivation and involvement, the ability to look at an object from different points of view, and take information from different sources. Students may take on different roles and responsibilities within their groups, such as mediator, researcher, or facilitator. This helps develop teamwork and leadership skills and promotes equal distribution of knowledge.

As a result, by working together, students better absorb information, build strong relationships with their classmates, and develop the skills necessary to apply the acquired knowledge in their daily tasks (Tettamanzi et al., 2023).

Adaptive methods involve the introduction of technology to create an individual experience for each student. This approach is based on the thesis that each student has his own needs, interests, predispositions and abilities, which means that the tools must be adaptable. Using this method, you can find gaps in knowledge and determine how best to address them. This helps students overcome obstacles and achieve results more easily.

To provide an individual approach, Machine Learning algorithms, data analytics, and artificial intelligence are used. These systems can adapt to pace, skill level and learning style. They provide real-time feedback, personalize content and change the way you interact with an educational product. Gamification is one of the main trends in distance education. It relies on the idea that games are a good learning tool because they give students the opportunity to interact with content in a fun way. Against this background, a whole direction has emerged—edutainment, which combines leisure with study. This can be used in different ways: from introducing individual mechanics, for example, ratings, an achievement system, battles, to game logic at the heart of the entire course. In game-based learning, students are given problems to solve. They can be designed to teach skills ranging from basic math and literacy to critical thinking. As they progress, students receive feedback and support, allowing them to learn from mistakes and improve their results. Gaming tools increase motivation, involvement, and make it easier to remember information. Such study does not cause negativity, therefore it helps to reduce the stress, anxiety, and rejection that students experience when completing traditional tasks. In addition, game-based learning can be used to reinforce positive behaviors such as persistence and cooperation (Pettersson, 2021, 26).

When describing the main methods, it is necessary to mention synchronous and asynchronous learning. The difference between them is the time factor. The synchronous approach involves students and teachers interacting in real time. In this type, students attend classes or lectures at specific times and participate in discussions, activities, and assessments with their fellow students. The asynchronous model, on the other hand, operates on the principles of autonomy, with students accessing course materials, lectures, and other resources at their own convenience. They can participate in discussions and complete assignments on their own schedule without being tied to a specific schedule Sannen et al. (2021).

Due to the difference in approaches, the set of methods is also different. With synchronous logic this is:

- Video lectures or webinars in real time;
- Group discussions or debates;
- Simulations, role-playing games that require immediate participation;
- Collaborative projects or presentations that involve simultaneous work;
- Online meetings, conferences, calls to discuss complex issues.
- Examples of asynchronous methods:
- Recorded video lectures or podcasts that can be viewed at any time;
- Independent assignments or projects with flexible deadlines;
- Chat rooms or other communication spaces where students can comment and respond whenever they want;
- Interactive simulations or virtual labs that students can access and study on their own schedule;

3 Research Method

The purpose of the very research is to determine the educational needs of the above mentioned categories of entrants and students according to the individual regions of Georgia, in order to organize a digital school on the basis of Sukhumi State University. The authors of the research have focused on the following opinions:

Organizing a digital school is an interesting and useful project for students and entrants of the specified category, as it allows us to provide this category of students and youth with an opportunity for education and development Mack (2021), Thomas et al. (2019). While organizing a digital school, we should take into account the following aspects: (1) What are the goals of the digital school and the concept of the educational program. The specificity of the target audience, the list of subjects to be studied and the level of teaching of these subjects. (2) A digital school definitely needs an online platform that will allow us to create and run online courses. Currently, there is a wide variety of such interactive platforms. (3) A high quality of teaching materials and video lessons, textbooks, presentations and, most importantly, diverse tasks must be created for the digital school. It should be noted that the learning process should be fun and diverse for students of different categories. (4) It is important to attract experienced and highly qualified teachers for teaching, because their qualifications will significantly increase the quality of teaching in the school. (5) There must be a student registration system in the school, where the price policy of training courses will be taken into account. It should also be noted that trial lessons and short free courses should be offered to students. This opportunity is a tool for attracting new students. (6) During the learning process, students must be evaluated and given feedback in order to improve their achievements. (7) It is useful to create an online school forum or community in a social network, where students and teachers will get to know each other informally, share different kinds of experiences, and etc. (8) When organizing a digital school, it is useful to use a marketing campaign and advertising, to create a digital school blog, in order to attract students. (9) Students should give us feedback regarding the educational process in any form. The purpose of this feedback is to improve the quality of learning and to see the new needs of the school. (10) The digital school must be continuously developed and the list of its training courses must be constantly updated. Each course should gradually add certain functions, in order to widely use the latest technologies integrated in the field of education as for some students, the digital school is the only educational space.

Managers and students of Public schools in several regions and the capital city (# 52, 128, 12, 118, Zugdidi district, Gali district), state and private universities of Georgia, program coordinators, students, a manager of a German university, a lecturer, a master student of London University have participated in the research.

The survey has mainly been conducted through the Google Form application, because this type of survey does not require personal contact with the organizers of the survey and excludes bias. Cooperation between different universities and schools will contribute to the development of digital capabilities in institutions. In our research, we have developed a digital school action plan and budgeting guide. By selecting several universities and schools, we have determined the main factors that will affect the effective work of the school, we have investigated positive and negative characteristics of the digital school. We have been monitoring the initiative to launch a digital school to develop digital management. The electronic platform Studlab of Sokhumi State University is used as a learning platform for the operation of the digital school. The very electronic platform has been created by the staff of the Computer Innovations Laboratory and the students of the Informatics department. Based on educational needs, new functions are periodically added to the Studlab platform, in which students of the target level take an active part. The platform is used for the management and administration of the educational process, as well as for informing students and entrants, for providing various types of educational materials, for evaluation, for contacting lecturers and course participants in any way. The e-learning system Moodle and the anti-plagiarism system Turnitin are built into the platform. Software products such as ZOOM, Google Meet, Microsoft Teams are used for online meetings. The set of software products listed above is quite sufficient for effective management of the digital school.

We have organized meetings with leading university and school managers, entrants, and students, both online and face-to-face, where we have discussed digital competencies and the digital school development plan, challenges and ways to overcome them. In order to ensure the validity and reliability of the received information,

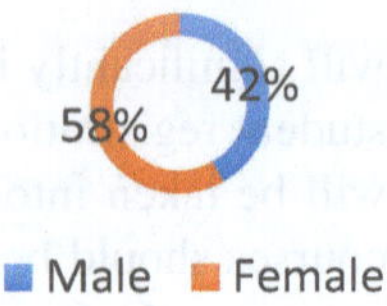

Fig. 1 Gender distribution of respondents

we have had another discussion of the very information and analyzed the results with a small group of participants.

We have created questionnaires in Google forms format for pupils and students in order to analyze the relevant factors for the development of the action plan of the digital school. Surveys have been conducted in Georgian/English language (The total number of respondents is 103).

The data collected as a result of the research were analyzed using the statistical software package SPSS-23. Identification data were obtained from the registry of students and schoolchildren. Respondents consented to the use of their data in the study and expressed willingness to participate in the research.

The analysis of the research results revealed that 58% of the total participants were women, 42% were men (see Fig. 1). The research participants belonged to different age groups: 48% were younger than 18 years old, 49% were between 19 and 27 years old, and 3% were older than 27 years.

When asked which distance learning platforms did you use? 50% of respondents said it was ZOOM, while 24% said it was Teams. Some of them talked about social networks. When asked how effective distance learning is, a large number of respondents (60.2%) consider it partially effective (see Fig. 2), because they believe that the methods and techniques of distance learning should be further improved. Only 14.6% of the respondents consider distance learning to be fully effective, while a quarter of the respondents consider it ineffective, which is thought-provoking because the distance learning methodology used so far clearly needs to be improved.

The next question was about the quality of access to the Internet. As mobile Internet is available practically in all regions of Georgia, and in cities and large settlements it is possible to use the optical cable of any Internet provider, 51.5%

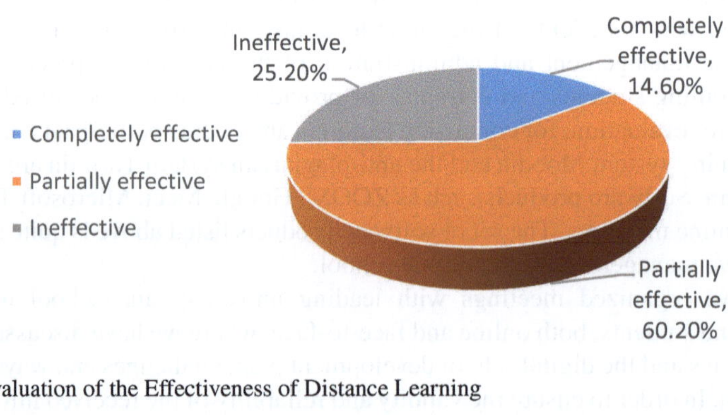

Fig. 2 Evaluation of the Effectiveness of Distance Learning

expressed full satisfaction with this question, and 38.8% expressed the desire for a better quality connection. Dissatisfaction with the quality of the Internet was noted by only 9.7% of respondents.

The next question was about the availability of devices. How accessible are the electronic devices which are necessary for learning (desktop computer, notebook, netbook, tablet, mobile phone, etc.)? 78.6% of the respondents gave a positive answer to this question, and 21.6% noted more or less availability in their answers.

The next question was: Do you have the necessary education for distance learning?

75.7% gave a positive answer to this question, and 22.3% indicated that they had partial knowledge. Only 2% indicated that they didn't have such education.

The next question was about the quality of distance learning. 28.2% of respondents answered "yes" to this question, 46.6% indicated "partially", 25.2% answered "no".

To the question: "Which subjects would you like to study in an online school?" (see Fig. 3) the answers were distributed as follows: Georgian language—36.9%, mathematics—28.2%, history—31.1%, English 61.2%, computer technologies—58.3%, computer graphics—45.6% and others—9.7%.

The respondents have expressed their needs via text messages. For example, they have mentioned the following ones: the necessity of constantly turning on cameras, long-term storage of video recordings of classes, the ability of the lecturer/teacher to conduct classes remotely, the importance of proper time for the learning process, full access to the Internet, and equipping pupils/students with appropriate equipment. The fact that hybrid teaching is considered a quite effective way has been emphasized. The requirements also include the development of skills necessary for distance learning on the part of teachers/lecturers, strict planning and understanding of the structure of online learning, reference of all types of tasks or sources of information, and beforehand preparation before the lesson, refinement and maintenance of educational platforms, use of digital board, preparation and publication of various illustrated electronic visual materials. Also, the respondents have highlighted the importance of conducting surveys and exams with high quality, raising

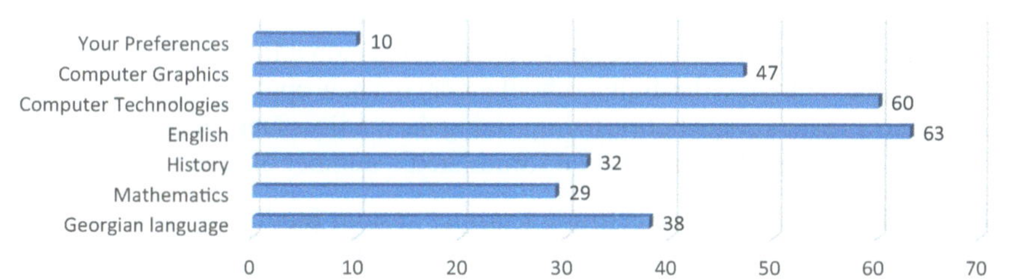

	Georgian language	Mathematics	History	English	Computer Technologies	Computer Graphics	Your Preferences
Number of students	38	29	32	63	60	47	10

Fig. 3 Preferred subjects for online school study

the control of the exam process. Strengthening the practical component at the lessons and explaining the new material in the form of a presentation, getting comprehensive answers to all kinds of questions related to the explained issue. Respondents consider distance learning to be quite a good and necessary opportunity, it is an effective tool for overcoming learning difficulties, it requires the development or maintenance of certain software in order to automate the learning process and bring it into one system. It is necessary to develop modern learning platforms with elements of artificial intelligence (Machine Learning, Natural language processing), which will fundamentally change the existing possibilities. Pupil/teacher, student/lecturer should be focused on the teaching result, plagiarism detection software should be implemented, while composing exam questions the possibility of copying should be minimized.

The staff (lecturers/teachers) and managers have also been interviewed. The results of their survey are essentially close to the results of the students' survey. A large part of the respondents believe that distance learning is a partially effective form of education. A large part believes that the evaluation system and tools need to be improved. Basically, in the case of teaching, Zoom or Teams platforms are used. A part of the respondents expressed a desire to work in some kind of paid or free platform with a flexible interface. The staff believe that it is partially possible to accurately evaluate the effectiveness of a training program with currently available distance learning tools. It is also difficult for the staff to prepare the budget for the training program.

Additionally, interviews were conducted with German experts who visited Georgia in 2023 as part of a research project and shared their views on digital education (see the Annex, Table 1).

4 Results and Discussion

Based on the analysis of answers we have developed some recommendations. The results of the study have showed that it is necessary to review the digital practice taking into account institutional, organizational and personal factors. With extensive use of digital technologies, the digital school model is a new opportunity for education and can make a serious contribution to improving the quality of teaching and learning. In particular, based on the analysis, we formulated a number of recommendations:

- For the digital school, the electronic learning system Studlab in Sukhumi State University, which is a software product developed and created entirely by the university staff, should be improved and adapted to the needs of the digital school. Students of all three levels participated in the development of this software product. Currently, the Moodle system is used simultaneously with Studlab, but in the future new possibilities will be added to the Studlab system. Informatics department staff and students participate in debugging and testing its code.

- For the operation of the digital school, academic staff with high digital skills should be selected, and the working staff should deepen their digital skills. If necessary, the teachers of the schools participating in the research will be actively involved in the work of the digital school.
- For the digital school, the curriculum should be refined, the constituent components of the program's training courses should be reviewed and written in detail, a realistic budget should be developed, a school operation business plan should be created, and risks of implementing the plan should be assessed. An advertising campaign should be conducted in order to attract digital school students.
- Within the scope of the possibility, the university should ensure the updating and refinement of appropriate study materials and survey tools in accordance with modern requirements.
- Permanent control of training programs in terms of quality assurance should be carried out, in this regard, active cooperation with experts living in Georgia and abroad is necessary.
- The experience of previous years should be studied and shared, as well as the experience of existing international digital schools should be used.
- The educational platform of the digital school should be adjusted as much as possible to the needs of the pupils/students, convenient tools for placing educational materials and online surveys, and an AI-based information system should be built into it.
- Learning outcomes of digital school students should be visible, measurable and relevant to modern requirements.
- It is important to develop a digital school and update training courses in order to introduce the latest educational methodologies.

5 Conclusions, Limitations and Further Research

We are going to conduct further research on behalf of Sokhumi State University in order to offer digital school services to youth from some regions of Georgia.

For our further research, we are planning to:

Conduct market research, organize a high-level campaign on digital education in order to ensure the involvement of beneficiaries; strengthen internationalization, develop joint programs; offer beneficiaries a variety of modern educational courses, trainings, seminars within the framework of partnership and cooperation, where inclusivity will be taken into account.

Taking into consideration the outcome of the conducted research, we are planing to describe all of the costs in detail, including the hourly rate/payment of teachers in the budget of digital educational programs. Employees of the university's computer science department have developed a trial mobile application for a digital school with built-in AI (using MIT App Inventor and Android Studio technology). We have already made a decision on creating a web application.

Table 1 Questionnaire is intended for experts

The purpose of the study: to identify problems related to distance learning in education
In your opinion, what main challenges did the education system face during distance learning?
How would you evaluate the effectiveness of distance learning?
What do you think about the role and importance of digital technologies in the preparation of entrants? (Foreigners, Cross-border Regions, repatriates, ethnic minorities, and residents of the occupied territory)
What should be done in the education system in order to improve distance learning that will contribute to the development of our future society?
What should different types of distance learning include?
What major changes should be carried out in the field of higher education in order to implement innovative approaches in distance learning?
What are the strengths and weaknesses of distance learning?
In your opinion, what are the opportunities and threats associated with distance learning?
What important new strategies and approaches should be developed and implemented in order to ensure the quality of distance education?
What is your opinion on open educational resources?
What kind of quick reply should the government and relevant institutions give in order to speed up all the processes that will support the development of open education and open educational resources?
What are challenges of digital education of higher education nowadays?
Share your experience regarding the budgeting of the Education program

We are planning to: develop a digital monitoring system for the teaching/learning process, improve the knowledge assessment system; create prerequisites for the sustainability and spread digital education.

6 Annex

See Table 1.

References

Aesaert, K., van Braak, J., Van Nijlen, D., & Vanderlinde, R. (2015). Primary school pupils' ICT competences: Extensive model and scale development. *Computers & Education, 81*, 326–344.

Angelova, M. (2020). Students' attitudes to the online university course of management in the context of COVID-19. *International Journal of Technology in Education and Science (IJTES), 4*(4), 283–292.

Bacos, C., & Grove, K. (2019). Using online education to improve traditional classroom instruction: A blended learning approach. In *Society for Information Technology & Teacher Education*

International Conference. Association for the Advancement of Computing in Education (AACE) (pp. 374–379).

Bateson, G. 1972. *Steps of an ecology of mind.* The University of Chicago Press.

Brown, C., & Poortman, C. L. (2018). *Networks for learning: Effective collaboration for teacher, school and system improvement.* Routledge.

Burden, K., Kearney, M., Schuck, S., & Hall, T. (2019). Investigating the use of innovative mobile pedagogies for school-aged students: A systematic literature review. *Computers & Education, 138*, 83–100. https://doi.org/10.1016/j.compedu.2019.04.008

Gavaldon, G., & McGarr, O. (2019). Exploring pre-service teachers' future intentions to use technology through the use of comics. *Teaching and Teacher Education, 83*, 99–109. https://doi.org/10.1016/j.tate.2019.04.004

He, W., Xu, G., & Kruck, S. E. (2014). Online IS education for the 21st century. *Journal of Information Systems Education, 25*(2), 101–106.

Iivari, N., Sharma, S., & Ventä-Olkkonen, L. (2020). Digital transformation of everyday life—How COVID-19 pandemic transformed the basic education of the young generation and why information management research should care? *International Journal of Information Management, 55*, 102183.

Irimias, A. R., Mitev, A. Z., & Volo, S. (2022). Digital arts-based collaborative learning in management education. *The International Journal of Management Education, 20*(3), 100727. https://doi.org/10.1016/j.ijme.2022.100727

Mack, K. S. (2021). Studio practices in management education: Creative adventures in aesthetic formativeness. *Journal of Management Education, 45*(6), 889–915. https://doi.org/10.1177/1052562920962544

Maya-Jariego, I., Holgado-Ramos, D., Santolaya, F., Villar-Onrubia, D., Cachia, R., Herrero, C., & Giannoutsou, N. (2023). Teachers' personal network analysis reveals two types of pioneers in educational digitalization: Formal and informal intermediaries at schools. *Computers and Education Open, 4*, 100137.

Mishra, L., Gupta, T., & Shree, A. (2020). Online teaching-learning in higher education during lockdown period of COVID-19 pandemic. *International Journal of Educational Research Open, 1*, 100012.

Papagiannidis, S., Harris, J., & Morton, D. (2020). WHO led the digital transformation of your company? A reflection of IT related challenges during the pandemic. *International Journal of Information Management, 55*, 102166. https://doi.org/10.1016/j.ijinfomgt.2020.102166

Paudel, P. (2021). Online education: Benefits, challenges and strategies during and after COVID-19 in higher education. *International Journal on Studies in Education (IJonSE), 3*(2), 70–85. ISSN: 2690-7909

Pettersson, F. (2021). Understanding digitalization and educational change in school by means of activity theory and the levels of learning concept. *Education and Information Technologies, 26*(1), 187–204. https://link.springer.com/article/10.1007/s10639-020-10239-8

Pramila-Savukoski, S. (n.d.). *The influence of digital learning on health sciences students' competence.*

Pramila-Savukoski, S., Kärnä, R., Kuivila, H. M., Juntunen, J., Koskenranta, M., Oikarainen, A., & Mikkonen, K. (2023). The influence of digital learning on health sciences students' competence development—A qualitative study. *Nurse Education Today, 120*, 105635. https://doi.org/10.1016/j.nedt.2022.105635

Sannen, J., De Maeyer, S., Struyf, E., De Schauwer, E., & Petry, K. (2021). Connecting teacher collaboration to inclusive practices using a social network approach. *Teaching and Teacher Education, 97*, 103182. https://doi.org/10.1016/j.tate.2020.103182

Tettamanzi, P., Minutiello, V., & Murgolo, M. (2023). Accounting education and digitalization: A new perspective after the pandemic. *The International Journal of Management Education, 21*(3), 100847. https://doi.org/10.1016/j.ijme.2023.100847

Thomas, L., Tuytens, M., Devos, G., Kelchtermans, G., & Vanderlinde, R. (2019). Beginning teachers' professional support: A mixed methods social network study. *Teaching and Teacher Education, 83*, 134–147.

Uvarov, A. (2019). *Difficulties and prospects of digital transformation of education* (343 p.). HSE Publication.

Zakharov, K., Komarova, A., Baranova, T., & Gulk, E. (2022). Information literacy and digital competence of teachers in the age of digital transformation. In *XIV International Scientific Conference "INTERAGROMASH 2021" Precision Agriculture and Agricultural Machinery Industry, Volume 2* (pp. 857–868). Springer International Publishing.

The New Institutional Economics and Digitalization

Marine Natsvaladze

Abstract The New Institutional Economics (NIE) offers a crucial framework for understanding the impact of digitalization and its impact on economies and societies. This process, as mentioned earlier, involves incorporating digital technologies into various aspects of life, including business, government, education, healthcare, and social interactions. The NIE framework helps us understand how institutions, rules, and norms interact with digitalization and shape its outcomes. Digitalization disrupts traditional institutions and requires adaptation to leverage the benefits of new technologies effectively. Consequently, existing rules, regulations, and governance structures often require modification to accommodate digital processes, such as online transactions, electronic signatures, and data protection. Moreover, digital technologies can significantly reduce transaction costs in various economic activities and address information asymmetry by providing access to vast amounts of information through the internet. The rise of dominant digital platforms can create lock-in effects, where users become heavily dependent on a specific platform, potentially limiting competition and innovation. This can be seen in cases where users rely heavily on certain social media platforms, search engines, or e-commerce websites, which can have implications for market competition. Digitalization has the potential to exacerbate existing inequalities and create a digital divide between those who have access to digital technologies and those who do not. Addressing this divide is crucial to ensure that all members of society can benefit from digitalization's opportunities. Digital technologies often exhibit network effects, where the value of the technology increases as more people use it. Additionaly, digitalization poses important questions about regulation and governance. Governments must strike a balance between fostering innovation and protecting consumers and society from potential risks associated with emerging technologies. Trust and reputation play a significant role in digital transactions. Digital platforms frequently leverage user reviews and ratings to establish trust between buyers and sellers.

M. Natsvaladze (✉)
Tbilisi State University, Tbilisi, Georgia
e-mail: marine.natsvaladze@tsu.ge

R. C. Geibel and S. Machavariani (eds.), *Digital Management to Shape the Future*,
Springer Proceedings in Business and Economics,
https://doi.org/10.1007/978-3-031-66517-2_3

Keywords ·Institutional economics · New Institutional Economics (NIE) · Digitalization · E-Government

1 Introduction

The New Institutional Economics (NIE) provides a framework for analyzing the economic and social institutions that govern economic behavior. In recent years, digitalization has posed new challenges and opportunities for NIE. New Institutional Economics emphasizes the importance of institutions in shaping economic outcomes. Institutions refer to the formal and informal rules that structure economic activity, such as property rights, contracts, and governance structures. NIE also highlights the role of transaction costs in shaping economic behavior Arwani and Priyadi (2024).

Institutional economics is a broad and longstanding school of thought that emerged in the late nineteenth and early twentieth centuries. It emphasizes the significance of social, cultural, and political factors in shaping economic behavior and outcomes. Institutional economists argue that economic processes cannot be fully understood without considering the impact of institutions like laws, customs, norms, and organizations. They often critique traditional neoclassical economics for oversimplifying human behavior and neglecting the importance of these institutions.

New Institutional Economics, as the name suggests, is a more recent development that emerged in the latter half of the twentieth century, particularly in the 1970s and 1980s. It builds upon the ideas of institutional economics but introduces a more formal and analytical approach. NIE seeks to understand how institutions affect economic behavior, transaction costs, and market efficiency.

NIE incorporates elements from other economic schools, such as game theory and information economics, to analyze how institutions influence economic outcomes. Ronald Coase, Douglass North, and Oliver Williamson are key figures in the development of New Institutional Economics.

NIE distinguishes between "formal institutions," which are explicitly defined and codified, and "informal institutions," which are unwritten norms, traditions, and customs. It also delves into the concept of "transaction costs," which are the costs associated with making economic exchanges, and how institutions can impact these costs.

While both, institutional economics and New Institutional Economics are concerned with the role of institutions in economics, NIE represents a more structured and analytical approach that evolved from the broader ideas of institutional economics. NIE incorporates modern economic methodologies to study the impact of institutions on economic behavior, efficiency, and outcomes.

Institutional economics emphasizes the role of power, distribution, historical context, and social relationships in economic decision-making. Prominent figures associated with institutional economics include Thorstein Veblen, John Commons, and Clarence Ayres.

Digitalization has had a profound impact on society, affecting various aspects of life. It refers to the transformation of traditional processes, services, and interactions into digital formats, enabled by advancements in technology. The widespread adoption of digital technologies has revolutionized the way people communicate, work, learn, access information, and conduct business.

Digitalization has significantly influenced society. It has made communication faster and more accessible. Social media platforms, messaging apps, and video conferencing tools have connected people worldwide, facilitating real-time communication across of geographical boundaries.

The Internet has become a vast repository of information, allowing people to access news, research, educational resources, and knowledge on a wide range of topics with just a few clicks. Governments have embraced digitalization to provide online services, such as tax filing, permit applications, and access to public records, making interactions with government agencies more convenient for citizens.

E-government, also known as electronic government or digital government, refers to the use of digital technologies by governments to provide public services, engage with citizens, and improve overall governance. It aims to enhance the efficiency, accessibility, transparency, and responsiveness of government operations. E-government offers a range of online services that citizens can access through government websites or dedicated portals. These services include applying for official documents, paying taxes, renewing licenses, and accessing public records. Citizens can complete these tasks from the comfort of their homes, reducing the need for physical visits to government offices.

Digital technologies enable governments to engage with citizens through social media, online forums, and interactive websites. This fosters a two-way communication channel, allowing citizens to provide feedback, participate in surveys, and contribute to public decision-making processes.

E-government often involves making government data open and accessible to the public in machine-readable formats. Open data initiatives promote transparency and enable citizens, businesses, researchers, and journalists to analyze and use government data for various purposes. E-government systems typically employ digital identity and authentication mechanisms to ensure secure access to online services. These systems may use methods such as two-factor authentication or digital signatures to verify the identity of users.

E-government initiatives must prioritize data security and privacy to protect sensitive information and prevent unauthorized access. Robust cybersecurity measures and compliance with data protection laws are essential to build public trust in digital government services.

The New Institutional Economics (NIE) provides a framework for analyzing the economic and social institutions that govern economic behavior. In recent years, digitalization has posed new challenges and opportunities for NIE. The New Institutional Economics is a large and relatively new multidisciplinary field that includes aspects of economics, history, sociology, political science, business organization and law.[1]

Douglass North, along with Ronald Coase and Oliver Williamson, transformed the early intuitions of new institutional economics into powerful conceptual and analytical tools that spawned a robust base of empirical research.[2] NIE largely adopts the definition of institutions given by North, for whom they "are the rules of the game in a society, or more formally, are the humanly devised constraints that shape human interaction".[3]

The New Institutional Economics (NIE) is an economic theory that focuses on understanding how institutions influence economic behavior and outcomes. It emphasizes that economic transactions and activities are shaped by the rules, norms, and organizations that govern human interactions. When applied to the context of E-government, the NIE framework helps analyze how digital technologies and institutional arrangements influence the functioning and effectiveness of government services in the digital era.

The main features of the relationship between New Institutional Economics and E-government are the following:

1. Institutional Frameworks—The NIE framework emphasizes that the success of E-government initiatives depends on the underlying institutional arrangements. Effective digital governance requires clear rules, property rights, contract enforcement mechanisms, and accountability structures. The design and implementation of E-Government services need to align with existing institutional frameworks to ensure legitimacy and acceptance.
2. Transaction Costs—NIE places a strong emphasis on transaction costs, which are the costs incurred during economic exchanges. In the context of E-government, the adoption of digital technologies can lead to reduced transaction costs, making public services more efficient and accessible to citizens. For example, online applications and payments can streamline bureaucratic processes and reduce paperwork, resulting in cost savings for both the government and citizens. Reducing transaction costs is a central issue in modern economic organization and economic policy.[4]
3. Information Asymmetry—Information asymmetry occurs when one party has more information than the other during economic interactions. E-government can address information asymmetry by providing citizens with access to comprehensive and timely information. Open data initiatives, transparency in government operations, and digital communication channels can bridge the information gap between the government and citizens, fostering better decision-making.

[1] The new institutional economics: Applications for agricultural policy research in developing countries Kherallah and Kirsten (2002).

[2] Ménard and Shirley (2011).

[3] North (1990).

[4] Williamson (1981).

4. Trust and Social Capital—NIE recognizes the importance of trust and social capital in economic transactions. Trust is essential for citizens to engage with E-government services and share sensitive information online. Governments must build and maintain trust by ensuring data security, privacy protection, and reliable service delivery.
5. Path Dependence and Lock-in Effects—NIE highlights the concept of path dependence, wherein historical decisions and events can lock an institution into a particular trajectory. Governments must be aware of lock-in effects when adopting E-government systems to avoid becoming dependent on inefficient or outdated technologies. Flexibility and adaptability are crucial to ensure that E-government initiatives evolve in response to changing needs and technological advancements.
6. Public–Private Partnerships—NIE also examines the role of public–private partnerships in shaping economic outcomes. In the context of E-government, collaborations between government agencies and private technology companies can lead to innovative solutions and efficient service delivery. However, these partnerships must be carefully designed and regulated to avoid potential conflicts of interest and ensure public interests are prioritized.
7. Digital Divide—The NIE framework highlights that institutions can create winners and losers. In the context of E-government, the digital divide can exacerbate inequalities, as certain segments of the population may lack access to digital technologies or digital literacy. Addressing the digital divide becomes crucial to ensure that E-Government initiatives benefit all citizens.

2 Methodology

Based on the modern economic theory, the paper utilizes the theoretical-scientific research. In the research were used publications in the field of New Institutional Economics, opinions of foreign scientists and experts, Internet resources and electronic books.

3 Results

Digitalization has the potential to create both opportunities and challenges for economic development. It can increase connectivity, reduce transaction costs, and lead to greater productivity. However, it also raises questions about income inequality, job displacement, and cybersecurity risks (Table 1).

Digitalization presents both opportunities and challenges for economic development. It can increase connectivity, reduce transaction costs, and lead to greater productivity. However, it also raises questions about income inequality, job displacement, and cybersecurity risks.

Table 1 Influence of digitalization on economic development

	Advantages	Disadvantages
Increased connectivity	• Greater access to information • Increased market efficiency	• Digital divide • Increased competition
Automation	• Increased productivity • Greater customization	• Job displacement • Cybersecurity risks

The adaptation of institutions refers to the process by which formal and informal rules, norms, and structures evolve and change in response to shifts in economic, social, technological, and political contexts. Institutions are not static; they often need to adapt to remain effective and relevant in an ever-changing environment. This concept is central to both institutional economics and New Institutional Economics (NIE).

The adaptation of institutions refers to the process by which formal and informal rules, norms, and structures evolve and change in response to shifts in economic, social, technological, and political contexts. Institutions are not static; they often need to adapt to remain effective and relevant in an ever-changing environment. This concept is central to both institutional economics and New Institutional Economics (NIE).

How should institutions adapt?

1. Institutions need to adapt when the external **environment** they operate in changes. This could be due to technological advancements, shifts in social values, changes in economic conditions, or alterations in political regimes.
2. NIE emphasizes the role of institutions in reducing **transaction costs**—the costs associated with making and enforcing agreements. When the environment changes, transaction costs may also change. Institutions evolve to address these changes and help minimize the costs of economic exchange.

   The impact of digitalization on transaction costs can lead to adaptations in institutional frameworks:

   - As digital transactions become more prevalent, legal and regulatory frameworks may need to be adapted to address issues like online contracts, intellectual property rights, and data protection.
   - Institutions may need to evolve to protect consumers in digital transactions, ensuring that online platforms provide accurate information, uphold product quality, and maintain fair competition.
   - Global digital transactions may require international institutions to standardize rules for e-commerce, intellectual property, and cross-border data flows.
   - As digital payments become more common, institutions overseeing financial systems and payment methods may need to adapt to ensure security and stability.

Digitalization can help businesses minimize transaction costs by automating business processes and improving supply chain management. For instance, e-commerce platforms eliminate the need for physical store locations and the associated costs such as rent, utilities, and taxes. Additionally, digital payments reduce human error associated with transactions, while blockchain technology eliminates middlemen associated with transactions (Table 2).

3. Changes in technology or economic conditions can impact **property rights**. For instance, the rise of digital assets has led to discussions about how traditional property rights concepts should adapt to this new form of ownership.
4. Institutions influence how contracts are formulated and enforced. As economic activities evolve, such as the growth of e-commerce, institutions may need to adapt to ensure that **contracts** are relevant and enforceable in these new contexts.
5. Informal institutions, like **social norms**, also adapt over time. As societies change, what is considered acceptable or unacceptable behavior may shift, and institutions must adjust to reflect these changes.
6. Formal institutions often include **regulations** and laws. These need to be updated to address emerging challenges, ensure consumer protection, and maintain a fair and competitive economic environment.
7. **Globalization** has led to the need for international institutions that regulate cross-border transactions, trade, and investment. These institutions must adapt to changing economic and political dynamics among nations.
8. **Technological innovation**, Rapid technological advancements can disrupt existing economic processes and create the need for new rules and norms. For example, the emergence of blockchain technology has spurred discussions about the need to adapt financial and legal institutions to accommodate cryptocurrencies and smart contracts.
9. **Changes in political leadership** and ideologies can lead to shifts in the priorities of institutions. Governments may revise regulations, trade agreements, and other policies to align with their new agendas.
10. Institutions often adapt based on the feedback loop of **experience and learning**. As individuals and organizations interact within institutional frameworks, they may identify areas for improvement, leading to changes in rules and practices.

The adaptation of institutions is a complex and ongoing process. Successful adaptation requires a balance between preserving the stability and predictability that

Table 2 How digitalization reduces transaction costs

Supply chain management	E-Procurement	Virtual collaboration
Digitalization enables better supply chain management. Sensors and AI software can track inventory levels and automate procurement processes, lowering transaction costs	Electronic procurement (e-procurement) streamlines procurement by eliminating the need for manual processes such as filing paperwork and making in-person visits	Virtual collaboration platforms reduce the need for physical meetings through video conferencing and real-time data collaboration, which lowers travel and accommodation costs

Table 3 Applications of NIE

Public policy	NIE has been applied to a range of public policy issues, including antitrustlaw, environmental regulation, and property rights
International development	NIE has been used to explain and inform policies related to economic development and international trade
Corporate governance	NIE has been applied to the analysis of corporate governance, including the role of boards of directors and executive compensation

institutions provide while allowing for flexibility and responsiveness to changing circumstances. It's a dynamic interplay between formal and informal institutions and the economic, social, and political contexts they operate within (Table 3).

4 Conclusions

Digitalization is challenging traditional economic theory, particularly in regards to property rights, transaction costs, and governance structures. While there are significant opportunities for economic development, there are also notable risks and challenges. Future research should focus on developing new frameworks for analyzing the intersection between digitalization and institutional economics.

The New Institutional Economics (NIE) provides valuable insights into how digitalization affects economic behavior, institutions, and outcomes. When examining the relationship between New Institutional Economics and digitalization, we can understand how the adoption and impact of digital technologies are shaped by existing institutions and how digitalization, in turn, influences institutions and economic activities. The key aspects of this relationship are:

- Impact on Transaction Costs—Digitalization can significantly reduce transaction costs in economic activities. By automating processes, eliminating paperwork, and enabling real-time communication, digital technologies streamline transactions between individuals, businesses, and governments. Lower transaction costs can lead to increased efficiency and productivity in the economy.
- Institutional Adaptation—The adoption of digital technologies requires institutions to adapt and adjust their rules, norms, and governance mechanisms. As digitalization disrupts traditional industries and practices, institutions may need to respond with new regulations, intellectual property rights, and data privacy laws.
- Digital Platforms and Network Effects—Digitalization often gives rise to platform-based business models, where intermediaries facilitate exchanges between multiple users. These platforms can create network effects, where the value of the platform increases as more users join. NIE helps explain how these digital platforms and network effects impact competition, market power, and the dynamics of economic interactions.

- Information Asymmetry and Transparency—Digitalization can address information asymmetry by making information more accessible to all participants. Through data transparency and open data initiatives, digital technologies enable more informed decision-making and can enhance market efficiency.
- Path Dependence and Lock-in Effects—NIE highlights that historical decisions can create path dependence, wherein the trajectory of economic activities is influenced by past choices. In the context of digitalization, early technology adoption or investment decisions can lead to lock-in effects, where organizations become reliant on specific digital solutions, making it challenging to switch to more efficient alternatives.
- Trust and Reputation—Digitalization relies on trust and reputation mechanisms. Online transactions, e-commerce, and digital services require trust between parties. Institutions play a critical role in establishing and maintaining trust in digital environments.
- Digital Inclusion and the Digital Divide—The NIE framework can help analyze the impact of digitalization on inclusivity. It highlights how unequal access to digital technologies can create a digital divide, potentially exacerbating existing economic disparities.
- Government Regulation and Digital Markets—Digitalization raises questions about the role of governments in regulating digital markets and platforms. NIE can provide insights into how regulatory institutions must adapt to address issues such as data privacy, competition, and consumer protection in the digital era.

Implications of Digitalization on New Institutional Economics is:

- Increased Efficiency—Digitalization has the potential to reduce transaction costs, making markets more efficient. For instance, blockchain technology can reduce the need for intermediaries in transactions.
- New Forms of Property Rights—Digital goods, such as software and music, have led to the development of new forms of property rights. Digitalization has challenged traditional notions of ownership and control.
- Disintermediation—Digital platforms like Uber and Airbnb have disrupted traditional industries, challenging existing governance structures and regulatory frameworks. These platforms have also raised questions about the future of work and worker protections.

The New Institutional Economics offers a useful lens to understand how digitalization interacts with existing economic institutions and how these institutions respond to the challenges and opportunities presented by digital technologies. Understanding this relationship is crucial for policymakers, businesses, and society to harness the full potential of digitalization while addressing its potential pitfalls and ensuring its benefits are broadly shared.

E-government and Digital Services have the potential to enhance government efficiency, reduce bureaucratic red tape, and provide citizens with more convenient access to essential services. However, successful implementation requires careful planning, investment in technology infrastructure, cybersecurity measures, and continuous efforts to bridge the digital divide to ensure equitable access for all citizens.

While digitalization has brought numerous benefits, it has also raised concerns about data privacy, cybersecurity, digital divide, and potential job displacement due to automation. Striking a balance between embracing technological advancements and addressing the challenges it presents is an ongoing task for society.

In conclusion, digitalization has the potential to significantly reduce certain transaction costs, reshape economic behaviors, and prompt adaptations within institutional frameworks. However, managing the balance between the benefits and challenges introduced by digitalization remains an ongoing process for individuals, businesses, and policymakers.

Digitalization can both mitigate and exacerbate information asymmetry, depending on how it's harnessed. While it offers tools to reduce information imbalances, it also presents new challenges that institutions need to address to ensure fair and transparent economic interactions in the digital age.

The digital divide contributes to various forms of inequality, limiting opportunities and access to essential resources for those without access to digital technologies. Addressing the digital divide is crucial for creating a more equitable society and ensuring that everyone has the opportunity to fully participate in the digital age.

By applying the principles of New Institutional Economics to E-government, policymakers and researchers can gain valuable insights into the factors that influence the success and impact of digital governance initiatives. Understanding the institutional context and dynamics helps shape effective strategies for designing, implementing, and evaluating E-government services that align with the needs and expectations of citizens while promoting transparency, efficiency, and accountability.

References

Arwani, A., & Priyadi, U. (2024). The role and contribution of the new institutional economics in economic system performance. *Jurnal Simki Economic, 7*(1), 271–288. https://doi.org/10.29407/jse.v7i1.508

https://www.jstor.org/stable/40751586

https://www.sciencedirect.com/science/article/abs/pii/S0956522105000138

Kherallah, M., & Kirsten, J. F. (2002). The new institutional economics: Applications for agricultural policy research in developing countries. *Agrekon, 41*(2), 110–133.

Ménard, C., & Shirley, M. M. (2011). *The contribution of Douglass North to new institutional economics.* https://shs.hal.science/halshs-00624297/file/2011--Menard_Shirley_North_and_NIE--CUP.pdf

North, D. C. (1990). *Institutions, institutional change and economic performance* (Vol. 10). Cambridge University Press.

Williamson, O. E. (1981). The economics of organization: The transaction cost approach. *American Journal of Sociology, 87*(3), 548–577. http://www.jstor.org/stable/2778934

Digitalization and International Collaborations in Higher Education: Fostering a Global Academic Community (the Case of Georgia)

Vasil Kikutadze and Tamta Lekishvili

Abstract In an era characterized by globalization and the digital revolution, the landscape of higher education has witnessed a profound transformation in the way academics collaborate, exchange knowledge, and experience global perspectives. This research paper investigates the role of digitalization in fostering international collaborations, cross-cultural exchanges, and global experiences for academics. Utilizing a comprehensive literature review, case analysis, and primary data collected from academic institutions and international collaborative projects, this study explores the impact of digital technologies in transcending geographical barriers and connecting scholars from diverse cultural backgrounds. It analyzes how digital platforms, virtual research networks, online conferences, and webinars enable seamless communication and collaboration among academics across the globe. Key findings underscore the critical role of digitalization in fostering a global academic community. Academics collaborate on joint publications, participate in international research networks, and engage in virtual exchange programs, cultivating a culture of collaboration, diversity, and inclusivity. In conclusion, this research offers valuable insights into the transformative power of digitalization in advancing global collaboration and cross-cultural education for academics. By harnessing digital tools and virtual experience, academics can build meaningful connections with their global counterparts, fostering a culture of international collaboration and contributing to the advancement of knowledge in an interconnected world.

Keywords Global collaboration · Cross-cultural education · Digitalization · International collaborations · Virtual research networks

V. Kikutadze (✉) · T. Lekishvili
East European University, Tbilisi, Georgia
e-mail: v.kikutadze@eeu.edu.ge

T. Lekishvili
e-mail: t.lekishvili@eeu.edu.ge

R. C. Geibel and S. Machavariani (eds.), *Digital Management to Shape the Future*, Springer Proceedings in Business and Economics,
https://doi.org/10.1007/978-3-031-66517-2_4

1 Introduction

The landscape of higher education is undergoing profound transformations, driven by the dual forces of globalization and the digital revolution (Mense et al., 2018). Over recent decades, these transformative dynamics have reshaped how academics collaborate, share knowledge, and engage with diverse global perspectives (Altbach & Knight, 2007; Daniel, 2012). The infusion of digital technologies into academic practices has emerged as a transformative force, transcending traditional geographical constraints and nurturing a heightened sense of global community among scholars (Bates, 2019; Weller, 2020). As the contours of higher education continue to evolve, this research paper endeavors to unravel the intricate layers of digitalization's role in not just facilitating but fundamentally shaping international collaborations, cross-cultural exchanges, and the cultivation of a vibrant global academic community.

The significance of digitalization in driving international collaborations within higher education has assumed increasing prominence against the backdrop of globalization (Teichler, 2017). As the world becomes more interconnected, the imperative for a globalized approach to higher education intensifies (Deardorff & Jones, 2012). The advent of digital technologies has not only facilitated real-time communication but has also dismantled traditional barriers, paving the way for a seamless exchange of ideas and collaboration among academics worldwide (Hatos, 2019). This paper positions itself at the intersection of technological innovation and the changing landscape of international collaboration, aiming to dissect the intricate interplay between digitalization and the creation of a global academic community.

Despite the increasing discourse on digital transformation in recent years, there remains a notable gap in the literature concerning explicit identification and characterization of digital transformation initiatives within universities, the paper seeks to contribute valuable insights that extend beyond a mere examination of technological integration. Instead, it aims to uncover the nuanced ways in which digitalization acts as a catalyst, propelling higher education institutions towards the forefront of global engagement and collaboration. As the global academic community continues to evolve, understanding the multifaceted role of digitalization becomes paramount, offering a roadmap for institutions committed to fostering cross-cultural education and advancing collaborative knowledge creation in an increasingly interconnected world.

2 Theory

2.1 Globalization and Higher Education

Globalization has brought about significant changes in higher education, leading to the internationalization of academia. As universities and academic institutions seek to provide students with a more global perspective, they are increasingly engaging in international collaborations (Knight, 2004). Globalization has created a need for academic institutions to prepare students for a world where intercultural competence and global awareness are crucial (Maringe & Woodfield, 2013). Digitalization plays a pivotal role in supporting these goals by providing tools and platforms that enable academics to connect across borders.

Digitalization and the Transformation of Education:

The digital revolution has transformed higher education in fundamental ways. The use of digital technologies, including the Internet, online learning platforms, and collaborative software, has reshaped traditional teaching and learning methods (Garrison & Kanuka, 2004). Digitalization has opened up opportunities for educators to transcend physical boundaries and engage in innovative teaching practices. It has also enabled students and scholars to access resources and expertise from around the world, enriching the educational experience (Shohel et al., 2021).

Digital Platforms for International Collaboration:

Digital platforms have become indispensable for international collaborations in higher education. Platforms like Zoom, Skype, and Microsoft Teams have made it easier for academics to conduct virtual meetings, webinars, and online conferences with colleagues from different parts of the world. These platforms facilitate real-time communication, allowing academics to share ideas, collaborate on research projects, and participate in cross-cultural exchanges (Tozini, 2020). They also enable the creation of virtual research networks that connect scholars globally.

Virtual Research Networks:

Virtual research networks have become essential for fostering global collaborations in higher education. These networks consist of scholars and researchers who collaborate on joint projects, share research findings, and exchange knowledge using digital tools. They may focus on specific academic disciplines or interdisciplinary topics and provide a platform for academics to build international partnerships and engage in cross-cultural research (Madden, et al., 2022).

Online Conferences and Webinars:

Online conferences and webinars have become popular alternatives to traditional in-person academic conferences. Digital platforms have made it feasible for academics to participate in international conferences without the need for physical travel. This has broadened opportunities for scholars to present their work, network with peers, and engage in cross-cultural dialogue (Inês & Márcia, 2023).

Virtual Exchange Programs:

Virtual exchange programs are another outcome of digitalization in higher education. These programs enable students and academics to interact with counterparts from different countries without leaving their own institutions. Virtual exchanges provide a cost-effective way to internationalize education and promote cross-cultural understanding (Proctor & Rumbley, 2018). Digital tools and platforms support virtual exchange programs by facilitating communication and collaboration.

2.2 Diversity and Inclusivity

Digitalization in higher education heralds a transformative era where the promotion of diversity and inclusivity emerges as a key outcome. The advent of digital platforms has revolutionized the academic landscape, providing unprecedented opportunities for scholars from diverse cultural backgrounds to collaborate and engage in meaningful academic activities. This paradigm shift fosters a culture of inclusivity, breaking down traditional barriers and broadening the perspectives of both students and academics.

The potential of digital platforms to enhance diversity and inclusivity in higher education is underscored by the work of Kryklii (2021). In his research, Kryklii delves into the profound impact of digitalization on academic collaboration, emphasizing how it transcends geographical constraints and cultural boundaries. The ability of scholars from different corners of the globe to connect and collaborate in virtual spaces is pivotal in dismantling traditional barriers that often impede inclusivity in academic endeavors.

Digital platforms, ranging from collaborative online spaces to virtual research networks, create a level playing field where individuals from diverse cultural backgrounds can contribute to academic discussions, share insights, and engage in collaborative research projects. This democratization of academic spaces aligns with the principles of inclusivity, ensuring that voices that might have been marginalized in traditional academic settings now find a platform for expression and contribution.

Moreover, the inclusivity facilitated by digitalization extends beyond cultural diversity to encompass a broader spectrum of learners and educators. The flexibility offered by online learning platforms accommodates diverse learning styles, preferences, and needs. Learners who might face challenges in traditional classroom settings, whether due to geographical remoteness, physical disabilities, or other constraints, find an accessible and inclusive environment through digitalized education.

The work of scholars such as Selwyn (2016) and Bates (2019) further supports the assertion that digitalization enhances inclusivity in higher education. Selwyn emphasizes the need to critically examine the intersection of technology and education, questioning assumptions about universal access and participation. Bates, in his exploration of teaching in a digital age, acknowledges the role of digital technologies in making education more accessible to a broader and more diverse audience.

In conclusion, the promotion of diversity and inclusivity stands as a significant hallmark of the digitalization wave sweeping through higher education. As scholars from various cultural backgrounds seamlessly collaborate in virtual spaces, and as online learning platforms cater to a diverse array of learners, the digital era in education is shaping a more inclusive and equitable academic landscape.

3 Research Methods

This study employs a quantitative approach to investigate the role of digitalization in fostering international collaborations and cross-cultural experiences among academics. The research includes a comprehensive literature review, analysis of academic institutions, and primary data collected through surveys and interviews with academics and institutional representatives engaged in international collaborative projects. By utilizing these approaches, the study explores the impact of digital technologies in transcending geographical barriers and connecting scholars from diverse cultural backgrounds.

The instrument of the study for the quantitative research was the survey using the structured questionnaire, which was allocated to academics of thirty-three existing Universities in Georgia.

A thorough analysis and synthesis of data from all sources were undertaken, resulting in the formulation of conclusive findings.

4 Results and Discussion

The research findings confirm that digital platforms, virtual research networks, online conferences, and webinars have played a pivotal role in facilitating international collaborations. Academics across the globe use these tools to connect with colleagues from diverse cultural backgrounds, share research findings, and engage in collaborative projects.

The study highlights the critical role of digitalization in fostering a global academic community. Academics collaborate on joint publications, participate in international research networks, and engage in virtual exchange programs, thereby cultivating a culture of collaboration, diversity, and inclusivity, which in any other case would be more complicated without digital technologies.

The level of internationalization of education in Georgia is gradually increasing and it is becoming even more scalable with digital technologies. According to the National Statistics Office of Georgia (Geostat.ge, 2023) the number of foreign students in Georgian state and private universities is as follows (Fig. 1).

In total, 87 country representatives were engaged in the education process in Georgia, for the 2022–2023 academic year, which is very impressive and significant progress for Georgia.

The study explored 51 academics from 18 Georgian Universities (out of 33 existed) to provide a quantitative understanding of the impact of digitalization.

Figure 2 provides a visual representation of the diverse array of universities under examination, offering a glimpse into the geographical (as some universities are located in the regional parts of Georgia) and institutional variety encompassed by the study. This breakdown is essential for contextualizing the findings within the broader landscape of higher education and digitalization, highlighting the inclusive nature of

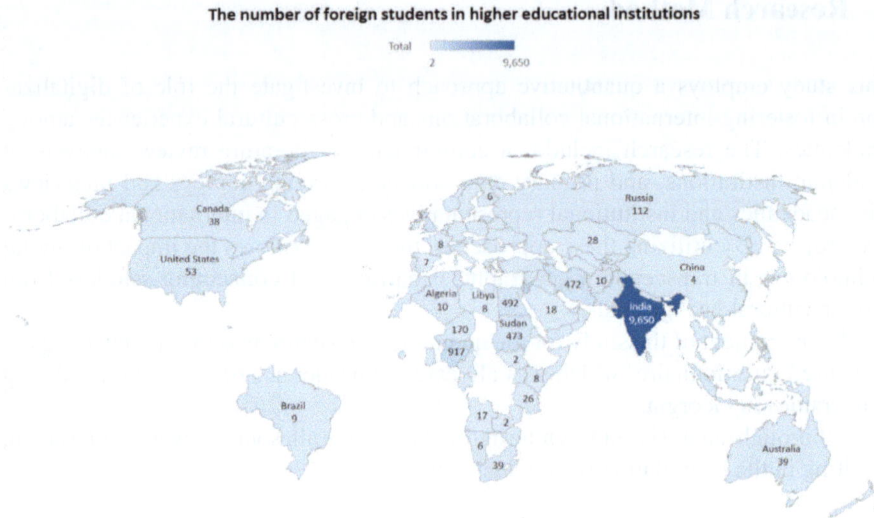

Fig. 1 Number of foreign students in Georgia by country (*Source* Own Graphic based on geosta t.ge Data)

the research in considering multiple academic institutions. The study showed that the degree of internationalization by using digital technologies is higher in the capital city of Georgia and in private universities compared to the universities in the regional areas, where in several cases they face the lack of modern technologies and in some cases the limited access to the internet. This has been an issue during pandemics and there are many governmental and non-governmental support programs to deal with this problem (Fig. 3).

The chart highlights the diversity of academic titles within the sample, offering a comprehensive view of the professional composition of the study participants. This variety is instrumental in understanding the perspectives and experiences of individuals at various stages of their academic careers within the context of digitalization and international collaborations in higher education. The study showed that the reliance on digital tools, recognition of the value of international collaborations, and the positive impact of these collaborations on research quality and diversity are confirmed across all academic titles. Whereas, junior academics highlight personal growth and skill development, while senior academics focus on strategic leadership and institutional impact. The comparative analysis uncovers how perspectives evolve with career progression.

The distribution of responses in Fig. 4 provides valuable insights into the prevalence of international collaborations among academics within the study. The varying frequencies reported shed light on the diverse engagement levels in global academic endeavors. Here are key observations and interpretations:

High Engagement Levels:

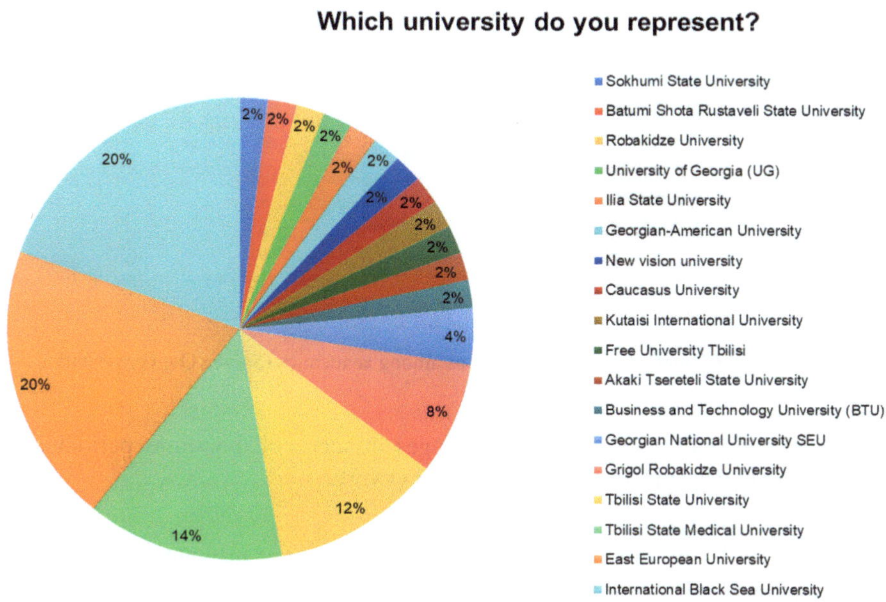

Fig. 2 Universities in the study (*Source* Own presentation)

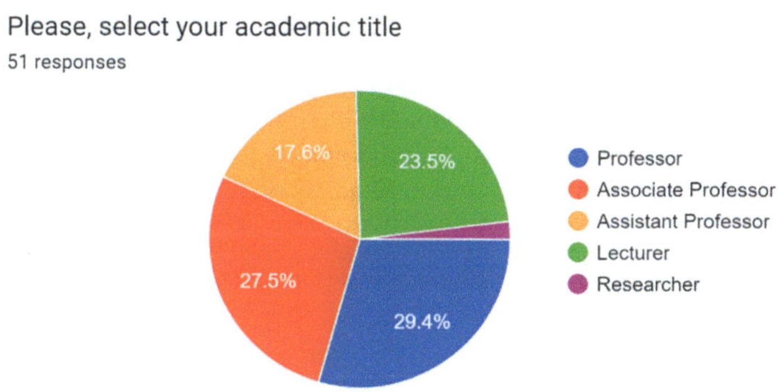

Fig. 3 Academic titles of the respondents (*Source* Own presentation)

The combined percentage of respondents indicating "Very Frequently" and "Frequently" (49%) suggests a substantial portion of academics actively participate in international collaborations. This heightened engagement aligns with the contemporary emphasis on global knowledge exchange.

Moderate Engagement Levels:

The "Occasionally" category, representing 27.5% of respondents, reflects a moderate but consistent level of international collaboration. This indicates that

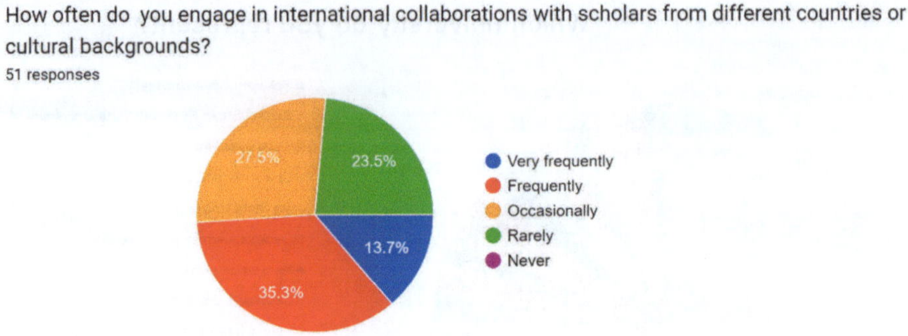

Fig. 4 Frequency of international collaborations among academics (*Source* Own presentation)

a considerable portion of academics engages in such collaborations periodically, contributing to a sustained global academic network.

Low Engagement Levels:

The "Rarely" category, at 23.5%, indicates a segment of respondents with infrequent participation in international collaborations. This might be influenced by various factors, such as institutional constraints, disciplinary nature, or personal preferences.

Zero Non-Engagement:

Notably, the "Never" category reports zero percent. This absence suggests a general openness or inclination among the surveyed academics toward international collaborations, with no respondents explicitly stating a complete lack of engagement.

The analysis of Fig. 5 reveals a pronounced reliance on digital tools for international collaboration among surveyed academics.

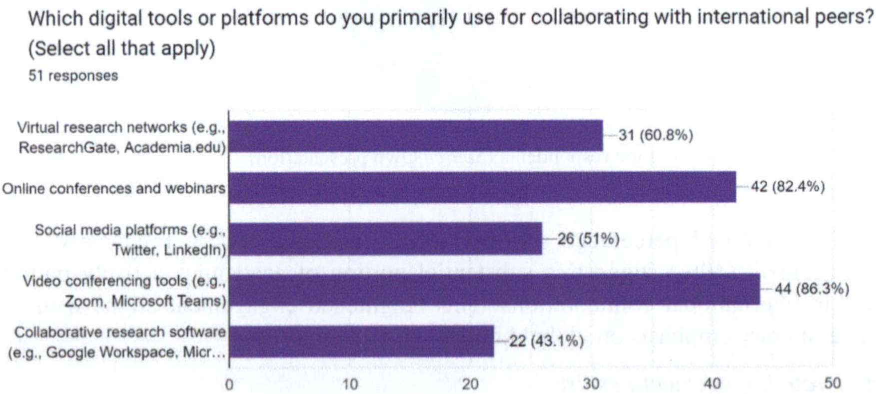

Fig. 5 Digital tools used for international collaboration (*Source* Own presentation)

Video conferencing tools emerge as paramount, with an overwhelming adoption rate of 86.3%, indicating the central role of real-time, face-to-face interaction in overcoming geographical barriers. Online conferences and webinars follow closely at 82.4%, emphasizing their efficacy in facilitating academic exchanges. Virtual networks, with a 60.8% adoption rate, signify their significance in building and sustaining global academic communities. However, moderate adoption rates for social media platforms (51%) and collaborative research software (43.1%) suggest opportunities for training and awareness initiatives. These insights offer institutions valuable guidance for optimizing digital infrastructure and support mechanisms to enhance international collaboration within the academic community.

Figure 6 illuminates the substantial benefits derived from digital collaboration among surveyed academics. A staggering 90.2% highlight faster communication as a paramount advantage, underscoring the pivotal role of digital tools in expediting information exchange and overcoming temporal constraints. The access to a broader spectrum of expertise, endorsed by 74.5%, signals the transformative impact of digital collaboration on knowledge acquisition and dissemination. Furthermore, 70.6% acknowledge increased research productivity, emphasizing the efficiency gains afforded by collaborative digital platforms. Although slightly less pronounced, the recognition of enhanced cross-cultural understanding by 54.9% attests to the role of digital collaboration in fostering a globalized academic community, enriching perspectives and transcending cultural boundaries. These findings underscore the multifaceted advantages of digital collaboration, offering institutions valuable insights into the diverse ways in which technology enhances academic endeavors.

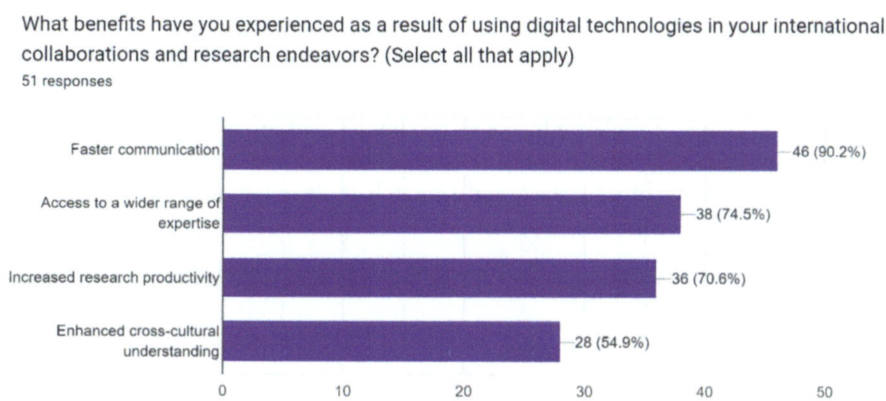

Fig. 6 Benefits of digital collaboration (*Source* Own presentation)

4.1 Building a Global Academic Community

While discussing the issue of building a global academic community, the study showed an extensive engagement of academics in the virtual exchange programs as well as working on joint publications.

The combined findings of Figs. 7 and 8 showcase a robust engagement in collaborative initiatives facilitated by digital platforms, signifying a significant stride towards building a global academic community. With 62.7% affirming their participation in collaborative projects and a notable 70.6% indicating joint publications, the results underscore a widespread commitment to leveraging digital tools for scholarly cooperation. This high participation rate not only emphasizes the willingness of academics to embrace global collaboration but also highlights the efficacy of digital platforms in fostering joint research endeavors. These outcomes collectively point to the transformative impact of digitalization in transcending geographical constraints, promoting knowledge exchange, and fostering a cohesive global academic community through collaborative initiatives and shared publications. It is also very promising that almost 90% of the respondents who have positive answers to the questions on Figs. 7 and 8. Consider this having either "very positive" or "positive" impact on their academic development (see Fig. 9).

5 Conclusions and Recommendations

In conclusion, this research paper has explored the profound impact of digitalization on international collaborations and cross-cultural exchanges within higher education. It has demonstrated that digital tools and platforms have become indispensable in fostering a global academic community. As the digital revolution continues to shape the landscape of higher education, academics and institutions must leverage these technologies to promote collaboration, diversity, and inclusivity, ultimately enhancing the quality of education and research in an interconnected world. The

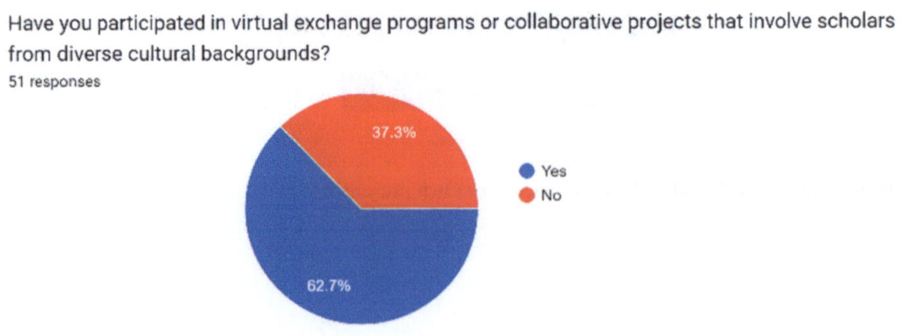

Fig.7 Participation Rate in Collaborative Projects

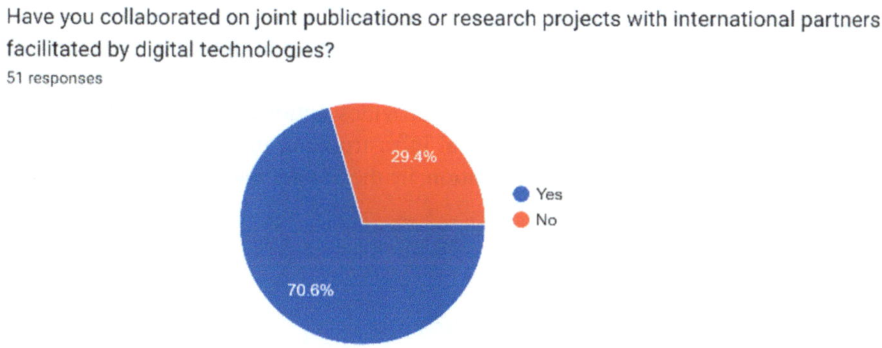

Fig. 8 Rate of Joint Publications (*Source* Own presentation)

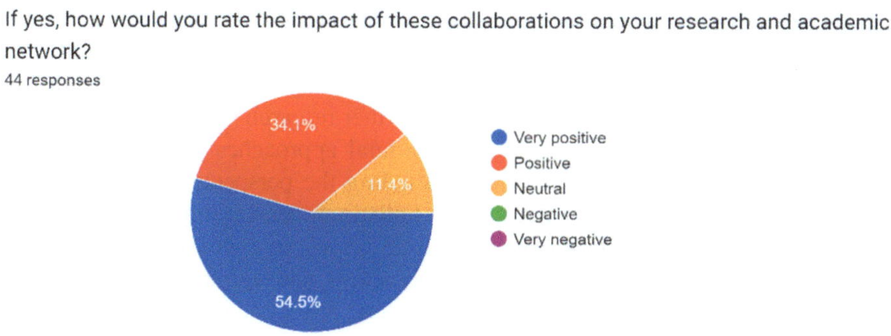

Fig. 9 Impact of virtual events on academic development (*Source* Own presentation)

implications and considerations drawn from the analysis offer a comprehensive roadmap for institutions seeking to cultivate a dynamic global academic community through digital platforms. The high participation rates in collaborative projects (62.7%) and joint publications (70.6%) underscore a widespread commitment to leveraging digital tools for scholarly cooperation, signaling a transformative stride towards building a cohesive international academic network. To enhance this engagement further, institutions should seize the opportunities presented, providing additional support and resources to nurture the enthusiasm for global collaborations. Identifying and addressing potential barriers, especially those contributing to occasional or rare engagement, becomes crucial for fostering more widespread and frequent collaborations. Disciplinary variances in engagement levels suggest tailoring strategies based on academic cohorts, and optimizing resource allocation for targeted support programs. Recognizing the preference for real-time, interactive communication through video conferencing tools, institutions can invest in robust infrastructure to facilitate collaborative engagements. Additionally, fostering virtual networking initiatives and providing training programs for social media platforms and collaborative research software can further optimize the use of digital tools, enriching the global academic community.

In conclusion, this integrated analysis provides actionable insights for institutions to strategically enhance their digital infrastructure, thereby advancing global collaboration and cross-cultural education in the interconnected realm of higher education.

5.1 Limitations and Further Study

While this study contributes valuable insights into digitalization and international collaborations in higher education in Georgia, certain limitations warrant consideration. The study's focus on specific academic institutions and collaborative projects may limit the generalizability of findings to a broader context. Additionally, the cross-sectional design captures a snapshot, potentially overlooking the dynamic nature of long-term digital transformations. Further research should explore diverse institutional settings and incorporate longitudinal approaches to track the evolution of digital collaborations over time. Including the perspectives of administrative staff and students would offer a more holistic understanding of collaborative dynamics. Addressing these limitations in future research endeavors and including other countries' cases will enhance the robustness and applicability of findings in guiding effective strategies for fostering global academic communities through digital platforms.

References

Altbach, P. G., & Knight, J. (2007). The internationalization of higher education: Motivations and realities. *Journal of Studies in International Education, 11*(3–4), 290–305.

Bates, A. (2019). *Teaching in a digital age—Second edition.* Tony Bates. https://pressbooks.bccampus.ca/teachinginadigitalagev2/

Daniel, J. (2012). Making sense of MOOCs: Musings in a maze of myth, paradox and possibility. *Journal of Interactive Media in Education, 3*(2012), Art. 18. https://doi.org/10.5334/2012-18

Deardorff, D., & Jones, E. (2012). Intercultural competence: An emerging focus in international higher education. In D. Deardorff, & E. Jones, *The SAGE handbook of international higher education* (pp. 283–304). Sage Publications.

Garrison, D. R., & Kanuka, H. (2004). Blended learning: Uncovering its transformative potential in higher education. *The Internet and Higher Education, 7*(2), 95–105.

Geostat.ge. (2023). *Number of foreign students in Georgia.* National Statistics Office of Georgia. https://www.geostat.ge/

Hatos, A. (2019). The impact of digitalization on educational achievement: A literature review from a sociological perspective. *Calitatea Vieții, 30*(1), 3–16.

Inês, M., & Márcia, S. (2023). Challenges and strategies of digital communication in an educational organization in Portugal, in the COVID-19 pandemic period. *Open Edition Journals—Comunicação e sociedade, 43*, e023013.

Knight, J. (2004). Internationalization Remodeled: Definition, approaches, and rationales. *Journal of Studies in International Education, 8*(1), 5–31.

Kryklii, O. (2021). The role of education in bridging the digital divide and ensuring digital inclusion. *Scientific opinion: Economics and Management.*

Madden, D. G., Alghader, M., C. C., Arniella, G., Cortez-Weir, J., Rose, B., ... Vangeepuram, N. (2022). Going virtual: building online collaborations to understand COVID-19's psychosocial impacts on New York City Adults. *Journal of Participatory Research Methods, 3*(2).

Maringe, F., & Woodfield, S. (2013). Contemporary issues on the internationalisation of higher education: Critical and comparative perspectives. *A Journal of Comparative and International Education, 43*(1), 1–8.

Mense, E. G., Lemoine, P. A., Garretson, C. J., & Richardson, M. D. (2018). The development of global higher education in a world of transformation. *Journal of Education and Development, 2*(3), 47.

Proctor, D., & Rumbley, L. E. (2018). The future agenda for internationalization in higher education: Next generation insights into research, policy, and practice. *Education.*

Selwyn, N. (2016). Is technology good for education? *Canadian Journal of Educational Administration and Policy*, 42–45.

Shohel, M., Ashrafuzzaman, M., Islam, M., S. S., & Mahmud, A. (2021). Blended teaching and learning in higher education. In M. Shohel, M. Ashrafuzzaman, M. T. Islam, S. Shams, & A. Mahmud (Eds.), *Blended handbook of research on developing a post-pandemic paradigm for virtual technologies in higher education.* IGI Global.

Teichler, U. (2017). Internationalisation trends in higher education and the changing role of international student mobility. *Journal of International Mobility, 4*, 177–216.

Tozini, K. (2020). Global perspectives on international student experiences in higher education. *Journal of International Students, 10*(2), 549–552.

Weller, M. (2020). *25 Years of Ed tech.* https://doi.org/10.3325/cmj.2020.61.477

The Impact of Cultural Differences on Consumer Behavior in Individualist and Collectivist Societies: A Study of Advertising Effectiveness and Brand Loyalty in Germany and Turkey

Laçin Serra Ateş

Abstract This paper examines the impact of cultural orientation—specifically individualism and collectivism—on brand loyalty and advertising effectiveness, focusing on a comparative study between Turkey and Germany. The study hypothesizes and explores the role of cultural orientation in shaping these aspects using self-administered survey data and statistical analysis. The findings highlight moderate levels of individualism and collectivism in both societies, reflecting shifts influenced by education and socio-political factors. Brand loyalty was high in both cultures, with Turkish consumers showing emotional connections to brands and Germans prioritizing quality. Despite comparable scores in advertising effectiveness, Turkish consumers favored emotional and socially responsible ads, while Germans leaned towards recommendations and word-of-mouth marketing.

Keywords Consumer behavior · Individualism · Collectivism · Brand loyalty · Advertising effectiveness

1 Introduction

In the current globalized landscape, companies eagerly seek international market penetration. However, the onset of the COVID-19 pandemic altered the global marketplace dynamics and profoundly impacted consumer behavior, especially in terms of heightened nationalism and an amplified understanding of cultural nuances (Su & Shen, 2020). The effects of cultural differences on advertising effectiveness and brand loyalty are well-documented. Yet, their implications in a pandemic context

L. S. Ateş (✉)
Hochschule Fresenius, Berlin, Germany
e-mail: lates15@ku.edu.tr

R. C. Geibel and S. Machavariani (eds.), *Digital Management to Shape the Future*, Springer Proceedings in Business and Economics,
https://doi.org/10.1007/978-3-031-66517-2_5

remain less explored. This study targets this gap, comparing Germany and Turkey—two nations with contrasting cultural orientations of individualism and collectivism, respectively.

In a post-COVID setting, grasping these cultural nuances becomes essential for companies. Tailored marketing strategies can forge stronger ties with consumers by recognizing and addressing their evolving preferences. Thus, our research explores the influence of individualism and collectivism on advertising and brand loyalty, especially within the unique contexts of Germany and Turkey. This study elaborates on cultural influences and culture's role in brand loyalty, building on the existing literature. Yoo (2009) posited that irrespective of national culture, collectivist-oriented consumers exhibit stronger brand loyalty than their individualistic counterparts. Furthermore, Lam (2007) highlighted that consumers from societies valuing individualism and discomfort with ambiguity often form stronger attachments to specific brands. This study aims to expand on these findings, comparing German and Turkish cultural settings. In parallel, this research assesses advertising effectiveness in the cultural spheres of Germany and Turkey. The study by Pergelova and Angulo-Ruiz (2017) revealed differences in advertising effectiveness across nations with distinct cultural dimensions. This study aims to supplement this knowledge, aligning with work that emphasizes the role of cultural orientations, like individualism and collectivism, in advertising strategies and consumer behaviors (Pham, 2022).

Recent societal changes, from rising anti-racism movements (Bundesregierung, 2023) to increased societal inclusivity (Knight, 2023), combined with significant migration patterns, like the intellectual migration from Turkey to Europe, suggest that past research findings might require reevaluation. This study explores the interplay between these societal evolutions and cultural values in the present context.

2 Theory

This section explores existing literature and theory, focusing on key concepts related to the study: Individualism and Collectivism, Brand Loyalty, and Advertising Effectiveness.

2.1 Individualism and Collectivism

Geert Hofstede's Cultural Dimensions Theory encompasses six cultural dimensions and provides a foundational framework for understanding the cultural variations between nations. This study focuses on the Individualism versus Collectivism dimension (IDV). In this dimension, Hofstede characterizes individualism as personal autonomy, independence, and self-expression, while collectivism emphasizes group harmony, interdependence, and a strong sense of belonging (2014). These cultural orientations shape various aspects of human interaction and decision-making, offering valuable insights into their implications on consumer behavior.

Individualistic cultures prioritize individual rights, self-reliance, and the pursuit of personal goals. These societies value personal achievements and independence. Relationships in individualistic cultures are often based on mutual interests and benefits, highlighting the priority of personal preferences and individual choice (Hofstede et al., 2010). In contrast, collectivist cultures prioritize group welfare over individual interests. Family plays a central role, and individuals are part of well-knit in-groups from birth onwards in collectivist societies. Maintaining harmony within the group and fostering close relationships are essential in collectivist cultures, and direct confrontation is avoided to preserve group harmony (Hofstede et al., 2010).

This study compares Germany and Turkey, representing individualist and collectivist cultural orientations. Germany strongly prioritizes personal freedom, self-realization, and direct communication, with a high individualism score of 67. Concepts like "Selbstverwirklichung" (self-realization) underscore the significance of fulfilling individual potential and creativity (Müssig, 2023). Direct communication is highly regarded, as evident from numerous German idioms that align with this preference (Erdoğan, 2022). Turkey leans towards collectivism with a score of 37, emphasizing group cohesion, familial loyalty, and indirect communication. The Turkish tradition of "Imece" underscores communal collaboration and shared responsibility, especially in rural areas. Turkish communication style tends to be more nuanced and indirect to maintain group harmony, as reflected in the language and idioms (Erdoğan, 2022). This comparative analysis provides a theoretical foundation for examining how these cultural differences in individualism and collectivism may influence advertising effectiveness and brand loyalty in Germany and Turkey.

2.2 *Brand Loyalty*

Brand loyalty is linked to cultural factors, beliefs, and values, which shape communication styles, thought processes, and message interpretation. Culture also molds how people view and engage with brands, affecting brand perception and resonance. Brand resonance is the emotional link between customers and a brand, characterized by intensity and activity dimensions. Intensity reflects the psychological connection, while activity measures customer engagement. This connection can manifest as behavioral loyalty, attitudinal attachment, a sense of community, and active engagement (Keller & Swaminathan, 2020). Brand loyalty differs from behavioral loyalty, encompassing a profound emotional attachment to a brand. It can be classified as true brand loyalty, rooted in conscious decision-making and commitment, or spurious brand loyalty, often stemming from inertia or familiarity (Bloemer & Kasper, 1995). Another perspective defines brand loyalty across three dimensions: behavioral (repeat purchases), attitudinal (positive brand attitudes), and attachment (emotional connection and brand identification) (Baldinger & Rubinson, 1996).

Brand loyalty benefits businesses with repeat purchases, positive word-of-mouth, cost-efficient feedback, and increased customer lifetime value. Loyal customers offer consistent revenue and act as brand advocates, providing valuable feedback to enhance products and services (Kumar, 2022; Reichheld, 2001).

Various factors shape brand loyalty, such as brand name, image, product quality, price, promotions, service quality, and store environment. Brand name and image build trust and familiarity (Keller & Swaminathan, 2020). The perceived value is influenced by product quality and pricing, whereas loyalty programs, such as promotions, have the potential to enhance loyalty and mitigate price-based competition (Melnyk & Bijmolt, 2015). The store environment, physical or digital, influences purchase intent and consumer perceptions of the brand (Liang & Lai, 2002; Liu, 2014).

In global markets, brands must adjust strategies for cultural differences and preferences. Cultural context significantly shapes brand perception and should be factored into marketing strategies (Boris, 2020). Brand culture, driven by history, leadership, and corporate social responsibility, offers a cultural context for brand comprehension and can impact customer loyalty and reputation (Schroeder et al., 2004).

2.3 Advertising Effectiveness

Advertising effectiveness is a complex concept encompassing essential elements for understanding its impact. Over the centuries, advertising has evolved as a tool for brand building and differentiation. Brands, as defined by the American Marketing Association, are identifiers that distinguish products or services from competitors. Brand visual identity, including logos, color schemes, and typography, helps create consistency in communication and fosters brand recognition and recall (Keller & Swaminathan, 2020, 124). It's essential to convey the brand's values, personality, and positioning through visual identity. A consistent and memorable brand experience, encompassing sensory, emotional, intellectual, and behavioral interactions with the brand, can lead to stronger brand attachment and increased advocacy (Brakus et al., 2009, 65). Effective brand messaging fosters an emotional connection and shapes consumer perceptions.

Advertising pursues multiple communication goals, like boosting brand awareness, creating positive brand attitudes, and stimulating purchase interest (Belch & Belch, 2021, 224). The DAGMAR framework by Russel H. Colley (1961) emphasizes measurable objectives tied to stages like awareness, comprehension, conviction, and action. Despite its influence, DAGMAR faces criticism for its potential limitations in capturing consumer behavior in the digital media era and its perceived impact on creativity and budget considerations.

Measuring advertising effectiveness includes pretesting and post-testing methods. Laboratory and field tests each have their own pros and cons. Various techniques, like consumer juries, portfolio assessments, theater trials, readability checks, comprehension and reaction assessments, and physiological measurements, reveal different aspects. Field tests, like dummy advertising vehicles, on-air tests, inquiry assessments, recognition evaluations, recall assessments, and tracking studies, offer real-world insights but can have limitations (Belch & Belch, 2021, 602). In online advertising, impression, effectiveness, and hybrid models assess campaign success, considering factors like ad cost, user interactions, conversions, and ROI (Rzemieniak, 2015, 981).

According to Nielsen (2017), creative content, reach, brand, recency, and campaign targeting influence advertising campaign effectiveness. Moreover, understanding cultural nuances is essential. Differences in values, traditions, customs, and language can shape consumer reactions to advertising. To maximize the effect and prevent cultural insensitivity, marketers must tailor their strategies to local contexts, understanding local values and norms (Belch & Belch, 2021, 638).

3 Research Method

This study targets participants from Germany and Turkey, aiming to recruit 100 participants from each country. Participants will be sourced via websites like Survey Circle, Survey Swap, and personal and professional networks. The primary instrument for data collection is a self-administered qualitative survey created via Microsoft Forms. Participants will be stratified by nationality using a random selection method to ensure representativeness. The survey is structured into four sections: individualism/collectivism, brand loyalty, advertising effectiveness, and demographics, designed to be completed in 8–10 min.

Rooted in Hofstede's framework, the first section explores a participant's inclination towards individualistic or collectivistic cultural values. The brand loyalty section dives into the depth of commitment to specific brands, examining trust, emotional connection, and repetitive purchasing behavior. The advertising effectiveness section assesses participants' perceptions and responses to advertising, measuring aspects like purchase influence and memory recall. Participants will use a 7-point Likert scale to indicate their agreement with twenty statements in the first three sections. The final section gathers demographic data for further subgroup analyses. The questionnaire includes negative questions to mitigate positivity bias effects and ensure data accuracy.

The initial survey, composed in English, will be translated into German and Turkish to maintain linguistic consistency. Sascha Sturm, a native German, will take charge of the German translation. Meanwhile, Dr. Arzu Ateş, with twenty years of expertise in teaching Turkish as a foreign language, will manage the Turkish translation. Yaren Öztürk, fluent in all three languages, will review the translations to ensure accuracy, thereby upholding cross-cultural validity.

Before widespread dissemination, a pre-test will be conducted with a small group to ensure the survey's validity and reliability. Feedback from this phase will fine-tune the questionnaire. Once refined, the updated survey link will be distributed. Any survey responses completed in less than five minutes will be excluded to maintain the integrity of the data. All collected data will then be stored in Excel.

During data preparation, each variable will be coded from 1 to 7 for analysis. Statistical analyses will be conducted in R, with the Mann–Whitney U test applied to compare scores between the German and Turkish respondents. Participants identifying as both German and Turkish will be excluded to prevent confounding factors. The test will determine the statistical significance of observed group differences, with a p-value under 0.05 indicating significant distinctions. Subsequently, it will generate descriptive statistics for brand loyalty and advertising effectiveness. Using Spearman's rank-order correlations, the associations between variables will be measured, aiming to understand correlations between individualism/collectivism, brand loyalty, and advertising effectiveness.

4 Results and Discussion

The German sample was composed of 100 participants, whose ages ranged from 18 to 65+. A significant majority, 91%, had at least an undergraduate degree. The gender distribution showed that 59% were female, and 91% lived in the country of their birth. From the questionnaire, scores indicated moderate levels of individualism/collectivism (3.22), brand loyalty (3.92), and advertising effectiveness (3.39).

In comparison, the Turkish sample, also consisting of 100 participants, had 41% aged between 25 and 34. A significant portion, 68%, held an undergraduate degree, and 87% lived in their birth country. The mean scores for the three categories were 3.06 for individualism/collectivism, 4.20 for brand loyalty, and 3.36 for advertising effectiveness. The results suggest a slightly lower score for collectivism and advertising effectiveness than the German sample but a higher score for brand loyalty.

Statistical analyses using the Mann–Whitney U test showed no significant differences between the German and Turkish participants in individualism/collectivism, brand loyalty, and advertising effectiveness since all p-values were above the significance level of 0.05. The Spearman's Rank Order Correlation also revealed no significant associations between individualism/collectivism and brand loyalty and between individualism/collectivism and advertising effectiveness.

4.1 Discussion of the Individualism and Collectivism

Several intriguing observations arose from the analysis. While both German and Turkish participants showed moderate levels of individualism and collectivism, 44% and 46% respectively, these figures deviate from Hofstede's cultural dimensions insights. Germany typically scores much higher in individualism (67%) than Turkey (37%). However, the Turkish sample displayed a markedly high level of education. Contrary to the Turkish Statistical Institute, which states only 23.9% of individuals aged 25 and over had a tertiary education in 2022, this survey showed a significant skew towards higher education levels. This discrepancy can be tied to colleges and similar institutions emphasizing independence as an ideal (Stephens & Townsend, 2021), suggesting that the educated may possess more individualistic traits.

The socio-political landscape in Turkey further complicates matters. The nation is currently politically polarized (Khrimian, 2022), with recent presidential election results showing a split between the electorate. This, coupled with bans on public celebrations that traditionally promote national unity, might have influenced feelings of individualism among respondents (İlknur, 2020). Additionally, the current immigrant crisis in Turkey and an increasing inclination towards emigration, especially among the educated (Yılmaz, 2022), could also influence the higher individualism scores.

The German sample, on the other hand, showed surprising results. Instead of scoring 67% in individualism, as Hofstede's insights suggest, they scored 44%, indicating a trend towards more collectivism. The survey results provide more nuanced insights into this shift. For instance, several statements received high scores that indicate a more collectivist mindset. A notable proportion of respondents agreed with the statement, "*I consult with my family and close friends before making important decisions*," illustrating the importance placed on collective decision-making over individual choices. Similarly, responses to the statement, "*I sacrifice my personal interests for the good of my group*," underline the growing inclination towards prioritizing group welfare over personal gain.

Other statements indicating a collectivist lean include, "*I prefer working alone rather than in a team*" (in reverse scoring) and "*I believe it is necessary to maintain harmony in my group or community*." These statements demonstrate a group-oriented approach to work and a significant emphasis on maintaining collective harmony. Furthermore, responses to "*I feel comfortable conforming to my group's norms and expectations*" and "*Having close connections with people from my cultural or social background is important*" showcase the value placed on social conformity and the importance of strong relational ties in their societal context. Lastly, the statement "*The conventions and rules of the group I belong to influence my behavior*" was met with significant agreement, further highlighting the shift towards collectivist values.

The shift towards a more collectivist mindset in German society may, in part, be traced back to certain societal trends and movements. For instance, Germany's fight against racism, its multicultural ethos (Bundesregierung, 2023), and inclusive political policies, like the 'Opportunity Card' (Knight, 2023), might be nurturing collectivist tendencies.

4.2 Discussion of the Brand Loyalty

Several statements in the brand loyalty section received high scores that indicate strong brand attachment and loyalty among Turkish respondents. These statements align with elements contributing to brand loyalty and reflecting the importance

Turkish consumers place on their relationship with particular brands. The brand loyalty chapter of the paper explains these elements in detail.

A notable proportion of respondents agreed with the statement, "*There are brands I consider myself loyal to*," illustrating their tendency to establish long-term relationships with particular brands and their repetitive purchase behavior. This sentiment speaks to the commitment component of brand loyalty, where customers stick to a brand over time. Similarly, the agreement with the statement, "*There are brands I buy whenever I can*," further underscores this loyalty, highlighting the behavioral element of repeated purchases.

Another statement receiving high scores was, "*I can identify with certain brands that come to my mind when I hear a product category*" suggesting that specific brands have become top-of-mind and have strong associations with particular product categories. This cognitive loyalty indicates brand resonance and positioning in consumers' minds. Furthermore, the respondents' agreement with the statement, "*I am interested in learning more about my favorite brands*," demonstrates an active engagement and interest in their chosen brands, reflecting their emotional connection and involvement.

The statement, "*I am proud to have others know that I like using certain brands and identify with people who use the same brands*," shows social identity theory, where individuals identify with the membership in certain groups, in this case, brand communities. Lastly, the agreement with the statement, "*There are some brands I have happy memories with*," illustrates the power of nostalgia and positive past experiences in forging emotional connections with brands, further enhancing brand loyalty.

As for the German respondents, it is interesting to note the prominence of one particular brand loyalty statement, "*I trust my favorite brands to produce high-quality products*." This statement was highly rated among German respondents, pointing to a crucial element of German consumer psychology: the importance of quality. As mentioned before, product quality is one of the crucial elements contributing to brand loyalty. According to a report, 58% of Germans are increasingly willing to pay more for quality products (2019).

Nevertheless, while Turkish and German participants displayed high levels of brand loyalty, their emotional attachment and connection to brands manifested in different ways. As previously discussed, Turkish participants showed a higher average score for brand loyalty ($M = 4.20$) compared to German participants ($M = 3.92$). This discrepancy may be explained by examining the unique elements of brand loyalty that resonated more with the Turkish respondents. The Turkish participants identified more with affective aspects of brand loyalty, such as social identification with a brand, deriving pride from brand use, and the presence of positive memories associated with certain brands. These aspects paint a picture of brand loyalty that is deeply rooted in emotional engagement, group identity, and nostalgic connections, contributing to the higher loyalty scores observed in the Turkish sample. While both German and Turkish consumers display brand loyalty, their pathways to developing and maintaining this loyalty may diverge based on cultural factors.

4.3 Discussion of the Advertising Effectiveness

The advertising effectiveness scores were closely matched for the Turkish and German samples, with mean scores of 3.36 and 3.39, respectively. These averages imply a similar receptiveness towards advertising in both cultural contexts. However, the specific aspects that produced strong agreement within each group highlight their distinct advertising preferences and offer a richer understanding of the unique consumer behaviors within these nationalities.

Both Turkish and German participants agreed highly with the statement, "*Ads that evoke emotions (e.g., happiness, nostalgia) impact my purchase decisions*," suggesting that emotionally-driven advertising could be an effective strategy in both markets. Similarly, both groups demonstrated trust in products advertised with sustainability or social responsibility messaging, aligning with global trends towards ethical consumerism and underscoring the role of socially responsible advertising in shaping consumer trust and brand loyalty in both nationalities.

The responses from the Turkish sample in the survey highlight several points related to advertising effectiveness, emphasizing a variety of marketing objectives that particularly resonate with this audience. To begin, most respondents agreed with the statement, "*I find advertisements entertaining and engaging*," reflecting the importance of creating captivating and interactive content in advertising.

The survey also found that advertising contributes to shaping Turkish consumer preferences, as indicated by the agreement with the statement, "*I believe that ads influence my preferences and tastes*." This statement implies that well- structured advertising campaigns can sway consumer choices and foster brand preference. Lastly, the tendency to interact with social media advertisements reflects the effectiveness of digital marketing in encouraging consumer engagement, highlighting the crucial role of social media platforms in modern advertising strategies. On the other hand, German participants showed a marked tendency towards favoring recommendations when deciding on purchases, indicating the potential effectiveness of word-of-mouth marketing in the German market.

5 Conclusion, Limitations and Further Research

The survey analysis of individualism/collectivism, brand loyalty, and advertising effectiveness offers a detailed perspective on German and Turkish cultures, diverging from Hofstede's insights. Turkish and German samples reflected changing cultural orientations, with Turkish education levels and Germany's inclusive policies influencing results. While both nationalities showed strong brand loyalty, Turks were more emotionally attached to brands, whereas Germans prioritized quality. Advertising effectiveness was similar, but preferences differed: emotionally charged and socially responsible ads appealed to both, with Turks finding ads influential and Germans favoring personal recommendations.

This study, however, has limitations. The chosen samples were highly educated, potentially skewing results. The Turkish-German cultural overlap due to the significant Turkish population in Germany might also influence outcomes. Future research could examine cultures with more distinct individualism/collectivism differences and incorporate other cultural dimensions like power distance and uncertainty avoidance. Additionally, future studies should dive deeper into varying advertising strategies, assessing their impact across cultures to optimize marketing efforts.

References

10 minutes with Geert Hofstede on Individualisme versus Collectivisme 10112014. (2014). YouTube. https://www.youtube.com/watch?v=zQj1VPNPHIl&t=29s. Accessed 19 May 2023.

Baldinger, A. L., & Rubinson, J. (1996). Brand loyalty: The link between attitude and behavior. *Journal of Advertising Research*, 22–34. https://rubinsonwhitepapers.s3.us-east-2.amazonaws.com/96+12+JAR+Baldinger+Rubinson+Brand+Loyalty.pdf. Accessed 19 March 2023.

Belch, G. E., & Belch, M. A. (2021). *Advertising and promotion: An integrated marketing communications perspective*. McGraw-Hill.

Bloemer, J. M. M., & Kasper, H. D. P. (1995). The complex relationship between consumer satisfaction and Brand Loyalty. *Journal of Economic Psychology, 16*(1195), 311–329. https://doi.org/10.1016/0167-4870(95)00007-b

Boris. (2020). *Mr. Clean's strategy to become global brand with name change, High names—International naming service, brand name, product name*. https://highnames.com/mr-cleans-strategy-global-brand-with-name-change/. Accessed 6 April 2023.

Brakus, J. J., Schmitt, B. H., & Zarantonello, L. (2009). Brand experience: What is it? How is it measured? Does it affect loyalty? *Journal of Marketing, 73*(3), 52–68. https://doi.org/10.1509/jmkg.73.3.52

Country Comparison Tool. (no date). *Hofstede Insights*. https://www.hofstede-insights.com/country-comparison-tool?countries=germany%2Cturkey. Accessed 20 May 2023.

Erdoğan, E. (2022). Türkçe ve Almanca Deyimlerde i letişim Biçemleri—Kültürdilbilimsel Bir i nceleme, Dil Araştırmaları [Preprint]. https://doi.org/10.54316/dilarastirmalari.1163351

German Consumers Willing to pay More for Quality Produce. (2019). *Hortidaily*. https://www.hortidaily.com/article/9096085/german-consumers-willing-to-pay-more-for-quality-produce/. Accessed 07 July 2023.

Hofstede, G., Hofstede, G. J., & Minkov, M. (2010). *Cultures and organizations: Software of the mind: Intercultural cooperation and its importance for survival*. McGraw-Hill.

İlknur, M. (2020). Ya çeşitli Bahanelerle iptal Ettiler Ya da Içini Boşaltarak Cumhuriyet ve atatürk'le Hesaplaşma Yolunu Seçtiler, Cumhuriyet. https://www.cumhuriyet.com.tr/haber/ya-cesitli-bahanelerle-iptal-ettiler-ya-da-icini-bosaltarak-cumhuriyet-ve-ataturkle-hesaplasma-yolunu-sectiler-1761614. Accessed 01 July 2023.

Kein Platz für Rassismus: Bundesregierung. 2023. Die Bundesregierung informiert | Startseite. https://www.bundesregierung.de/breg-de/suche/tag-gegen-rassismus-2172570. Accessed 06 July 2023.

Keller, K. L., & Swaminathan, V. (2020). *Strategic brand management: Building, measuring, and managing brand equity*. Pearson.

Khrimian, A. (2022). *Democratic backsliding in the Middle East's former beacon of democracy: Polarization and media control by Erdoğan and the AKP, democratic erosion*. https://www.democratic-erosion.com/2022/04/30/democratic-backsliding-in-the-middle-easts-former-beacon-of-democracy-polarization-and-media-control-by-erdogan-and-the-akp/. Accessed 01 July 2023.

Knight, B. (2023). *German parliament reforms skilled work immigration law, dw.com.* https://www.dw.com/en/german-parliament-reforms-skilled-work-immigration-law/a-66010566#:~:text=Those%20who%20are%20awaiting%20asylum,here%20on%20a%20tourist%20visa. Accessed 06 July 2023.

Kumar, S. (2022). Customer retention versus customer acquisition, forbes. *Forbes Magazine.* Available at: https://www.forbes.com/sites/forbesbusinesscouncil/2022/12/12/customer-retention-versus-customer-acquisition/?sh=783861421c7d. Accessed: 24 March 2023.

Lam, D. (2007). Cultural influence on proneness to brand loyalty. *Journal of International Consumer Marketing, 19*(3), 7–21. https://doi.org/10.1300/j046v19n03_02

Liang, T.-P., & Lai, H.-J. (2002). Effect of store design on consumer purchases: An empirical study of on-line bookstores. *Information & Management, 39*(6), 431–444. https://doi.org/10.1016/s0378-7206(01)00129-x

Liu, Y. (2014) Store environment and consumer purchase behavior: Mediating role of consumer emotions, Psychology and Marketing. https://www.academia.edu/6568382/Store_Environment_and_Consumer_Purchase_Behavior_Mediating_Role_of_Consumer_Emotions. Accessed 5 April 2023.

Melnyk, V., & Bijmolt, T. (2015). The effects of introducing and terminating loyalty programs. *European Journal of Marketing, 49*(3/4), 398–419. https://doi.org/10.1108/ejm-12-2012-0694

Müssig, L. V. (2023). *Selbstverwirklichung: So Entfalten Sie Ihr wahres ich, Vogue Germany.* https://www.vogue.de/lifestyle/artikel/selbstverwirklichung. Accessed 20 May 2023.

Nielsen. (2017). *When it comes to advertising effectiveness, what is key?* https://www.nielsen.com/insights/2017/when-it-comes-to-advertising-effectiveness-what-is-key/. Accessed 7 May 2023.

Pergelova, A., & Angulo-Ruiz, F. (2017). Comparing advertising effectiveness in south-American and north-American contexts: Testing Hofstede's and Inglehart's cultural dimensions in the higher education sector. *International Journal of Advertising, 36*(6), 870–892. https://doi.org/10.1080/02650487.2017.1364032

Pham, T. (2022). Individualism and collectivism in advertising—An overview. *Journal of English Language Teaching and Applied Linguistics, 4*(1), 30–36. https://doi.org/10.32996/jeltal.2022.4.1.3

Reichheld, F. (2001). *Prescription for cutting costs, Bain & Company.* https://www.bain.com/insights/prescription-for-cutting-costs-bain-brief/. Accessed 24 March 2023.

Rzemieniak, M. (2015). Measuring the effectiveness of online advertising campaigns inthe aspect of e-entrepreneurship. *Procedia Computer Science, 65*, 980–987. https://doi.org/10.1016/j.procs.2015.09.063

Schroeder, J. E., Salzer-Mörling, M., & Askegaard, S. (2004). *Brand culture.* Routledge.

Stephens, N. M., & Townsend, S. (2021). Research: How you feel about individualism is influenced by your social class. *Harvard Business Review.* https://hbr.org/2017/05/research-how-you-feel-about-individualism-is-influenced-by-your-social-class. Accessed 01 July 2023.

Su, R., & Shen, W. (2020). Is nationalism rising in times of the covid-19 pandemic? Individual-level evidence from the United States. *Journal of Chinese Political Science, 26*(1), 169–187. https://doi.org/10.1007/s11366-020-09696-2

Yılmaz, F. (2022). Yükselen Bir fenomen: Türkiye'den Avrupa'ya Beyin Göçü, Perspektif. https://perspektif.eu/2022/12/01/yukselen-bir-fenomen-turkiyeden-avrupaya-beyin-gocu/. Accessed 01 July 2023.

Yoo, B. (2009). Cross-national invariance of the effect of personal collectivistic orientation on brand loyalty and equity. *Asia Pacific Journal of Marketing and Logistics, 21*(1), 41–57. https://doi.org/10.1108/13555850910926236

Enhancing Economic Growth Through Digital Technologies: A Focus on Customs Risk

Rusudan Seturidze

Abstract This paper delves into the significance of digital technology not only in terms of technological advancements but also its role in process modernization, particularly evident in the customs risk system. The customs risk system plays a pivotal role in identifying and assessing risks, developing response plans, and streamlining risk management processes. In the realm of digital technology, customs risk management has undergone significant transformation. The adoption of web portals by taxpayers has revolutionized the way they interact with customs authorities, providing them with a lots of advantages. These advantages include resource-saving, reduced risk of document processing errors, enhanced data accuracy, cost reduction, minimal reliance on paper documentation, and substantial time savings. Moreover, the implementation of digital services has made interactions between taxpayers and customs authorities more convenient, accessible, and user-friendly. The ultimate goal of customs authorities is to ensure that all taxpayers fulfill their tax obligations promptly and accurately. This objective can only be effectively achieved by reducing the risk of tax evasion. Consequently, paramount importance is given to the system's correctness, convenience, and accessibility, which together contribute to time and cost savings, data accuracy, compliance, secure data storage, and protection. The continuous drive for improved service delivery is underscored, together withthe importance of accommodating the human factor, which remains indispensable in digital administration. This paper presents a case study on the Georgian Customs Service and its successful development of a robust risk management system. The study details the strategies employed in this process. Additionally, quantitative data on the outcomes of digital customs and risk management initiatives are provided to support the efficacy of the approach. Based on the analysis of the Georgian Customs Service case study, this paper formulates recommendations that can be applied to enhance electronic customs services in various countries.

Keywords Customs risk management · Digital services · Electronic customs · ICT · Economic growth

R. Seturidze (✉)
Ivane Javakhishvili Tbilisi State University, Tbilisi, Georgia
e-mail: rusudan.seturidze@tsu.ge

R. C. Geibel and S. Machavariani (eds.), *Digital Management to Shape the Future*, Springer Proceedings in Business and Economics,
https://doi.org/10.1007/978-3-031-66517-2_6

1 Introduction

In today's global landscape, the pertinence of digital transformation is paramount, particularly in the context of advancing information and communication technologies. The process of digitalization, wielded effectively within the economic realm, has assumed ever-increasing significance for the economic prosperity and competitive edge of nations.

Scientists Hikmet A. et al. conclude in their work that the results of their research support the theoretical and empirical literature, which claims that digitization will have a positive effect on economic growth (Hikmet et al., 2023). Also, the empirical results of research conducted by scientists Qu J. et al. suggest that the spread of digital technologies has significantly improved economic output in Australia and beyond, contributing to a steady increase in gross domestic product per capita (Qu et al., 2017).

The exponential surge in international trade has catalyzed the evolution of customs risk management strategies. This imperative arises from the need to proficiently navigate potential risks in light of the escalating movement of goods across borders.

Pohjola (2001) found that a positive relationship between ICT and economic growth existed in 23 OECD countries, however, this was not the case for the other 16 countries, based on data covering 39 countries from 1980 to 1995. Yousefi (2011) examined contributions of ICT and other production factors on economic growth in 62 countries, displaying that ICT can improve economic growth in high- and upper-middle income countries, but not in lower-middle income countries.

With the help of information systems, the customs department has successfully started to solve the issues of customs control and also customs supervision. The Customs Department was also actively involved in the modernization of the risk management system. The author R. Seturidze noted in her published scientific work that risk profiles in the "ASYCUDA" system work on the basis of existing materials on violations of customs legislation, information provided by international organizations, various state bodies, and international experience in the field of risk management. Risk profiles are created for a certain period of time or for life and represent confidential information. The existing risk profiles are updatedor removed periodically (Seturidze, 2017).

In the article, scientists Jovanka Biljan et al. described that in the Macedonian customs administration, as in all customs administrations in the world, the practice of risk management began in the direction of "risk analysis". It is important that knowledge about the business environment, expert assessment and common sense should not be neglected when analyzing risks (Biljan & Trajkov, 2012).

In recent years, the Customs Service of Georgia has witnessed a notable expansion in its efforts pertaining to digital technologies and the implementation and enhancement of various modern information systems. The Georgian aim is to establish a fair administration system, thus making the country a reliable partner in international trade and a progressive member of the international commonwealth of states (Seturidze & Lekashvili, 2012).

This paper delves into the significance of digital technology not only in terms of technological advancements but also its role in process modernization, particularly evident in the customs risk system. The development of a web-portal was a notable achievement for the Revenue Service, with the portal providing numerous services and saving significant taxpayer time, energy, and financial resources (Seturidze, 2021). The customs risk system plays a pivotal role in identifying and assessing risks, developing response plans, and streamlining risk management processes. For instance, let us examine the customs system of Georgia, where in the realm of digital technology, customs risk management has undergone significant transformation. The adoption of web portals by taxpayers has revolutionized the way they interact with customs authorities, providing them with a lots of advantages. These advantages include resource-saving, reduced risk of document processing errors, enhanced data accuracy, cost reduction, minimal reliance on paper documentation, and substantial time savings. Moreover, the implementation of digital services has made interactions between taxpayers and customs authorities more convenient, accessible, and user-friendly.

2 Research Method

This document has been prepared using general and specific research methods, in particular: analysis, synthesis, induction, deduction, scientific comparison, and statistical methods, as well as expert assessment. In order to ascertain consistent patterns between analytical and statistical assessments, the paper have uses latest databases released by the National Statistics Office of Georgia. The data is analyzed and correlation analysis is conducted between various ICT indicators.

The author, who brings forth a wealth of experience garnered over 16 years in diverse roles within the customs system, has great practical experience in operating the information systems introduced to the Revenue Service of Georgia, which ensures the originality of the paper. The author moreover has established, and currently delivers, university-level academic courses on information systems and e-services in the field of customs.

3 Discussion and Results

3.1 The Formation and Evolution of Digital Technologies and Risk Management in the Customs System

There were no information systems in the customs system until 1998, and customs declarations for imported and exported goods in Georgia were filled manually or by typewriter (Seturidze, 2012). In 1998, the first stage of implementation of the automated customs data system ASYCUDA (Automated SYStem for CUstoms DAta) began (Seturidze, 2011a), which was created within the framework of the United Nations Conference on Trade and Development (UNCTAD). Initially, it included the computerization of the main procedure that was performed in customs bodies (Seturidze, 2015). These are: declaration, pre-declaration, registration certificate for cargoes and their removal from control, registration of TIR shipments, data processing and others. With the introduction of the "ASYCUDA" system, it became possible to complete accounting of imported and exported goods in the customs system.

The foundations for EU-Georgia relations were laid as far back as the disintegration of the Soviet Union and the restoration of Georgia's state independence. The European Union and the United States government regularly pledged to support Georgian economic, social, and political ongoing reforms. The European Union was one of the first to have rendered significant assistance to Georgia during its difficult transition years (Meskhia & Seturidze, 2013). Since 2003, the customs system has been reformed in Georgia.

The first stage of ASYCUDA installation was completed in 2004, the system was updated and various modules were added, next the version of ASYCUDA ++ was launched, the gradual simplification of customs procedures began, which allowed for effective management of the customs system. If earlier the time duration of the registration procedure was 2–10 days, then the duration of the registration procedure was reduced to 2 h. The automated risk management system excludes the possibility of any kind of transaction between the customs officer and the importer, which is an effective mechanism in the fight against corruption.

The presence of inconsistencies in customs legislation can be attributed to numerous legislative changes, primarily influenced by specific interest groups advocating for additional preferences. These legislative alterations often served the personal interests of particular groups.

Investors were enticed by promises of tax benefits, leading to the influx of short-term speculative capital of dubious origin into the country. The implementation of large-scale corrupt practices introduced instruments where the budget was merely executed on paper, and legislation assumed a largely formal character. Fictitious companies served as conduits for numerous criminal transactions.

The customs, tax departments, and financial police within the Ministry of Finance operated with disparate databases, characterized by poor synchronization. Data input into the database underwent manual processing by revenue service employees, and the compiled report was transmitted to higher echelons in manuscript form. As information ascended the hierarchy, distortions occurred, resulting in the Ministry of Finance receiving inaccurate information.

After 2007, a modern Public Financial Management Information System was implemented within the customs system, consolidating both the customs and tax systems. Initially, certain provisions of the Customs and Tax Codes exhibited contradictions among themselves and with other regulations. Instances arose where the same issue was treated disparately across various articles or provisions of the law. The proliferation of numerous taxes led to interactions with customs officers and instances of corruption. Consequently, the legislation underwent a gradual process of clarification and simplification. It is noteworthy that with each legislative amendment, the text and video versions of the new legislation were disseminated on the websites www.mof.ge and www.rs.ge.

Through collaborative efforts between the Ministry of Finance and the World Bank, the corporate web portals of the Ministry of Finance (www.mof.ge) and the Revenue Service (www.rs.ge) were established. This project facilitated the integration of electronic resources, available throughout Georgia in the central office of the Ministry of Finance and its structural divisions (customs and tax departments, financial police, treasury) into a unified information space. A central data warehouse and a unique data storage structure were established. The integrated database and corporate web portal represent the initial phase in the establishment of the Unified Tax Service of the Ministry of Finance.

An integral component of the tax service, the strong financial and analytical service at www.fas.ge, was fortified. This service successfully implemented the "EDocument"—an electronic document management system, offering a straightforward and efficient electronic office product that ensures paperless exchange of official information. Additionally, the Human Resource Management System (HRMS) was introduced, encompassing the Ministry of Finance and all its structural divisions, among other innovations.

Subsequently, the 'one window' principle was instituted, eliminating the detrimental practice of preliminary approval of customs documentation with a customs officer. Customs services such as electronic declaration, internet payments, and online submission and tracking of declarations and documents are now operational, fostering electronic relations with importers and exporters through the website www.rs.ge. The gradual standardization of payer's personal registration cards simplified procedures for receiving and submitting documents, enabling the offset of excess payments for one type of tax against another or the automatic utilization of the amount for the same tax.

In order to facilitate the pre-processing of data, strengthening of customs control and effective implementation of customs control measures (including the detection, suppression and prevention of violations of tax legislation) in 2016 passenger data (API-PNR) and cargo selection (WCO CTS) were implemented in the system.

In 2021, a series of strategic enhancements were introduced to fortify the control mechanisms for customs and tax risks. This included the incorporation of number recognition video cameras and a bespoke software solution tailored for vehicles within the customs framework. Additionally, video systems overseeing customer flow management underwent a comprehensive upgrade in the economic zones of the customs checkpoints and service centers. Moreover, the customs service has been actively engaged in the progressive integration of the Advance Passenger Information (API) and Passenger Name Record (PNR) system for air travelers.

3.2 *The Impact of Digital Technologies in the Customs System on Economic Growth*

The Revenue Service conducts customs control over declared goods through a risk management system to be applied through the eCustoms automated data system or the Oracle tax administration information system (Revenue Service of Georgia, 2023). The objectives of the risk management system encompass several key aspects, including: Streamlining all customs procedures to enhance efficiency; Prioritizing attention to the handling of dangerous goods; Optimally allocating customs resources for effective utilization; Minimizing the possibility of importing undeclared, unaccountable, and contraband goods; Ensuring immediate detection of dangerous goods; Safeguarding intellectual property rights and other pertinent considerations.

When the goods declaration is made, the system compares the data of the declaration and the risk profiles in the program, and if they match, the declaration is moved to the corridor of the corresponding color. The color of the corridor is determined by the content of the risk profile and also by the principle of random selection. Green—means the release of goods without the office check of the declaration and enclosed documents or visual examination of the goods. Yellow—means the release of goods without the office check of the declaration and enclosed documents, but with visual examination of the goods. Red—means the release of goods with the office check of the declaration and enclosed documents and with visual examination of the goods. Blue—means the release of goods without the office check of the declaration and enclosed documents or visual examination of the goods on condition of examining the validity of the documents and correctness of the charged tax amounts in the future (Seturidze, 2017). Initially, only the yellow and red corridor worked, and later the green and blue. This led to the reduction of customs clearance time, effective distribution of resources and, most importantly, minimal subjectivity in the clearance process reduced.

The outcomes of the customs control measures conducted within the declared goods corridor are mandatory and electronically recorded in the "ASYCUDA" information system.

Risk criteria encompass variables such as the exporting/importing country, the specific HS code classification (The Harmonized Commodity Description and Coding System) assigned to a particular product by the customs authorities of Georgia [4], identification codes of legal or natural persons, the type of packaging of goods, the quantity of goods, and others.

Risk profiles are formulated through the processing of "ASYCUDA" data, available materials documenting violations of customs legislation and international conventions, information sourced from various international organizations, other state entities, and global experiences in risk management.

The Risk Management Division of the Revenue Service is actively developing an automated risk management system designed for deployment during the state control of declared goods. This system involves the implementation of post-audit procedures, processing and analysis of preliminary information related to the payer and/or declared goods, planning of measures to be undertaken, integration and monitoring of relevant risk management elements within the system, processing and analysis of information on export–import operations received from authorized bodies of foreign states, monitoring the operation of the risk management system, and leveraging other available databases through the automated data system "ASYCUDA" during the implementation of state control over goods declared in the economic territory of Georgia. This includes integrating risk profiles and parameters for random selection into the "ASYCUDA" system, as well as modifying or canceling existing risk profiles and random selection settings. New risk modules are progressively being developed, contributing to the enhanced efficacy of the service's risk system. Consequently, there has been a reduction in the number of physical documents required for customs procedures.

The www.rs.ge portal in the customs system has been updated. The portal allows for full automation of the customs system.

In 2022, the Revenue Service implemented significant measures, including the establishment of an information and methodological hub, in accordance with the latest digital requirements, known as infohub.rs.ge. This platform serves as a centralized repository for various types of continuously updated information and documentation related to tax and customs issues. The information available on this online platform is accessible to both service employees and taxpayers.

Given Georgia's status as a crucial transit country, the Revenue Service is actively engaged in enhancing infrastructure to align with international customs standards. Efforts are directed towards improving the analytical capabilities of customs control.

Ongoing collaboration with the strategic partner, the United States of America, under the Export Control and Border Security (EXBS) program, remains active across various fronts. Notably, a significant project involves the modernization of customs information systems. In coordination with the Korean Customs Administration, an independent evaluation document for the customs system was developed, enabling the Revenue Service to objectively assess its progress moving forward.

As a small country, Georgia relies heavily on international trade, especially imports, as the country has a negative trade balance. Over the years, imports have shown a significant increase from 752 million USD in 2001 to 10,099 million in 2021. However, tax revenue from imports (exports are tax-free) has been declining over the years.

Figure 1 illustrates total imports (in millions of US dollars) and international trade payments in Georgia for the period 2001–2021.

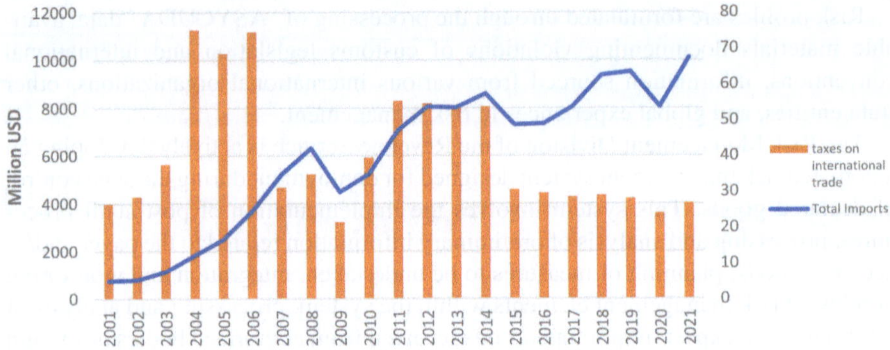

Fig. 1 Total Imports and taxes on international trade (2001–2021) (*Source* Figure has been developed by author)

The GDP of ICT sector has been steadily increasing from 2017. Real growth rate for 2022 constituted 50%, which made ICT sector one of the main drivers for economic growth for 2022. The share of GDP fo ICT in total GDP has increased from 2.6% in 2016 to 4.1% by 2022. This showcases the increased significanvy of ICT sector for Georgia's economic growth (Fig. 2).

The Fig. 3 clearly shows the growth of GDP of the information and communication sector (Fig. 3), which will undoubtedly affect the overall GDP. Even though the growth in the ICT sector in Georgia is evident over the recent years, the country lost its positions in number of international rankings. In Global Innovation index, which measures measuring a country's capability to produce innovative outputs, Georgia lost 11 positions and ranks as 74th out of 132 economies (from 2021 to 2022). In Frontier Technologies Readiness Index, which measures countries abilities for adopting frontier technologies, Georgia ranks 79th out of 166 nations and has remained at this positions since 2019 when it lost 4 positions. At last, in Network

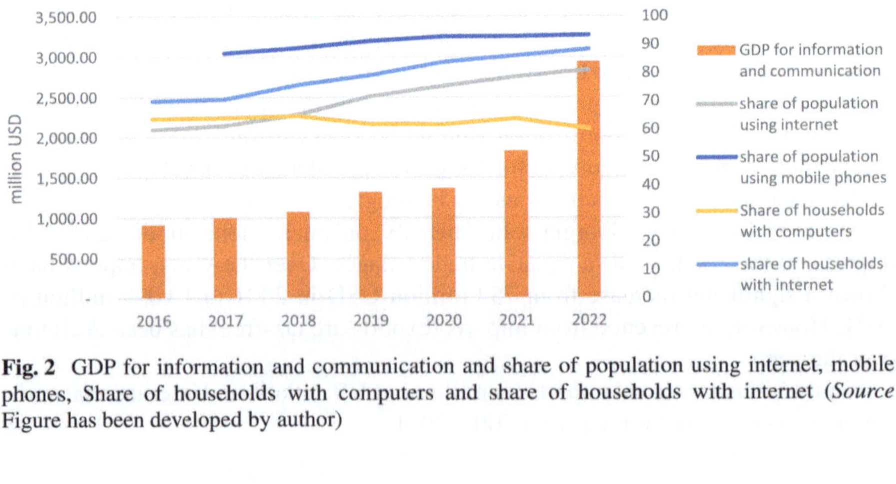

Fig. 2 GDP for information and communication and share of population using internet, mobile phones, Share of households with computers and share of households with internet (*Source* Figure has been developed by author)

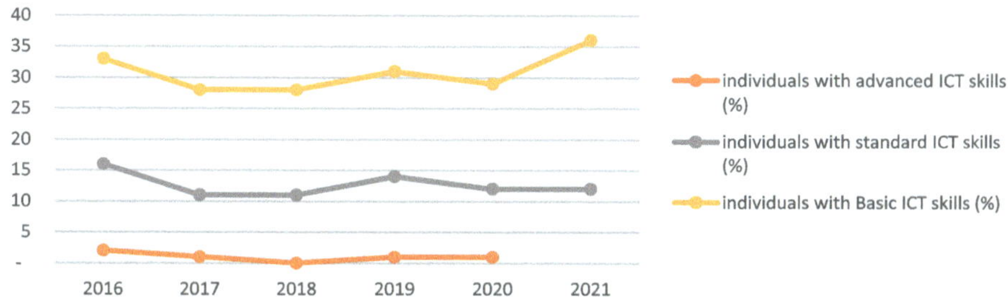

Fig. 3 ICT skills in Georgia (*Source* Figure has been developed by author)

Readiness Index, which measures ICT utilization for increasing in country's competitiveness, Georgia ranks 75th out of 131 countries in 2022, positions behind from 2021 ranking (Georgia—Digital Development Country Profile, 2022).

Table 1 shows a comparative analysis of the GDP of the "Information and Communication" sector in 2017–2022 (data on the use of mobile phones in the National Statistical Service of Georgia is available only from 2017) with the % share of the population using the Internet and mobile phones.

From the foregoing analysis, it can be inferred that a robust correlation exists between the GDP of the information and communication sector, the percentage of time spent using the Internet (0.822), and the percentage of mobile phone use (0.705).

To mitigate the persistent shortcomings associated with periodic malfunctions of electronic customs services, it is advisable to bolster efforts towards the implementation of artificial intelligence. This can involve the integration of chat-bots or specialized support tools, encompassing a comprehensive array of potential questions or instructions that taxpayers might encounter while utilizing electronic tax services. Introducing artificial intelligence and innovative Internet of Things (IoT) elements is deemed beneficial when implementing changes to the electronic tax system. This approach facilitates timely communication with ratepayers. However, it is imperative to note that the implementation of these systems necessitates specialized knowledge and skills. Provision of adequate training is recommended to ensure effective utilization and interpretation of insights generated by artificial intelligence. The ongoing evolution of technology foretells the convergence of artificial intelligence and customs risk management as a pivotal force shaping the future landscape of international trade oversight.

4 Conclusions and Further Research

It can be concluded that the introduction and integration of digital technologies in the customs system had a positive impact on economic growth. This positive effect is evident through several key indicators, including a substantial reduction in the time required for customs clearance, a decrease in the number of physical documents

Table 1 Correlations

		Information and communication, GDP, million GEL	Using the Internet, %	Total Trade_ ICT	Use of mobile phones, %
Information and communication, GDP, million GEL	Pearson Correlation	1	0.822[a]	0.854[a]	0.705
	Sig. (2-tailed)		0.045	0.030	0.118
	N	6	6	6	6
Using the Internet, %	Pearson Correlation	0.822[a]	1	0.461	0.978[b]
	Sig. (2-tailed)	0.045		0.357	0.001
	N	6	6	6	6
Total Trade_ICT	Pearson Correlation	0.854[a]	0.461	1	0.282
	Sig. (2-tailed)	0.030	0.357		0.589
	N	6	6	6	6
Use of mobile phones, %	Pearson Correlation	0.705	0.978[b]	0.282	1
	Sig. (2-tailed)	0.118	0.001	0.589	
	N	6	6	6	6

Source Table has been developed by author
[a]Correlation is significant at the 0.05 level (2-tailed)
[b]Correlation is significant at the 0.01 level (2-tailed)

necessary for customs procedures, and an increase in the volume of imports and exports. Moreover, a notable correlation has been established between these positive outcomes and key economic factors, such as the GDP of the information and communication sector, internet and mobile phone use. Following the implementation of digital technologies in Georgia's customs system, there has been a discernible improvement in economic growth trends compared to the period before these technological advances. The preceding era was marked by challenges such as corruption and artificial delays. The positive trajectory in economic indicators underscores the transformative impact of digital technologies on the efficiency and effectiveness of the customs system, contributing to the overall economic development of the country.

Based on the research, the following recommendations were made:

- For digital technologies to exert a positive impact on the economic growth of the country, it is imperative that the government actively promotes the adoption and modernization of digital technologies within the customs system. Furthermore, collaboration between the government and stakeholders is essential to maximize

the facilitation of international trade and foster the economic development of the country.
- The prudent utilization of artificial intelligence is advisable, requiring specialized knowledge and skills. The successful integration of artificial intelligence necessitates that customs officials and stakeholders possess the requisite expertise. To fully leverage the potential of these tools, it is crucial to strategically plan comprehensive training initiatives and promote developmental efforts in this domain.
- It is paramount to consider that artificial intelligence systems should be designed for seamless integration with the customs systems of other countries, facilitating effective cross-border risk assessment.
- The implementation of risk management assumes a pivotal role in ensuring the smooth functioning of the customs system. Introducing artificial intelligence represents a progressive step in this context, as customs risk management heavily relies on high-quality data. Ensuring the accuracy and consistency of data is critical, as incomplete data can lead to erroneous risk assessments.

The aforementioned recommendations can be employed to enhance the electronic services of customs systems in developing countries. Upon their implementation, electronic customs services are poised to become more convenient, efficient, secure, and reliable. This transformation could serve as a catalyst for the economic growth of the country. While working on the article, it became evident that specific statistical information in Georgia is not available. For instance, the National Statistical Service of Georgia's website provides data for the last 7 years of internet usage and 6 years of mobile phone usage. Consequently, the study encountered limitations in conducting various analyses. However, the future exploration of these endeavors is planned.

References

Automated System for Customs Data (ASYCUDA). www.asycuda.org

Biljan, J., & Trajkov, A. (2012). Risk management and customs performance improvements: The case of the Republic of Macedonia. *Procedia-Social and Behavioral Sciences, 44*(212), 302–312. https://www.sciencedirect.com/

Challenges and Strategies for the Reform of Customs Administration. Edited by Michael Keen. (2003). International Monetary Fund. https://www.imf.org/external/pubs/nft/2003/customs/

Cheng, C.-Y., Chien, M.-S., & Lee, C.-C. (2021). ICT diffusion, financial development, and economic growth: An international cross-country analysis. *Economic Modelling, Elsevier, 94*(C), 662–671.

Dominici, G., & Gagnidze, I. (2021). Effectiveness of entrepreneurial universities: Experiences and challenges in digital era (a systemic approach). *Interdisciplinary Description of Complex Systems, 19*(1), 13–30. https://doi.org/10.7906/indecs.19.1.2

Georgia—Digital Development Country Profile. (2022). https://georgia.un.org/sites/default/files/2022-05/Digital%20Development%20Country%20Profile_Georgia_final_02.22.pdf

Georgia Ranking in the Global Innovation Index. (2023). https://www.wipo.int/edocs/pubdocs/en/wipo-pub-2000-2023/ge.pdf

Hikmet, A., Tuba, A., & Gökhan, A. (2023). *Digitalization and economic growth: New evidence from EU countries*. https://doi.org/10.31795/baunsobed.1234251

Krabina, B., Liu, P., Meyerhoff-Nielsen, M., Millard, J., Reichstädter, P., & Wimmer, M. A. (2014). *Digital Georgia: E-Georgia strategy and action plans 2014–2018* (p. 97).

Meskhia, I., & Seturidze, R. (2013). The European Union's Generalized System of Preferences (GSP) and the prospect of a unified database. In *World Academy of Science. Engineering and Technology. Barcelona ISSUE 82* (pp. 445–449).

Meskhia, I., & Seturidze R. (2016). The use of ERP systems in international business management in Georgia. In *III International Scientific and Practical Conference "strategic Imperatives of Modern Management" Review, SIMM-2016 Kyiv*. ISBN 978-966-926-069-7.

Ministry of Finance of Georgia. www.mof.ge.

National Statistics Office of Georgia. https://www.geostat.ge/en.

Pogarcic, I., Jankovic, S. R., & Seturidze, R. (2017). How does the help desk quality improve customer satisfaction? In *ATINER's Conference Paper Series MED2017-2255* (pp. 3-22). Athens, Greece by the Athens Institute Education and Research. ISSN: 241-2891

Pohjola, M. (Ed.). (2001). *Information technology, productivity, and economic growth: International evidence and implications for economic development*. OUP Catalogue, Oxford University Press, number 9780199243983.

Qu J., Simes R., & O'Mahony J. (2017). *How do digital technologies drive economic growth?* https://doi.org/10.1111/1475-4932.12340

Revenue Service of Georgia. https://www.rs.ge/Home-en.

Seturidze, R. (2011a). New trends in development of Georgia's Economic border information systems. In *New trends of development of V4 Countries & Ukraine*. III International Internet conference Volyn Institute for Economics and Management, Ukraine.

Seturidze, R. (2011b). *Modern information technologies in customs System*. Georgian Economics in the works competitiveness indicators: Problems, perspectives, II inter-university Collection of Reports of Scientific-Practical Conference, Tbilisi, Georgia.

Seturidze, R. (2012). *Information technologies in customs system*. Secondary text-book, Publishing house "Universal", Georgia.

Seturidze, R. (2014). Information Systems, as one of the tools to improve the Customs System Management of Georgia. *Refereed and Reviewed International Scientific and Practical Journal of the Faculty of Economics and Business Ivane Javakhishvili Tbilisi State University, N6*, 101–118.

Seturidze, R. (2015). Role of the informational technologies in the improvement of the state sector (on the example of the customs of Georgia). In *Business Systems Laboratory. Third international Symposium Advances in Business Management Towards Systemic Approach*. Italy, Perugia e-Book of ABSTRACTS Business Systems Laboratory (pp. 11–13). ISBN: 9788890824227

Seturidze, R. (2016a). Improving customs control efficiency through the automated risk control system. In *The international scientific conference "Challenges of Globalization in Economic and Business"* (pp. 450–453). Publishing house "Universal", Georgia.

Seturidze, R. (2016b, August). *Role of the ERP systems in the successful management of Georgian companies, BOOK OF ABSTRACTS Business Systems Laboratory Review, Vilnius, Lithuania*. http://bslab-symposium.net/Vilnius.2016/BSLab-Vilnius2016-e-book_of_Abstracts.pdf

Seturidze, R. (2017). *The role of the information systems in the risk management model (On the example of the customs system of Georgia)* (pp. 177–181). ISBN: 9788890824258. http://bslab-symposium.net/BSLab-Sydic-2017/Book-Abstracts-BSLab-Sydic-2017-final.pdf

Seturidze, R. (2018). *Challenges and problems of e-customs in developing countries: The case of Georgia*. ISBN: 9788890824265.

Seturidze, R. (2021). Trends in teaching modern information systems in the field of taxation within higher educational institutions. *Progress in Education, 68*, 203–227. ISBN: 978-1-68507-230-8.

Seturidze, R., & Lekashvili, E. (2012). The reforms realized in the customs system of GEORGIA and CONTRADICTIONS. In *XVI IRSPM International Conference "Contradictions in public management" Managing in volatile times* (p. 669).

Seturidze, R., & Mikiashvili, N. (2012). Role of information technologies in operational risk management. In *Research proceedings of the IX KIMEP international conference* (pp. 190–192). Almaty, Kazakhstan.

Seturidze, R., & Paresashvili, N. (2012). Role of information technologies in operational risk management. In *The 9th KIMEP International Research Conference (KIRC 2012) at Almaty, Kazakhstan*. https://www.kimep.kz/kirc/files/2012/05/BCB-proceedings.pdf#page=190.

Seturidze, R., & Topuria, N. (2020). Cooperation between the businesses and the universities—Unified data management using the business intelligence portal. In *Business Systems Laboratory—7th International Symposium, Socio-Economic Ecosystems: Challenges for Sustainable Development in the Digital Era*. University of Alicante, Alicante, Spain, ISBN: 9788890824296.

Seturidze, R., & Topuria, N. (2021). A way of developing collaboration between universities and businesses in a time of COVID-19. *Kybernetes, 50*(5), 1661–1678. https://doi.org/10.1108/K-08-2020-0518

Seturidze, R., Topuria, N., & Bokhashvili, K. (2024). Enhancing economic growth through digital technologies: A focus on electronic tax services. *E-Book of Abstracts Business Systems Laboratory—8th International Symposium, "Great Reset. Opportunity or Threat?"* (pp.111–114). University of Palermo. ISBN: 9788890824289.

Tax Code of Georgia. https://matsne.gov.ge/ka/document/view/1043717

Taxation and Customs Union. https://ec.europa.eu/taxation_customs/index_en

The Association Agreement on the one hand between Georgia and on the other hand the European Union and the European Atomic Energy Union and their Member States. (2014). Official Journal of the European Union. https://eur-lex.europa.eu/legal-content/en/TXT/PDF/?uri=CELEX:22014A0830(02)

The program of the Government of Georgia "Basic data and directions of the country for 2017–2020", 2017. https://www.mof.ge/images/File/BDD/BDD-saboloo-2017-2020-30.01.2017-BOLO.pdf

United Nations Conference on Trade and Development. www.unctad.org.

World Customs Organization. (2012). *Risk management in the custom context*. World Customs Organization. http://www.wcoomd.org/-/media/wco/public/global/pdf/topics/enforcement-and-compliance/activities-and-programmes/risk-management-and-intelligence/risk-management-compendium-volume-1.pdf

World Customs Organization. *Customs and the UN 2030 agenda for sustainable development*. http://www.wcoomd.org/ru-ru/topics/key-issues/customs-in-support-of-sdgs.aspx

World Customs Organization. *Customs' role in achieving sustainable development goals*. WCO.

Yousefi, A. (2011, November). The impact of information and communication technology on economic growth: Evidence from developed and developing countries. *Economics of Innovation and New Technology, Taylor & Francis Journals, 20*(6), 581–596.

The Evolving Workforce: Technological Advancements and Their Impact on Employee Skills and Characteristics

Lia Kvirchishvili

Abstract In this era of rapid technological advancement, it is undeniable that technology has had a profound impact on various aspects of human life. One particular area greatly affected by this progress is the workforce, where technological developments have significantly influenced the required professional skills and personal characteristics of individuals. The traditional work landscape, once characterized by routine tasks and linear career paths, has been thoroughly transformed by the integration of new technologies, automation, artificial intelligence, and data-driven decision-making processes (Acemoglu & Restrepo in Robots and jobs: evidence from U.S. Labor markets, 2017; Aspan in International Journal of Innovation, Creativity and Change 13:761–774, 2020). Technology has not only altered the way we work but has also transformed the skills and attributes necessary to thrive in the modern workplace. The traditional set of professional skills that were once sufficient for success has expanded to include digital literacy, adaptability, and proactive thinking in the face of constant change. Similarly, personality traits that were previously deemed desirable, such as stability and hierarchical thinking, have now been replaced by creativity, critical thinking, collaboration, and resilience (Ashutosh Jani in HRM Review 45–57, 2016). The objective of this paper is to study and analyze the profound impact of technological development on individuals' professional skills and personal characteristics. By understanding the changes brought about by technology, individuals, organizations, and policymakers can gain valuable insights into the evolution of work and effectively address the demands of the digital age. The research in this paper will delve into various aspects, including the role of automation in altering skill requirements, the emergence of new skills in technology-driven fields, the importance of adaptation and continuous learning, the significance of skills in the age of artificial intelligence, and the importance of training and skills development (Coley in Science 365:6453, 2019).

Keywords Technological advances · Skills · Employee development

L. Kvirchishvili (✉)
East European University (EEU), Tbilisi, Georgia
e-mail: Lia_kvirchishvili@yahoo.com

R. C. Geibel and S. Machavariani (eds.), *Digital Management to Shape the Future*,
Springer Proceedings in Business and Economics,
https://doi.org/10.1007/978-3-031-66517-2_7

1 Introduction

The rapid advancement of technology has undeniably brought about a profound impact on various facets of human life, particularly in the realm of the workforce. This progress has significantly altered the requisite professional skills for individuals. The traditional work landscape, once characterized by routine tasks and linear career trajectories, has undergone a metamorphosis due to the infusion of novel technologies, automation, artificial intelligence, and data-driven decision-making processes (Acemoglu & Restrepo, 2018; Office, 2019).

Technology has not solely revolutionized our work methods; it has also reshaped the proficiencies and attributes necessary for thriving in the contemporary workplace. The erstwhile conventional suite of professional skills, which was once deemed sufficient for achieving success, has expanded to encompass the imperative need for digital literacy, adaptability, and forward-thinking acumen in the face of ceaseless change (McGee & Thompson, 2015). Similarly, personality traits that were once held in high regard, such as stability and hierarchical thinking, have yielded ground to qualities like creativity, critical thinking, collaboration, and resilience (Brin & Nehme, 2019).

The objective of this paper is to thoroughly investigate and analyze the profound ramifications of technological advancements on both individuals' professional proficiencies and personal characteristics. By comprehending the transformations wrought by technology, individuals, organizations, and policymakers can glean invaluable insights into the evolution of work and adeptly tackle the requisites of the digital age (Brynjolfsson & McAfee, 2014).

The research contained herein will delve into multifarious aspects, including the role of automation in reshaping skill prerequisites, the emergence of novel skills within technology-driven domains, the pivotal significance of adaptability and perpetual learning, the relevance of skills in the era of artificial intelligence, and the import of training in fulfilling skill development needs (McKinsey Global Institute, 2017). Through a comprehensive examination of these dimensions, we aim to fathom the multifaceted nature of technology's impact on individuals and to formulate strategies that harness its potential while concurrently nurturing the competencies and traits necessary for thriving in the ever-evolving professional sphere (Cappelli, 2015; Davenport, & Ronanki, 2018; Samarasinghe & Medis, 2020).

The infusion of technology into the workplace has fundamentally revolutionized the anticipated professional skills and personal attributes of human resources (Dulebohn & Johnson, 2013). Adapting to this novel paradigm is imperative for individuals striving to maintain relevance in their careers, for organizations endeavoring to preserve their competitiveness in the marketplace, and for policymakers tasked with cultivating an environment conducive to skills enhancement. Grasping the repercussions of technological progress on human resources is an indispensable stride toward forging a workforce primed for the future, capable of navigating challenges and capitalizing on opportunities engendered by technological strides (Autor, 2015).

2 The Impact of Technology on the Workplace

Technological advancements have revolutionized organizations, streamlining business processes and enhancing integration. This has enabled companies to operate efficiently and effectively (Schulte & Howard, 2019). The global collaboration of multinational employees in real-time stands as a testament to the transformative power of technology. In the workplace, technology acts as a facilitator, ensuring smooth and accurate workflows. Tools like QuickFMS aid leaders in organization and information management, contributing to overall business profitability (Prasad, https://www.quickfms.com/, 2019).

Historically, companies grappled with paperwork, physical meetings, and travel costs for client interactions. Communication within organizations was also challenging. Technology has propelled businesses forward, simplifying operations and communication. Barriers like communication, task execution, management, and outsourcing have been surmounted through technology's evolution. The Internet and various software solutions have enabled businesses to maintain focus on goals without disruption.

The impact of technology on the modern workplace:

2.1 Communication Transformation

Technology has redefined workplace communication. Smartphones, social networks, and chat apps have elevated communication. Employees can now instantly connect, collaborate, and communicate via emails, texts, video chats, and conferences through platforms like WhatsApp and Skype. Physical presence at the workplace is no longer a constant requirement.

2.2 Enhanced Organization

Technology enables comprehensive business organization. Project management software systems aid companies in structuring, assigning, reviewing, and assessing tasks. This fosters accountability, efficiency, and timely task completion. Employers and managers can easily monitor activities, ensuring smooth progress and alignment with goals.

2.3 *Efficient Operations*

Modern businesses rely on productivity software to address daily strategic challenges. Managers use these tools to track goal progress, offer immediate feedback, and maintain on-task performance. Technology boosts productivity by enabling faster and more accurate task execution.

2.4 *Cost Management Support*

Revenue improvement is a universal business goal. Innovative technology fosters fiscal health by optimizing cost-effectiveness. Automation via software minimizes manual tasks, reducing costs. Automated processes yield accurate results, facilitating easy record retrieval. This reduction in expenses increases overall income.

2.5 *Enhanced Security*

Security is paramount across all business levels. Technology reinforces workplace safety through data encryption, allowing authorized access. Biometric features like fingerprint and facial recognition heighten system security. Cutting-edge technology and security software safeguard sensitive information from malicious cyber threats (Howard, 2017).

2.6 *Enhanced Cooperation*

Technology has revolutionized corporate collaboration, enabling seamless connectivity anytime, anywhere. This heightened collaboration fosters flexibility in communication, facilitating interaction among employees, colleagues, and managers. Improved teamwork and understanding result from this enhanced connection, benefiting both leaders and employees.

2.7 *Employee Efficiency Boost*

Effective time management is crucial in today's workplace to avoid missed deadlines and client dissatisfaction. Modern technological tools simplify time management, optimizing daily routines and focusing employees on essential tasks. This efficiency improvement leads to timely task completion and customer contentment. Reduced time spent on routine tasks allows for increased creativity and idea development.

2.8 Remote Work Flexibility

New technologies have ushered in remote work, teleconferencing, and collaborative digital spaces, fundamentally altering the modern workplace. Jobs are no longer tied to a single location but are facilitated by virtual conferencing, complete connectivity, and portability. Cloud technologies and advanced instant messaging systems enable employees to work from anywhere. Video conferencing ensures coordination across distances.

In conclusion, technology's impact on the workplace is profound, reshaping traditional work dynamics. Business leaders are tasked with effectively managing its evolution. To maintain productivity, profitability, and security, businesses must embrace new technology solutions and facility management software. These implementations ensure optimal modern workplace efficiency and profitability (Prasad, www.quickfms.com, 2018).

3 Research Method

A mixed methods approach was employed in this research, incorporating both quantitative and qualitative methodologies. This combination allowed for the collection of statistical data through quantitative research and in-depth insights through qualitative research. This chapter offers a comprehensive outline of the empirical approach utilized for the quantitative research segment, as well as the data processing procedures employed for the 150 participants who were interviewed using Google Form.

The quantitative research segment aimed to investigate the correlation between technological advancements and employee skills. Additionally, it sought to explore how different generations perceive the rapid technological evolution within the workplace. The choice of an empirical methodology was deliberate, as it facilitates the collection of numerical data for the purpose of analyzing statistical trends and interrelations.

To amass quantitative data, a self-administered survey was devised using Google Forms. The utilization of Google Forms was deemed fitting due to its convenience, accessibility, and broad reach to a substantial respondent base. The survey instrument underwent a meticulous development process, including pilot testing, to ensure both clarity and validity.

The quantitative data gathered were subjected to descriptive statistical analysis, which encompassed an examination of frequencies, means, and standard deviations of the variables under scrutiny. Furthermore, inferential statistics like correlation and regression analyses were conducted to delve into the connections between technological advancements, employee skills, and personal attributes.

Complementing the quantitative insights, a qualitative study was carried out to gain a more profound comprehension of the subject matter. Semi-structured interviews were conducted with a subset of participants from the quantitative research phase. The selection of interviewees was purposive, aiming to encompass a diverse spectrum of industries, organizational levels, and technological expertise. These interviews were conducted via the Zoom platform and transcribed verbatim for subsequent analysis.

4 Results and Discussion

The demographic data pertaining to the ages of the respondents is represented as follows (Fig. 1).

A notable portion of the respondents, as evidenced by their work experience, has been engaged in employment for a period of 10 years or more. Consequently, the robustness of the presented research is heightened, given that these respondents possess the capacity to thoroughly assess the impact of technological advancements on their work environment (Fig. 2).

Based on the categorization by organizational type, a significant majority of respondents are employed within the private sector (Fig. 3).

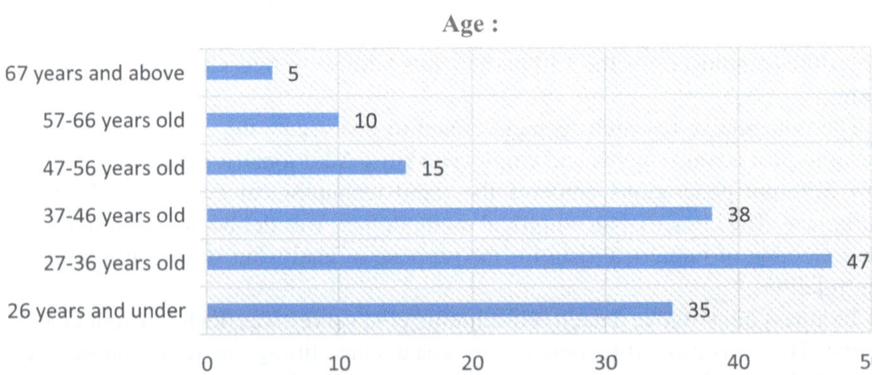

	26 years and under	27-36 years old	37-46 years old	47-56 years old	57-66 years old	67 years and above
Total:	35	47	38	15	10	5

Fig. 1 Age distribution

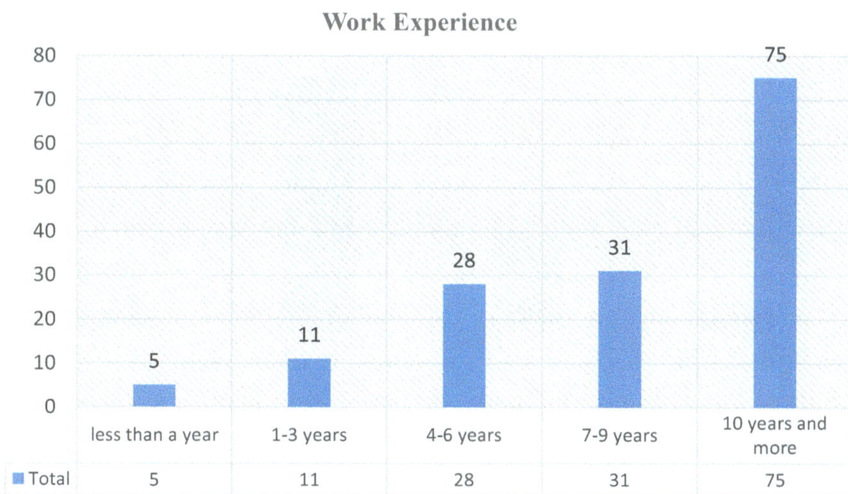

Fig. 2 Distribution of work experience

Fig. 3 Distribution by type of organization

Furthermore, it is crucial to emphasize the extent of technology utilization by the respondents themselves. The outcomes of the quantitative research underscore that the respondents predominantly engage with various technologies (Fig. 4).

The subsequent question unveiled the respondents' perspectives regarding the utilization of technology. The outcomes varied notably, reflecting a lack of uniformity in the respondents' attitudes or viewpoints toward this matter. Consequently,

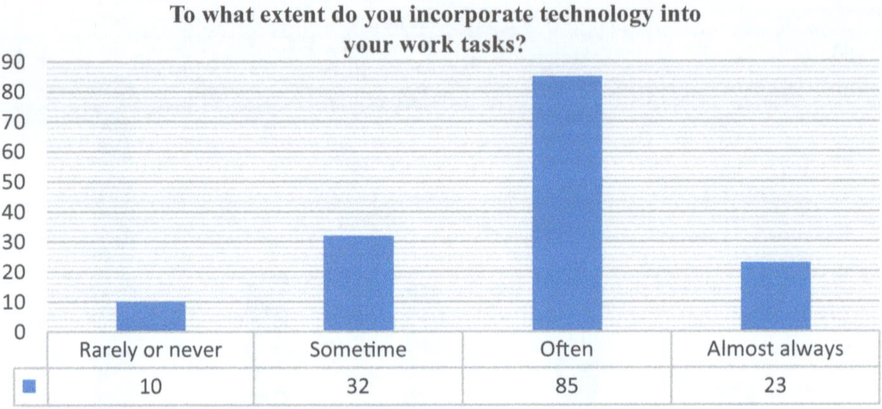

Fig. 4 Technology usage tendency

it could be contended that a more in-depth investigation is warranted to comprehend the underlying reasons for their divergent attitudes. Potential factors might encompass apprehension, lack of familiarity with suitable technologies, among other possibilities (Fig. 5).

Through the subsequent question, "Please rate your proficiency in using specific technologies relevant to your job (e.g., software, tools, equipment) on a scale of 1 to 5 ("1" indicating "very poor," and "5" indicating "very good")," it becomes evident that the observation highlighted in connection with the prior question is prominently underscored. Specifically, respondents appear to lack the requisite knowledge for the comprehensive utilization of technology, thereby giving rise to a sense of unease toward its use (Fig. 6).

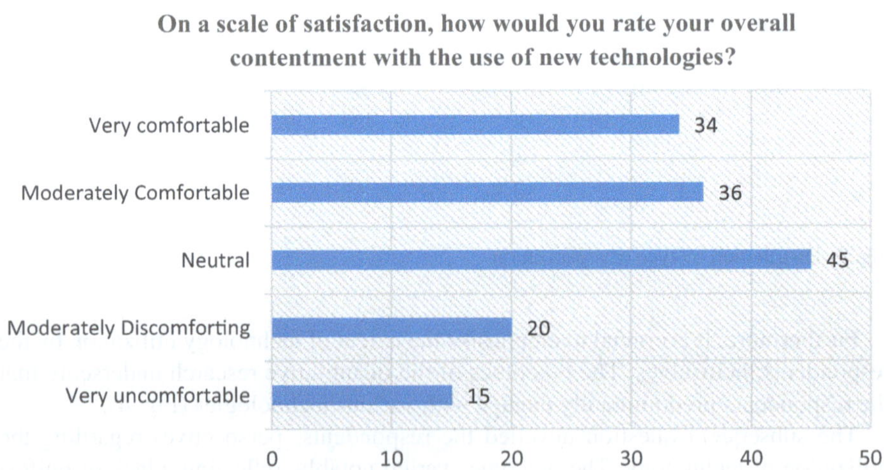

Fig. 5 Satisfaction levels with technology usage

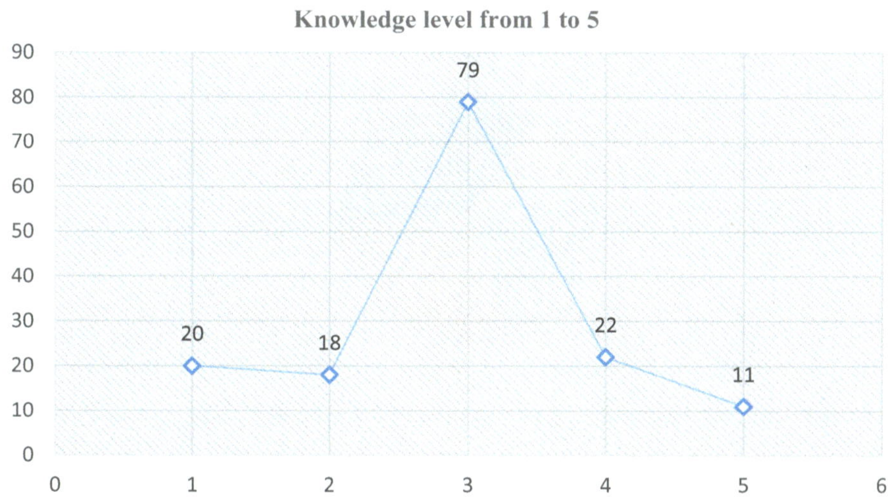

Fig. 6 Proficiency levels in technology usage

Regarding the skills cultivated among the respondents due to technological advancements, drawing a definitive conclusion proves challenging. This complexity arises from the even distribution of responses across various skills. Consequently, the identification of specific skills significantly enhanced among the respondents remains elusive. An argument can be made that technological progress has equally influenced the development of diverse skills such as communication, adaptability, analytical abilities, and more (Fig. 7).

The question concerning the influence of technologies on the overall work performance of the respondents yielded intriguing outcomes. Similarly, the results obtained exhibit a blend of responses. A deeper analysis is merited for this question, given its significance in spotlighting the state of affairs within Georgian companies. This inquiry delves into the extent to which they align with the prevailing trends that advocate for maximal process automation (Fig. 8).

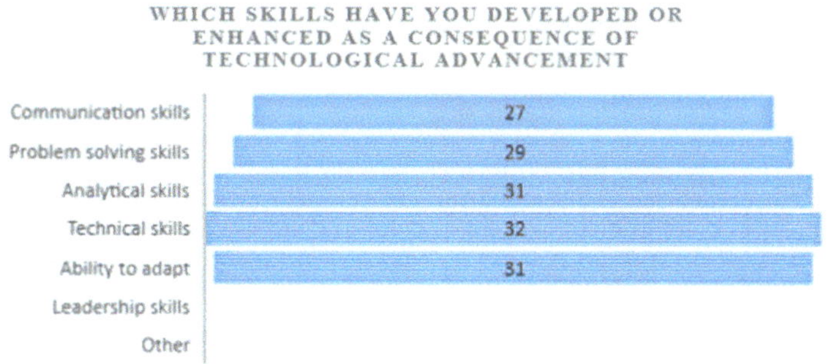

Fig. 7 Skill development in relation to technology

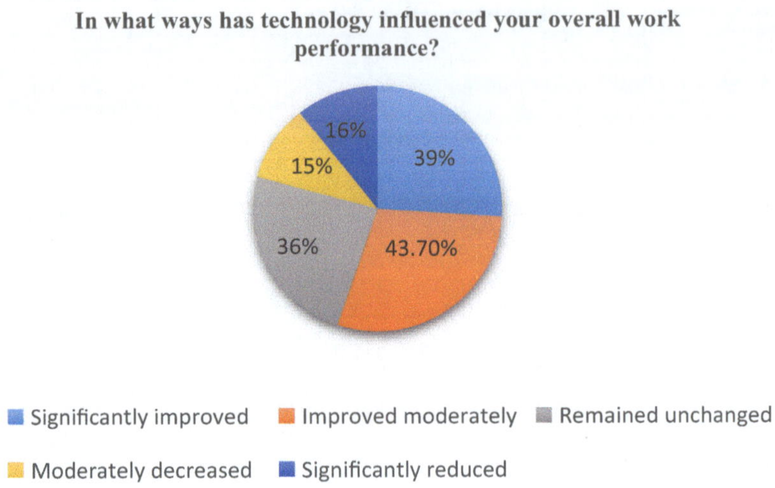

Fig. 8 Technology's impact on work performance

In the current dynamic landscape, fostering employee support and organizing training or educational initiatives concerning recent advancements hold paramount significance. To elucidate this aspect, respondents were queried about their exposure to training or professional development opportunities aimed at accommodating technological transformations in the workplace. The majority of respondents in the survey conveyed that they had occasionally received comparable training. Furthermore, a noteworthy portion of these respondents reported that the efficacy of such training sessions ranged from either being ineffective or moderately effective in most instances (Susskind & Susskind, 2015) (Fig. 9).

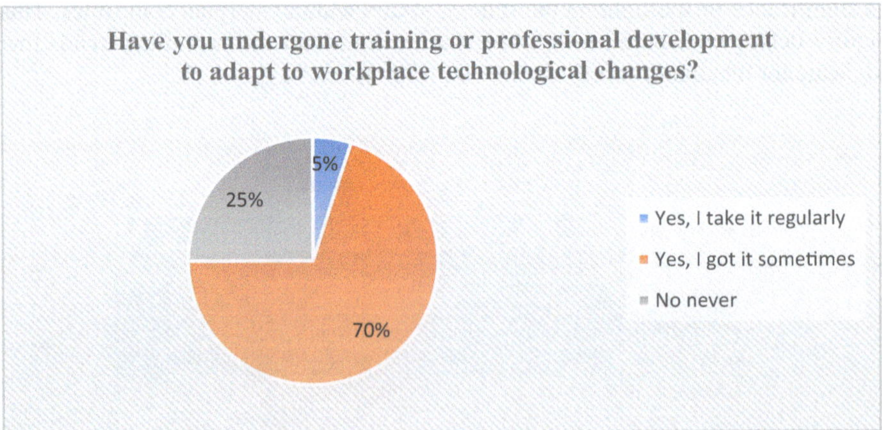

Fig. 9 Statistics on Receiving Training and Support

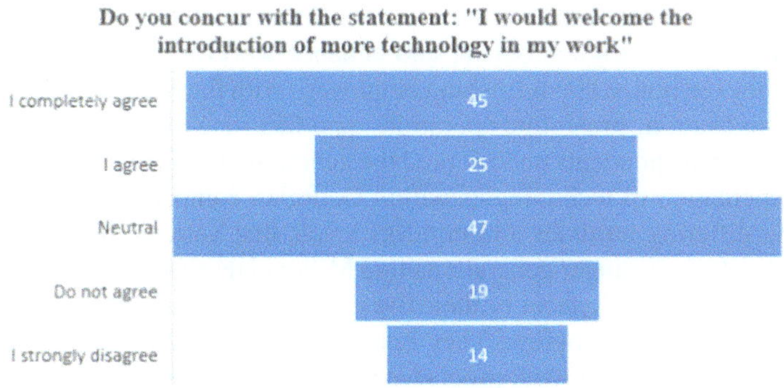

Fig. 10 Readiness for implementing technology in the contemporary work environment

Examining respondents' perspectives on the desirability of increased technology integration in their work environment yielded intriguing insights. The findings revealed generational disparities, particularly with Generation Z expressing a strong inclination toward heightened technology adoption. In contrast, respondents from other generations depicted a varied outlook. The majority held a neutral stance on the matter, while some expressed reluctance toward the necessity of extensive technological integration.

This scenario underscores the necessity for a comprehensive analysis, as the scope of technological transformation continues to expand significantly. Increasingly, numerous processes are transitioning towards automation and digitization. The workforce's preparedness for these shifts is pivotal. However, the present scenario suggests that many respondents currently resist such a transformation within their professional milieu (Fig. 10).

In the qualitative research phase, respondents highlighted the remarkable technological advancement shaping today's landscape. Their insights underscored the sweeping progress made across industries and sectors. Technological innovations have led to substantial alterations in business operations, affecting manufacturing processes, communication methods, customer engagement, and service delivery dynamics (Oeij et al., 2017).

However, a respondent also noted a distinction between companies that merely employ technology to meet obligations and those that genuinely recognize its necessity, prioritizing employee well-being in the process. This differentiation reflects the varied attitudes and approaches that companies adopt toward technology.

Certain organizations may adopt technology as a standard industry practice or to meet market expectations. Their primary motivation might be competition or regulatory compliance. While such companies incorporate technology solutions, their focus may lean toward surface-level implementation, rather than considering its holistic impact on employee productivity, contentment, and development.

Conversely, certain entities comprehend the transformative potential of technology, viewing it as a potent tool to empower employees and enhance the work environment. These companies transcend conventional solutions, actively investing in technological avenues that bolster and enhance workforce efficiency and effectiveness. They recognize that furnishing employees with the right resources and tools can foster innovation, streamline operations, and facilitate improved collaboration.

Furthermore, respondents underscored the generational disparities in the adoption and implementation of technologies within Georgian companies. This observation mirrors the differing attitudes and comfort levels that various age groups exhibit toward technology. Younger generations like Millennials and Gen-Z, accustomed to technology as an intrinsic facet of their lives, manifest greater openness and adaptability to technological progress. They readily embrace novel tools and platforms, employing them to elevate work processes and communication.

Conversely, older generations might display skepticism or resistance to technology, stemming from limited exposure during their formative years or perceived complexities linked to new digital tools. Nonetheless, it is important to acknowledge that these generalizations might not encompass all individuals, as attitudes toward technology vary widely regardless of age.

Comprehending these generational nuances holds paramount importance for companies navigating the effective implementation of new technologies. Organizations can address such disparities through robust training initiatives, fostering a culture of perpetual learning, and cultivating an inclusive milieu where employees feel empowered and supported in adapting to technological changes.

5 Conclusion

This study has illuminated the transformative impact of technological advancements on employee skills. The findings accentuate an existing lack of preparedness among employees for the technological metamorphosis within their work environments, marked by resistance and apprehension toward the incorporation of additional technologies. Furthermore, the insufficiency of measures taken by companies, including the absence of requisite training programs and support mechanisms, contributes to the challenge's employees confront when adapting to technological shifts (Towers-Clark, 2020).

The study has underscored the critical significance of addressing these issues to facilitate a seamless transition into a technologically advanced workplace. It is evident that the absence of employee skills and readiness can impede their ability to keep pace with technological transformations, potentially eroding organizational productivity and competitive prowess (Vogels, 2019).

To surmount these challenges, a proactive approach is imperative for companies. This involves crafting comprehensive technology readiness initiatives encompassing structured learning endeavors, nurturing a culture of technological adoption and innovation, forging a supportive organizational framework, and executing effective change management strategies. By doing so, organizations can empower employees, endowing them with the essential skills and fostering an environment that embraces technology as a catalyst for growth and advancement.

Ultimately, by bridging the gap between employee preparedness and technological transformation, organizations can position themselves for triumph in the digital era, concurrently empowering employees to flourish within an ever-evolving work milieu (Younis & Adel, 2020).

6 Recommendations

This paper offers a glimpse into the trajectory of the contemporary work landscape. Drawing from the insights derived from a limited study conducted in the Georgian context, it becomes evident that employees are ill-prepared for the impending technological transformation, and companies are yet to adopt suitable measures to address this challenge. In light of these observations, several specific areas warrant consideration for further research, alongside recommendations tailored for both employees and companies (Vincent, 2023).

6.1 Recommendations for Further Research

- Conduct comprehensive studies to discern the underlying causes of employees' resistance to technological transformation.
- Explore the primary factors contributing to employees' discontent with technology, such as apprehension over fundamental work alterations, uncertain circumstances, loss of a secure work environment, and unstable conditions.
- Investigate the influence of cultural and organizational elements on employees' inclinations toward technology adoption.
- Examine the role played by employee demographics, including age, tenure, and educational level, in shaping their readiness for technology adoption.
- Analyze the potential repercussions of technological resistance on employee well-being and organizational performance.
- Investigate the impact of technological resistance on employees' job satisfaction, engagement, and stress levels.
- Examine how employees' technological readiness influences their career progression and long-term employability.
- Evaluate the correlation between organizational preparedness for technology adoption and overall performance, productivity, and competitiveness.

6.2 Recommendations for Employees

- Cultivate a growth-oriented mindset and proactively pursue skill development opportunities.
- Recognize the paramount significance of ongoing learning and adaptability in the face of technological progress.
- Enroll in personal skills enhancement training programs, online courses, or other avenues for professional growth.
- Seek out mentors well-versed in technological advancements to bolster skill acquisition.
- Actively engage in change endeavors and provide constructive input when encountering challenges.
- Participate in candid dialogues with both management and peers regarding the merits and hurdles associated with technological transformation.
- Articulate any reservations or concerns about technology adoption in a constructive manner, while also suggesting potential solutions or supportive measures.
- Leverage their own experiences and insights to bolster the effective implementation of technology-driven initiatives within the organization.

6.3 Recommendations for Companies

- Cultivate a culture of perpetual learning and innovation.
- Nurture a supportive environment that urges employees to embrace technology and engage in continuous skills enhancement.
- Establish routine training programs or seminars to enhance employees' technological proficiencies.
- Promote employee experimentation with new technologies and provide platforms for the dissemination of best practices and lessons learned.
- Develop comprehensive change management strategies.
- Implement change management processes addressing employees' emotional and psychological concerns tied to technology adoption.
- Clearly and transparently communicate the advantages of technological transformation to employees at all hierarchical levels.
- Involve employees in decision-making processes concerning technology implementation to ensure their perspectives are valued and their feedback is heeded.
- Provide requisite resources and support measures.
- Allocate adequate resources to guarantee employees' access to training, mentorship, and technical assistance during the transitional phase.
- Establish dedicated help centers or support teams to address employee queries and apprehensions about technology.
- Extend opportunities for employees to test and offer feedback prior to the full-scale implementation of new technologies.
- Foster collaboration and knowledge exchange.

- Encourage cross-functional collaboration and the sharing of knowledge to enhance employee comprehension and acceptance of new technologies.
- Acknowledge and reward employees actively contributing to the integration of technology and innovation within the organization.

References

Acemoglu, D., & Restrepo, P. (2017). *Robots and jobs: Evidence from U.S. Labor markets* (NBER Working Papers No. 23285).

Acemoglu, D., & Restrepo, P. (2018). *Artificial intelligence and work* (NBER Working Paper No 24196).

Ashutosh Jani, A. M. (2016). HR and technology. *HRM Review*, 45–57.

Aspan, H., Wahyuni, E. S., Prabowo, A., Zahara, A. N., Sari, I. N., & Mariyana. (2020). Individual characteristics and job characteristics on work effectiveness in the state-owned company: The moderating effect of emotional intelligence. *International Journal of Innovation, Creativity and Change, 13*, 761–774.

Autor, D. H. (2015). Why are there still so many jobs? The history and future of workplace automation. *Journal of Economic Perspectives, 29*, 3–30.

Brin, P. V., & Nehme, M. N. (2019). *Corporate social responsibility: Analysis of theories and models.*

Brynjolfsson, E., & McAfee, A. (2014). *The second machine age: Work,progress and prosperity in a time of brilliant technologies.* WW Nordon and Co.

Cappelli, P. H. (2015). Skill gaps, skill shortages and skill mismatches evidence and arguments for the United States. *ILR Review, 68*(2), 251–290.

Coley, C. W., Thomas, D. A., Lummiss, J. A. M., Jaworski, J. N., Breen, C. P., Schultz, V., Hart, T., Fishman, J. S., Rogers, L., Gao, H., Hicklin, R. W., Plehiers, P. P., Byington, J., Piotti, J. S., Green, W. H., Hart, A. J., Jamison, T. F., & Jensen, K. F. (2019). A robotic platform for flow synthesis of organic compounds informed by AI planning. *Science, 365*(6453).

Davenport, T. H., & Ronanki, R. (2018). Artificial intelligence for the real world. *Harvard Business Review*, 108–116.

Dulebohn, J. H., & Johnson, R. D. (2013). Human resource metrics and decision support: A classification framework. *Human Resource Management Review, 23*(1), 71–83.

Howard, J. (2017). Nonstandard work arrangements and worker health and safety. *American Journal of Industrial Medicine*, 1–10.

McGee RE, T. N. (2015). *Unemployment and de pression among emerging adults in 12 states.* მოპოვებული Behavioral Risk Factor Surveillance System 2010: http://dx.doi.org/10.5888/pcd12:140451-დან

McKinsey Global Institute. (2017). *Jobs lost, jobs gained: Workforce transitions in a time of automation.*

Oeij, P., Rus, D., & Pot, F. D. (2017). *Workplace innovation: Theory, research and practice.* Springer International Publish AG.

Office, I. L. (2019). ILO global commission on the future of work. In *Working for a brighter future.* Geneva.

Prasad, A. (2018 წლის 8 10). მოპოვებული www.quickfms.com: https://www.quickfms.com/blog/how-technology-has-reshaped-the-workplace-დან

Prasad, A. (2019 წლის 21 November). *https://www.quickfms.com/.* მოპოვებული https://www.quickfms.com/blog/quickfms-the-best-facility-management-software-დან

Samarasinghe, K. R., & Medis, A. (2020). Artificial Intelligence based Strategic Human Resource Management (AISHRM) for Industry. 4.0. *Global Journal of Management and Business Research, 20*(2), 7–13.

Schulte, P., & Howard, J. (2019). *The impact of technology on work and the workforce.* USA.
Susskind, R., & Susskind, D. (2015). *The future of the profession: How technology will transform the work of human experts.* Oxford University Press.
Towers-Clark, C. (2020 წლის 10 12). *Human Skills Will Be Most Important In The Digital Future Of Work.* მოპოვებული www.forbes.com: https://www.forbes.com/sites/charlestowersclark/2020/12/10/human-skills-will-be-most-important-in-the-digital-future-of-work/?sh=78cd29c07721-დან
VINCENT, J. K. (2023 წლის 26 June). *Hope, fear, and AI.* მოპოვებული www.theverge.com: https://www.theverge.com/c/23753704/ai-chatgpt-data-survey-research-დან
VOGELS, E. A. (2019 წლის 9 September). *Millennials stand out for their technology use, but older generations also embrace digital life.* მოპოვებული www.pewresearch.org: https://www.pewresearch.org/short-reads/2019/09/09/us-generations-technology-use/-დან
Younis, R. A. A., & Adel, H. M. (2020). Artificial intelligence strategy, creativity-oriented HRM and knowledge-sharing quality: Empirical analysis of individual and organisational performance of AI-powered businesses. In *Proceedings of the British Academy of Management (BAM) 2020 Annual International Conference: Innovating for a Sustainable Future.* London, United Kingdom.

Social Commerce Revolutionizes Electronic Commerce

Victoria Frings and Richard C. Geibel

Abstract The growing importance of constant developments in e-commerce, and thus the restructuring of the online consumer market, leaves users and companies curious about what new technologies will emerge, take hold, and promise to add value to people's lives. One important answer to this question is social commerce, a new field in e-commerce. Social commerce combines e-commerce with social media and thus exploits enormous potential in areas that are becoming increasingly important. Due to its current stage of development, social commerce is still considered by many companies to be a potential phenomenon, but one that is already actively changing the market. The added value that social commerce offers users, influencers, small businesses, and large corporations alike is transactions, sales, and the purchase of products directly via social media, as well as awareness for products or services. Customers are intercepted directly on social media and, with a proper trigger of the content from the brand and company, can directly purchase and carry out the transaction on the platform. Many companies are now investigating: in what form can these visions of the future be put into practice, and to what extent can this revolutionize the market structure in the long term? This article takes a closer look at the core of social commerce, investigates its functions, and looks at it especially in relation to the beauty industry. These research questions are examined in detail and answered through an as-is and to-be analysis and illustrated using the beauty industry as an example. The selected industry is considered a pioneer of digital innovations and can also serve as a case study for other segments in this field. This article shows that social commerce is restructuring and revolutionizing the consumer market. Social commerce offers enormous added value for companies and users. It adapts to changing consumer behavior by shifting power from companies to consumers, benefiting users and enabling companies to increase reach and sales. At the same time, this new, very complex area must be actively shaped and organized, and in doing so, it is essential to avoid costly mistakes and prevent incorrect developments.

V. Frings · R. C. Geibel (✉)
E-Commerce Institute, Cologne, Germany
e-mail: geibel@ecommerceinstitut.de

V. Frings
e-mail: frings@ecommerceinstitut.de

R. C. Geibel and S. Machavariani (eds.), *Digital Management to Shape the Future*, Springer Proceedings in Business and Economics,
https://doi.org/10.1007/978-3-031-66517-2_8

Keywords Social commerce · eCommerce · Customer journey · Customer moment · Social media

1 Introduction

Anyone interested in digitization and the increasing improvement of electronic commerce (e-commerce), in general, will sooner or later come across the topic of social commerce. This topic has been at the center of conversations among e-commerce stakeholders for several years and may be described as a future phenomenon in the industry (Roschmann, 2022, p. 4). Due to the current restructuring of the market with a focus on digitalization, it can be observed that more and more people are using social platforms as search engines to find products. Regarding future developments and innovations that will change entire industries and commerce, it must be admitted that social commerce is much bigger than predicted. This area will encompass and revolutionize the sales market in the future, offering innovations in customer satisfaction at the consumer level and satisfying the needs of the mobile-first generation (Schmider, n.d.). This potential favors a boom in the social commerce industry starting now (Roschmann, 2022, p. 4). However, what factors are driving its future development? Moreover, to what extent can these visions of the future be translated into reality? How exactly should this new area be designed? What mistakes should be avoided? Social commerce and its functions still seem to be a fictitious glimpse into the future. Nevertheless, companies that dare to expand the social commerce segment of e-commerce and take actions that drive social commerce in the future can rise in market value and position. These can lead to a change in the general corporate structure but there are also challenges and risks involved.

Social commerce is arguably the most controversial and debated topic in e-commerce. This research paper, therefore, focuses on the development of social commerce and sheds light on the difficulties that can arise, its areas, and progress in selected areas. The beauty industry and many other industries can benefit from the functions of social commerce. Therefore, research deals with definitions, boundaries, and all tangible information on social commerce and offers a reference to the beauty industry, which serves as a case study to understand fast developments better. In addition, the market, and the market potential of social commerce in connection with various social media platforms are examined. Can social commerce establish itself equally on all platforms, or does one platform favor its growth? Today, the direct sale of products and services via social media is no longer fiction due to constant development. Users in Germany have been shown to spend around 90 min daily on social media (Eger, 2022). Social media users often use social media as inspiration for subsequent purchases. What innovation could better serve customer needs and their transformation than social commerce?

2 Theory

A change in consumer behavior due to ongoing digitalization forces the market to drive change and create innovative ways to satisfy needs. On the other hand, these changes in behavior also offer great potential for companies to develop creative solutions and adapt to customers' behavior. They also indicate that consumer acceptance of these innovations is relatively high. This presents companies with the significant challenge of satisfying customer needs online in a trend-oriented manner in the face of constantly changing consumer behavior. Therefore, it is more important than ever to stand out (Eger, 2022). This creates high pressure on companies to distinguish themselves with a consumer-oriented unique selling proposition (USP).

As a result of ongoing digitalization and the constant change in market structures, social media continue to boom and are continuously gaining users. For companies, this also means achieving and driving interaction, customer acquisition, and sustainable customer loyalty on such platforms. Thus, the companies that perform better with their content on social media can build a customer base and direct customers to the company's website to buy its products. Since it has been proven that most users are only looking for inspiration on social media, the company must use triggering content to persuade the users to buy the product on its website (Eger, 2022). The website link can direct users from social media to the company's website to make a purchase. This feature poses risks to companies and is a multi-step approach. A long customer journey with multiple touchpoints risks the customer losing interest in the product and abandoning the purchase process. Therefore, this feature cannot be described as really user-friendly (Roschmann, 2022, p. 31). Moreover, social media does not benefit companies trying to attract customers to their websites via a link. Customers should stay on social platforms and not switch to another activity because of the stickiness of the page.

Due to these difficulties, a suitable long-term solution to the described problem must be found. Social Commerce is one crucial answer to improve this situation and is an innovative solution to increase sales through social media content. Social commerce thus favors shopping on social media and allows users to stay on the platform and thus make impulse purchases (Roschmann, 2022, p. 31). Ideally, there is no longer a need to switch to another website. However, this raises the question of what exactly shopping via social media such as *TikTok* and *Instagram* might look like and to what extent companies will change the nature of content creation in the long term. What steps does a company need to take to generate sales via social media, and to what extent does such technology need to be implemented in a company to meet the needs of users? To operate as a company in the industry, a social commerce strategy must be implemented and developed. So far, the transaction functions required for this have only been available and implementable on e-commerce platforms and sites. Therefore, constant technical development is required to enable social commerce transactions on social media platforms.

The topic of trust must also be covered to give customers the feeling of a secure shopping experience. It can uniquely affect transactions on social platforms (Lee,

2016). More than ever, a company must perform on social platforms to generate increased sales, increasing pressure on every company. The points mentioned may act as hurdles for companies in the future and must be solved by innovative solutions from companies to turn users into customers (Roschmann, 2022, p. 4).

In the following analyses of the problem and the general definition of social commerce are illuminated based on the beauty industry on social media.

3 Research Method

The specific research objective of this article is to analyze the field of social commerce in detail and gain a deeper understanding of the functions of social commerce and its implications through a case study of the beauty industry in social media, as well as upcoming risks. The overall goal of this research is to use this case study to trace the developments and implementation steps of social commerce on the most popular social media platforms to understand the future transformation of the market. In addition, influencing factors that affect the performance of social commerce are highlighted. In addition, the influence of social commerce on user decision-making will be examined. This leads to the research question: To what extent can the technological advances, potentials, and innovations around social commerce and its possibilities be implemented and the everyday life of companies and provides added value for customers? To what extent will the market structure and hierarchy change due to these innovations, and what critical impact will this have on society? As social commerce is currently described as revolutionary in the industry, expectations are rising. To what extent can these expectations be met, and what will be possible in the future? How exactly should this new area be designed? What mistakes should be avoided? In the context of these areas to be highlighted, this research paper critically examines possible difficulties in implementation as well as risks and changes to the same. Another focus of this article is the investigation of the two currently most popular social platforms, as well as a comparison of the enforcement of social commerce on both platforms. Can social commerce establish itself equally well on every platform, or can specific platforms be found to be more promising? Thus, this thesis aims to examine the field of social commerce based on developments in e-commerce, analyze functions and future developments, apply them to the industry and compare the associated potential on different platforms.

This study examines the acceptance of social commerce and its state of development on the German market. It uses a ***qualitative approach*** based on existing information and an extensive survey of experts. The focus of the study is on how companies can benefit from the development of social commerce and what challenges are associated with the implementation of social commerce. Questions relating to the role of social media in companies' e-commerce strategy and the importance of customer ratings and recommendations for the success of social commerce are also considered. In addition, the study analyzes and discusses potential future developments in social commerce to help companies plan their strategies and prepare for upcoming trends. The results of this study can help companies develop successful social commerce strategies and position themselves in the competitive environment.

4 Case Study

Developments in e-commerce due to digitalization are leading to constant change in the industry and thus to ever-new potential arising from technical innovations (Eger, 2022). Due to the increasing tolerance for new online technologies and online shopping, e-commerce is booming (E-Commerce Institute, 2022). The development of social commerce and its functions offer companies a direct route to the customer. In this process, the functions of e-commerce, which represent the online transaction function, are transferred to the area of social media. At the same time, functions and features of social media are also transferred and used in other areas of e-commerce, such as live shopping (Mundt, 2022). Social media have many users and thus a broad spectrum of different target groups, which offers great potential for social commerce and its implementation.

Social commerce represents a fusion of efficient e-commerce functions and combines them with social networks (Eger, 2022). Nevertheless, social commerce embodies a different form of online selling and thus differs from commercial e-commerce and its shopping experience (Roschmann, 2022, p. 4). While traditional e-commerce enables digital transactions on a company's websites or platform models, social commerce involves purchasing directly through social media (Roschmann, 2022, p. 4). It combines online selling with online buying and integrates it firmly into consumers' daily lives. The social commerce sector has a global market volume of nearly $492 billion (Eger, 2022). Transactions are integrated into social media, providing users with a familiar environment that is already part of their daily routine (Roschmann, 2022, p. 4). This provides a high revenue opportunity and a social buying experience that can be shared with others. Due to the social nature of transactions on social platforms, this allows for direct customer feedback and interaction between customers (Roschmann, 2022, p. 4).

Since most users use social media as a source of inspiration and do not go directly to the company's website, they can now combine the search for inspiration and the purchase of products in one transaction directly on social media. This also shortens the customer journey, meaning that in the future, users will be able to find inspiration on social media, incorporate the opinions of others into the buying process, consider influencer feedback and general reviews, and make a purchase on a single platform. In this way, social commerce creates an integrated shopping experience for customers, making users' everyday lives easier and simplifying online shopping. Customers get the information they need to make a purchase decision and feel that the buying process is seamless and straightforward (Grote, 2022). Social commerce has great potential to shape online shopping in the long term. It enables all stakeholders, such as users, consumers, manufacturers, sellers, and influencers, to participate in innovation and add value. As social commerce changes the nature of online shopping, any company with an online presence will be affected by its potential and prospects (Eger, 2022). This represents an inevitable change for the industry that will determine which companies will lead the market and compete in the marketplace in the future (Roschmann, 2022, p. 16). Companies that integrate social commerce into their social media strategy benefit from the potential and the added value it offers for increasing their sales. Social commerce represents a unique form of online shopping and holds the potential of a revolutionary concept that will change the online sales market and dominate it in the future (Roschmann, 2022, p. 34). However, the implementation of social commerce on social media depends on the further development of the infrastructure and the technical functions of social media (Laing, 2022). The development of social commerce is equally dependent on customer acceptance. For a deeper and more detailed understanding of social commerce, its possibilities and technical implementation will be explained in the further course of the research using a three-stage model. This leads to a more comprehensive understanding of the current state of development of social commerce and its future potential.

4.1 Customer Journey

Digital innovations in the field of e-commerce promote changes in a customer journey and thus benefit companies and corporations. The customer journey describes the path of a potential customer and his various touchpoints with a product or service. The customer journey thus embodies the process from the discovery of a product with all its touchpoints to the purchase decision and the final purchase of a product on the Internet (Fig. 1). The purchase of a product represents the overarching goal of the Customer Journey. An average customer journey consists of five to six steps. These describe various contact points with the product, for example, through online advertising, social media advertising, word of mouth, or recognition marketing (Roschmann, 2022, p. 17). Digitization-driven innovations in e-commerce, apps, and social media, as well as other developments, help to extend the customer journey and create new touchpoints. These touchpoints represent friction points and, therefore, opportunities for a customer to decide not to purchase the product. Extending the customer journey, therefore, means more opportunities to change traditional opinions about buying the product (Roschmann, 2022, p. 17). A traditional social media ad leads the customer to the desired product via the website (Instagram, 2022a, 2022b). The customer must follow this link and then add the product to the shopping cart. The customer must then enter the checkout area. To finally buy the product, the customer's data is needed, profiles are created, and shipping and payment options are set (Advidera GmbH & Co. KG, 2022). This effort on the customer's part provides many opportunities to abandon the purchase decision. Thus, a company can lose the customer's attention and interest at each touchpoint. Therefore, the nature of such a customer journey with more and more touchpoints represents a risk for a company (Roschmann, 2022, p. 18).

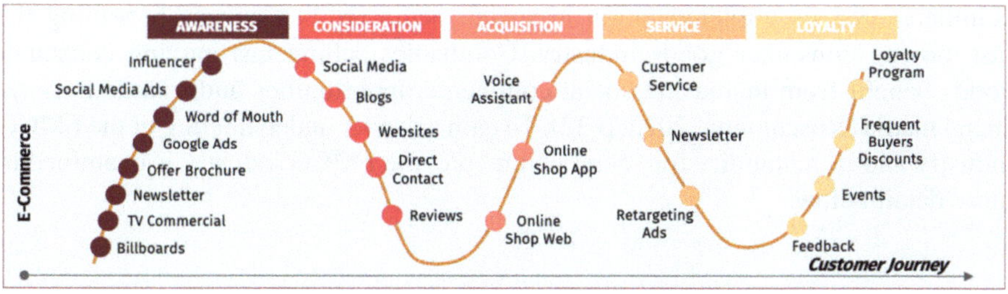

Fig. 1 The traditional customer journey (*Source* Own presentation)

4.2 Consumer Moment

The social commerce approach is changing and revolutionizing the nature of the traditional customer journey. It removes friction points, the so-called touchpoints, and thus additional effort on the part of a potential buyer from the traditional customer journey. This makes it different from the customer journey of regular online shopping. It revolutionizes the customer journey approach and serves the customer directly on social media (Roschmann, 2022, p.17). The customer journey can thus be reduced to a minimum through social commerce and is limited to a **single step** (Fig. 2). This eliminates the lengthy process of the traditional customer journey and avoids the risk of losing a customer before the purchase is completed. Above all, this offers companies great potential and enables customer engagement. The results presented above show that this **consumer moment** approach replaces the traditional e-commerce Customer Journey and shortens it by a maximum (Roschmann, 2022, p. 18). Social commerce creates a unique approach that dissolves the risks and difficulties of the commercial Customer Journey and eliminates all friction points. The consumer moment describes the discovery of a product and the purchase at the same time and thus offers future potential and market advantages, favoring the use of social commerce (Roschmann, 2022, p. 17). In summary, the social commerce customer journey begins and ends in social media (Roschmann, 2022, p. 18).

In the further course of the work, the relevant markets are examined. The following section focuses on the fast-moving consumer goods industry to identify the key industry that benefits from social commerce innovation. Developments in social

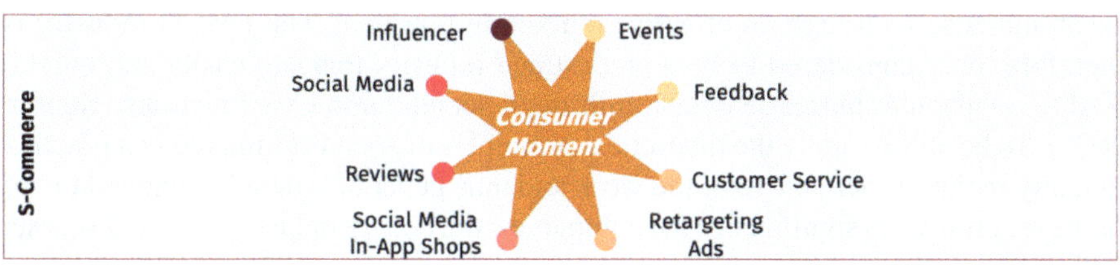

Fig. 2 The social commerce customer journey is the consumer moment (*Source* own presentation)

commerce and its implementation in social media are particularly benefiting the fast-moving consumer goods industry. Companies selling fast-moving consumer goods benefit from increasing social commerce opportunities and transactions via social media (Roschmann, 2022, p.32). To gain a deeper understanding of the FMCG industry and its suitability for social commerce, the FMCG industry is examined in more detail below.

4.3 Fast Moving Consumer Goods

Fast-moving consumer goods (FMCG) sell quickly and at a comparatively low price (Goeken, 2022). They are often purchased in large quantities and are also quickly repurchased. Because of their relatively low price, the products sell quickly and therefore have a high turnover rate in a store (Kenton, 2021). Therefore, these products are considered commodities and are part of consumers' frequent or daily consumption. Companies in this sector benefit from high potential, as their goods are regularly used and repeatedly purchased by customers (Roschmann, 2022, p. 32). Due to the frequent use and low price of the products, these products are also considered low-involvement products, where customers make a purchase decision without thinking about it for longer or comparing substitute products. Fast-moving consumer goods are generally divided into durable goods, non-consumer goods, and services (Goeken, 2022). Due to the great potential and high sales in the market, more and more companies are also getting involved in fast-moving consumer goods. Brands such as Coca-Cola and Pepsi are examples of fast-moving consumer goods in the supermarket. However, other industries such as fashion, gaming, entertainment, and beauty are also FMCG companies that can benefit from this potential (Kenton, 2021). Social commerce developments are particularly relevant for consumer brands, beauty, fashion, entertainment, and other industries. Using social media marketing, the right trigger at the right time can trigger impulse purchases for an FMCG company (Roschmann, 2022, p. 33).

The unique features and relatively low prices of FMCG products entice users to buy more quickly than a high-engagement product. However, it is more than just the FMCG industry that can benefit from the features and goals of social commerce (Roschmann, 2022, p. 32). Instead, all industries that sell a product or service can benefit from the possibilities of social Commerce and increase online sales immensely through an effective marketing presence. The FMCG industry is, therefore, only considered to be a predestined industry that can easily and quickly lead to a customer purchase decision through social commerce functions (Kenton, 2021). To be able to apply the theoretical principles of social commerce to a practical industry in the further course of the work and thus generate a detailed understanding of the functions and significance for companies, the beauty industry will be discussed in the next section.

4.4 *Beauty Industry—Social Media*

The beauty industry is also undergoing a transformation due to digitalization and is being given the opportunity to further expand online shopping with new opportunities and customer satisfaction, as well as increased awareness and sales online (Rivas, 2022). Due to the changes in the digital shopping industry, a change in the character of shopping can be observed, offering a new digital transaction experience to customers. Due to the high use of social media by customers and the potential of social media marketing for companies, the beauty industry and its players are already taking advantage of the potential offered by the social media environment (Douglas, 2022). The success of the beauty industry on social media is due to its strong visual component (Rivas, 2022). Therefore, the industry can benefit from high potential in the social commerce sector, not only because it is one of the fast-moving consumer goods but also because of the nature of the products, which are highly visual and therefore ideal for marketing on social media (Goeken, 2022). For this reason, companies in the beauty industry can connect with their customers on social platforms through videos, photos, and stories, turning platform users into potential customers (McKinsey & Company, 2022). In addition, social media marketing strategies are highly adopted, including influencer marketing. This allows companies to drive platform interaction and increase sales (Rivas, 2022). In the following, the opportunities, and developments of social commerce in the beauty industry will be examined in more detail and the changes brought about by digitalization will be presented. In addition, this will be applied to the Instagram and TikTok platforms, as well as substantiated and proven with examples from the industry. The rapid changes in the sales market and the digitization-driven changes in the shopping industry are also creating new potential and challenges in the beauty industry (Goeken, 2022). The rapid changes in the sales market and the digitization-related changes in the shopping industry are also creating new potential and challenges in the beauty industry. Through the social commerce approach and its developments, the beauty industry can already be described as the most purchased product category on social media in America (Rivas, 2022). Through the functions of social commerce, users can be served directly and seamlessly on the respective social media platform and thus be inspired by the companies' content (Roschmann, 2022, p. 5). Also, the needs of the social component in an online purchase can only be met through the social media space and the companies' content (Goeken, 2022). Live shopping and live interaction are also integrated into the social media content of the beauty industry and can give customers a realistic impression of the products due to the high visuality of the products (McKinsey & Company, 2022). The beauty industry is considered a fast-moving and adaptable sector when it comes to digitization-related changes (Rivas, 2022).

These features and other ways of engaging with customers and building a community are essential for the beauty industry on the Instagram and TikTok platforms. The TikTok presence has become an essential tool for companies due to the platform's development, digitalization, and innovations. Especially for companies in the beauty industry and their online presence, the entertainment platform is essential (Rivas,

2022). To build a functioning social commerce strategy for a company in the beauty industry, it is vital to create a trusting and seamless buying experience for consumers. Trust is an important aspect that can be increased through referral marketing, influencers, and customer interaction (Roschmann, 2022, p. 17). In this way, beauty brands can also create user-generated content, and customers can be addressed individually. The beauty industry not only represents a case study for the implementation of social commerce on social media, as it is active in the field of FMCG, but also already shows steady developments in this area (Goeken, 2022).

In summary, the characteristics of beauty products increase the opportunities and possibilities for the beauty industry in social commerce. Nevertheless, companies in the beauty industry take a pioneering role and show customers what they need but do not yet know themselves (Roschmann, 2022, p. 18). These characteristics predestine the beauty industry to exploit the full potential of social commerce with an effective digital marketing strategy and, in the future, to record a new type of transaction and thus an increase in sales and brand awareness.

For a company to fully utilize social commerce on a social media platform, technical processes must be assumed. Users must expand their user profile and add personal data such as an address, payment options, etc. to carry out a smooth transaction on social media. In the following, the potential, and the development status of the respective platforms Instagram and TikTok are highlighted. The above results show that the beauty industry is taking advantage of the power and potential of social media and new technologies that are trending. Both platforms also serve as examples due to high metrics, such as growth rate, user numbers, engagement rate, and the type of content, as well as general characteristics of the platforms that enable sales and transformation into an integrated sales platform. In addition, the general potential of the respective platforms is analyzed in order to filter out which medium offers the most significant application possibilities and potential for companies and customers.

Instagram is currently one of the most used social media. Due to the constant digital progress and the boom of e-commerce as well as the increasing online transactions, it is important for companies to establish an online presence (Eger, 2022). To be competitive in the market, companies show their online presence on social media (Dahlke, n.d.). Establishing an Instagram account for a business creates awareness, builds a customer base and community, and increases sales through presence. Instagram can provide a business with a wide reach and therefore a high potential to increase sales. For example, Instagram can already serve as a sales platform to drive customers from a product post to a company's website with one click. This feature is called Shoppable Posts (Instagram, 2022a, 2022b). Since 2018, features like Shoppable Posts have allowed businesses to make sales on the platform with just a few clicks and redirects (Gatto, 2023). These Shoppable Posts integrate with the Instagram experience and add value for customers and businesses (Grote, 2022). This feature can be considered a precursor to social commerce and can be further expanded in the future (Douglas, 2022). Instagram offers the possibility of creating one's own Instagram store, which acts as a kind of digital shop window for companies. The Instagram store, which displays individual content, offers customers the opportunity to be inspired, and learn about new products, and gives companies the

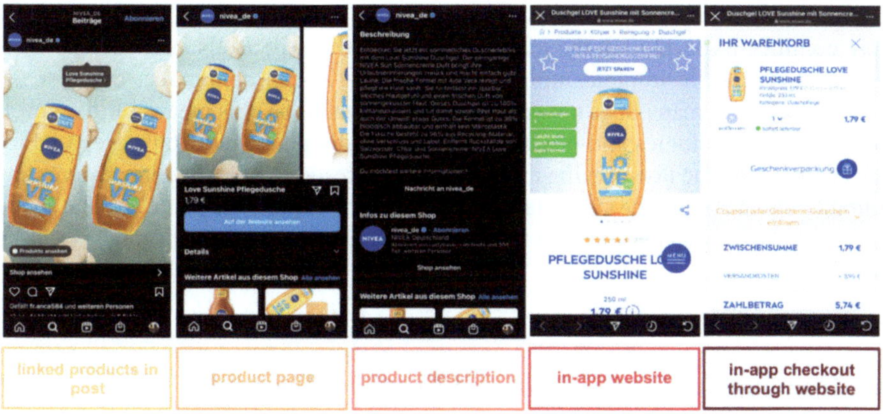

Fig. 3 Social commerce functions on Instagram

chance to win new customers through their own customer loyalty (Grote, 2022). Digitization-related new features, such as the Shoppable button in Instagram stories, offer a particularly important role in the use of influencer marketing. With shoppable story stickers, it is possible for every user to get to a landing page by clicking on the sticker (Online Haendler News, 2020). These stickers serve as an alternative or additional channel to the swipe-up links that take users to the company's own platform. However, the feature can only be activated and used by companies or users with a larger follower base of at least 10,000 followers (Grote, 2022). Looking at the evolution of social commerce, the platform Instagram (Fig. 3) can be seen as an ideal sales and transaction environment (Grote, 2022). The company demonstrates social commerce through its early response and integration.

In addition, social commerce features can increase sales and provide fewer touch points where customers abandon a purchase. In summary, Instagram is already making initial progress toward social commerce by already offering users the ability to conduct virtual transactions nearly on social media via shoppable posts. This offers the opportunity to increase customer acceptance of the combination of e-commerce and social media.

5 Results and Discussion

Social commerce offers extreme potential and market opportunities and will change the sales industry in the future. In addition, the majority stated that social commerce would prevail and ensure satisfaction among users and companies by shortening the customer journey. Furthermore, they are aware that the use of social media will continue to increase in the future and that social commerce functions will therefore continue to develop in the market. However, the experts also see specific difficulties and risks in implementing and developing social commerce. Since social commerce in Germany does not yet offer mature functions, this means further development of technologies and progress in social media platforms. To be prepared for the changes and the fast-moving market in the future, companies are already creating suitable social commerce strategies. In summary, the experts are confident that social commerce will revolutionize the market and offer high opportunities and potential for the future.

6 Conclusion, Limitations and Further Research

As the work results have shown, social commerce has the potential to revolutionize the digital sales market and offers immense added value for companies, users, customers, and influencers. The development of social commerce in Europe and especially in Germany, is still very different from the development in China. With its developed infrastructure, acceptance, and technical achievements, the Chinese market offers a kind of preview or glimpse into the future of the European market and its social commerce developments. The necessary technologies will make social commerce a seamless transaction on social media in the future and make it possible to serve customers directly on social media. Nevertheless, due to the different technical requirements and the differences in customer interests and acceptance, it is not possible to conclude directly from the Chinese market to the German market. Since customers in China trust digital commerce more than offline commerce, the latter differs from the offline-oriented commerce of the German market. German online retail thrives on the development from offline retail to online retail and the steady growth of the acceptance of online transactions.

The authors assume that the market for e-commerce in Germany can be divided into three major segments by 2030 (Fig. 4). In the online segment, the importance of platforms will continue to increase and reach a market share of a good 60%. On the other hand, the share of traditional websites will continue to decline and fall below 30%. The third segment, social commerce—including the important area of live shopping—will continue to grow and together account for around 10%. This means that social commerce is becoming increasingly important as the fastest growing segment of e-commerce (Roenisch, 2023). There is of course a need for further research here.

This assessment is also supported by the fact that the two hyper scalers Meta and Amazon have recently agreed on intensive cooperation in this segment in order to promote social commerce (Vanian, 2023). Amazon announced: "For the first time, customers will be able to store Amazon's Facebook and Instagram ads and check out with Amazon without leaving the social media apps." This would be an important step towards integrating the important fulfillment and e-payment functions into the world of social media. This will benefit both users, who would enjoy a smooth shopping

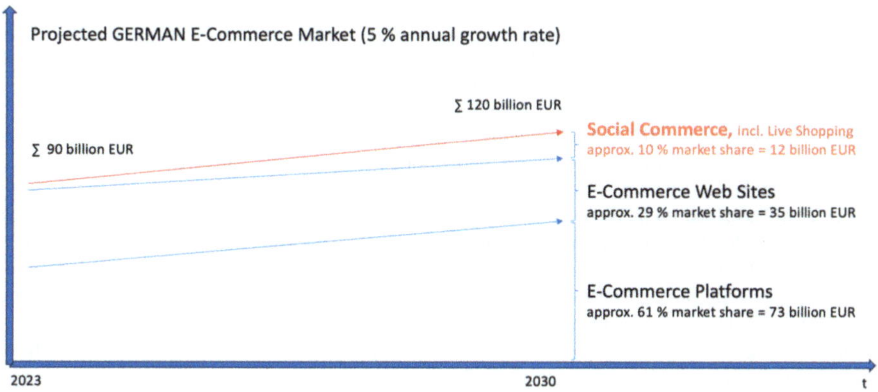

Fig. 4 Expected size and breakdown of the e-commerce market in Germany (*Source* own presentation)

process, and platforms, which would further expand and combine their respective strengths.

Nevertheless, offline retail plays a significant role for customers in their everyday lives. An omnichannel strategy can continue to benefit from social commerce, and customer needs can be satisfied online. Since social commerce reaches users directly where they spend their free time online daily, a broad mass of existing and new customers can be reached. Since customers are already on social platforms and looking for inspiration or entertainment, this desire can be implied directly on the platform through social commerce. Younger target groups expect social commerce in the future and look forward to being able to conduct transactions as quickly and seamlessly as possible. After the analysis, it is found that not all international market developments are transferable to other markets—there is still a need for further research. However, it is already clear that social commerce, as a combination of social media and e-commerce, is playing an increasingly important role and will continue to do so in the future.

References

Accenture. (2022). *The future of shopping and social commerce*. Retrieved November 11, 2022, from https://www.accenture.com/us-en/insights/software-platforms/why-shopping-set-social-revolution

Advidera GmbH & Co. KG. (2022). *Customer journey explained simply: Definition & examples*. ADVIDERA. Retrieved December 12, 2022, from https://www.advidera.com/glossar/customer-journey/

Dahlke, D. (n.d.). *Why you should include social commerce in your marketing strategy*. Retrieved November 16, 2022, from https://www.printful.com/de/blog/warum-social-commerce

Douglas. (2022). *DOUGLAS live shopping, new trends every day*. Retrieved December 20, 2022, from https://www.douglas.de/de/cp/videos/video-overview

Douglas Marketing Solutions. (2022). *The next big thing: Social commerce & live shopping on social media and other platforms.* Retrieved October 28, 2022, from https://www.douglas-marketing-solutions.com/de/the-next-big-thing-social-commerce-live-shopping-on-social-media-and-other-platforms/

E-Commerce Institute. (2022). *Scientifically supported definition of social commerce.* Retrieved October 16, 2022, from https://ecommerceinstitut.de/scientifically-supported-definition-of-social-commerce/

Eger, A. (2022). *Was ist social commerce? Diese trends und plattformen solltest du kennen*. Retrieved October 20, 2022, from https://de.wix.com/blog/amp/social-commerce?utm_source=google

Fleming, M. (2020). Instagram launches shoppable posts as it looks to play a bigger role in ecommerce. *Marketing Week.* Retrieved December 18, 2022, from https://www.marketingweek.com/instagram-launches-shoppable-posts-looks-play-bigger-role-ecommerce/

Flora, L. (2022a). *Beauty brands embark on TikTok shopping.* Retrieved November 21, 2022, from https://www.glossy.co/beauty/beauty-brands-embark-on-tiktok-shopping/

Flora, L. (2022b). *TikTok searches for 2022.* Retrieved November 10, 2022, from https://www.glossy.co/pop/tiktoks-influence-dominates-googles-top-trending-beauty-searches-for-2022/?utm_medium=email

Gatto, E. (2023). *Social know how—Social media marketing services.* https://socialknowhow.com

Goeken, C. (2022). *Winning the Sustain Game—5 hypotheses on the future of the consumer goods an retail industry.* https://www.rolandberger.com/en/Insights/Publications/Winning-the-Sustain-Game.html

Geibel, R. (2022). *Social commerce: Emergence and importance.* Retrieved November 8, 2022, from https://ecommerceinstitut.de/social-commerce-emergence-and-importance-2/

Geibel, R., & Kracht, R. (2023). Social Commerce—Origin and meaning, In Geibel/Machavariani (eds.), *Digital Management in COVID-19 Pandemic and Post-Pandemic Times, Proceedings of ISPC 2021* (pp. 49–67).

Grote, S. (2022). *What is social commerce? Definition, examples and tips.* Retrieved November 10, 2022, from https://www.meltwater.com/de/blog/social-commerce-definition-beispiele-tipps

Harju, N. (2022). *Live shopping: The future of e-commerce?* Retrieved December 4, 2022, from https://blog.hubspot.de/marketing/live-shopping

Instagram. (2022a). *Douglas_cosmetics.* Retrieved December 10, 2022 from https://instagram.com/douglas_cosmetics?igshid=YmMyMTA2M2Y=

Instagram. (2022b). *nyxcosmetics_de.* Retrieved December 10, 2022, from https://instagram.com/nyxcosmetics_de?igshid=YmMyMTA2M2Y=

Kenton, W. (2021). *Fast-Moving Consumer Goods (FMCG) industry: Definition, types, and profitability.* Retrieved November 3, 2022, from https://www.investopedia.com/terms/f/fastmoving-consumer-goods-fmcg.asp

King, D., Outland, J., Turban, E., & Whiteside, J. (2017). *Introduction to electronic commerce and social commerce* (4th ed.).

Laing, J. (2022). *What does social commerce mean.* Retrieved December 12, 2022 from https://www.bytedance.com/en/

Lee, J. (2016). *Research Gate | Trust and Social Commerce.* Retrieved December 12, 2022, from https://www.researchgate.net/publication/292211943_Trust_and_Social_Commerce

McKinsey & Company. (2022). *Beauty is booming: Cosmetics industry successfully relies on digitization.* Retrieved October 6, 2022, from https://www.mckinsey.de/news/presse/beauty-boomt-kosmetikbranche-setzt-erfolgreich-auf-digitalisierung

Mundt, E. (2022). *What is social selling? Definition, strategy and examples in B2B marketing.* Retrieved November 2, 2022, from https://www.marconomy.de/was-ist-social-selling-definition-strategie-und-beispiele-im-b2b-marketing-a-820096/

Nordqvist, C. (2018). What is social commerce. Definition and meaning. *Market Business News.* Retrieved December 10, 2022, from https://marketbusinessnews.com/financial-glossary/social-commerce-definition-meaning/#:%7E:text=Social%20commerce%20refers%20to%20new%20online%20marketing%20strategies,it%20is%20where%20social%20media%20and%20shopping%20meet

Online Haendler News. (2020). *Instagram as a sales channel—Rise of social commerce*. Retrieved October 12, 2022, from https://www.onlinehaendler-news.de/e-commerce-trends/marketing/133217-instagram-vertriebskanal-social-commerce
Rivas, C. (2022). *#TikTokMadeMeBuyIt: Why social commerce is the next big thing for beauty brands—Ingenuity*. Retrieved November 7, 2022, from https://www.thgingenuity.com/resources/blog/tiktokmademebuyit-social-commerce-next-big-thing-for-beauty-brands
Roenisch, S. (2023). *Prognose: So entwickelt sich der E-Commerce bis 20230*. Retrieved September 21, 2023, from https://www.versandhausberater.de/members/aktuell/db/124083bma.html
Roschmann, U. (2022). *Red Paper Social Commerce*. Retrieved December 1, 2022, from https://pixelpark-pwa.e-spirit.cloud/Landingpages/Social-Commerce/
Schmider, A. (2017). *Mobile first—What's behind the trend?* Retrieved December 12, 2022, from https://www.bitfactory.io/de/blog/mobile-first/
Terstiege, M. (2020). Digital marketing. Success models from practice. In *Concepts, instruments and strategies in the context of digitalization* (1st ed.). Springer Gabler.
Vanian, J. (2023). *Meta lets Amazon shoppers buy products on Facebook and Instagram without leaving the apps*. CNBC article. Retrieved November 11, 2023, from https://www.cnbc.com/2023/11/09/meta-lets-amazon-users-buy-on-facebook-instagram-without-leaving-apps.html

Digitalization of the German Legal System from the Perspective of a District Court

Mia Alikhah, Jan Baumann, Richard C. Geibel, and Christian Schlicht

Abstract Increasing digitalization is affecting all areas of life, including the German legal system. As in other areas, it is becoming clear that digitalization in the justice system brings great advantages in terms of speed, cost and quality, but at the same time it is associated with major challenges, e.g., with regard to data protection and security. This article first looks at the initial situation and traces the increasing digitalization of the German legal system. Recently, the experience gained during the Corona pandemic in the administration of justice has played a significant role in this. Particularly noteworthy are electronic legal transactions (ERV), electronic record keeping and court hearings via videoconferencing. After an interim summary of the status quo, the necessary measures for further digitalization of the justice system are presented and evaluated. The experience gained so far in the successive implementation of further digitalization measures will be highlighted and explained in detail on the basis of the working methods of a large German district court. Finally, an outlook on possible future developments in the judiciary is given. All digitalization efforts must take into account aspects relevant to society as a whole—such as continued proximity to citizens, effective legal protection and sustainability.

Keywords Digitalization · Legal system · Regional court · Digital transformation · Sustainability

M. Alikhah · J. Baumann · C. Schlicht (✉)
District Court of Cologne, Cologne, Germany
e-mail: christian.schlicht@lg-koeln.nrw.de

R. C. Geibel
E-Commerce Institute and IU—International University, Cologne, Germany
e-mail: geibel@ecommerceinstitut.de

R. C. Geibel and S. Machavariani (eds.), *Digital Management to Shape the Future*,
Springer Proceedings in Business and Economics,
https://doi.org/10.1007/978-3-031-66517-2_9

1 Initial Situation and Developments During the Corona Pandemic

Until 2018, pleadings were always received by the court in paper form by post. Court files were kept exclusively in paper form. Oral proceedings generally took place in the courtroom in the presence of all parties.

This has begun to change even before the pandemic and is very different today: Fully digital proceedings are no longer the exception. Lawyers communicate with the court in electronic form, case files are largely kept electronically in the civil sector. Oral hearings are often held via videoconference. Especially in cases where there is no need to take evidence, the parties often enjoy the benefits of digital proceedings. The following legislative and technological milestones have made this development possible.

1.1 Electronic Legal Transmission (ERV)

A key component of today's digitalization of the justice system is the electronic legal transmission of documents and files ("*Elektronischer Rechtsverkehr*"—ERV). This includes all electronic communication between the courts and the parties involved in the legal proceedings. In addition to lawyers, this includes citizens, companies, notaries, public authorities, hospitals, and caregivers. The electronic transmission of pleadings, letters and other files has been possible for the legal profession in Germany since 1 January 2018, and is mandatory since 1 January 2022 (see, for example, Section 130d ZPO: active obligation to use).

As of 1 January 2023, this obligation has also been extended to tax advisors.[1] Since 2018, federal, state and local authorities have been able to participate in electronic legal transactions with the judiciary via the special electronic public authority mailbox (beBPo). Although the various authorities are making increasing use of this option in view of the obvious advantages of electronic legal transactions, there is currently still a lack of nationwide connectivity. In addition to DE-Mail access, citizens and companies can participate in electronic legal transactions via the electronic citizen and organization mailbox (eBO) since the beginning of 2022.[2] But in view of the costs involved (approx. 12 to 20 euros per month[3]), this is currently of interest mainly to companies and professionals.[4]

[1] Cf. *Müller*, Active duty of use for tax consultants from 1.1.2023, https://ervjustiz.de/aktive-nutzungspflicht-fuer-steuerberater-ab-1-1-2023.

[2] For the technical and organizational requirements, see https://egvp.justiz.de/buerger_org.anisationen/2022_08_04_Sicherer_Uebermittlungsweg_Buerger_Organisationen_V1-4.pdf.

[3] Status of price determination: September 2023.

[4] A free P.O. box called "My Justice P.O. Box" is scheduled to be available in mid-October 2023 according to current plans, see https://egvp.justiz.de/buerger_organisationen/index.php.

In the ERV, documents are transmitted from the senders' electronic mailbox to the electronic court and administrative mailbox (EGVP). The further processing of electronic submissions at the court depends to a large extent on whether the court has implemented electronic files. If this is not the case, the electronic submissions must be printed out and added to the file in paper form. Otherwise, the electronic submissions are processed directly in the electronic file.

German courts are not yet obliged to send parts of the court files and notifications to the parties involved electronically.[5] However, to the knowledge of the authors, all courts in Germany already have the technical means. In some courts, electronic transmission for service units[6] has been ordered by service directive.

As soon as the courts communicate completely electronically with the parties to the proceedings, this will ultimately mean a digitalization—explicitly not a digitalization—of the analog transmission processes from the "paper world". However, this mere transfer of previous processes into the "digital world" has been aptly described as the "digitization of the stagecoach".[7] In the civil process of the future, there will be other possibilities for a reliable and rapid exchange of information between the court and the parties involved.

1.2 Electronic Case Files

The various procedural codes allow courts to keep case files electronically.[8] From 1 January 2026, electronic case files management will be mandatory in Germany (see, for example, Section 298a (1a) of the German Code of Civil Procedure[9]). In the meantime, *all* German federal states have started to keep case files electronically, at least in some courts.[10] A few federal states already keep all new civil proceedings as electronic files.[11]

In practice and discourse, the buzzword "*electronic case file*" (short for: electronic file) refers to the digitalization process as a whole, not just the digital case file itself.

---

[5] The active usage obligation of the judiciary is not a requirement of the Act to Promote Electronic Legal Transactions (BR-Drs 500/13) (so-called eJustice Act).

[6] Service units take care of file maintenance, execute decrees and send documents.

[7] *Köbler*, Auf der grünen Wiese der Wissenschaft - Ansätze zu einer Verfahrensordnung für originär elektronisch geführte Gerichtsverfahren, JurPC Web-Dok 157/2014 para 2.

[8] Cf. for example § 298a ZPO, § 32 StPO, § 65b SGG, § 46e ArbGG, § 14 FamFG, § 55b VwGO, § 110a OWiG, §135 GBO, § 52b FGO.

[9] Henceforth, reference is made only to provisions on civil procedure.

[10] While some of the pilot projects used "hybrid files," i.e., a paper file and an electronic (second) file in parallel, the majority of cases that have been created as paper files up to the changeover date will continue to be handled in paper form until the instance has been legally concluded. Only new proceedings—even if only within one instance during the transitional period until the comprehensive management of e-files—are managed exclusively electronically.

[11] Cf. for example *Schlicht*, Zum Stand der Digitalisierung der Justiz in Köln, NRW und darüber hinaus, KAV Magazin 3/2022, 24 (24 f), also available at koelner-anwaltsverein.de/kav-magazin.

Nevertheless, the current electronic case file largely replicates the paper file and continues to meet its requirements: In particular, it preserves the requirements of file integrity and completeness, traceability and truthful file management, integrity and authenticity, and security.[12] The structure of the electronic case file is linear and chronological.

In addition, the electronic case file electronic case file provides digital tools to better understand and structure its content. This included functions for searching, marking, grouping, or setting bookmarks, notes or links facilitate file entry. Due to the fact, that several users at court can work on the court file simultaneously, there are additional tools for multiple task creation and workflows.[13] In addition, the file contains a structuring tool. This tool recognizes marked sections and can create a structured file extract with the particularly important factual information.[14]

Basic data relevant for further processing (e.g., data on the parties or witness addresses, internal chamber assignments, amount in dispute) is stored in so-called judicial programs. This data is inserted and automatically used during further processing of the electronic case file.

A significant advantage of the electronic case file over the paper file is its availability anytime, anywhere, which allows parallel processing. This leads to a profound change in working methods and workflows.[15] Simultaneous availability, even outside the court, speeds up the process considerably. For example, it is now common for a file to be sent to several experts during trail. They can prepare their respective expert reports simultaneously and parallel to the ongoing proceeding. The acceleration potential is immense, especially in the case of construction processes or claims involving medical experts from different disciplines. As a result, proceedings can be completed more quickly. Flexible access for judges and service staff can also significantly increase their satisfaction and significantly reduce absenteeism due to illness, etc.

The electronic case file was initially introduced at six courts in North Rhine-Westphalia in 2018. In 2019, 19 further rollouts took place—in the Cologne district at Wipperfürth Local Court. At the Cologne District Court, the electronic case file was introduced in civil proceedings chamber by chamber between September 2020 and September 2021. Since the end of August 2022, all civil courts in the district of the Cologne Regional Court are using the electronic case file. The electronic case file is also increasingly being used in the various departments at the district court.[16] With regard to the electronic file, the criminal area remains as a major project—by 2026, all courts must keep their files completely electronically.

The electronic case file represents an unprecedented restructuring of workflows in the justice. It is situated in a field of tension between the familiar and progress. In

[12] *Jansen/Schlicht*, Elektronische Akte, in *Dörr/Riehm* (eds.), Handbuch Digitalisierung und Zivilverfahren (2023) § 16 Rz 4.

[13] For details, see in particular *Jansen/Schlicht* in *Dörr/Riehm* (eds.) § 16 Rz 33, 35 f, 43 ff.

[14] *Jansen/Schlicht* in *Dörr/Riehm* (ed.) § 16 Rz 56 et seq.

[15] *Jansen/Schlicht* in *Dörr/Riehm* (ed.) § 16 Rz 24.

[16] Family, guardianship, chattel execution, probate and land registry matters, etc.

this area of tension, however, the electronic case file does not contradict the judicial independence of the judiciary, but rather extends it. It allows to work even more flexibly in terms of time and place. In this way, the electronic case file increases the attractiveness of the profession and contributes to a better work-life balance.[17]

For Cologne Regional Court, as the largest regional court in North Rhine-Westphalia, the introduction of the electronic case file posed a particular challenge. A considerable part of the service operation—from processing incoming mail to file submission—had to be reorganized. In addition, 135 civil court judges and more than 100 service staff, bailiffs, judicial officers, and costs officers had to be trained to use the electronic case file securely and familiarize themselves with the new efficient workflows. The challenge was to anticipate the possible problem areas as comprehensively as possible without having any practical experience with the electronic case file. The primary objective was, and still is, to ensure that operation of the court service is not compromised in the interest of citizens seeking justice.

It was only with the electronic case file that the judiciary was able to say goodbye to the previous use of large printers purchased specifically for this purpose. The electronic case file makes it possible to receive, process and send electronic submissions.[18]

However, this potential can only be fully realized if all parties can participate in secure electronic legal transactions. This is the case for lawyers, who are legally obliged to do so. This leads to enormous efficiency gains in the practice of a district court, before which the parties must generally be represented by lawyers in accordance with Section 78 (1) of the Code of Civil Procedure (Zivilprozessordnung).[19]

1.3 Video Hearings

In the wake of the Corona pandemic, video hearings finally awoke from their "deep sleep".[20] The ZPO Reform Act of 2001 had already introduced video and audio transmission of hearings in civil proceedings (Section 128a ZPO). Before the Corona pandemic, however, the provision had little practical relevance.[21] After the proportion of video hearings during the pandemic was estimated at 40–60% according to

[17] Schlicht/Wiemer, Die elektronische Akte beim LG Köln Teil II: Die Arbeit mit der eAkte, https://legal-tech.de/die-arbeit-mit-der-eakte.

[18] Schlicht/Wiemer, Die Einführung der elektronischen Akte beim Landgericht Köln in Zivilverfahren, https://le-gal-tech.de/einfuehrung-der-elektronischen-akte-beim-landgericht-koeln/.

[19] There is still considerable potential, especially at the district courts, if the other parties have to file electronically or can do so cost-effectively, see above.

[20] *Windau*, Gerichtsverhandlung per Videokonferenz: Keine Angst vor § 128a ZPO, https://anwaltsblatt.anwaltverein.de/de/anwaeltinnen-anwaelte/anwaltspraxis/gerichtsverhandlung-per-videokonferenz-keine-angst-vor-128a-zpo.

[21] BeckOK ZPO/von Selle ZPO § 128a Vor Rn. 1.

individual judges,[22] the extent of their use has presumably settled at a lower level hereafter. The actual extent to which video hearings are currently used is not statistically recorded and is likely to vary widely between courts, chambers, and judges. At the Cologne Regional Court, all courtrooms are equipped with the necessary technical equipment, so that it is possible to make full use of it. Video hearings are therefore now an integral part of the judicial landscape and are used on a daily basis in all major city courts.

In the face of increasing Europeanisation and globalization, parties to proceedings and witnesses are no longer regularly based in Germany. It is true that, with the consent of all parties and representatives, video hearings can be held across national borders and witnesses can be heard directly in other EU countries on a voluntary basis.[23] Since requests for mutual assistance in other cases are still cumbersome and time-consuming, it would be worth considering—at least from an economic point of view—to further remove administrative and technical obstacles to video hearings abroad.

2 Interim Conclusion

The status quo proofs that digital civil proceedings are not a dream of the future, but already a living reality. Communication with the legal profession takes place electronically in already digitized files, as does the recording and processing of the file itself. Even after the pandemic, hearings are still regularly conducted by video, especially in simple cases or cases with predominantly legal contentious issues. As a result, important milestones have already been reached. The "digital foundation" has been laid.

3 Further Digitalization of the Judiciary

However, the digitalization steps taken so far only pave the way for further digitalization and, in particular, automation. The focus is on promoting the following areas:

- Video hearings will be further promoted, and cross-border video hearings facilitated.
- Digital complaint channels will be developed and tested.

[22] Cf. With regard to the Dortmund Regional Court, the order of the President of the Higher Regional Court of Hamm, Mündliche Zivilverhandlungen im Wege der Videokonferenz - Länderumfrage des BMJV.

[23] *In detail:* Fabig/Windau: Die Neufassung der Europäischen Zustellungs- und Beweisaufnahmeverordnungen, NJW 2022, 1977; Windau: Die Verhandlung im Wege der Bild- und Tonübertragung, NJW 2020, 2753.

- Mass litigation in small claims will be accelerated through efficient online procedures.
- A further focus will be on the uniform structuring of the parties' submissions, e.g., by means of an electronic basic document.
- AI-based legal tools for procedural support, especially in mass litigation, will be developed and tested.
- The civil procedure should evolve from the pure text level to the (more efficient) evaluation of metadata.
- Legal language models will be used for faster generation of draft e-mails, simple letters, or even first draft decisions.
- The automatic anonymization of decisions is intended to promote the publication rate and thus the predictability of case law.

Some of the many specific development steps are to be outlined below.

3.1 Draft of the Federal Government to Promote the Use of Videoconferencing Technology

At the end of May, the government published a draft of the "Act on the Promotion of the Use of Video Conferencing Technology in Civil and Specialized Courts".[24] In addition to a number of "fine points" (concerning the taking of evidence and inspection, flat-rate costs, etc.), the main provision is that video hearings "shall" be ordered if the parties so request, and that any refusal must be justified and appealable. In the case of an order for video participation by the chairperson, there should be an "opt-out" provision. To some extent, video and audio recording should be possible.[25] The "fully virtual hearing"—in which the court does not participate from the courtroom—should be tested.

3.2 Digital Legal Action

In April, the Budget Committee of the German Bundestag, as part of the BMJ's digitalization initiative, approved 6.1 million euros for the development and testing

[24] The government's draft and the draft bill, as well as the comments received to date, are available at https://www.bmj.de/SharedDocs/Gesetzgebungsverfahren/DE/Videokonferenztechnik.html?nn=6705022.

[25] The BWD, for example, is critical of individual regulations. The statement is available at https://www.bundes-verband-wirtschaftskanzleien.de/wp-content/uploads/2023/01/BWD-Positionspapier-13.01.23_L.pdf.

of an online civil court procedure, as well as for the development of a digital legal application center[26] and a video portal for the judiciary for the period up to 2023.[27]

As a logical development of the ERV, it will in future be possible for citizens to file complaints electronically via a common justice portal. In order to improve access to justice, it is worth considering combining this option with model procedures (online complaint tools). A first prototype has been developed and presented on behalf of the BMJ for air passenger compensation and rental defects.[28] It is to be welcomed if citizens can obtain low-threshold information on legal options and, if necessary, access sample letters. An intuitive, user-friendly design in the simplest possible language is particularly important.

For individuals and businesses without the necessary legal expertise, such procedures will only be appropriate if the legal situation is evidently in their favor and they do not need to seek further legal advice. In all other cases, a concept would have to be developed how to make the further course of civil proceedings—especially for consumers—similarly simple.[29]

3.3 Accelerated Online Procedure for Handling Mass Proceedings in the Small Claims Area

The idea of an accelerated online procedure was already included in the discussion paper "Modernization of Civil Procedure".[30] The core idea is to lower the practical hurdles for using state courts in order to overcome the so-called rational disinterest[31] and, in mass cases with low amounts in dispute, to transfer the civil procedure in principle completely into the digital domain—from the filing of the complaint to the hearing and ultimately the decision. For reasons of jurisdiction, such proceedings should be concentrated in central online courts.[32]

---

[26] Elements for implementation can also be found in the federal government's draft presented earlier.

[27] https://www.bmj.de/SharedDocs/Pressemitteilungen/DE/2023/0525_Digitalgipfel.html.

[28] Cf. the associated project page at https://tech.4germany.org/project/digitale-klagewege-bmjv/. The prototype is currently no longer available.

[29] Cf. also *Riehm*, Online-Klage und elektronischer Verfahrensraum, presentation on 15.10.2022 at the Legal Tech Tagung 2022 of LMU/MLTech, available at: https://www.youtube.com/watch?v=lnIE-ImV-NE.

[30] *Working Group "Modernization of Civil Procedure" on behalf of the Presidents of the Higher Regional Courts, the Court of Appeal, the Bavarian Supreme Court and the Federal Supreme Court*, Modernization of Civil Procedure—Discussion Paper, https://www.justiz.bayern.de/media/images/behoerden-und-gerichte/oberlan-desgerichte/nuernberg/diskussionspapier_ag_modernisierung.pdf.

[31] See also *Meller-Hannich*, Wenn die Klage sich nicht lohnt - Effektiver Rechtsschutz bei geringen Streitwerten, NZM 2022, 353 (353 ff).

[32] Cf. in particular the white paper of the *Mass Proceedings Working Group in the DRB*, Proposals for Better Management of Mass Proceedings by the Judiciary, https://www.drb.de/fileadmin/DRB/pdf/Stellungnahmen/2022/Loesungsvorschlaege_AG_Massenverfahren.pdf; see in detail *Albrecht*,

Simplification of procedures should also be discussed. This includes, for example, the proposal to allow more free evidence. In small claims litigation, it is often argued that the ZPO is too complex and therefore not in the interests of the parties.[33] At present, the limit for the admission of free evidence is a amount in dispute of not more than 600 Euros (cf. Section 495a ZPO). The Federal Ministry of Justice is currently working together with the Digital Service as the central digitalization unit of the Federal Government on the development of an online civil court procedure for small amounts in dispute and on the establishment of digital legal application offices.[34]

3.4 *Electronic Base Document*

The idea of a structured submission by the parties has been around for decades. Pleadings should no longer be presented chronologically. Instead, the parties are supposed to place their arguments and positions in a relational table in the "right" place. The aim is to provide a better overview of disputed and uncontested facts and legal opinions. To this end, the research project "Reallabor Strukturvorgaben für den Parteivortrag im Zivilprozess" was launched in 2023. The prototype[35] is being tested at four regional courts.[36] Using technology, the lawyer's presentation is "guided" according to the model of a relational table, without rigidly limiting it. The process also includes an independent structuring session where the court and the parties agree on a common structure.[37]

Ein Reallabor Beschleunigtes Online-Verfahren, https://anwaltsblatt.anwaltverein.de/de/zpoblog/beschleunigtes-onlineverfahren-reallabor-strategie-bundesregierung-julian-albrecht.

[33] Cf. only *Windau/Bert*, Zukunft der ZPO, AnwBl 2022, 75.

[34] Cf. *BMJ,* DigitalService des Bundes startet Projekte für die Justiz, https://www.bmj.de/SharedDocs/Arti-kel/DE/2022/1026_Digitalservice.html.

[35] Cf. https://app.parteivortrag.de/ (last accessed 9/4/2023).

[36] These are the regional courts of Hanover, Landshut, Osnabrück and Regensburg; Cf. https://www.uni-regensburg.de/forschung/reallabor-parteivortrag-im-zivilprozess/startseite/index.html (last accessed Mar. 4, 2023)... Cf. in detail *Bert*, Structured Party Lecture: What Happens in the Real Lab, https://anwaltsblatt.anwaltverein.de/de/anwaeltinnen-anwaelte/anwaltspraxis/strukturierter-parteivortrag-was-passiert-im-reallabor#collapse_598213 (last accessed 3/4/2023).

[37] Cf. in this context also *Greger*, Erörterungstermin im Zivilprozess - warum nicht? NJW 2014, 2554; *ders*, Struk- turierung von Parteivortrag und Verfahren, AnwBl 2021, 284.

3.5 AI-Based Support in Mass and Bulk Processes

Several federal states are currently testing programs that enable judges to structure the content of the proceedings.[38] Large volumes of documents can be automatically checked for specific (legal) requirements using integrated knowledge management tools, and relational tables can be created with the help of checking assistants. Other tools make it possible to structure the file inventory across proceedings in order to identify, group and process similar cases (especially in mass proceedings). Still other programs can read metadata from the pleadings and integrate them into predefined building blocks.

In Bavaria, the Codefy software is used at the Ingolstadt Regional Court in so-called "diesel proceedings" and complex construction disputes. In Baden-Württemberg, the same software is being piloted at Hechingen Regional Court in various civil proceedings. The OLGA software has been piloted at the Stuttgart Higher Regional Court since December 2022.[39] In Hesse, the Frankfurt Ruling Configurator Electronic (FRAUKE) supports the judiciary, particularly in proceedings relating to the Air Passenger Rights Ordinance.

Equipping the judiciary with appropriate AI-supported capabilities appears to be urgently needed, given that even lawyers' submissions in mass litigation are increasingly being prepared or generated using AI. Without technical support, such submissions, which are considerably larger and more complex than those prepared by hand, are difficult to process, which can have a negative impact on the provision of effective and speedy legal recourse.

3.6 The Data-Based Civil Process: From Text to Metadata

The tools used and planned today are only a first step on the way to a digital civil process. In particular, the tools presented for AI-based structuring and support show the lack of submissions in a uniform—machine processable—way. For example, in airline passenger cases, consumers enter their data digitally into query masks. The service providers receive the metadata, which they have to spell out in text form in

[38] Cf. the basic paper for the 74th Annual Meeting of the Presidents of the Higher Regional Courts, the Court of Appeal, the Bavarian Supreme Regional Court and the Federal Supreme Court, May 23–25, 2022, in Rostock, Germany, entitled "Use of AI and Algorithmic Systems in the Judiciary," available at: https://www.justiz.bayern.de/media/images/behoerden-und-gerichte/oberlandesgerichte/nuernberg/einsatz_von_ki_und_algorithmischen_systemen_in_der_justiz.pdf. On the technical, systemic and legal challenges further Rühl, KI in der gerichtlichen Streitbeilegung, in Kaulartz/Braegelmann (eds.), Rechtshandbuch Artificial Intelligence und Machine Learning (2020) ch. 14.1 Rz 11 et seq. In addition, from a legal perspective, there is the planned regulation by the EU AI Regulation.

[39] Cf. the presentation of OLGA by *Spoenle* at the Göttingen Colloquia on the Digitalization of Civil Procedure Law, Feb. 17, 2023, available at https://www.youtube.com/watch?v=iXb3qkHlscA&t=5255s.

PDF files in order to send the pleading(s) electronically to the court. The judiciary uses programs to extract the metadata back from the pleading. It would be simpler to provide the metadata directly.[40] Evaluation tools would not be needed if, instead of PDF files, file formats were chosen for the transmission of pleadings in which the content structure is already provided in the form of metadata, for example as XML files. This—as a mandatory requirement—is being discussed under the heading of "data-based civil procedure", particularly in mass litigation in the legal profession.[41] In a first step, this would enable the automatic creation of a relation table by the court.

3.7 Use of Language Models

ChatGPT, Bard and their successors cannot and must not yet be used for traditional judicial activities due to data protection aspects. Nevertheless, their use is conceivable for service units or general information offerings of the judiciary for efficient answers to standard inquiries.

In addition, North Rhine-Westphalia and Bavaria have decided to jointly develop and test a legal language model.[42] At the academic level, the project is being developed by the University of Cologne and the Technical University of Munich. This Generative Language Model of Justice (GSJ) has been prioritized.[43] It is to be tested on the basis of several pilot projects, which are to be designed using legal design thinking.

3.8 Predictive Justice

Automatic anonymization of court decisions is already technically possible. The publication rate of court decisions will rise sharply.[44] As a result, decision forecasting

---

[40] For a detailed and more in-depth discussion, see *Riehm*, Digital First! Visions for the communication of the Staats mit seinen Bürger:innen, in *Reuß/Windau* (eds.), Göttinger Kolloquien zur Digitalisierung des Zivilverfahrensrechts, Kolloquien im Sommersemester 2021 (2022), 123 (123 ff).

[41] Cf. *Riehm*'s presentation on the subject of "Online lawsuits and electronic procedural space" of 15.10.2022 at the LMU/MLTech Legal Tech Conference 2022, available at: https://www.youtube.com/watch?v=lnIE-ImV-NE. On the "digital process architecture" based on structured data, see also *Fries*, ELSTER für Fluggastrechte: Skizze für ein europäisches Online-Bagatellverfahren, in *Breidenbach/Glatz* (eds.), Rechtshandbuch Legal Tech (2021) Teil 7.3 Rz 4 et seq.

[42] https://www.land.nrw/pressemitteilung/einsatz-kuenstlicher-intelligenz-der-justiz-nordrhein-westfalen-und-bayern.

[43] Resolution at the 2nd Federal-Länder Digital Summit on 25.05.2023, which took place on the occasion of the Conference of Ministers of Justice (JuMiKo).

[44] See *Hamann*, Der blinde Fleck der deutschen Rechtswissenschaft - Zur digitalen Verfügbarkeit instanzgerichtlicher Rechtsprechung, JZ 2021, 656 (656 ff); *Fobbe*, Open Legal Data:

will become much more accurate, especially in mass litigation with few legal issues and a large number of available decisions. This will enable the legal profession and legal tech companies to conduct a comprehensive digital litigation risk analysis, including the targeted filing of lawsuits with specific courts where procedurally possible.[45]

This development is accompanied by important questions, such as how it will affect judicial activity as such (keyword: "transparent judge"). Interdisciplinary research on this, for example in the fields of (work) psychology and philosophy, and more generally on the increasing automation of judicial activity and the use of AI[46] is still in its infancy along the lines of current court practice.

4 Summary and Outlook

The German judiciary is already taking bold and important steps to fully digitize its procedures. But there is no time for stagnation. The rapid pace of technological progress allows and demands that we continue to think and act boldly on this manner.

As the third branch of government and a pillar of democracy, the judiciary must continue to keep pace with technological progress in society and the needs it creates. Digitalization and automation are not an end in themselves but serve to promote the rule of law through simple and citizen-friendly access to justice and through accelerated, efficient and, as far as possible, cost-effective proceedings.

The sometimes lamented decline in the number of court cases is attributed, among other things, to excessively long proceedings, excessive costs and the perceived unpredictability of the outcome. Increasing digitalization can help in all these areas. Largely digital case management makes proceedings cheaper, faster, and more predictable. Travel costs can be saved, superfluous steps can be minimized and access to the court system can be facilitated for individuals.

In particular, the procedural maxims of speed and the right to be heard will benefit directly. It is also conceivable that the principle of openness will take on new dimensions, for example through the comprehensive online broadcasting of proceedings and extensive publication of court decisions.

The path to full digitalization and progressive automation has been paved by important milestones in the German justice system in recent years. After initial adjustment difficulties, the potential of digitalization is now impressing even former

Das Fundament des Rechtsstaates, https://www.drb-berlin.de/themen-und-positionen/justizthemen/justizthema/news/open-legal-data-das-fundament-des-rechtsstaates; *Braegelmann*, Ein Gesetz für mehr Gerichtstransparenz, https://www.libra-rechtsbriefing.de/L/gerichtsoeffentlichkeit/.

[45] Cf. *Quarch*'s lecture on the topic of "Digital Process Risk Analysis" from 9.11.2022 as part of the lecture series Legal Tech at the University of Passau, available at: https://player.vimeo.com/video/774666273?h=50391ace38&title=0&byline=0&portrait=0&speed=0&badge=0&auto-pause=0&player_id=0&app_id=171734.

[46] Cf. for example the research project "Explainable Intelligent Systems", https://explainable-intelligent.sys-tems/ which is composed of various disciplines and universities.

sceptics of digitalization, regardless of their age, simply because of the independence and flexibility it offers, as well as the even faster and better possibilities of providing people with appropriate access to justice.

Rich Overnight? A Critical Review of Online Business Coaching in Germany

Jonas Polfuß

Abstract On platforms such as YouTube, Instagram, and TikTok, offers promising straightforward strategies for rapid wealth for aspiring entrepreneurs are ubiquitous. More and more self-proclaimed sales gurus and business coaches are marketing seminars and workshops on social media, some with significant price tags. What exactly are the coaching services these providers offer and what marketing strategies do they use? Are their business coachings as questionable as several media reports suggest, and is it possible to discern from the outside whether a provider is credible? This study examines select coaching services in Germany, focusing on their program offers and advertising tactics, their testimonials and customer reviews, and their website and social media data. The paper discusses what traditional and established training providers can learn from the rapidly emerging coaching firms and which aspects of online business coaching require exploration in future research.

Keywords Coaching · Online coaching · Business coaching · Marketing · Social media · Analytics

1 Introduction

Business coaching has become pervasive in today's digital landscape. Providers actively promote their programs across various media channels, some with a high price tag. While numerous users express enthusiasm, others recount less-than-satisfactory experiences. In addition, journalistic outlets are increasingly publishing critical reports on the methodologies employed by certain coaching firms. The surge in coaching providers appears to address the demand for innovative knowledge formats centered on entrepreneurship, potentially filling the voids and shortcomings of governmental educational initiatives. However, some argue that these coaching enterprises prioritize their profit motives over the genuine needs of the participants,

J. Polfuß (✉)
IU Internationale Hochschule, Essen, Germany
e-mail: mail@jonas-polfuss.de

R. C. Geibel and S. Machavariani (eds.), *Digital Management to Shape the Future*, Springer Proceedings in Business and Economics,
https://doi.org/10.1007/978-3-031-66517-2_10

contrary to their promotional claims. This raises the question of how to assess contemporary online business coaching from a marketing science perspective. This paper first elucidates the potential advantages and disadvantages of business coaching. Subsequently, it provides a marketing-centric analysis of select coaching offerings. Drawing on this analysis, the study offers practical insights and highlights avenues for future research on online coaching.

Modern online business coaching, which leverages cutting-edge communication and sales technologies, is an emerging and evolving domain that remains relatively under-researched. This is partly because of the rapid evolution and continuous emergence of new trends and phenomena. In contrast, there is a more extensive body of research on coaching in general and trends in (digital) self-improvement. A recurring critique in the literature is the absence of standardized coaching practices. Several authors have noted that certain corporate coaches lack the requisite training and have proposed enhancements from both psychotherapeutic and psychological standpoints (e.g., Holm-Hadulla, 2002).

Concerning the digital delivery of coaching sessions, research has highlighted potential drawbacks, such as technical challenges and limitations in nonverbal communication, as well as offering solutions (Berninger-Schäfer, 2018). Other studies have underscored the benefits of digital coaching, emphasizing its spatial and temporal flexibility and the augmentation of traditional communication methods using digital tools (e.g., Geißler, 2022). While some authors have reported positive behavioral shifts among coaching participants, the cult-like following of certain successful coaches has been met with skepticism (e.g., Bradley, 2021; Lawrence, 2023). To date, a comprehensive data-driven analysis of diverse coaching services and their marketing strategies and resources remains unexplored.

2 Research Method

This empirical investigation provides a case study approach with market and content analysis, drawing on the publicly accessible content of coaching companies, consumer feedback, and data from the (social) web. Through this methodology, the sales and marketing strategies of coaching providers were scrutinized in depth. Specific advertising messages were dissected, and various marketing channels employed by coaching firms were assessed using advanced analytical tools. Building on this analysis, the paper deliberates whether coaching services are dubious, as some media narratives imply, and outlines the criteria to gauge the credibility of a coaching proposition from an external perspective. The research explores the potential economic advantages that emerging coaching and media formats might offer the next wave of entrepreneurs, despite prevailing criticism. In conclusion, in addition to advocating heightened transparency in coaching services, this study pinpoints further research avenues pertinent to the coaching sector.

3 Online Business Coaching: An Overview

Recently, online business coaching has solidified its position as an influential medium for enhancing professional expertise and entrepreneurial proficiency. Tracing its roots back to the 1960s, primarily in the United States, professionally oriented coaching has gained widespread recognition. It embodies a targeted process in which a coach aids an individual or group in realizing specific personal or professional objectives through structured training and mentorship. By probing questions, providing insightful feedback, and using various techniques, the coach facilitates the coachee's journey towards solution discovery and progression (Ives, 2008). This study focuses primarily on coaching scenarios in which coachees receive guidance from individual external experts on strategic matters related to their business endeavors over a defined timeframe.

3.1 Profiles and Services of Business Coaches

The online business coaching under consideration here emphasizes the commercial success of the coachee. Initial contact and subsequent interactions occur predominantly through digital platforms, although they can occasionally be complemented by in-person sessions. Business coaches have diverse backgrounds and varying levels of training. This diversity stems from the fact that the term "coach" is not legally protected or associated with specific qualifications in Germany. While some business coaches have recognized credentials in coaching, mediation, or even comprehensive psychological training, many do not. The rise of social media, messaging services, and learning management systems since the 2010s has significantly boosted online business coaching. The COVID pandemic has further accentuated the shift toward online learning modalities, culminating in an e-coaching surge, evident not just in Germany (cf. Passmore et al., 2023).

Estimating the exact number of online business coaches in Germany by 2023 is challenging because of the absence of registration requirements. However, it is reasonable to posit that their count extends to several tens of thousands (e.g., Deters, 2021). Some digitally active coaches have been service providers since before the social media era, focusing on conventional consulting areas such as strategic business directions. Notably, younger coaches, particularly those visible on platforms such as YouTube, Instagram, and TikTok, underscore in their promotional content their commitment to integrating the latest technological trends into their business or marketing coaching (e.g., Jackson, 2023). The spectrum of content provided by coaching entities ranges from hands-on resources, such as business plan blueprints, marketing campaign templates, guides, and (e-)books, to multimedia components, such as video sessions and interactive live coaching modules for individuals or groups. Many companies offer both offline and online networking avenues to fellow coachees. From a pricing perspective, the spectrum is vast; it starts with basic packages available for free or at nominal costs and extends to premium packages marketed as exceptionally exclusive and priced in the upper five-figure euro bracket (e.g., Jüttner, 2023).

3.2 Potential Advantages of Online Business Coaching

As initially highlighted, digital learning modalities offer participants a number of advantages, primarily through enhanced flexibility. Moreover, one-on-one coaching sessions can cultivate a private environment conducive to pivotal learning, ideation, and transformative processes that may be more challenging in alternative settings (Bozer & Jones, 2018). For younger people, online media engagement aligns more closely with their media consumption habits and the reality of everyday life.

Within the business context, precise coaching can be a catalyst for navigating present-day challenges without committing to lengthy training sessions or full-fledged degree programs that might, in some instances, lack practical applicability. Many young individuals in Germany express dissatisfaction with their financial education, which is a cornerstone of business success (Verbraucherzentrale Bundesverband e. V, 2023). Ideally, effective coaching bridges the divide between conventional scholastic and academic education and the ever-evolving requisites of the contemporary business world (Trenner, 2013). Online business coaching has the potential to democratize business acumen that may otherwise be exclusive to boardrooms of large corporations or consulting firms. This accessibility can demystify the entrepreneurial realm, which is often perceived as intricate. Particularly in Germany, with its social market economy foundation, the tenets of entrepreneurial endeavors remain relatively obscure for certain segments of the population, occasionally drawing unwarranted criticism without a genuine understanding.

Arguably, the most significant benefit is the tailored support provided to the coachees. Numerous entrepreneurs, particularly startups, grappling with unique challenges are seldom addressed comprehensively in generic advisory literature, standardized business courses, or academic curricula. Professional online business coaches, equipped with years of analogous industry experience, are poised to offer bespoke guidance that is meticulously aligned with the coachee's specific needs and hurdles (cf. Wiginton & Cartwright, 2020).

3.3 Criticism of Online Business Coaching

Online business coaches often face criticisms that extend beyond potential inadequacies in their qualifications. Several critical media reports garnered significant attention and sparked further debate in Germany. This section summarizes the primary criticisms, setting the stage for a subsequent discussion on the necessity for further investigation.

Recurrent critiques have addressed the pricing structure of online business coaching. While traditional coaching sectors offer transparent and comparable average fees, the same cannot be said for online business coaching—a discrepancy that some argue is intentional. The stark contrast between free initial offers for lead generation and the subsequent, sometimes exorbitant, coaching fees is another point of contention. For high-priced services, critics often point out that genuine one-on-one coaching sessions, which can potentially yield significant results, constitute only a minor portion of programs. Instead, many program elements would consist of prerecorded content or limited group sessions (cf. Webers & Zickermann, 2019). Another prevalent criticism targets promises made through coaching programs. Accusations range from fostering unrealistic expectations to employing questionable advertising tactics that use superlatives without success (e.g., Wittmann-Naun, 2022). Critiquese argue that potential clients are enticed into expensive programs that may not align with their needs, financial capacities, or long-term profitability. In addition, the technological systems and contractual terms employed by coaching companies have come under scrutiny for their lack of transparency and flexibility, seemingly benefiting providers more than participants (e.g., ZDF, 2023). Concerns also arise regarding the quality of coaching materials and content, which some believe do not justify the high fees or meet the promised standards.

While many of these criticisms appear valid and are supported in part by credible testimonials, it is essential to approach them from a discerning scientific lens. Every product or service, especially high-priced ones, inevitably has both satisfied and dissatisfied customers. Moreover, most of the negative reports are isolated or sporadic. Although critical journalism is invaluable, journalists may not represent the typical demographic for business coaching. Online business coaching, a relatively new digital phenomenon, often faces initial skepticism, a trend not just observed in Germany. This is not an attempt to discount any malpractice by coaching companies or to downplay the grievances of unsatisfied clients. Instead, it underscores the importance of thoroughly examining coaching firms and their offerings. One goal is to provide potential consumers with informed recommendations for selecting the appropriate services whenever possible.

4 Analysis of Five Selected Coaching Providers in Germany

In this study, the online presence of five of the best-known German-language online business coaches was scrutinized in October 2023. The selection was based on criteria such as general media visibility, social media presence, and website rankings. Emphasis was placed on providers specializing in marketing, sales, automation, and scaling. Coaching companies that focused on areas such as motivation, mindset, lifestyle, or rhetoric were excluded. Companies that prominently featured a specific coach or mentor as their public face were prioritized. To ensure scientific neutrality and to avoid influencing purchasing decisions, the identities of the providers were kept anonymous during the analysis.

The content, offerings, and promotional messages on the websites and social media profiles of the coaching providers were analyzed and evaluated from a marketing science perspective. Ratings on websites and customer portals were then considered along with a discussion of the relevance of these platforms in the context of the study. Finally, the websites and Instagram profiles of the providers were examined in detail using professional web analysis tools. Based on the collected data, the marketing strategies of the companies were further analyzed, and the relevance of the tools used for these scientific investigations was assessed.

4.1 Coaching Offers from a Marketing Perspective

Many coaching providers label themselves with superlatives such as the "No. 1" in their (sub-)industry, even though such claims seem hard to validate with data, given that the coaching industry lacks comprehensive statistical documentation. To showcase quality, providers highlight their business achievements, some of which are validated by growth awards from external media sources (e.g., Focus Business, 2023). TÜV seals, which are quality certifications, are also displayed as evidence of quality, even if their relevance to the actual coaching service is tangential. Positive mentions in the media are showcased as endorsements, although several ones likely stem from paid partnerships. Many coaches share parts of their life stories, often emphasizing a rise from significant setbacks. These narratives are frequently paired with striking visuals showcasing the coaches' current affluence.

As anticipated, the offered services are portrayed in a positive light. Here too, we find performance promises like "rapid" or "first-class," which seem nebulous and often lack direct evidence to support them. Detailed service offerings are typically concealed behind lead forms that invite potential clients to a "free initial consultation" or a preliminary "potential analysis." Empirical reports suggest that these sessions not only assess the needs of potential clients but also gauge their financial capacity to afford the services. The costs of seminars, consultations, and coaching are not immediately visible on the websites. Prices are only mentioned for specific products, such as discounted (e-)books. Certain products are promoted as "gifts," but when ordering, a "shipping fee" is added, exceeding standard postal charges. Similar promotional tactics are evident during major coaching events. Tickets are often sold at a fraction of their official price, raising questions regarding the authenticity of the original price. Several providers, directly or indirectly, claim that their services surpass those available elsewhere, without providing evidence. Some affiliated media hint at intensifying competition among major coaching firms, where competitors are openly criticized for perceived unethical business practices.

From a marketing science viewpoint, the strategies and techniques employed by coaching firms exemplify contemporary adaptations of classic funnel marketing. They initiate contact and lower the initial purchase barriers by offering free or discounted introductory products. This can set potential clients on a path from a free e-book to a reasonably priced video course, progressing to group coaching, and eventually to individual coaching. The culmination of this upselling journey often involves high-end coaching and consultation subscriptions. This process typically leverages modern marketing and sales automation tools (cf. Beco & Zeren, 2023). Moreover, coaching firms endeavor to elevate coaching personalities to brand icons, sometimes even cultivating cult-like followers around the founders. Sales promotions employ well-established psychological tactics such as creating a sense of scarcity and urgency. These tactics are further optimized in online marketing through tracking and retargeting.

In summary, coaching providers utilize the contemporary digital marketing and sales techniques expected from entities positioning themselves as industry innovators. Based on their growth awards, the examined coaching firms seem to have achieved significant success using these methods. However, strategies such as aggressive discounting can potentially undermine a company's pricing strategy in the mid to long term (e.g., Holden, 2008). While critiques of rival coaching firms might be justified in the interest of upholding industry standards, they could also backfire, casting a shadow of skepticism over the coaching industry as a whole, a topic further explored in subsequent sections.

4.2 Specifics of Coaching Clients Reviews Online

When considering feedback from coaching clients, it is essential to differentiate between testimonials featured on provider websites and those featured on independent review platforms. All five companies displayed select customer testimonials on their sites, which predictably lauded the services provided, either in written form or through videos. In some instances, clients are given the opportunity to promote their businesses through these videos, likely serving as an added incentive to provide public endorsement of the coaching services. In several instances, these client testimonials are framed as mini-case studies, briefly outlining how the coaching intervention facilitated the client's progress. For the most part, the successes attributed to coaching are described in broad terms. However, on two of the coaching websites, specific revenue growth figures are provided without disclosing the full names of the clients.

Several providers also highlight their favorable ratings on review platforms such as ProvenExpert and Trustpilot directly on their websites. One of the five sites has integrated the latest reviews from one of these platforms, lending an air of transparency to their presentation. More critical reviews are present on these external platforms. Unlike the curated testimonials on their own websites, external reviews

Table 1 Selected coaching provider reviews on the Internet

Provider/platform	Trustpilot	Google Maps
Coaching firm 1	4,3/5	4,9/5
Coaching firm 2	4,9/5	4,9/5
Coaching firm 3	4,8/5	4,9/5
Coaching firm 4	4,8/5	4,8/5
Coaching firm 5	–	5,0

Source Own presentation

are challenging for providers to alter or manipulate. Table 1 summarizes the five providers, accompanied by the available review platforms as of October 17, 2023.[1]

With only one exception, the providers, who have a minimum of 100 and in some instances over 2,000 ratings on each of the two platforms, have garnered overwhelmingly positive feedback from the reviewers. Despite the explicit prohibitions imposed by these platforms, there remains the possibility of ratings being manipulated or purchased, an issue not exclusive to coaching reviews. Platforms may ask reviewers to provide evidence to substantiate their claims, particularly if a company challenges a negative review (e.g., Trustpilot, 2023). Typically, platforms will only remove reviews if they are evidently fraudulent or breach their guidelines.

Assuming that most coaching reviews on these platforms are genuine, there appears to be a high level of satisfaction among the coachees. An interesting observation is the polarization of the ratings; many are extremely positive, whereas a few are distinctly negative. Some reviewers claim that the coaching programs exceeded their promises and objectives. The lowest score observed was 4.3 out of 5, with 11% of the reviews awarding just 1 out of 5 stars. Across various profiles, the negative comments echoed the previously mentioned criticisms, such as a perceived lack of individual attention or professionalism. Even among the predominantly positive reviews, there were occasional complaints regarding unscrupulous sales tactics. Several reviewers alleged that they were pressured by the coaching companies to give positive feedback, which would be a clear violation of the platform guidelines. Additionally, a few reviewers claimed that these companies attempted to remove their genuine criticism by labeling them fake, although these attempts were apparently unsuccessful. Considering the fierce competition in the industry, it is not entirely implausible that competitors might purchase products just to leave negative reviews and tarnish their rivals' reputations.

The coaching providers seem adept at showcasing satisfied customers on their websites. While the external platform reviews largely indicate a contented clientele, a few highly critical reviews are eye-catching. Beyond the general risk of fake reviews, both positive and negative, it is conceivable that in the competitive coaching industry,

[1] The ProvenExpert platform was not included here, because–although some companies have aggregated reviews there–the majority of these reviews originated from sources such as Amazon and Apple which are specifically related to coaching services.

where digital reputation is paramount, providers might go to great lengths to outshine their competitors in terms of ratings.

4.3 Analysis of the Websites and Social Media

On October 18, 2023, the open-source developer tool Lighthouse (Google Chrome, 2023) was used to evaluate the performance of the websites. Website performance, particularly its loading speed, increasingly affects its ranking in organic search results. Ahrefs (2023), an advanced analytics tool, was employed to assess the domain rankings and identify the top 100 keywords associated with these websites. This tool sheds light on the frequency with which a website is referenced by other reputable sites, which is a factor that enhances its Google ranking and bolsters its position in search engine results. Furthermore, the recognized analysis tool MOZ (2023) was used to determine the spam score of the webpages. This score indicates the likelihood of a website facing penalties from Google for deploying dubious tactics. All results are shown in Table 2.

It is evident that all coaching companies prioritize their websites as pivotal marketing channels and, in some cases, as sales channels. This emphasis is underscored by the detailed, current content and service descriptions, even though specific pricing details are often absent. Given this emphasis, it is startling that, barring one exception, the technological infrastructure of these websites is not aligned with contemporary standards, as indicated by the Lighthouse performance analysis. Scores below 50 are deemed problematic, scores above 80 reflect well-optimized websites, and those surpassing 90 are considered top-tier (Chrome for Developers, 2023).

In the realm of domain ranking, a metric that can be proactively enhanced through strategic link-building as an integral component of advanced search engine optimization (SEO), only coaching company 1 exhibits commendable performance. This favorable ranking could be attributed to the website's longevity and the coach's renown, which might have fostered increased link-building over time. Domain rankings hovering around 30 are deemed satisfactory, whereas a score of 3.3 is decidedly subpar. Companies 2 and 3 also exhibit suboptimal keyword positioning. Company

Table 2 Website performance of selected coaching providers

Provider/value	Lighthouse performance	Domain ranking	Top 100 keywords	Spam score (%)	Website traffic
Caoching firm 1	24/100	57/100	2,714	9	11,149
Caoching firm 2	51/100	28/100	94	1	3,949
Caoching firm 3	49/100	3.3/100	27	1	2,113
Caoching firm 4	42/100	15/100	136	1	796
Caoching firm 5	80/100	34/100	1.217	1	667

Source Own presentation

1 is ardently endeavoring to secure a robust ranking and traffic flow, and while achieving this aim, it is concurrently elevating its spam suspicion. In contrast, despite its impressive performance and ranking metrics, company 5 witnesses limited traffic. This discrepancy could be ascribed to the site's infrequent content updates, such as the addition of new blog articles.

The data imply that none of the five coaching firms have executed a comprehensive approach to website marketing and management. Company 1 stands out in terms of traffic but fails in technical performance, which could potentially affect the site's long-term success. Company 5, despite having the most technically adept website, fails to capitalize on content marketing opportunities. Given that these companies aim to provide marketing consultation and, in some instances, technical expertise, the lack of holistic website optimization is perplexing. These companies may prioritize sales through third-party platforms and lean more toward search engine advertising (SEA) than toward search engine optimization (SEO) to drive traffic. However, even under such a strategy, neglecting to maximize organic website success is strategically imprudent. An optimized website not only bolsters the brand's online presence, but also solidifies the company's digital footprint in the long run. However, this long-term vision does not appear to be the primary consideration for these firms.

With regard to social media presence, Instagram channels will be examined here as an example, which can provide information about the digital marketing skills of companies and the genuine enthusiasm of coaching fans. The personal profiles of the coaches were examined, on which they overtly presented themselves as coaching providers. For this purpose, the well-established analysis tool InfluData was used on October 19, 2023. Using this tool, it is possible to see from which country the followers of a profile originate and which share of followers looks suspicious (e.g., bots) or is inactive. It is also possible to view the engagement rates and the overall score of the profiles, which are based on a mixture of all the criteria that the platform considers central to its success on Instagram.

Given the consistent and dynamic promotion of coaching services in their profiles, it is evident that these coaches consider this platform significant. Table 3 shows that while all profiles are curated in German, coach 4 has a notably high percentage of non-DACH (i.e., Germany, Austria, Switzerland) followers. The presence of non-native, suspicious, or inactive followers could indicate the possibility of purchasing followers, with coaches 2 and 3 being particularly conspicuous in this regard. Regarding post-engagement, profiles with a larger number of followers often exhibit lower engagement. This observation might partially explain the suboptimal engagement of coach 1 but does not entirely account for coach 4's commendable performance. Coach 5's metrics are particularly concerning, given the mediocre engagement despite a moderate follower count, coupled with a relatively high percentage of foreign and inactive followers.

These coaches have discernible scope for improvement. Coach 2, who has the best overall score, has a significant proportion of less-than-ideal followers. When comparing the engagement metrics of these coaches with those of other Instagram experts, their performance does not stand out as particularly impressive. Financial expert Bodo Schäfer had a Reels engagement rate of 2.6% with 431,000 followers,

Table 3 Instagram performance of selected coaching providers

Provider/ value	Followers in thousands	DACH follower (%)	Suspicious / inactive followers (%)	Engagement for posts (%)	Engagement for reels (%)	Total score
Coach 1	146	79,9	10,5	0,1	1,5	6,4/10
Coach 2	71	78,4	24,9	1,6	1,8	7,6/10
Coach 3	84	84,7	25,1	2,4	1,1	7,4/10
Coach 4	12	65,1	8,7	2,7	1,1	7,2/10
Coach 5	47	73,4	17,2	0,2	1,0	4,9/10

Source Own presentation

and mindset coach Christian Bischoff recorded a rate of 2.1% with 178,000 followers as of October 18, 2023 (InfluData, 2023). Despite their self-portrayal as business and marketing pioneers, the analyzed coaches seem to hover around the (decent) average range in their Instagram presence. The notably high number of suboptimal followers for some coaches suggests their potential purchase of followers. However, this remains speculative and not exclusive to coaching accounts (Nizri, 2022).

When leveraging tools such as InfluData, the precision of data analyses is not absolute. Although one can manually verify post-engagement rates, follower analysis is contingent on these tools. Moreover, as fake follower bots become increasingly sophisticated, even the most advanced tools may fail to detect them. Consequently, the actual number of dubious followers is likely to be higher. While these followers are often purchased, they sometimes latch onto profiles without the knowledge or intent of the account owner.

5 Discussion and Implications

An examination of the online offerings reveals that the coaching firms in focus adeptly combine traditional and modern marketing strategies and promotional narratives to captivate a broad audience. However, there is a noticeable lack of transparency in terms of services and pricing on their websites. This approach is presumably designed to gather as many leads as possible from which the most promising prospects can be identified and targeted. While one should exercise caution when interpreting customer feedback on websites and portals, the reviews on independent evaluation platforms suggest that a significant majority of coaching clients are either satisfied or highly satisfied with the services they receive. However, isolated instances of intense criticism shed light on the aggressive customer acquisition tactics employed by these coaching companies and underscore the cutthroat nature of the industry. The tool-based analysis of the websites and Instagram profiles further indicates that even coaches who position themselves as business and marketing experts have significant room for improvement. This is particularly evident in the areas of sustainable website and social media marketing.

5.1 Problem of Measuring Coaching Success

The analysis presented here does not corroborate the perception conveyed by some media outlets that online business coaching inherently poses an economic risk to participants. However, this study underscores the challenges associated with quantifying coaching success. The success stories of coaching participants, when available, are seldom detailed or transparent and often resemble brief promotional snippets. It is plausible that successful coachees opt not to publicize their achievements, perhaps because of concerns about their strategies being replicated, or out of respect for the confidentiality of the coaching firms. A more comprehensive understanding of the tangible successes achieved by coachees will enhance the evaluation of the industry and its offerings.

Beyond measurable outcomes such as revenue growth and sales milestones, some coaching clients may primarily derive psychological benefits such as bolstered self-confidence. Assessing the value of these intangible gains against the coaching fees is a subjective task for individual coachees. A shift in mindset, while potentially indirectly boosting business success, is not readily quantifiable. From a psychological perspective, it is conceivable that coachees who do not find coaching beneficial might refrain from public criticism. This could be attributed to cognitive biases, such as the sunk cost fallacy, in which individuals continue a behavior due to previously invested resources, or buyer's remorse, in which they feel regret or guilt after making a purchase. Such individuals might retrospectively justify or even embellish their high investments in coaching or feel embarrassed about having allocated significant funds to a less-than-satisfactory coaching experience (cf. Dijkstra & Hong, 2019).

5.2 Reasons for the Coaching Image Problems

Given that most coachees appear to be satisfied, it is interesting to consider why the broader public perceives online business coaching negatively. Research indicates that a significant portion of the German population harbors skepticism towards capitalism (e.g., YouGov, 2017) and, naturally, media outlets cater to their audience's sentiments to a certain extent. Investigative journalism, adopting a critical stance towards consumerism or capitalism, often seeks to unveil instances of deceit that undeniably occur in the coaching realm. When media outlets delve into negative individual experiences, such narratives tend to overshadow potential success stories that either remain unheard of or are not amplified by the media. Media platforms that portray coaching in a positive light may also face allegations of covertly promoting commercial entities. Furthermore, media representatives, despite their commitment to impartiality, may struggle to empathize with coaches boasting of multi-million-dollar sales, assuming that these claims are genuine. A cultural undercurrent in Germany, often described as an "envy culture" (Neidkultur) regarding affluence, might also likely hinder the dissemination of narratives centered on rapid wealth accumulation (e.g., Zitelmann, 2019).

Compared to other countries, the achievements of founding personalities often receive limited respect in German society. This backdrop probably makes the coaching scene's euphemisms and exaggerations appear especially shrill. However, it is crucial to acknowledge that coaching providers play a role in shaping their own public image. Even if negative accounts of aggressive sales tactics and unscrupulous business practices are isolated incidents, they still highlight the ethically questionable behaviors prevalent in segments of the industry. The intensifying rivalry among coaching companies may further taint the sector's reputation. The assertive posturing of numerous male coaches may resonate with certain individuals and inspire them. However, for others, such behavior might be arrogant and overbearing, raising concerns about the perpetuation of toxic masculinity.

5.3 Recommendations for Coaching Selection

Those considering coaching should meticulously assess the qualifications and offerings of the potential firms. Consumer organizations and recognized coaching associations emphasize the presence of both good and less commendable coaches, suggesting that quality credentials can guide selection (BDVT, 2023; EVZ, 2023). Discerning the exact pricing of sessions is challenging in online business coaching. It is desirable for coaching firms to enhance transparency to ensure that potential clients do not waste time on services misaligned with their needs or budgets. One should be wary of sales tactics such as limited availability or exclusivity claims. Despite the often hefty fees, expecting miraculous results from coaches is unrealistic. As analyzed above, in terms of website and social media presence, coaching companies sometimes only match the average. This does not negate their potential expertise in areas such as digital advertising and sales automation. After sharing contact details with a coaching firm, prospective clients must anticipate persistent outreach. Contrary to their promotion of digital sales automation, these firms often revert to traditional communication methods such as phone calls or basic messaging. Indeed, with a combination of enthusiastic marketing, opaque offerings, potentially biased client testimonials, and occasionally overly critical media coverage, navigating to an informed choice regarding a coaching service becomes a complex task.

6 Limitations and Outlook

The present study offers content-based and data-driven insights into the often enigmatic or stigmatized online business coaching industry, shedding light on the structure, credibility, and reputation of providers and the sector as a whole. It is crucial to note that the analysis focused on only five coaching firms and did not examine the actual coaching services, which are seldom detailed in the firms' public presentations. Although the selected firms are prominent players in the field, they do not cover the entire sector. As with many online reviews, the customer feedback assessed in this study was predominantly polarized, complicating the task of extrapolating an average customer experience (cf. Schoenmueller et al., 2019).

Given these findings, there is a need for further research to comprehensively understand online business coaching and identify its potential benefits and pitfalls for participants. A thorough exploration of specific coaching structures, teaching materials, and daily operations would be particularly insightful. Participatory research can explore coaching from the perspective of emerging entrepreneurs. A deeper look at the coachees' before- and after-scenarios would also be enlightening. Coaching firms are likely to possess extensive data that could be shared with researchers. An anonymized academic evaluation of coaching outcomes could also bolster the coaching firms' reputations if the results align with their self-portrayed success. Beyond detailed studies on coaching modalities and outcomes, a comprehensive market overview, which has so far been based on broad estimates, would be invaluable (e.g., Deters, 2021).

In summary, based on current understanding, there is no reason to believe that online business coaching by adept professionals cannot yield significant results for well-informed and financially apt clients. The industry's growth underscores the need for traditional educational institutions to revamp and tailor their offerings, communication strategies, and platforms. Countries such as Germany undeniably require more youths to be inclined toward successful entrepreneurship. It is widely recognized that these individuals gravitate towards hands-on role models in contemporary case studies rather than relying on outdated or excessively theoretical resources. By adopting modern methodologies and marketing strategies, both state and private educational entities can effectively appeal to future businesses. It is imperative to ensure that future business experts recognize the importance of refining their skills not only for self-employment or the corporate world but also to contribute to research, politics, or the nonprofit sector. While the allure of online business coaching might appear enticing, it also has its disadvantages, and there are countless other paths worth exploring.

References

Ahrefs. (2023). *Marketing intelligence tools powered by big data*. https://ahrefs.com

BDVT (Professional Association for Training, Consulting and Coaching e.V.). (2023). *Statement business coaching*. https://www.bdvt.de/bdvt/aktuelles/meldungen/statement-business-coaching.php

Beco, J., & Zeren, E. (2023). Funnel performance management. In U. Hannig & U. Seebacher (Eds.), *Marketing and sales automation: Management for professionals* (pp. 347–360). Springer. https://doi.org/10.1007/978-3-031-20040-3_22.

Berninger-Schäfer, E. (2018). *Online-Coaching*. Springer.

Bozer, G., & Jones, R. J. (2018). Understanding the factors that determine workplace coaching effectiveness: A systematic literature review. *European Journal of Work and Organizational Psychology, 27*(3), 342–361. https://doi.org/10.1080/1359432X.2018.1446946

Bradley, S. (2021). Understanding attendees' transformative experiences following Tony Robbins's Unleash the Power within seminars. *Consciousness, Spirituality and Transpersonal Psychology, 2*, 47–59. https://doi.org/10.53074/cstp.2021.26

Chrome for Developers. (2023). *Lighthouse performance scoring: How Lighthouse calculates your overall Performance score*. https://developer.chrome.com/docs/lighthouse/performance/performance-scoring

Deters, J. (2021). Psychologe über Coaching. "Ich habe viele unsinnige Sachen gesehen" [Psychologist on coaching. "I've seen a lot of nonsense"]. *Wirtschaftswoche*. https://www.wiwo.de/erfolg/management/psychologe-ueber-coachings-ich-habe-viele-unsinnige-sachen-gesehen/26126980.html

Dijkstra, K. A., & Hong, Y. Y. (2019). The feeling of throwing good money after bad: The role of affective reaction in the sunk-cost fallacy. *PLoS ONE, 14*(1), e0209900. https://doi.org/10.1371/journal.pone.0209900

EVZ. (2023). *Unseriöse Coaching-Angebote: So schützen Sie sich* [Untrustworthy coaching offers: How to protect yourself]. https://www.evz.de/presse/pressemitteilungen/unserioese-coaching-angebote-so-schuetzen-sie-sich.html (European Consumer Centre Germany e.V.).

Focus Business. (2023). *Entdecken Sie Deutschlands Wachstumschampions* [Discover Germany's growth champions]. https://focusbusiness.de/wachstumschampions

Geißler, H. (2022). E-coaching: An overview. In S. Greif, H. Möller, W. Scholl, J. Passmore, & F. Müller (Eds.), *International handbook of evidence-based coaching*. Springer. https://doi.org/10.1007/978-3-030-81938-5_22.

Google Chrome. (2023). Lighthouse. https://chrome.google.com/webstore/detail/lighthouse/blipmdconlkpinefehnmjammfjpmpbjk?hl=de

Holden, R. K. (2008). Kick the discounting habit: Step one for more effective pricing. *Journal of Business Strategy, 29*(6), 14–18. https://doi.org/10.1108/02756660810917192

Holm-Hadulla, R. M. (2002). Coaching. *Psychotherapeut, 47*(4), 241–248. https://doi.org/10.1007/s00278-002-0236-7

InfluData. (2023). *Empowering your creator marketing*. https://www.infludata.com/de/

Ives, Y. (2008). What is "coaching"? An exploration of conflicting paradigms. *International Journal of Evidence Based Coaching and Mentoring, 6*(2), 100–113.

Jackson, A.-L. (2023). Starting a company? Better sign up for video coaching. *Bloomberg*. https://www.bloomberg.com/news/articles/2023-03-28/video-coaching-for-instagram-youtube-and-tiktok-grows-fast?embedded-checkout=true

Jüttner, J. (2023). *Wie Verkaufstrainer Dirk Kreuter gegen einen Kleinunternehmer vor Gericht verlor* [How sales trainer Dirk Kreuter lost to a small businessman in court]. https://www.spiegel.de/panorama/justiz/dirk-kreuter-die-fragwuerdigen-akquise-methoden-des-verkaufstrainers-a-6b4c00aa-2ea1-4831-b6bb-5ded42ca6385

Lawrence, S. (2023). I am not your guru. In *Digital wellness, health and fitness Influencers* (Vol. 1, pp. 1–15). Routledge. https://doi.org/10.4324/9781003256021-1

MOZ. (2023). *Spam score*. https://moz.com/help/moz-pro/links/spam-score

Nizri, E. (2022, September 9). Council post: New study: One in four influencers bought fake followers. *Forbes*. https://www.forbes.com/sites/forbestechcouncil/2022/09/09/new-study-one-in-four-influencers-bought-fake-followers/.

Passmore, J., Liu, Q., Tee, D., & Tewald, S. (2023). The impact of COVID-19 on coaching practice: Results from a global coach survey. *Coaching: An International Journal of Theory, Research and Practice, 16*(2), 173–189. https://doi.org/10.1080/17521882.2022.2161923

Schoenmueller, V., Netzer, O., & Stahl, F. (2019). The extreme distribution of online reviews: Prevalence, drivers and implications. Columbia Business School Research Paper no. 18–10. *SSRN Electronic Journal*. https://doi.org/10.2139/ssrn.3100217

Trenner, L. (2013). Business coaching for information professionals: Why it offers such good value for money in today's economic climate. *Business Information Review, 30*(1), 27–34. https://doi.org/10.1177/0266382113480020

Trustpilot. (2023). *Richtlinien für Bewerter* [Guidelines for reviewers]. https://de.legal.trustpilot.com/for-reviewers/guidelines-for-reviewers

Verbraucherzentrale Bundesverband e. V. (2023). *Verbraucherumfrage: Finanzbildung an Schulen Reicht Nicht aus* [Consumer survey: financial education in schools is not enough]. https://www.vzbv.de/pressemitteilungen/verbraucherumfrage-finanzbildung-schulen-reicht-nicht-aus

Webers, T., & Zickermann, R. (2019). Training vs. Coaching – über Aporien in der Professionalisierungsdiskussion [Aporia in the debate of professionalization]. *Coaching | Theorie and Praxis, 5*(1), 35–50. https://doi.org/10.1365/s40896-019-00030-z

Wiginton, J. G., & Cartwright, P. A. (2020). Evidence on the impacts of business coaching. *Journal of Management Development, 39*(2), 163–180. https://doi.org/10.1108/JMD-09-2018-0266

Wittmann-Naun, J. (2022). *Pseudo-Coaches bei Instagram sind eine der größten Plagen unserer Zeit* [Pseudo-coaches on Instagram are one of the biggest plagues of our time]. https://www.welt.de/iconist/partnerschaft/article238371935/Pseudo-Coaches-bei-Instagram-sind-eine-der-groessten-Plagen-unserer-Zeit.html

YouGov. (2017). *Was die Deutschen vom Kapitalismus halten* [What Germans think of capitalism]. https://de.statista.com/infografik/10660/was-die-deutschen-vom-kapitalismus-halten/

ZDF. (2023). *ZDF Magazin Royale vom 24 Februar 2023*. https://www.zdf.de/comedy/zdf-magazin-royale/zdf-magazin-royale-vom-24-februar-2023-100.html

Zitelmann, R. (2019). *Die Gesellschaft und ihre Reichen* [Society and its wealthy]. FinanzBuch Verlag.

The Digital Future of Healthcare

Ulrich Arnold and Richard C. Geibel

Abstract In the vast majority of countries, national healthcare systems are facing major challenges and are suffering from a considerable cost explosion, which, combined with a significant increase in demand—especially due to demographic change and the effects of Covid 19—has led to an extreme burden on the healthcare system. One promising approach to improving this problematic situation is to significantly promote outpatient treatment over inpatient treatment in hospitals. In this way, the efficiency of the system can be increased and the burden on healthcare resources reduced. Many positive results support this view and confirm the premise. However, this approach alone is not enough to significantly alleviate the challenging situation in the healthcare system in the long term. The logical continuation of this recognized strategy is the expansion of the approach through consistent and sustainable digitalization at all levels. In this context, digitalization is prioritized over outpatient treatment, as it offers a wide range of benefits. This leads to the following conclusion: "*Digital* prioritized before *outpatient* prioritized before *inpatient*". This article will structure and analyze the resulting benefits based on four dimensions from the perspective of a large IT service company. The focus is placed on the material, financial, personnel and motivational dimensions in order to describe and examine the potential benefits in detail.

Keywords Digitization · Service company · eHealth · Healthcare · Health insurance

U. Arnold (✉)
gkv informatik, Wuppertal, Germany
e-mail: ulrich.arnold@gkvi.de

R. C. Geibel
E-Commerce Institute, Cologne, Germany

IU International University, Cologne, Germany

R. C. Geibel
e-mail: geibel@ecommerceinstitut.de

R. C. Geibel and S. Machavariani (eds.), *Digital Management to Shape the Future*, Springer Proceedings in Business and Economics,
https://doi.org/10.1007/978-3-031-66517-2_11

1 Introduction

The German healthcare system is of a high standard and provides many people with high-quality medical care. At the same time, there are significant problems and challenges in German healthcare. Demographic change and the associated ageing population are increasing the need for medical care. This puts enormous pressure on scarce resources, in particular on the finances of the healthcare system. People of advanced age and with chronic illnesses account for 80% of healthcare expenditure in Germany (German Trade & Invest, 2022). According to the German Federal Statistical Office, the number of over 67-year-olds in the German population is set to rise by up to 42% (German Medical Association, 2021).

People of advanced age and with chronic illnesses account for 80% of healthcare expenditure in Germany (German Trade & Invest, 2022). According to the German Federal Statistical Office, the number of over 67-year-olds in the German population is set to rise by up to 42% (German Medical Association, 2021). This is reflected in rising healthcare expenditure. In 2021, expenditure in the German healthcare system has already risen by 7.5% to over 474 billion euros. The forecast for 2023 shows similar trends. It is estimated that healthcare expenditure in Germany will be around 500 billion euros in 2022 (Federal Statistical Office, 2023c).

In addition to rising healthcare costs and the increased need for care, there is also the trend of increasing urbanization. More and more people are moving to the cities. This is also increasingly the case for the younger generation of doctors and medical graduates. The shortage of doctors in Germany is reflected in particular in rural areas and in individual specialties. This significantly restricts access to healthcare and leads to ever longer waiting times for specialist appointments. The additional shortage of qualified nursing staff and the often difficult working conditions place an additional burden on the healthcare system.

Digitization represents a sustainable approach to relieving the burden on the healthcare system. Modern information and communication technologies can be integrated into both medical care and the management of health data to improve performance. This opens up new, more comprehensive possibilities for providing healthcare services. Improved patient care, increased efficiency and greater accuracy will fundamentally reduce the burden on the healthcare system. The advancement of digitalization in the healthcare system can not only help to reduce the burden on the healthcare system, but also to further improve the performance of the healthcare system (German Science and Humanities Council, 2023). However, there are a number of significant challenges and hurdles standing in the way of the immediate implementation of digitalization.

2 Problem Definition

In addition to the many benefits that digitalization brings to the healthcare sector, it also poses a number of challenges. A particular challenge for digitalization in the healthcare sector is the need for appropriate data protection and data security measures to ensure the protection and confidentiality of patient data. The integrity of patient data is of explicit importance and represents a fundamental principle for high-quality and secure healthcare. This includes various aspects such as the relationship of trust between patients and doctors. Patients must be able to assume that their personal medical data will be treated confidentially and that only authorized persons can access it. The relationship of trust described above is extremely important both for successful treatment and for intensive care. Fundamentally, the protection of patient data is not only an ethical but also a legal obligation (Schirmer, 2022). Data protection laws regulate the protection of privacy and the confidentiality of health data at national level (EU-DSGVO, 2023). This creates a complex requirement for the establishment of digitalization. A lack of data security and data protection increases the risk of personalized data being disclosed to unauthorized third parties. This data can be misused for criminal purposes, which can have serious consequences for the individuals concerned. The aim is therefore to provide sufficient preventive protection against identity theft and fraud. The safeguarding of valid and complete patient data must also be fundamentally protected, as medical decisions are often based on the available data. Incorrect data can lead to misdiagnoses, inappropriate treatment methods or generally dangerous situations for patients. At the same time, healthcare professionals must also be able to rely on error-free data in order to make informed decisions. The challenge remains to keep patient data up-to-date and error-free at all times in order to ensure a continuous treatment chain. Continuous care is particularly important, for example, when there is an exchange between different healthcare facilities. Furthermore, false or distorted research results can occur in research, which means that the validity of studies is no longer guaranteed and further medical development is negatively affected (Schirmer, 2022).

3 Dimensions of Digitalization

The digitalization of the healthcare system is progressing rapidly. There are numerous advantages for the development of the healthcare system if the associated challenges can be successfully overcome at the same time. These benefits can be divided into resource-oriented and behavior-oriented benefits. At the resource-oriented level, there are material, financial and personnel benefits, whereas all motivational aspects can be found at the behavior-oriented level (see Fig. 1).

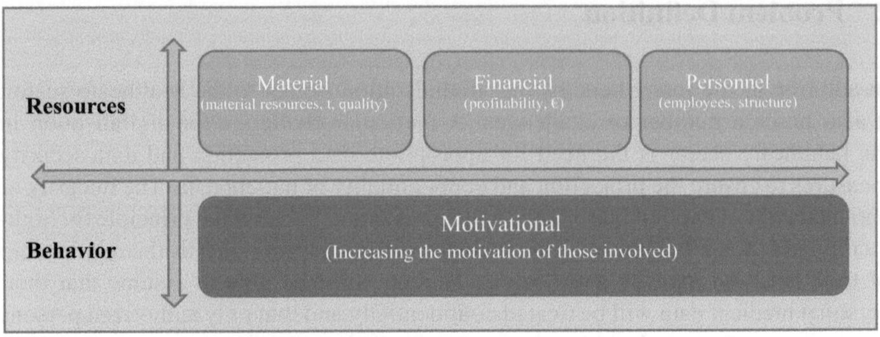

Fig. 1 Illustration of the advantages of digitization in two dimensions

3.1 Material Dimension

With regard to the material dimension, the focus is on the spatial and temporal perspective in order to illuminate and examine the possibilities and opportunities of digitalization in more detail. The matrix in Fig. 2 uses four fields to structure the possible forms of support for digitalization in medical care.

3.1.1 Synchronous and Centralized Communication

The doctor and patient meet at the same time and in the same place via a synchronous and centralized communication channel. The scenario corresponds to the classic approach in healthcare as soon as a patient consults a doctor in person during a visit to the hospital or doctor's surgery. The participants meet face-to-face. The special feature of this form of communication is the personal contact, in which the participants are in the same room, have eye contact and can also communicate via body language.

3.1.2 Synchronous and Decentralized Communication

In the synchronous and decentralized form of communication, the participants meet at different locations at the same time. This takes place, for example, via a camera using digital media such as computers, tablets or smartphones. Telemedicine is a growing area in the field of digital health applications that enables patients to communicate online with doctors, obtain medical advice and even receive remote medical diagnoses. Through the additional use of remote monitoring tools, healthcare professionals can provide patients with telemedical advice by transmitting health data, especially in less severe cases—largely without compromising the quality of care. This is often done through the use of tablet computers.

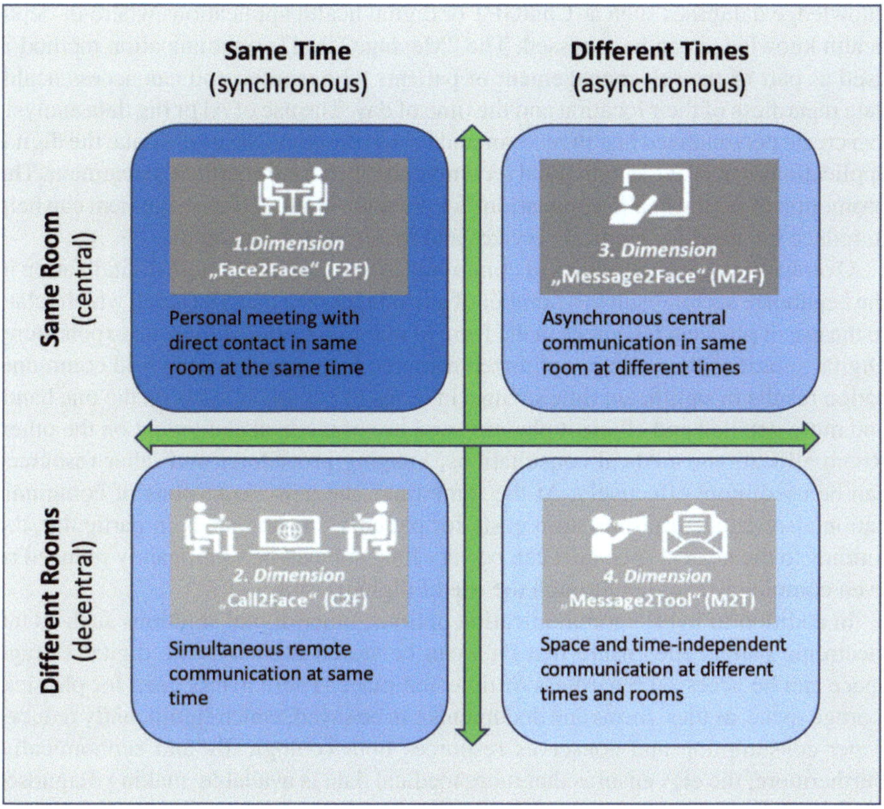

Fig. 2 Illustration of the four fields of possible spatial and temporal types of communication and treatment

3.1.3 Asynchronous and Central Communication

Another option for communication can be asynchronous and centralized. Typical examples of communication between participants at different times in the same place are a digital bulletin board, an online community or other collaboration tools. Treatment in a medical center without a doctor is—to a certain extent—possible with "Dr. Google". Access to information is always possible for everyone involved in the same place and improves information procurement in particular, such as researching the latest research results and progress or finding the right doctor or hospital.

3.1.4 Asynchronous and Decentralized Communication

In asynchronous and decentralized communication, the participants communicate with each other at different times and in different places. A typical example is access to knowledge databases such as ChatGPT or digital health applications where in-depth health knowledge can be accessed. The "Message2Tool" communication method is used as part of the self-management of patients who want to and can access health data regardless of their location and the time of day. The use of AI or big data analysis can create personalized health recommendations. Based on the user's data, the digital applications can provide individual recommendations for the patient's treatment. The promotion of digital health applications for prevention and self-management can help to reduce the need for medical services and materials for treatments.

Overall, the new possibilities of communication channels through digitalization in the healthcare sector result in a number of advantages on a material level, which relate to the use of physical resources in the form of material resources or time expenditure. Digital solutions thus ensure optimized resource management, as hybrid communication results in significant time savings in terms of personnel costs on the one hand, and more detailed and efficient planning and use of medical equipment on the other. Room allocations, medical consultations, imaging procedures and other resources can be used more effectively. At the same time, the new dimensions of communication also reduce transportation costs for patients. In rural areas in particular, the journey to the nearest specialist can be very long and can be significantly reduced or even completely avoided through the use of digitalization.

In addition to hybrid communication options, other digital solutions such as the electronic patient file ensure that data can be stored digitally. The digital storage space can be accessed regardless of time and place. There is less need for physical storage space, as files, forms and documents can be saved, which significantly reduces paper consumption and conserves resources both ecologically and economically. Furthermore, the ePA ensures that more medical data is available, making diagnoses easier and avoiding duplicate examinations, among other things (Gerlach et al., 2021).

Digitization can therefore make a significant contribution to optimizing the material use of resources in the healthcare system, which not only saves costs (aspect of increasing efficiency), but also contributes in particular to qualitatively improved and more sustainable healthcare (aspect of improving effectiveness).

3.2 Financial Level

Annual healthcare expenditure amounts to many hundreds of billions of euros and continues to grow. Most recently, healthcare expenditure amounted to 474 billion euros in 2021. This is estimated to have risen to almost 500 billion euros in the following year 2022, and the trend is still rising (Federal Statistical Office, 2023a). A closer examination of healthcare expenditure shows that inpatient treatment in the healthcare system is by far the most expensive. It has been proven that outpatient treatment can be provided more cheaply than inpatient treatment (Dorner, 2018). If we go one step further, there is an opportunity to save further costs by using digital tools for remote treatment. Although these are not applicable in every case, there are more and more digital applications that make it possible to save costs without having to reduce the quality of treatment. In addition to digital support in the treatment of patients in the healthcare system, there are also all the accompanying organizational and administrative, digitalized measures that need to be taken into account and are responsible for a large proportion of indirect costs (Federal Statistical Office, 2023b). At a financial level, the benefits of digitalization can therefore be differentiated between the perspective of healthcare facilities on the one hand and the perspective of patients on the other. There are financial benefits for both perspectives.

Healthcare facilities achieve an increase in efficiency through digitalization by reducing operational costs. For example, automated administrative processes, savings on paper costs and the minimization of manual errors ensure more efficient work. Administrative costs can also be reduced by increasingly dispensing with material goods such as paper files. Electronic patient files and other digital databases can help here. From an organizational point of view, resources can be better planned and used more economically thanks to digital technologies. Medical equipment, hospital beds and staff planning can be optimally utilized thanks to digitalization. Likewise, the increasing use of telemedical consultations reduces inpatient stays, which can also increasingly save costs for care here (Federal Ministry of Health, 2023).

Digitalization in the healthcare sector also offers financial benefits for patients themselves. The preventive use of digital health applications or health apps for the early detection of illnesses can improve their own health literacy and thus prevent long-term health problems. The associated costs can be saved. Improved medication management through appropriate health apps also helps to adhere to treatment plans and counteract unnecessary treatments or hospital stays. Telemedical consultations (see Chapter 3.1.2) can also save travel costs from the patient's perspective, for example when it comes to preliminary and follow-up consultations that do not require a personal presence or concerns that can be coordinated remotely. Overall, this not only reduces costs for healthcare facilities, but also the patient's co-payment.

In summary, digitalization in the healthcare sector can ensure that costs are reduced for both healthcare facilities and patients, resources are used more efficiently, and significant financial benefits can be achieved in the long term.

3.3 Personnel Level

Increasing digitalization also makes it possible to make professions in the health care sector more attractive by ensuring that those involved can focus less on administrative processes and more on the actual content-related tasks. In this way, the working conditions for professionals can be sustainably improved.

Administrative processes such as appointment scheduling, patient management and billing are automated using digital technologies, which frees up time for medical staff to focus on other tasks. The focus can be better placed on clinical activities and patient care. At the same time, digital platforms ensure an easier flow of information and seamless communication between different employees such as doctors, nurses and therapists. The exchange of information in real time ensures more effective patient care and consequently better collaboration. In addition, collected data can be documented more precisely thanks to new applications such as the electronic patient record (ePA). Healthcare professionals can access essential data more easily and medical decisions can be made on the basis of more detailed information, as medical examinations themselves have limited time capacity. The ePA stores complete information from previous examinations. Communication with patients can also be made more effective. Digital solutions can send appointment or prescription reminders as well as general health information. Through telemedicine and the possibility of remote monitoring, patients can attend telemedical consultations and document their own health data. Patients with chronic illnesses or complaints in particular need more intensive medical advice and care, which often cannot be provided by medical professionals in the conventional form in terms of time (Federal Ministry of Health, 2023). Digitalization generally ensures faster handling processes. Be it data transmission or access to information. There are even more possibilities in the future. The use of artificial intelligence and big data can be used to create personalized treatment plans based on individual health data. Here, too, the workload for medical professionals will be considerably reduced and the quality of care for patients will also be improved.

In summary, digitalization in the healthcare sector ensures more efficient, more precise and more patient-oriented workflows, which in turn allows medical professionals to focus more productively on clinical activities, including patient care.

3.4 Motivational Level

The use of modern technologies and health solutions in medicine offers those affected and their relatives the opportunity to receive constant information through feedback on the course of treatment, which provides additional motivation (Federal Ministry of Education and Research (BMBF), 2021). From a behavioral science perspective, the willingness to deal with problems is significantly strengthened. Digitalization enables increased self-management for patients. Future precise and personalized data will enable personalized recommendations. These can be validly derived based on digitally collected data. The personalized recommendations give patients increased health literacy. They gain knowledge on how to better manage their health and consciously influence it positively through preventive measures (Federal Ministry of Health, 2017). Increased health literacy therefore has a positive effect on patients' self-management. As a result, existing health problems can be minimized independently without the need for outpatient or inpatient treatment, thus reducing the risk of future complaints. The "digital before outpatient before inpatient" approach therefore suggests that digital care will be an important addition—and in many cases also an alternative—to the healthcare system in the future (Dorner, 2018).

Various digital health applications are setting a positive example here. These are also known as health apps or medical apps and are software applications that can be played on mobile devices (smartphones, tablets or wearables). The main focus is on access to secure health information, medical services and the possibility of self-management of health. Some health apps record and document patient health data such as heart rate, blood pressure, blood sugar, sleep patterns or other data. Collected data helps to determine the development and possible changes and thus supports medical professionals in the diagnosis and treatment of patients. A large number of health insurance companies are already promoting a wide range of digital health applications for their policyholders. Since October 2020, e-health can be prescribed on prescription. The digital health apps (DiGA) meet prescribed quality and safety criteria and vary depending on the health condition and complaint. Some examples of DiGA are apps to support the treatment of people with diabetes, obesity or mental illness. A range of many other apps can be prescribed for other conditions. The doctor diagnoses the person concerned as usual and then the DiGA can be used to support the treatment. This allows patients to acquire more knowledge independently and have a greater influence on the course of their illness. Fitness, activity, relaxation and nutrition apps also help people to be more active and improve their physical and/or mental health as a preventative measure. Pedometers, calorie consumption or personalized training/nutrition plans are available to users (Federal Ministry of Health, 2023).

Digital health solutions create new opportunities for patients to self-manage prevention and treatment. Patients are more actively involved in their healthcare, which promotes patient participation. Medical progress and successes can also be documented more transparently, which also encourages patients to take personal responsibility. The often integrated immediate feedback on the achievement of health goals or adherence to treatment plans also has a positive effect on patient motivation. The same applies to the personalization of recommendations and solutions, which help users to feel better supported and understood. The opportunity for exchange that these applications offer in forums or chats also promotes connection with like-minded people, the feeling of support and dealing with one's own clinical picture. Additional elements of gamification ensure that users experience more joy in dealing with their health. Challenges, competitions and rewards have a positive effect on user motivation.

These expanded options can increase the interest, motivation and commitment of those involved to actively look after their own health. Overall, at a motivational level, digitalization can help to improve health literacy, strengthen personal responsibility and increase motivation.

4 Discussion

Even if the benefits of digitalization are clear and of enormous importance, there are still a number of challenges to holistic implementation. Many digital tools and applications have already been established, but are still not fully integrated into everyday life. For example, although the ePA is ready for use, according to a survey, only 6% of doctors surveyed use this application so far (Statista, 2022). It is also important for patients to show initiative so as not to slow down the progress of digitalization in the healthcare system. When drawing up the digitalization strategy, the Federal Ministry of Health launched the opt-out principle for the electronic health record, whereby everyone receives an electronic health record unless they explicitly object to it (Federal Ministry of Health, 2023). Further solutions and draft legislation are needed at national level to facilitate the implementation of further digital innovations. This includes minimizing the obstacles of data protection and security hurdles. According to a survey, 72% of respondents would like to see more speed in the process of digitalization in the healthcare sector overall (Wintergerst, 2023).

IT service providers can ultimately ensure that digital ideas and projects are realized. In addition to well-known introductions such as the ePA, DiGA or the ePrescription, it is important to continue on the path of digitalization and overcome the serious challenges. Digital change is a constantly advancing process. With the establishment of the first digital solutions, further areas of application must be created in the future. In the complex IT landscape, applications must meet national requirements and at the same time be made accessible to end users. In order to fully exploit the benefits of digitalization, it is necessary for all stakeholders involved to work together intensively.

5 Summary and Outlook

Digitalization in the healthcare sector is here to stay and irreversible. The multitude of new possibilities and advantages are obvious and clearly predominate. Some digital applications are already established in the healthcare sector, many are in the starting blocks and many more are being planned. There is a need for further action at several levels. Both at national level and on the part of the healthcare system, as well as on the part of patients. Digitalization is still in the starting blocks and must be further promoted and expanded. It is therefore primarily up to relevant stakeholders such as IT service providers to drive digitalization forward. As service providers for players in the healthcare sector, they play a key role in new applications to enable, develop and implement digital innovations. With their comprehensive digital IT expertise and many years of experience in the successful implementation of digitally supported processes, they have a key role to play in the digital transformation of the healthcare sector. After all, the primary goal should continue to be to create better quality and more efficient healthcare at all levels.

Bibliography

Dorner, C. (2018). "Digital before outpatient before inpatient": How digitalization will change our healthcare system. *kma—Klinik Management aktuell*, *23*(5), 22–23. https://doi.org/10.1055/s-0036-1595194

EU-DSGVO. (2023). *General Data Protection Regulation (GDPR).* https://dsgvo-gesetz.de/

Federal Ministry of Education and Research (BMBF) (ed.). (2021). *Innovations in medical technology. Successful projects of small and medium-sized enterprises.*

Federal Ministry of Health. (2017). *Alliance for health literacy.* https://www.bundesgesundheitsministerium.de/fileadmin/Dateien/3_Downloads/E/Erklaerungen/Allianz_fuer_Gesundheitskompetenz_Abschlusserklaerung.pdf

Federal Ministry of Health. (2023). *Gemeinsam digital: Digitization strategy for healthcare and nursing* (p. 44) [Final report]. Federal Ministry of Health. https://www.bundesgesundheitsministerium.de/service/publikationen/details/digitalisierungsstrategie-fuer-das-gesundheitswesen-und-die-pflege.html

Federal Statistical Office. (2023a). *Health expenditure in Germany.* https://www.destatis.de/DE/Themen/Gesellschaft-Umwelt/Gesundheit/Gesundheitsausgaben/_inhalt.html

Federal Statistical Office. (2023b). *Health expenditure by type of service* (Health expenditure). DESTATIS. https://www.destatis.de/DE/Themen/Gesellschaft-Umwelt/Gesundheit/Gesundheitsausgaben/Tabellen/leistungsarten.html

Federal Statistical Office. (2023c, August 17). *Health expenditure increased to over 474 billion euros in 2021.* Federal Statistical Office. https://www.destatis.de/DE/Presse/Pressemitteilungen/2023/04/PD23_136_236.html

Gerlach, F. M., Greiner, W., Jochimsen, B., Von Kalle, C., Meyer, G., Schreyögg, J., & Thürmann, P. A. (2021). *Expert report 2021 digitalization for health—Goals and framework conditions of a dynamically learning healthcare system.* https://www.svr-gesundheit.de/fileadmin/Gutachten/Gutachten_2021/SVR_Gutachten_2021.pdf

German Medical Association. (2021). *Results of the physician statistics as of 31.12.2021.* https://www.bundesaerztekammer.de/baek/ueber-uns/aerztestatistik/aerztestatistik-2021

German Science and Humanities Council. (2023). *Perspectives for the further development of the health professions | Recognizing and using scientific potential for health care* [Application/pdf]. 159 pages. https://doi.org/10.57674/6EXF-AM35

German Trade and Invest. (2022). *HealthCare Market.* https://www.gtai.de/en/invest/industries/healthcare/healthcare-market-65626

Schirmer, H. (2022). Opportunities and limits of digitization in healthcare for the sustainable promotion of population health in Germany: Digitization in healthcare leads to comprehensive changes and new innovations in the healthcare of the population. In T. Kümpel, K. Schlenkrich, & T. Heupel (Eds.), *Controlling & Innovation 2022* (pp. 281–334). Springer Fachmedien Wiesbaden. https://doi.org/10.1007/978-3-658-36484-7_12

Statista. (2022). *Use and distribution of electronic patient records among physicians in 2022.* Statista Research Department. https://de.statista.com/statistik/daten/studie/1352923/umfrage/nutzung-und-verbreitung-der-elektronischen-patientenakte-bei-aerztinnen/

Wintergerst, Ralf (2023). Bitkom zu den neuen Digitalgesetzen im Gesundheitswesen, 30. August 2023. https://www.bitkom.org/Presse/Presseinformation/Bitkom-zu-neuen-Digitalgesetzen-Gesundheitswesen

Cloud and Technology Services as Enablers of Digitalization in the Healthcare Sector

Markus vom Scheidt, Vanessa Hering, Alina Holle, Ulrich Arnold, and Richard C. Geibel

Abstract The German healthcare system faces a number of challenges that affect the provision of high-quality healthcare. Demographic change in Germany is leading to a growing prevalence of age-related diseases and increasing the demand for medical care. Due to the disproportionate rise in costs, the financial pressure on the healthcare system is increasing. The increase in chronic diseases, the shortage of healthcare professionals and rising healthcare costs are resulting in limited access to healthcare and an overall increased burden on the healthcare system. In addition, the Covid-19 pandemic has put healthcare systems around the world to the test. Further increases in expenditure are to be expected in the coming years in order to ensure adequate healthcare for the population. The digital transformation offers opportunities to relieve the burden on the healthcare system and further improve the quality of care. Technological innovations play a central role in overcoming these challenges. Digital healthcare services such as electronic patient records, e-prescriptions and telemedicine are already established and are helping to make the healthcare system more efficient. The following article takes a closer look at the opportunities and risks of cloud services and artificial intelligence in the healthcare sector from the perspective of an IT service provider.

M. Scheidt (✉) · V. Hering · A. Holle · U. Arnold
gkv informative, Wuppertal, Germany
e-mail: markus.vomscheidt@gkvi.de

V. Hering
e-mail: vanessa.hering@gkvi.de

A. Holle
e-mail: alina.holle@gkvi.de

U. Arnold
e-mail: ulrich.arnold@gkvi.de

R. C. Geibel
IU International University, Cologne, Germany

E-Commerce Institute, Cologne, Germany

R. C. Geibel
e-mail: richard.geibel@iu.org; geibel@ecommerceinstitut.de

R. C. Geibel and S. Machavariani (eds.), *Digital Management to Shape the Future*, Springer Proceedings in Business and Economics,
https://doi.org/10.1007/978-3-031-66517-2_12

Keywords Digitization · Service company · Cloud services · Artificial intelligence · Health insurance

1 Introduction

The ongoing demographic change in Germany in the form of an ageing population is leading to the increasing prevalence of age-related diseases. These go hand in hand with more intensive use of and increasing demand on the healthcare system. At the same time, Germany is facing a shortage of qualified medical professionals. The increasing demand for high-quality medical care among the population is becoming increasingly difficult to meet. The result is ever longer waiting times, an increasing burden on the remaining healthcare providers and a loss in the quality of patient care. The financial and logistical challenges for the healthcare system are becoming ever greater (German Science and Humanities Council, 2023; Federal Statistical Office, 2023). In 2021, healthcare expenditure in Germany totaled around 474.1 billion euros, according to data from the Federal Statistical Office. These figures show a sustained increase in healthcare expenditure in Germany in recent years. Similarly, the share of healthcare expenditure in gross domestic product has been steadily increasing in recent years (Statista, 2023). The digital transformation is opening up new opportunities to relieve the burden on the healthcare system in Germany. The opportunities relate to the administration of healthcare facilities, healthcare itself and medical research. The innovation of new technologies and information systems can be integrated into all aspects of medical care. Applications such as the electronic patient file, the e-prescription or telemedicine are already established in healthcare provision. Cloud services and the increasing use of artificial intelligence are the main driving forces behind the ongoing development of the healthcare sector. The seamless interlocking of technology and information opens up the possibility of alleviating the pressure on the healthcare system. At the same time, there is the potential to improve the quality of healthcare and administrative processes, facilitate access to medical information and promote collaboration between medical professionals. Efficiency, quality and reach in healthcare can be greatly enhanced through the use of cloud services and the application of artificial intelligence (German Science and Humanities Council, 2023; Lohmann, 2021; Schirmer, 2022).

The introduction of digital healthcare services and the creation of standardized electronic applications represent important opportunities for the German healthcare system. However, there are complex challenges for the implementation and security of digital health data (Federal Ministry of Health, 2023; EU GDPR, 2023; Statista Research Department, 2022a).

2 Problem Definition

While cloud services and the application of AI are undoubtedly promising for the digitalization of healthcare, they also come with a number of challenges, especially given the sensitive nature of data processed in the industry and strict regulatory requirements (Jäschke, 2018).

Health data is some of the most sensitive information in existence. Electronic patient records, medical images and laboratory data contain personal information that must be protected from unauthorized access. Data breaches can have serious consequences for patient privacy and trust. Storing such sensitive data in the cloud or analyzing personalized patient data through the use of AI raises legitimate concerns about data security. IT service providers must implement stringent security measures, including encryption of data at rest and in motion, access controls and continuous monitoring to ensure the confidentiality and integrity of data (Jäschke, 2023). The healthcare industry is subject to a variety of regulatory requirements, such as the Health Insurance Portability and Accountability Act (HIPAA) in the US or the General Data Protection Regulation (GDPR) in the EU. These regulations define how medical data may be collected, processed, stored and shared (EU GDPR, 2023; Feld, 2005). When using cloud services, healthcare facilities must ensure that cloud providers meet the required compliance standards. This includes aspects such as data storage in certain regions, transparency with regard to data processing and transfer, and the ability to delete data in accordance with the regulations (EU-DSGVO, 2023). The use of artificial intelligence in healthcare also requires careful planning, monitoring and regulation in order to reap the benefits of the technology while ensuring safety, ethics and data protection (Pechmann et al., 2022). Furthermore, it is of enormous importance to gain the trust of patients and healthcare professionals regarding the implementation of new digital innovations to ensure adherence to actual implementation.

Addressing these challenges requires close collaboration between IT service providers, healthcare organizations and regulators to ensure that the benefits of cloud use in healthcare do not come at the expense of security and compliance.

3 Cloud Services and Artificial Intelligence

3.1 Cloud Services

Cloud services play a key role in the digitalization of the healthcare sector. They enable further progress and make a significant contribution to the establishment of new technologies. For example, cloud services create the basis for the application of artificial intelligence. Digital innovations are based on cloud technologies, which enable the need for digitalization in the first place (AOK Rheinland/ Hamburg, 2023).

3.1.1 Types of Cloud Services

Cloud services, also known as cloud computing, are a key technological development that has changed the way companies and organizations manage their IT infrastructure and use resources. In healthcare, cloud services have become particularly important as they offer a number of benefits that contribute to the digitalization of the industry (Lohmann, 2021).

Cloud services are a collection of resources provided via the internet, including computing power, storage, databases, networks and software. These resources can be scaled as required without the need for an on-site physical infrastructure. There are different types of cloud services: Infrastructure as a Service (IaaS), Platform as a Service (PaaS), Software as a Service (SaaS). With IaaS, basic IT infrastructure components such as virtual machines, storage and networks are provided via the internet. This enables companies to outsource their existing infrastructure and add or remove resources as required. PaaS, on the other hand, provides a platform on which developers can create, test and deploy applications without having to worry about the underlying infrastructure. This speeds up development and allows you to focus on the application logic. With SaaS, users get access to applications over the internet without having to install them on their own devices. This enables easy scaling and maintenance of the applications by the provider (Corsten, 2022).

3.1.2 Advantages of Cloud Services in the Healthcare Sector

The use of cloud services in the healthcare sector brings with it a number of benefits that contribute to the modernization and increased efficiency of the industry. These benefits extend across various areas and help to promote patient-centered care and support healthcare professionals.

Compared to conventional local infrastructures, one of the outstanding features of cloud services is their scalability. In the healthcare sector, which can be characterized by seasonal fluctuations and unpredictable loads, cloud usage allows resources to be adapted quickly. In the event of a sudden increase in demand, such as during a flu epidemic, healthcare facilities can easily add additional server capacity or storage space to meet the increased demand. Resource requirements can be flexibly adapted using cloud services. Traditionally, building and operating an in-house IT infrastructure requires significant capital investment. Cloud services offer a pay-as-you-go model where users only pay for the resources they actually use. This reduces the need for expensive upfront investment and allows healthcare organizations to better plan and control their IT spend. The cloud enables seamless data sharing and improved collaboration between different healthcare professionals and facilities. Shared data and applications are accessible at all times. Electronic patient records can be securely stored in the cloud and accessed by authorized individuals in real time. This promotes continuous and coordinated care, regardless of location and specialty (Bork & Weitz, 2019). Setting up IT infrastructure in the cloud is much faster compared to conventional methods. New resources and medical innovations can be made available in the shortest possible time. Developers of medical applications can access a variety of tools and resources to create and test new solutions. This speeds up the innovation process and enables healthcare facilities to benefit from new technologies more quickly (Lohmann, 2021).

Overall, cloud services form a solid foundation for digital transformation in the healthcare sector. They offer the necessary flexibility to respond to the industry's constantly changing requirements and facilitate the introduction of innovative technologies and solutions.

3.2 Artificial Intelligence

Artificial intelligence (AI) is a field of computer science that deals with the development of computer systems and programs that are capable of performing tasks that normally require human intelligence. These tasks can include problem solving, learning, decision making, speech recognition, image processing and much more. AI systems use algorithms and models to analyze data and recognize patterns or correlations (Federal Ministry of Education and Research et al., 2020).

3.2.1 Types of Artificial Intelligence

The application of AI can be divided into different categories. Weak AI (narrow AI) is when the AI is limited to a specific task or a limited task area. Typical examples of this are virtual assistants such as Siri and Alexa, chatbots or image recognition algorithms. In contrast to weak AI, "strong AI" (general AI) refers to systems that are able to perform a variety of tasks and simulate human intelligence in a wide range of activities. This concept of artificial intelligence is hypothetical. There are currently no existing systems that fully embody the concept. Another type of AI is machine learning, where algorithms are developed to learn from data and make predictions or decisions. This is a sub-discipline of AI. It includes methods such as neural networks, decision trees and support vector machines. A special form of machine learning are "deep learning models", which are based on deep neural networks that handle complex tasks such as speech recognition and image processing (Harwardt & Köhler, 2023).

3.2.2 Advantages of Artificial Intelligence in Healthcare

The application of AI can be integrated both in the administrative area and in the area of healthcare to support doctors and clinics in diagnostics and treatment. In both areas, the use of AI can help to improve the accuracy, efficiency and accessibility of healthcare.

At an administrative level, the use of AI can optimize business processes. Speech and text recognition systems can make it easier to create and edit documents. At the same time, errors can be minimized by detecting incorrect data entry. Embedding automated conversation processes using chatbots or virtual assistants also supports healthcare staff. This reduces the workload for healthcare staff and provides them with more time resources, allowing them to optimize their time management and focus on other tasks. AI can also help to monitor compliance with legal regulations and data protection provisions in order to identify and prevent breaches in good time. In the area of healthcare research and quality assurance, the analysis of treatment pathways to improve the quality of treatment and increase the efficiency and cost-effectiveness of certain treatment methods can be promoted (Statista Research Department, 2022b). At the healthcare level, AI can serve as support for medical professionals and also optimize operational processes at this level. By analyzing complex medical data, the use of AI systems can facilitate the diagnosis of diseases by helping to read imaging procedures, such as X-rays or MRI scans, and detect abnormalities. There is also the possibility that AI models will be able to identify risk factors and trends by analyzing large amounts of patient data in the future, thus ensuring the early detection of diseases. Many diseases can be treated much better with early detection, which improves the prognosis and quality of treatment and reduces the resources required for care. In terms of patient treatment, AI can detect drug interactions and thus minimize treatment errors. AI systems can also support the adaptation of treatment plans to individual patient profiles, which can improve the chances of successful therapies (Illustration 1). The first robot-assisted AI applications are now also being used to support complex surgical procedures and increase precision and accuracy (Federal Ministry of Education and Research et al., 2020; Kalis et al., 2018).

10 AI applications that could change health care

Overall, the establishment of AI in the healthcare sector can increase efficiency in healthcare and significantly reduce financial, time and personnel resources through analyses, automated processes and other applications.

4 Case Studies

The use of cloud services in healthcare is just the beginning of a broader digital transformation that will fundamentally change the way medical services are delivered. The future outlook for cloud-based solutions in healthcare and the application of AI based on them is promising and still holds a lot of untapped potential. However, when using these services, it is crucial to prioritize data privacy and security to ensure the confidentiality of sensitive healthcare data. The security of healthcare data is a top priority, especially when it comes to the use of cloud services in the healthcare sector. Given the sensitivity of the information, it is crucial to implement strict privacy and security measures to ensure the confidentiality, integrity and availability of the data.

Illustration 1 AI applications that could change healthcare

Application	Potential annual value by 2026	Key drivers for adoption
Robot-assisted surgery	$40 B	Technological advances in robotic solutions for more type of surgery
Virtual nursing assistants	$20 B	Increasing pressure caused by medical labor shortage
Administrative workflow	$18 B	Easier integration with existing technology infrastructure
Fraud detection	$17 B	Need to address increasingly complex service and payment fraud attempts
Dosage error reduction	$16 B	Prevalence of medical errors, which leads to tangible penalties
Connected machines	$14 B	Proliferation of connected machines/devices
Clinical trial participation	$13 B	Patent cliff; plethora of data; outcomes-driven approach
Preliminary diagnosis	$5 B	Interoperability/data architecture to enhance accuracy
Automated image diagnosis	$3 B	Storage capacity; greater trust in AI technology
Cyber security	$2 B	Increase in breaches; pressure to protect health data

Source Own presentation based on Kalis et al. (2018)

IT service providers play a key role in supporting the progress of digitalization in the healthcare sector through cloud services and artificial intelligence. Their expertise is crucial to ensure that the implementation and use of these technologies meet the highest standards in terms of security, efficiency and patient care. Through their expertise, IT service providers can enable and deliver suitable cloud infrastructures. By specializing in the implementation and management of cloud platforms, they enable the secure storage and access of sensitive healthcare data. This includes the selection and consideration of suitable cloud providers and solutions. Basic measures to protect healthcare data include encrypting the data. Data should be encrypted both in transit and at rest to ensure that it is only accessed by authorized persons. Modern cloud providers offer encryption services that meet the highest security standards. The implementation of multi-level authentication methods and role-based access controls can also ensure controlled data access.

Similar to cloud services, IT service providers can also develop customized AI applications and algorithms that are specifically tailored to the needs and requirements of the healthcare sector. Depending on the players in the healthcare sector, the relevant framework conditions must be observed. Using health insurance companies as an example, this can include data analysis, the optimization of business processes and support in healthcare provision, as well as much more. If existing AI systems are to be integrated into existing IT infrastructures in the healthcare sector, a high level of expertise is required. IT service providers can help to ensure seamless integration. Furthermore, the security and data protection requirements of IT service providers can be ensured. They can implement security measures, access controls and encryption to ensure compliance and legal requirements are met while protecting the integrity of healthcare data and patient trust. Technical support provides assistance for problems that arise with established technical innovations. Because the systems are known, it is possible to react quickly if technical or application problems occur. Finally, in the long term, once successfully implemented, IT service providers can monitor the performance of the established cloud-based systems and AI applications and make adjustments as necessary to ensure they are operating efficiently and cost-effectively. In terms of strategic planning, decision support can be provided to uncover opportunities and difficulties relevant to future projects.

Overall, compliance with regulatory requirements, such as GDPR or SGB, is essential. It is important to ensure that the chosen provider provides the necessary certifications and compliance measures. The security of healthcare data in the cloud or in the use of AI requires careful planning, implementation and monitoring of security measures.

5 Discussion

Cloud technologies will continue to evolve and adapt to the specific requirements of the healthcare sector. This may include the introduction of advanced security mechanisms, better integration capabilities and improved analytics tools. The growing power of the cloud will help to enable more complex medical applications and services. In addition, cloud services will further promote the introduction of telemedicine services and decentralized healthcare applications. Patients can receive medical advice via video conferencing, diagnoses can be made remotely and medical devices can transfer data directly to the cloud. This enables more convenient and accessible healthcare. The combination of cloud services with artificial intelligence and machine learning opens up exciting opportunities for the healthcare sector. AI algorithms can analyze large amounts of healthcare data to identify patterns and make accurate diagnoses. Cloud platforms provide the computing power to perform these sophisticated calculations and train AI models. On the other hand, sensitive health data needs to be protected and secured. The use of cloud services can entail security risks, especially if providers do not pay sufficient attention to data protection and security. There are also concerns that patient data could be misused by third parties. In this context, it is important to consider the patient perspective. Although the technical aspects regarding data protection and data security are fulfilled, it is crucial that patients as end users have the same level of trust and acceptance in relation to the new digital applications. In a study on user acceptance of electronic patient records by Fischer (2019) it was found that a majority of participants were not sufficiently informed about the electronic patient record (EPR). Not surprisingly, 61% of respondents in another study rated the likelihood of doctors being able to provide sufficient information as low (Baxmann et al., 2018). These study results underline the importance and necessity of a high level of information with regard to the establishment of new digital applications. In a consumer survey, insufficient knowledge about digital innovations was cited as the main reason for non-use (an der Heiden et al., 2021). It is therefore essential to actively include the patient perspective in the development process of software solutions in order to increase patient trust in digital innovations. Sufficient trust makes a decisive contribution to increasing acceptance (Scheibner et al., 2021). In conclusion, it is important not to focus exclusively on the compliance of new applications, but at the same time to consider user-centered development in which the needs and wishes of patients are sufficiently taken into account. The challenge in implementation is to take advantage of the benefits of digital change without jeopardizing the privacy and security of patient data and at the same time making it attractive for patients to use.

In this context, IT service providers can act as the driving force behind digitalization in the healthcare sector. They support healthcare facilities in the introduction and integration of software solutions and ensure that these systems function smoothly. At the same time, they develop customized software solutions that are specially tailored to the needs of the healthcare sector and meet the specific requirements of healthcare stakeholders. Given the sensitivity of healthcare data, security and data protection are of paramount importance. IT service providers help with the implementation of security measures, encryption and protection against unauthorized access. More specifically in relation to cloud services, IT service providers offer cloud infrastructures to enable storage and access to healthcare data without healthcare facilities having to operate their own infrastructures. In this context, the integration and interoperability of different systems and applications is particularly important in order to implement standards for data exchange and ensure that different systems can interact with each other. After successful implementation, ongoing technical support ensures that IT systems in healthcare facilities can continue to function smoothly.

The role of IT service providers is crucial to the successful implementation of digitalization in the healthcare sector. They make a significant contribution to improving the efficiency, quality and safety of patient care and enable healthcare facilities to focus on their core competencies.

6 Summary and Outlook

The use of cloud services and artificial intelligence in healthcare has the potential to significantly transform the industry and improve the quality of medical care. The flexibility, scalability and increased efficiency offered by cloud services enable healthcare facilities to successfully overcome the challenges of digital transformation. Cloud services in particular act as an enabler of digitalization in the healthcare sector and provide the basis for the increasing use of artificial intelligence and other innovative technologies. Despite the numerous positive effects, it is a top priority to carefully consider data protection, security and regulatory compliance in order to maintain patient trust and protect the integrity of healthcare data. IT service providers can contribute significantly to a successful implementation by playing a major role in driving digitalization in healthcare, improving patient care, increasing efficiency and ensuring the smooth exchange of information between healthcare stakeholders.

With the further development of cloud technologies and the integration of artificial intelligence, the potential of digitalization in healthcare will continue to increase. The use of cloud services and artificial intelligence in healthcare is just the beginning of a broader digital transformation that will fundamentally change the way medical services are delivered. The future outlook for cloud-based solutions in healthcare is promising and still holds a lot of untapped potential, especially if it enables the increasing use of AI and other innovative technologies.

Bibliography

an der Heiden, I., Bernhard, J., & Otten, M. (2021). *Scientific evaluation of the productive operation of the telematics infrastructure applications—Study report*. IGES Institute.

AOK Rheinland/Hamburg. (2023). *Elephants club conference on the digitalization of healthcare met at the AOK Rheinland/Hamburg education center* (AOKs and their association). https://www.aok.de/pp/rh/pm/elephants-club/

Baxmann, K., Jerke, K., & Eicke, P. (2018). The digital patient record: Acceptance or rejection? In K. Butzer-Strothmann, A. Bork, & N. Forgö (Eds.), *Digitalization in healthcare* (Vol. 7, pp. 37–62). Cuvillier.

Bork, U., & Weitz, J. (2019). Cloud computing in healthcare: More opportunities than risks. *German Medical Journal*, *116*(14). https://www.aerzteblatt.de/archiv/206602/Cloud-Computing-im-Gesundheitswesen-Mehr-Chancen-als-Risiken

Corsten, H. (2022). Cloud services. In S. Roth & H. Corsten (Eds.), *Handbook of digitization*. Publishing house Franz Vahlen.

EU-DSGVO. (2023). *General Data Protection Regulation (GDPR)*. https://dsgvo-gesetz.de/

Federal Ministry of Education and Research, Federal Ministry of Health, & Federal Ministry for Economic Affairs and Energy (eds.). (2020). *Daten helfen heilen-Innovationsinitiative "Daten für Gesundheit": Roadmap for better patient care through health research and digitalization*. https://www.gesundheitsforschung-bmbf.de/files/Roadmap_Innovationsinitiative_Daten_fuer_Gesundheit_barrierefrei.pdf

Federal Ministry of Health. (2023). *Gemeinsam Digital: Digitization strategy for healthcare and nursing* (p. 44) [Final report]. Federal Ministry of Health. https://www.bundesgesundheitsministerium.de/service/publikationen/details/digitalisierungsstrategie-fuer-das-gesundheitswesen-und-die-pflege.html

Federal Statistical Office. (2023). *Health expenditure in Germany*. https://www.destatis.de/DE/Themen/Gesellschaft-Umwelt/Gesundheit/Gesundheitsausgaben/_inhalt.html

Feld, A. D. (2005). The Health Insurance Portability and Accountability Act (HIPAA): Its Broad Effect on Practice. *The American Journal of Gastroenterology, 100*(7), 1440–1443. https://doi.org/10.1111/j.1572-0241.2005.50621.x

Fischer, P. (2019). *Digital Health Study on the acceptance of electronic health data storage in the form of the electronic patient file (ePA) in Germany* (Vol. 17). MA Academy.

German Science and Humanities Council. (2023). *Perspectives for the further development of the health professions | Recognizing and using scientific potential for health care* [Application/pdf]. 159 pages. https://doi.org/10.57674/6EXF-AM35

Harwardt, M., & Köhler, M. (2023). Artificial intelligence. In M. Harwardt & M. Köhler (Eds.), *Artificial intelligence along the customer journey* (pp. 21–29). Springer Fachmedien Wiesbaden. https://doi.org/10.1007/978-3-658-39109-6_3

Jäschke, T. (2018). *Data protection and information security in healthcare: Basics, concepts, implementation*. Medizinisch Wissenschaftliche Verlagsgesellschaft.

Jäschke, T. (2023). *Data protection, information and cyber security in healthcare: Grundlagen-Konzepte-Umsetzung* (3rd, updated and expanded edition). MWV Medizinisch Wissensch.

Kalis, B., Collier, M., & Fu, R. (2018). 10 promising AI applications in health care. *Harvard Business Review*. https://hbr.org/2018/05/10-promising-ai-applications-in-health-care

Lohmann, U. (2021). Cloud computing in digitization. In U. Lohmann, *Architectures of administrative digitization* (pp. 189–214). Springer Fachmedien Wiesbaden. https://doi.org/10.1007/978-3-658-34522-8_9

Pechmann, L., Mildner, M., Suthau, T., & Leucker, M. (2022). Regulatory requirements for artificial intelligence solutions in healthcare. In M. A. Pfannstiel (Ed.), *Artificial intelligence in healthcare* (pp. 175–198). Springer Fachmedien Wiesbaden. https://doi.org/10.1007/978-3-658-33597-7_8

Scheibner, J., Sleigh, J., Ienca, M., & Vayena, E. (2021). Benefits, challenges, and contributors to success for national eHealth systems implementation: A scoping review. *Journal of the American Medical Informatics Association, 28*(9), 2039–2049. https://doi.org/10.1093/jamia/ocab096

Schirmer, H. (2022). Opportunities and limits of digitization in healthcare for the sustainable promotion of population health in Germany: Digitization in healthcare leads to comprehensive changes and new innovations in the healthcare of the population. In T. Kümpel, K. Schlenkrich, & T. Heupel (Eds.), *Controlling & Innovation 2022* (pp. 281–334). Springer Fachmedien Wiesbaden. https://doi.org/10.1007/978-3-658-36484-7_12

Statista Research Department. (2022a). *Barriers to digitization in the German healthcare system 2022*. Statista Research Department. https://de.statista.com/statistik/daten/studie/1352847/umfrage/hindernissen-fuer-die-digitalisierung-im-deutschen-gesundheitswesen/

Statista Research Department. (2022b). *Survey on AI application areas in healthcare worldwide in 2020*. https://de.statista.com/statistik/daten/studie/1248402/umfrage/ki-anwendungsbereiche-im-gesundheitswesen/#:~:text=In%20a%20worldwide%20survey%20conducted%20on%20application%20areas%20for%C3%BCr%20AI%20in%20healthcare.

Statista. (2023). *Annual healthcare expenditure in Germany in the years from 1992 to 2021*. https://de.statista.com/statistik/daten/studie/5463/umfrage/gesundheitssystem-in-deutschland-ausgaben-seit-1992/

The Sustainable Digitalization Community of a German Federal Ministry—intention, Structure and Progress

Noah Bilski and Ruth Geibel

Abstract The major megatrends of our time are digitalization, globalization and sustainable transformation. They are changing the lives of all people. In order for digitalization, which is progressing rapidly, to become an opportunity driver for prosperity, justice and the environment, it needs a social framework. For this reason, the German Federal Ministry for the Environment, Nature Conservation, Nuclear Safety and Consumer Protection (BMUV) is working intensively on this topic and, as part of these activities, a central project team is focusing on the orientation, growth and long-term anchoring of the "Sustainable Digitalization" community. In the Community, the Federal Ministry for the Environment brings together stakeholders from the start-up scene, business, administration, local authorities, research and NGOs. In various event formats, they take the opportunity to inform themselves, exchange ideas and network with each other. In addition, the community acts as an enabler of projects, provides experts for various participation processes in the ministry and develops publications and workshop series. The project team relies on a synthesis of traditional and agile project management methods and uses technically supported solutions such as AI-supported data analysis for its project work. This report deals with the work for and by the BMUV Community "Sustainable Digitalization" to raise awareness of these megatrends and how a positive influence for the benefit of the environment is possible.

Keywords Federal Ministry for the Environment · Nature conservation · Nuclear safety and consumer protection · Federal Ministry · Environment · Sustainability · Digitalization

N. Bilski (✉)
BMUV, Bonn, Germany
e-mail: noah.bilski@bmuv.bund.de

R. Geibel
Msg Systems Ag, Ismaning, Germany
e-mail: ruth.geibel@msg.de

R. C. Geibel and S. Machavariani (eds.), *Digital Management to Shape the Future*, Springer Proceedings in Business and Economics,
https://doi.org/10.1007/978-3-031-66517-2_13

1 Introduction and Political Background

Digitalization and sustainability are interwoven in a complex network of relationships. On the one hand, the technical possibilities of digital technologies offer enormous potential for solving various problems that threaten politically set sustainability goals such as the 2030 Agenda. On the other hand, the increasing use of digital applications brings with it new challenges for climate, resource and environmental protection. Digitally driven business models, such as e-commerce platforms, have recorded enormous sales gains in recent years—in 2018 alone, online retail grew by 9.4% to a total turnover of EUR 68.1 billion (Zimmermann et al., 2020).

This is accompanied by adverse effects on the climate and environment caused by, among other things, CO_2 consumption in logistics, new increased consumption patterns, energy consumption in data centers and increased packaging waste (Zimmermann et al., 2020).

At the same time, consumption patterns can be made more sustainable with the help of digital technologies by providing online repair instructions that increase the lifespan of products, a digital product passport that stores information that facilitates the recycling of products or end customers selling goods that are no longer needed on second-hand platforms. These measures offer great potential for generating positive environmental effects in the course of introducing a circular economy (Krause et al., 2020).

The example of e-commerce platforms that, on the one hand, digitalization can generate and promote non-sustainable behaviours and business models (Zimmermann et al., 2020). On the other hand, digital technologies can also represent the solution to many sustainability-related problems, provided that they and the associated business models are sustainable.

E-Commerce platforms are just one of a large number of fields of action in reaching more sustainability in digital technologies, ranging from sustainable data centers and AI-supported climate models to the design of a smart city. Aware of this multitude of challenges and the associated need for a political framework, the BMUV began developing the **"Environmental Policy Digital Agenda"** (UPDA) together with around 200 experts in the fall of 2019 and presented it to the public in March 2020 (BMUV, 2020). The UPDA contains more than 70 specific measures in four transformation fields and pursues the goals of steering digitalization in an environmentally friendly direction and exploiting the opportunities of digitalization for environmental protection. The Digital Agenda is the first strategy in Europe to combine digitalization and environmental protection so consistently. The development process of the Environmental Policy Digital Agenda was characterized by broad stakeholder participation. The Federal Environment Ministry's digital policy concepts were developed in an adaptive process together with the stakeholders as part of various expert interviews and specialist workshops.

Following the 2021 federal elections and the successful coalition negotiations between the SPD, FDP and Bündnis 90/Die Grünen parties, the coalition agreement of the so-called Ampel government was agreed in November 2021 (Federal

Government of Germany, 2021). Under the motto "Daring more progress", the parties involved agreed to promote a state model that "seeks cooperation with business and civil society" and "offers more transparency and participation in its decisions" (Coalition Agreement, 2021: 7). Furthermore, the new federal government committed to strengthen the role of civil society in digital policy decision-making and supporting it in its efforts (ibid.: 14).

Based on the positive experiences gained during the stakeholder process for the creation of the UPDA and the goal of involving more stakeholders in political processes, the BMUV developed the **concept** of **establishing a "Sustainable Digitalization Community"**. The community should act as a steering instrument and door opener for obtaining external perspectives in digital policy processes in the BMUV.

On the one hand, the project serves as a **digital policy communication tool for** the BMUV to make the Federal Ministry's messages, goals and projects known and, on the other hand, the ministry wants to act as a **transmission belt** between the various political players and the expert public. To this end, the community members are offered communication spaces and networking opportunities, firstly so that they can talk to each other and to the specialist departments of the ministry and share their concerns. Secondly, the BMUV wants to strengthen the topic of sustainable digitalization among its target group and raise awareness of the benefits and harms of digitalization for the climate and environment.

Thirdly, BMUV intends to have an impact on existing networks, hubs and initiatives, learn from them and enter into a **discourse** with them. Through knowledge exchange, networking and joint projects, the aim is to work towards strengthening efforts that harness the potential of digitalization for environmental and climate protection and at the same time contribute to mitigating the environmental damage caused by digital technologies. The focus here is on various stakeholder groups involved in sustainability and digitalization from different branches of the administration, research institutions, education and business. The ministry has also involved networks, committees, associations, administration and companies in order to support their efforts and strengthen the topics in their institutions. In addition to the political goal of strengthening sustainability in digitalization processes, the German Ministry for the Environment is thus purses the federal government's overarching goal of involving civil society and business more closely in political and bureaucratic processes.

2 Theory and Methodology of the Project

Civic participation and the inclusion of different perspectives in **political decision-making processes are** among the central characteristics of democratic political systems (Frevel, 2009: 65). However, these are not only a necessary prerequisite for the functioning of parliamentarism and the establishment of social pluralism, but also represent a systemic advantage of democratic systems.

Based on David Easton's (1953) systems theory and the **input–output model** of political systems that he developed, the authors draw the following conclusion: political systems that are open to demands, inputs and expertise from society produce more effective output in the form of policies and projects (Easton, 1953). For this to work, the political system must ensure the "accessibility of society to the political system" and be responsive to the input provided (Czerwick, 2011: 192).

This objective in relation to specialist topics is achievable by involving various stakeholders from different parts of the society. This process can take the form of hearings, collaborations, public meetings or "notice and comment rulemakings" (Ahn & Baldwin, 2022: 3). Using this systemic advantage of democracies is particularly promising in view of the political objectives of the German Ministry for the Environment. Previous studies have shown that these forms of **collaborative governance of environmental sustainability** have strengthened various government policies and projects (ibid.).

Based on these findings and with the aim of strengthening stakeholder engagement as the "core of democratic public governance processes" (ibid.) and promoting sustainability in digitalization processes, the BMUV launched the "**Sustainable Digitalization" community. The** project approach is based on the **hybrid project management method** (Agile Software Development, 2016; DIN, 2023; ISO, 2023), which combines traditional and agile elements. Classic project coordination and project phase planning is carried out with the aim of achieving defined milestones in each phase and an agile approach to implementation. To this end, the main activities, known as epics, the associated activities (stories) and their tasks are documented and planned as tasks via the Kanban board.

The sub-projects are set up as sprints and managed using **Kanban** via a digital whiteboard. With Kanban, the various tasks are clearly displayed, including a prioritization that can be adjusted at any time and the status of their processing. The Kanban board provides three content areas that display the current status, namely for the newly entered tasks, the tasks in progress and, in the third column, the items that have already been completed. New tasks and ideas are collected in the "task and idea parking lot" and discussed regularly. Depending on the target date, agreed tasks are placed in the "On Hold" backlog or dragged directly into the todo column. Each task is recorded on a (virtual) colored "sticky note" and given the name of the person responsible (task owner) and a due date. When the status of a task changes, the corresponding note is moved from left to right. The project team members, the so-called task owners, report on the degree of completion of their tasks at regular meetings (weekly meetings). This procedure provides a clear picture of the to-dos at all times and enables efficient coordination and consultation within the project team. Project management also combines the disciplines of **project marketing**, **quality, stakeholder and communication management**. Project marketing includes both the promotion of the project to increase awareness and the appealing formulation of content as messages to achieve the set goals. Stakeholder and communication management is about the 'how' of the content to be communicated to the stakeholders and thus the choice of communication spaces.

The potential target groups were identified, analyzed and clustered in order to sustainably build the community. To this end, the project team researched potential stakeholders for the community by contacting **them directly** and also utilized **AI-supported web research**. To define suitable starting points, the project researched potential interested individuals in relevant subject areas and then scraped the websites of the organizations for which the individuals work. To do this, the websites were downloaded and analyzed in two steps using software:

1. **Named entity recognition (NER):** Recognition of persons, organizations, dates, locations and other data points in the texts. The open source library for natural language recognition spaCy was used for this purpose. This identified new organizations and people, for which websites were also searched and analyzed. In this way, the data collection gradually grew.
2. **Embeddings:** For each of the websites, people and organizations found, so-called "embeddings" were calculated, high-dimensional representations that in this case depict linguistic relationships. With the help of the embeddings, the scraped websites could be arranged into suitable clusters in terms of content. For the people found with NER, the topic clusters can now be used to derive who is active in which topic areas. On this basis, people and organizations that appear in similar contexts can in turn be identified. The technology used for this was Transformer from HuggingFace.

In total, almost 500,000 websites were downloaded and more than 10,000 entities, clearly identifiable information objects, were identified. On this basis, the project was able to identify and categorize more than 1000 organizations and individuals. Figure 1 shows the process of AI-supported data analysis from data collection to the structured preparation of the results (see Fig. 1):

The people were contacted in order to obtain initial information about needs and currently relevant topics. With the help of this information, the project team developed various formats for community work and identified thematic priorities.

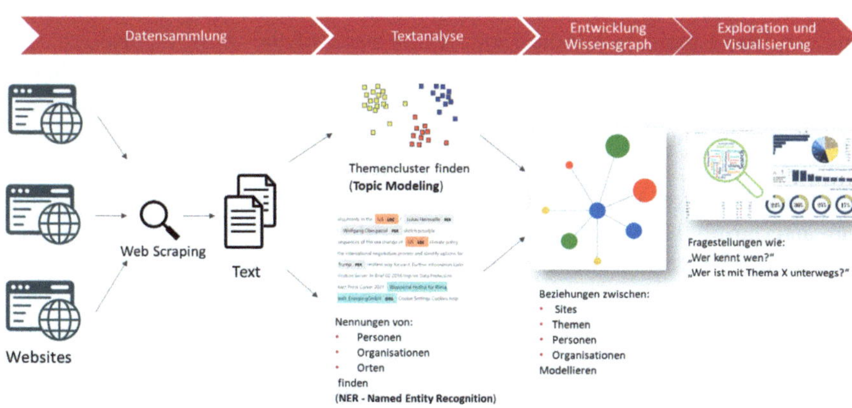

Fig. 1 Overview of the overall natural language processing and analysis workflow

This iterative approach ensured that the project work and the needs of the target group were congruent. In a further step, the people contacted were asked about their interest in becoming a member of the community and the vast majority expressed this interest. Consent to membership is given by entering the name and organization via a link on the BMUV website. The submitted data is collected in a mailbox and processed from there.

The concept for the "Sustainable Digitalization" community that emerged from this preliminary work is communicated through targeted project marketing and supported by a community corporate design for all publications on activities and results. Announcements, summaries of events and press releases are published both via social media and the BMUV community website—mailings are also sent to the community. These broad-based communication measures and individual discussions ensure the continuous growth of the community. The number of members is now growing organically.

3 Activities

With the start of the project at the end of August 2021, the results of the UPDA were jointly reflected on in various **presentations** from the BMUV in a professional-public circle at the first community meeting "Sustainable Digitalization". Topics included 'Data-driven environmental policy', 'OZG environment', 'AI for the environment and climate' and 'Europe as a field of action'. In the subsequent development work for the community, further exchange formats for expert discussions were developed to create networking opportunities. At the same time, **individual** and **AI-supported research** was carried out and potential target groups were approached in order to build and expand the community. The database also grew with the approval of community membership.

For the second event in December 2021, the decision was made to use the format of a virtual **barcamp** (BMUV, 2021), an interactive workshop format in which participants contribute their own topics and design parts of the event themselves. The focus was on challenges, visions and new concepts for the **digital and sustainable development of cities and municipalities**. The joint work on the topics contributed by the participants took place in breakout sessions on topics such as the 'necessity of standardization', 'digital product passport including product carbon footprint' or 'sustainable use of AI'. A digital whiteboard for personal profiles was available before and during the event to encourage networking. After the events, the participants received a report on the results of each breakout session and the summarized guiding principles.

In the following year, 2022, the focus continued to be placed on membership growth as well as on opportunities for new community members to network with each other through exchanges at events. As a result, the network doubled from around 500 members at the end of 2021 to around 1,000 members at the end of 2022. In 2022, the following activities in particular took place in the form of events.

- In April, the next event focused on **'Rebound effects as a challenge for sustainable digitalization'** with presentations on the social impact, the relativization of the ecological efficiency gains of digitalization and the need for transparency and education. The key points formulated were then communicated to the community (BMUV, 2022a, 2022b, 2022c, 2022d).
- The next Community event took place in barcamp format at the end of May 2022. Once again, networking was encouraged, while the topic of **'Corporate Digital Responsibility'** was discussed in several sessions on the effective and sustainable use of digital technologies in small and medium-sized enterprises (SMEs) after a brief introduction. The discussions were brought together in the concluding plenary session.
- The four presentations held in a workshop in July 2022 titled **'Into the next decade with Green IT!** In line with the political goal of the project—the exchange between society and administration—the speakers at the events were representatives from federal administration projects and community members (BMUV, 2022a, 2022b, 2022c, 2022d).
- This principle was continued at the annual event, the **Community Convention** on the topic of **'Together for green solutions'** in September 2022, where the Community celebrated its first birthday. Community members were able to apply for a speaker slot via a call for participation. At the same event, the BMUV used the occasion to inform the specialist public about the progress of its digital policy **lighthouse projects**, with exciting topics such as the five-point program **'AI for the environment and climate'**, the 'umwelt.info' portal, the 'DigiRess for resource-efficient and real-time data-based production' funding guideline and the 'Green-AI Hub Mittelstand'. Presentations from the community covered topics such as reusable solutions for food, rule-based circular economy, standardization for economic system development, digital product passports (DPP) and how open data can enable useful and sustainability-oriented applications (BMUV, 2022a, 2022b, 2022c, 2022d).
- A **panel discussion** on '**sustainable consumption in the digital space**' took place at the end of November 2022. The community get-together featured two presentations on 'sustainable consumption', with a project funded by the Federal Ministry to improve the visibility of sustainability labels in online retail and on the current status and solutions for e-commerce and sustainability (BMUV, 2022a, 2022b, 2022c, 2022d).

In the course of 2023, the **number of members has** grown **to over 1300 stakeholders**. The events this year, with their focus on sustainability and digitalization, are also intended to reach new target groups, for example student associations.

An application based on a Microsoft Excel file with macros was programmed to record the members of the community. This was used to create the **stakeholder database** as an.xlsm file, which fulfills the functionalities of a database. The members are divided into **stakeholder categories**. Table 1 below lists the main stakeholder categories:

Table 1 List of the 16 actor categories

Education, Research	Private
Financial institutions	Foundation
Freelancer	Association (small)
Non-profit organizations	Association (big)
Initiative/project	Administration (Federal Government)
Health insurance	Administration (municipality, state)
Press and media	Economy (large companies / SMEs / start-ups)
Politics	NGO

In addition, the thematic focus of the members' activities is recorded in the following **clusters**, which are shown in Table 2:

As state, one of the project goals for 2023 was to reach new target groups. To provide a low-threshold introduction to the topics of digitalization and sustainability, an event in **the format of a science slam** with three presentations was organized in February 2023. This format was intended to reach students and young professionals. The presentations focused on topics such as **'Visual rhetoric in sustainability reports'** and **'Digital twins'. The** aim of the event was to transfer knowledge from the community's expertise to society. The three presentations were recorded and are available on the YouTube channel (BMUV, 2023a, 2023b, 2023c, 2023d, 2023e, 2023f).

In March 2023, **msg's customer magazine for the public sector** (public, 2023) published an article by the project team entitled **'Networking for more radiance'** on the BMUV's objectives and activities for the "Sustainable digitalization" community. This publication promotes the sustainable digital transformation and also features four stakeholders who provide information on their support for the community and their activities in this area. In addition, guest lectures were held in various events such as the Greentech.Live conference series to promote the community and raise awareness.

This was followed in June by the community meeting **"Sustainability traps on the internet"** (BMUV, 2023a, 2023b, 2023c, 2023d, 2023e, 2023f), which featured

Table 2 List of the 21 clusters

Consulting	Industry 4.0	Mobility
Blockchain	IT infrastructure	Nature conservation
Services of general interest	Climate protection	Network policy
Digital product passport	Consumption	Smart City
Energy	Circular economy	Software
Geoinformatics	Agriculture	Environmental protection
Health	AI/ Big Data	Consumer protection

three presentations and discussions on the ecological, economic and social challenges of the internet. These focused on resource consumption, biases in AI applications and accessibility on the internet.

The Community **meet-up** at the **re:publica 23** (BMUV, 2023a, 2023b, 2023c, 2023d, 2023e, 2023f) digitalization conference in Berlin in June was another format to promote networking among members and recruit new ones (see Fig. 2). Under the title **'Bits & Bites: Connecting sustainable digital policy—locally and globally',** two representatives from different federal ministries led a dialog on sustainable digital policy at local and global level. Experts and interested parties came together to discuss the opportunities and challenges of digitalization in the context of sustainability. Along a so-called gallery walk, the participants were able to discuss and network using the illustrations on the above-mentioned range of topics.

In addition, a survey known as a **CFP (Call for Participation)** was launched in mid-2023 to involve the community. The aim was to find out about practical examples and pilot projects as well as interest in the joint development of guidelines on specific topics relating to sustainability and digitalization. The findings will be evaluated and made available to the public following a workshop with stakeholders. One outcome of this process will be the development of a guide for young people on the sustainable use of digital technologies. This paper will be developed at the end of 2023 together with experts from the community, people from the BMUV and representatives of youth organizations.

Another networking opportunity and the chance to join in the discussion was offered at the Community Treff in July during the lunch break on the topic of

Fig. 2 Meet Up at the re:publica

'Water and digitalization' (BMUV, 2023a, 2023b, 2023c, 2023d, 2023e, 2023f). In a **Learn&Lunch format,** Berliner Wasserbetriebe provided interesting insights into their work by presenting their innovative technologies and sustainable practices in dealing with the valuable resource of water.

To celebrate the Community's second anniversary, the second **Community Convention was** held in September 2023 on the premises of the BMUV under the motto **'Shaping digitalization'** (BMUV, 2023a, 2023b, 2023c, 2023d, 2023e, 2023f) in the presence of the Federal Minister. More than 130 people gathered to work together on solutions for a sustainable and digital future. The Federal Minister emphasized the important role that digitalization can play in overcoming ecological crises such as climate change, species extinction and environmental pollution. In addition to various workshops and presentations, a panel discussion focused on the challenges and potential of a **sustainable platform economy and the greening of e-commerce**. Important points of discussion included, for example, that interest in sustainable purchasing is increasing and that a major challenge is the task of obtaining data on various product components.

For community members and other interested software developers and software architects, a separate series of workshops was held as a **training program on the topic of "Learning Green Coding!"** (BMUV, 2023a, 2023b, 2023c, 2023d, 2023e, 2023f). It started in October 2023 with topics on basics, measurement tools, testing and operating platforms, case studies and study results from research projects. The focus was on resource-efficient software development and reducing the ever-increasing energy consumption (CO_2 footprint). The series of events met with great interest and was very well attended.

Over the past few years, the community has become an important exchange forum for stakeholders working on the intersections between sustainability and digitalization. In addition to the activities mentioned above, the project also acts as an intermediary between experts, disseminates scientific studies produced by the BMUV or community members and attempts to act as an enabler of projects between the stakeholders. The community thus fulfills its intended role as a transmission belt between the BMUV and society.

4 Results and Evaluation

In the more than two years since it was founded, the community has brought together over 1300 stakeholders. Over the project period to date, thirteen community meetings and two community conventions have been held, a series of workshops launched and an article published. The project has also managed to establish strategic cooperation with various civil society and political networks. The project has also succeeded in adapting the work of the community to the needs of its target group through personal discussions, surveys and other communication measures and reacting flexibly to new needs of the BMUV. These successes can be seen as positive project results and the project team has received corresponding feedback via emails, contributions and comments. Last but not least, the community is now growing organically, with interested people regularly registering via the website and other channels. These findings suggest that the BMUV project has come closer to achieving its goals.

At the same time, as part of a critical reflection, it must be determined that in the next step, the community should participate in the development of concrete results in a goal-oriented manner with the help of project management. To date, project work has focused primarily on events and other communication measures. As a result, the potential for expertise and knowledge as well as potential synergy effects that exist within the target group have not yet been fully exploited. In order to contribute to sustainability in digitalization processes, the members of the "Sustainable Digitalization" community will get more opportunities to participate in the development of policy papers and contribute their expertise as part of stakeholder participation. Ideally, the transfer of knowledge should also initiate the launch of other projects in the field of sustainable digital technologies. In this way, this project can act even more strongly as an enabler of projects and collaborations as well as a bridge builder between its members. As part of this, the project itends to reinforce contacts with other stakeholders within the federal authorities. Furthermore, research activities will be expanded in order to tap into parts of the potential target group that have not yet been identified.

5 Summary and Outlook

Digitalization, as a generic term for the digital transformation of our society and economy with the transition from the industrial age characterized by analogue technologies to the age of digitally supported technologies, is causing a profound process of change in the economy and society. At the same time, the importance of sustainability for the climate and environment is increasing to preserve and strengthen the natural regenerative capacity of the systems involved. In the political interplay between the two fields of action, it is important to develop ways and means of achieving sustainable digitalization that take both opportunities and risks into account.

The results presented in Chapter 4 show that the project has contributed to achieving the its objectives. On the one hand, it has acted as a door opener and facilitator of contacts between different stakeholders and the federal administration. On the other hand, it has strengthened existing sustainability efforts in the digitalization projects by providing the community with a platform for best-practices and networking opportunities for the specialist public.

Based on the successes to date, the project will be continued in 2024.

References

Agile Manifesto. (2016). Agile software development. http://agilemanifesto.org/iso/de/manifesto.html

Ahn, M., & Baldwin, E. (2022). Who benefits from collaborative governance? An empirical study from the energy sector. *Public Management Review, 1–25*. https://doi.org/10.1080/14719037.2022.2044505

BMUV. (2020). Environmental policy digital agenda. Ministry for the Environment, Nature Conservation, Nuclear Safety and Consumer Protection. de/fileadmin/Daten_BMU/Download_PDF/Digitalisierung/digitalagenda_bf.pdf

BMUV. (2021): Community Treff Barcamp, https://www.bmuv.de/meldung/bmuv-community-treff-nachhaltige-digitalisierung-am-10122021

BMUV. (2022a). Community Treff rebound effects. https://www.bmuv.de/meldung/bmuv-community-treff-nachhaltige-digitalisierung-am-04042022

BMUV. (2022b). Community Treff with Green IT into the next decade. https://www.bmuv.de/meldung/bmuv-community-treff-mit-green-it-ins-naechste-jahrzehnt-am-05072022

BMUV. (2022c). Community convention. https://www.bmuv.de/meldung/bmuv-community-convention-gemeinsam-zu-gruenen-loesungen

BMUV. (2022d). Community meeting on sustainable consumption in the digital space! https://www.bmuv.de/meldung/bmuv-community-nachhaltige-digitalisierung-online-shopping-nachhaltig-gedacht

BMUV. (2023a). Community Treff Science Slam. https://www.youtube.com/watch?v=oLNfDtcV6sg; https://www.youtube.com/watch?v=51UFv-zXo6I; https://www.youtube.com/watch?app=desktop&v=hcAHk-N938Q

BMUV. (2023b). Community Treff sustainability traps on the internet. https://www.bmuv.de/meldung/bmuv-community-nachhaltige-digitalisierung-nachhaltigkeitsfallen-im-internet

BMUV. (2023c). Community Treff at the re:publica 2023. https://www.bmuv.de/meldung/bmuv-auf-der-republica-so-profitieren-insekten-und-kmu-von-ki

BMUV. (2023d). Community Treff water and digitalization. https://www.bmuv.de/meldung/erfolgreicher-treff-der-bmuv-community-nachhaltige-digitalisierung-zum-thema-wasser-und-digitalisierung

BMUV. (2023e): Community Convention, shaping digitalization! https://www.bmuv.de/meldung/community-convention-digitalisierung-gestalten-2023

BMUV. (2023f): Learn green coding! https://www.bmuv.de/veranstaltung/workshop-reihe-green-coding

Czerwick, E. (2011). *Politics as a system: An introduction to the systems theory of politics*. De Gruyter.

DIN. (2023). Project management (DIN 69901-5:2009-01). https://www.din.de/de/meta/suche/62730!search?query=69901

Easton, D. (1953). *The political system. An inquiry into the state of political science*. Palgrave.

Frevel, B. (2009). *Demokratie*. Springer.

Federal Government of Germany. (2021). Coalition Agreement. https://www.bundesregierung.de/breg-de/service/gesetzesvorhaben/koalitionsvertrag-2021-1990800

ISO. (2023). Project management (ISO 21500:2016). https://www.iso.org/standard/50003.html

Krause, S., Fabian, M., Dicke, N., Köhn, M., Baumeister, H.J., Körber-Ziegengeist, G., Oehme, I., Bockhardt, I., Frien-Kossolobow, L., & Ebert, T. (2020). Extending the useful life of products. Approaches to waste prevention and resource conservation through reuse and preparation for reuse. In *UBA Background*. https://www.umweltbundesamt.de/sites/default/files/me-dien/1410/publikationen/hgp_verlangerung_produktnutzungsdauer_bf.pdf

Public. (2023). msg's customer magazine for the public sector: Sustainable and confidently digital. https://s3.msg.systems/Publications/Public%20Magazin/public_Ausgabe_01-23.pdf

Zimmermann, T., Hauschke, F., Memelink, R., Reitz, A., Pelke, N., John, R., Eberle, U., & Ninnemann, J. (2020). The greening of online trade. Second partial report. In *Federal environment agency texts* 227. https://www.umweltbundesamt.de/publikationen/die-oekologisierung-des-onlinehandels

The Use of Artificial Intelligence for Idea Generation in the Innovation Process

Ode Plätke and Richard C. Geibel

Abstract This presentation contains a systematic literature review, conducted using the PRISMA framework, examines the use of artificial intelligence (AI) for idea generation in the innovation process. To this end, fifteen articles from four databases were identified as appropriate and subjected to descriptive analysis, literature classification, and thematic synthesis as part of the consolidation of results. The focus of the analysis was to identify potential applications and limitations of AI for ideation in order to propose a framework for implementing AI in the innovation process to foster the ideation phase. The thematic synthesis revealed that current AI models at the time of the research, are best used to support and facilitate human innovators by leveraging their data analytics capabilities to provide human innovators with valuable information or to provide procedural support. Nevertheless, AI models are capable of independently generating new ideas based on combinations or own generations, but this capability is not advanced enough in current models to generate innovative ideas independently and reliably and fully replace human innovators. Therefore, validation by a human user is still recommended, which at the time of this research precludes a full replacement of the human component. Based on these findings, a hybrid intelligence model is proposed in which AI and human innovators collaborate in the idea generation phase. In this process, AI with its technical capabilities supports the human innovator in its human capabilities maintaining the key position human innovators hold in this process. However, due to the rapid development in the field of artificial intelligence, new research approaches are constantly emerging.

Keywords AI · Innovation · Idea generation · Ideation · Hybrid intelligence model

---

O. Plätke (✉) · R. C. Geibel
E-Commerce Institute, Cologne, Germany
e-mail: ode@plaetke.de

IU International University, Cologne, Germany

R. C. Geibel
e-mail: geibel@ecommerceinstitut.de

R. C. Geibel and S. Machavariani (eds.), *Digital Management to Shape the Future*, Springer Proceedings in Business and Economics,
https://doi.org/10.1007/978-3-031-66517-2_14

1 Introduction

The emergence of artificial intelligence has revolutionized a wide variety of sectors, and, through Chat GPT, it is also gaining traction with the general public. As this landscape continues to evolve, new applications of AI are constantly opening up (Mhlanga, 2023, n.p.). Thus, the innovative character of artificial intelligence may itself be a driver for innovation. This also emerges from a study by the auditing and consulting firm PwC, which recognizes a value generation through AI for the purpose of innovation of products and services (PwC, 2022, n.p.). The starting point of the innovation process is the generation of ideas. It is in this fertile ground that the seeds of potential are sown, germinating into concepts that eventually lead to the aspired innovations (Preez & Louw, 2008, p. 9).

Thus, in the wake of this rapid development of AI, it is important to ask what disruptive elements are impacting the innovation process and in what ways Artificial Intelligences are changing how ideas are generated and innovations emerge. From this claim to investigate the role of artificial intelligence for idea generation within the innovation process, the research question underlying this research is derived: How can artificial intelligence be used for idea generation in the innovation process?

This research question suggests the investigation and presentation of the relevance of the subsystem of idea generation in the innovation process, as well as the identification from the literature of possible applications and limitations of artificial intelligence for idea generation, in order to provide a multifaceted view of the topic and to round off the answer to the research question with a conceptual framework for the potential implementation of AI in the innovating process to support the generation of ideas.

Exploring this topic, a Systematic literature review is conducted by examining the research landscape for the object of inquiry and consolidating the thematically congruent contributions to illuminate a more nuanced understanding of the potential use of AI in the innovation process.

For the purpose of creating a compelling roadmap, this introduction is followed by the methodological approach to the Systematic Review with a stringent presentation of the individual steps of the review. After the presentation of the methodological background of the execution, the results of the review are treated on the basis of different synthesis methods. Finally, the results from the synthesis are evaluated in a conclusion.

2 Theory

The systematic literature review is characterized by a high degree of rigor, emphasizing the importance of validity, reliability, and objectivity. Internal validity is ensured through quality assessments, and reliability is upheld by transparent design, conduct, and analysis (Templier & Paré, 2018, p. 113).

The review adheres to the 'Preferred Reporting Items for Systematic Reviews and Meta-Analyses' (PRISMA) framework, a widely accepted guide for systematic literature reviews, prescribing the performance of a literature review and the content to be included (Page et al., 2021, p. 1).

3 Methodology

This chapter outlines the methodology used to address the central research question of this thesis. It employs a systematic literature review as a comprehensive approach to develop a conceptual framework for utilizing artificial intelligence (AI) in idea generation within the innovation process.

The research question centers on AI's role in idea generation within the evolving digital landscape. The review's objective is to identify and synthesize potential AI applications and limitations in idea generation, ultimately creating a theoretical framework for integrating AI into the innovation process.

3.1 Eligibility Criteria

The inclusion criteria specify that articles must be in English, published between 2013 and 2023, peer-reviewed, and thematically relevant to the research question.

3.2 Search Strategy

The search strategy relies on a keyword search in four electronic databases: EBSCO, ScienceDirect, Springer Link, and Wiley. The search string combines keywords related to AI, idea generation, and the innovation process using Boolean operators. Resulting in the following search string: ("artificial intelligence" OR "AI") AND ("idea generation" OR "ideation" OR "design thinking") AND ("innovation process" OR "innovating process" OR "innovation management").

3.3 Study Selection

A structured approach using the "Rayyan" platform is employed for screening and eliminating duplicates. Records are screened based on title, abstract, and full text to determine inclusion or exclusion, reducing the risk of bias.

3.4 Data Extraction

Data is extracted from eligible articles, encompassing both descriptive elements and conceptual evidence to offer a comprehensive overview of the research landscape.

3.5 Quality Assessment

A custom consolidated risk of bias assessment matrix is utilized, employing tools such as the Mixed Methods Appraisal Tool for empirical research (Hong et al., 2018), the AMSTAR 2 for review papers (Shea et al., 2017), and the criteria for theoretical conceptual papers by Margherita et al. (2022).

3.6 Methods of Synthesis

For the purpose of synthesizing the results, after a detailed presentation of the quantitative data of the yielded papers, a descriptive analysis is made of the thematic synthesis of the advantages and limitations of AI for idea generation.

4 Results

In this section, the results of the conducted literature search performed on the 10th of April 2023, the screening, and the data extraction as part of the review are presented, which was designed according to previously presented methodology.

The search, which included the four databases EBSCO, ScienceDirect, Springer Link and Wiley, yielded a total of 17,093 records, which represented a vast range of potentially relevant sources that could contribute to the review. However, to ensure that the selected literature was meeting the inclusion criteria, the following set of predetermined filters was set in the search masks of the databases to narrow down the scope of the literature: date range between 2013 and 2023, language English, as well as only peer reviewed journal articles.

For the purpose of narrowing down, the databases were filtered according to ("business") economic reference, if possible. This initial search and filtering procedure, resulted in the exclusion of 15,112 records, leaving 1981 records eligible for the Screening phase.

The screening process entailed a careful examination of the remaining records' titles and abstracts within Rayyan, to determine their relevance to the research question. The automated identification and manual reviewing of those potential duplicates resulted in 186 duplicate records, being excluded. Following this assessment, 1839 records were identified, based on the title and/or the abstract that did not address this thesis research topic or were otherwise unrelated, and thus, were excluded from the review. Being left with 142 reports that warranted a more detailed evaluation to ensure their suitability for inclusion in the synthesis. All 142 reports were successfully retrieved for a comprehensive evaluation, encountering no issues in accessing the full texts of these sources. During this stage, each report was assessed against the predetermined inclusion and exclusion criteria to confirm that they were both relevant to the research question and of appropriate quality. This resulted in 127 reports that did not meet the stringent criteria for inclusion.

The primary reasons for the exclusion of these 127 reports were twofold. First, 111 reports were found to be non-conforming to the subject matter, meaning that they did not directly address the research topic or were peripheral related at best, offering no contribution for the synthesis. Second, 16 articles were excluded on the rationale that the type of the article did not meet the requirements.

Ultimately, after this exhaustive and meticulous screening and selection process, a total of 15 papers was identified as eligible for inclusion in the systematic literature review. These carefully chosen sources provide valuable insights and contributions to a comprehensive understanding of the thesis topic.

The PRISMA flow diagram visualizing the rigor search and selection process is shown in Fig. 1.

The following Table 1 provides a comprehensive overview of all studies that met the eligibility criteria and were therefore included in this review. The table shows for each of the articles, the year of publication, the authors, the title of the publication, the hosting journal, issue, identifier of the article or the corresponding page numbers within the hosting journal, and the specific contribution each article made to this thesis and the underlying research question.

4.1 Risk of Bias Assessment

The Quality of each Article was assessed using a three-level rating system, represented by the following symbols:

- (✔): The criterion is met, indicating low risk of bias or high methodological quality.
- (?): It is unclear whether the criterion is met due to insufficient information, indicating unclear risk of bias or uncertain methodological quality.
- (X): The criterion is not met, indicating a high risk of bias or low methodological quality.

The evaluation of the individual domains was combined into an overall evaluation of the quality per article by determining an average value as seen in Fig. 2.

The risk of bias assessment results predominantly indicates a low risk of bias within the examined articles, reflecting a robust body of research and allowing for a non-discriminatory interpretation of the results. This assessment suggests that most

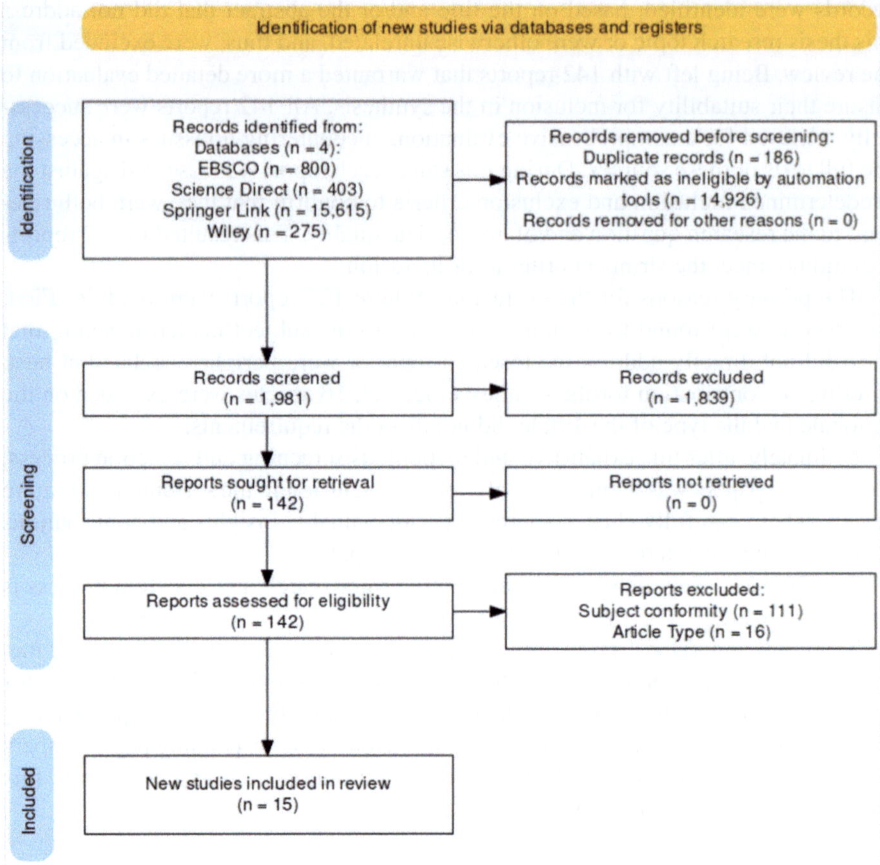

Fig. 1 PRISMA Flow Diagram (own presentation based on Haddaway et al., 2022, p. 5)

authors have employed sound methodologies and analytical techniques, contributing to the reliability of their respective research findings.

4.2 Thematic Synthesis of Applications

For the thematic synthesis of applications of AI for idea generation the scheme proposed by Thomas and Harden (2008, p. 1) was followed. Therefore, individual value concepts taken from the yielded papers were inductively combined to form higher-level themes. The individual codes were consolidated based on thematic correspondence to other codes. The codes extracted from the articles were checked for commonalities with other codes or for multiple mentions, aiming to infer, inductively, a category superordinate to the concepts that satisfies the classification of common

Table 1 Included studies

Year	Author(s)	Title	Journal	Issue	Article	Contribution
2023	Gimpel, H., Graf-Seyfried, V., Laubacher, R. & Meindl, O	Towards Artificial Intelligence Augmenting Facilitation: AI Affordances in Macro-Task Crowdsourcing	Group Decision and Negotiation	Volume 32, Issue 1	pp. 75–124	(Not really a contribution)
2019	Zhao, T., Yang, J., Zhang, H. & Siu, K. W. M	Creative idea generation method based on deep learning technology	International Journal of Technology and Design Education	Volume 31, Issue 2	pp. 421–440	Support human idea generation through AI
2022	Dkhil, A., Dammak, H., Mouatassim, M. & Gardoni, M	A new approach to ideation based on linkography combined with graph theory	International Journal on Interactive Design and Manufacturing	Volume 16, Issue 2	pp. 627–642	AI creativity enhancing techniques
2022	Poser, M. Küstermann, G. C., Tavanapour, N. & Bittner, E. A. C	Design and Evaluation of a Conversational Agent for Facilitating Idea Generation in Organizational Innovation Processes	Information Systems Frontiers	Volume 24, Issue 3	pp. 771–796	AI Conversational Agent to facilitate users idea generation
2021	Johannsen, F., Schaller, D. & Klus, M. F	Value propositions of chatbots to support innovation management process	Information Systems & e-Business Management	Volume 19, Issue 1	pp. 205–246	Chatbots for Idea Generation
2022	Wahl, J., Hutter, K. & Füller, J	How AI-Supported Searches Through Other Perspectives Affect Ideation Outcomes	International Journal of Innovation Management	Volume 26, Issue 9	pp. 1–24/22400 28	AI automated clustering to improve idea generation
2022	Clegg, M., Hofstetter, R. Blohm, I. & Bravin, M	Human–Machine Creativity: How AI Can Influence Human Creativity in Open Innovation	Marketing Review St. Gallen	Volume 6, Issue N/A	pp. 40–47	AI Idea generation facilitation by promoting creativity

(continued)

Table 1 (continued)

Year	Author(s)	Title	Journal	Issue	Article	Contribution
2020	Verganti, R., Vendraminelli, L. & Iansiti, M	Innovation and Design in the Age of Artificial Intelligence	Journal of Product Innovation Management	Volume 37, Issue 3	pp. 212–227	AI for solution development in design process
2021	Garbuio, M. & Lin, N	Innovative idea generation in problem finding: Abductive reasoning, cognitive impediments, and the promise of artificial intelligence	Journal of Product Innovation Management	Volume 38, Issue 6	pp. 701–725	Overcoming cognitive limitations in design thinking through AI
2021	Raisch, S. & Krakowski, S	Artificial Intelligence and Management: The Automation-Augmentation Paradox	Academy of Management Review	Volume 46, Issue 1	pp. 192–210	Augmenting and Automating Idea generation with AI
2023	Bouschery, S. G., Blazevic, V. & Piller, F. T	Augmenting human innovation teams with artificial intelligence: Exploring transformer-based language models	Journal of Product Innovation Management	Volume 40, Issue 2	pp. 139–153	Using language models to generate ideas
2023	Dwivedi, Y. K., Kshetri, N., Hughes, L., Slade, E. L., Jeyaraj, A. & Kar, A. K. et al	"So what if ChatGPT wrote it?" Multidisciplinary perspectives on opportunities, challenges and implications of generative conversational AI for research, practice and policy	International Journal of Information Management	Volume 71, Issue N/A	pp. 1–63/10264 2	Idea generation with ChatGPT
2023	Mariani, M. M., Machado, I. & Nambisan, S	Types of innovation and artificial intelligence: A systematic quantitative literature review and research agenda	Journal of Business Research	Volume 155, Issue B	pp. 1–14/11336 4	AI to help idea generation by reducing cognitive limitations

(continued)

Table 1 (continued)

Year	Author(s)	Title	Journal	Issue	Article	Contribution
2021	Haefner, N., Wincent, J., Parida, V. & Gassmann, O	Artificial Intelligence and innovation management: A review, framework, and research agenda	Technological Forecasting and Social Change	Volume 162, Issue N/A	pp. 1–10/12039 2	AI to overcome barriers in idea generation
2022	Füller, J., Hutter, K., Wahl, J., Bilgram, V. & Tekic, Z	How AI revolutionizes innovation management—Perceptions and implementation preferences of AI-based innovators	Technological Forecasting and Social Change	Volume 178, Issue N/A	pp. 1–22/12159 8	AI to overcome information processing constraints in idea generation

Source Own presentation

	Criteria / Articles	Gimpel et al (2023)	Zhao et al (2021)	Dkhil et al (2022)	Poser et al (2022)	Johannsen et al (2021)	Wahl et al (2022)	Clegg et al (2022)	Verganti et al (2020)	Garbuio & Lin 2021)	Raisch & Krakowski (2021)	Bouscherv et al (2023)	Dwivedi et al (2023)	Mariani et al (2023)	Haefner et al (2021)	Füller et al (2022)
Qualitative Study	Method approriate for research question?			✓	✓											
	Data collection method approriate?			✓	✓											
	Findings adequately derived from data?			✓	✓											
	Interpretation suffenciently substantiated?			✓	✓											
	Coherence between data sources, collection, analysis and interpretation?			✓	✓											
Quantitative Randomized Study	Randomization appropriately performed?															
	Groups comparable at baseline?															
	Complete outcome data?															
	Outcome assessors blinded to intervention provided?															
	Participants adhere to assigned intervention?															
Quantitative Non Randomized Study	Participants representative of target population?						✓									
	Measurements appropriate regarding outcome and intervention?						✓									
	Complete outcome data?						✓									
	Confounders accounted for in design and analysis?						✓									
	Intervention administered as intended?						✓									
Quantitative Descriptive	Sampling Strategy relevant to address research question?															✓
	Sample representative of target population?															✓
	Measurements appropriate?															✓
	Risk of nonresponse bias low?															✓
	Statistical analysis appropriate to answer research question?															✓
Mixed Methods	Adequate rationale for mixed methods design?	✓	✓			✓										
	Components of study effectively integrated to answer research question?	✓	✓			✓										
	Outputs of methods adequately interpreted?	✓	✓			✓										
	Divergences and Inconsistencies in the results adequately addressed?	✓	?			✓										
	Components of study adhere to quality criteria of each method involved?	✓	?			✓										
Review Paper	Appropriateness of methods?										✓			✓	✓	
	Comprehensive literature search?										✓			✓	✓	
	Risk of Bias Assessment?										X			?	X	
	Consideration of RoB in interpretation?										X			✓	X	
Theoretical Paper	Clarity and coherence?							✓	✓	✓		✓	✓			
	Logical reasoning?							✓	✓	✓		✓	✓			
	Use of evidence and literature?							✓	✓	✓		✓	✓			
	Originality and novelty?							✓	✓	✓		✓	✓			
	Quality of writing and organization?							✓	✓	✓		✓	✓			
	Overall Rating	✓	✓	✓	✓	✓	✓	✓	✓	✓	?	✓	✓	✓	?	✓

(✓): Criterion met. Low risk of Bias
(?): Unclear Risk of Bias
(X): Criterion not met. High Risk of Bias

Fig. 2 Quality assessment results (*Source* Own presentation)

codes. This process resulted in the identification of nine common value-describing concepts related to AI's role in idea generation, allowing for consolidation into a three-dimensional application space. In this application space, the concepts related to AI's use for idea generation were integrated into the categories "Informing", "Promoting" and "Generating" Furthermore, these three dimensions can be abstracted into a bilateral concept comprising the two dimensions of "Human Enablement" and "Autonomous Generator". For a comprehensive overview of the value propositions and dimensions, please refer to Table 2.

The first dimension, "Inform," encompasses four value propositions, namely data mining (I1), structuring (I2), data analysis (I3), and pattern recognition (I4). These value propositions underline the diverse ways AI technologies contribute to idea generation. For instance, AI technologies utilizing Natural Language Processing (NLP), such as chatbots, are shown to facilitate information collection and data retrieval from enterprise databases. Similarly, language models like BERT, developed by Google, have proven effective in mining data from social media platforms and identifying solution-oriented content.

Table 2 Uses of AI for idea generation

1st Level Dimension	2nd Level Dimension	Value Proposition		References
Human Enablement	Informing (I)	I1	Data Mining	Johannsen et al., (2021, p. 224, 225), and Wahl et al., (2022, p. 4)
		I2	Structuring	Gimpel et al. (p. 97), Wahl et al., (2022, p. 5, 12), and Johannsen et al., (2021, p. 225)
		I3	Data Analyzation	Bouschery et al., (2023, p. 146), Haefner et al., (2021, pp. 4,5), Wahl et al., (2022, p. 4), and Füller et al., (2022, p. 3)
		I4	Pattern identification	Verganti et al., (2020, p. 222), Füller et al., (2022, p. 3), and Haefner et al., (2021, p. 4)
	Promoting (P)	P1	Bias Mitigation	Clegg et al., (2022, p. 43), Verganti et al., (2020, p. 225), Garbuio and Lin (2021, pp. 712, 715), Mariani et al., (2023, p. 10), Haefner et al., (2021, p. 3), and Füller et al., (2022, p. 3)
		P2	Creativity stimulation	Zhao et al., (2019, p. 437), Dkhil et al., (2022, p. 628), Poser et al., (2022, p. 790), Clegg et al., (2022, p. 43), Dwivedi et al., (2023, p. 14, 27), and Garbuio and Lin (2021, p. 712)
		P3	Process Support	Johannsen et al., (2021, p. 225), Wahl et al., (2022, p. 12), Poser et al., (2022, p. 790), Dkhil et al., (2022, p. 628), and Garbuio and Lin (2021, p. 712)

(continued)

Table 2 (continued)

1st Level Dimension	2nd Level Dimension	Value Proposition		References
Autonomous Generator	Generating (G)	G1	Combination	Dkhil et al., (2022, p. 628), Clegg et al., (2022, p. 43)
		G2	Generation	Garbuio and Lin (2021, p. 713), Clegg et al., (2022, p. 43), Raisch and Krakowski (2021, p. 196), Bouschery et al., (2023, p. 140, 145, 146), Dwivedi et al., (2023, p. 15), and Haefner et al., (2021, pp. 5, 6)

Source Own presentation

The second subcategory within the “**Inform**” dimension, “Structuring (I2)”, involves the use of neural networks to categorize content and identify unique ideas. This capability is recognized for its ability to enhance idea generation by structuring solution-related content and efficiently identifying knowledge streams. Additionally, semantic categorization of idea content by AI is noted to promote the generation of novel ideas.

“Data analytics (I3)”, the third element of the “Inform” dimension, involves AI’s capacity to store, analyze, and encode large amounts of data. This capability facilitates the exploration of solution spaces, fostering divergent thinking in users to support idea generation. It is highlighted as a valuable aspect for innovation management.

AI-based “pattern recognition (I4)” plays a crucial role in identifying regularities and patterns in user behavior, which can lead to content recommendations tailored to user tastes. This benefit is recognized as a valuable utility aspect for generating ideas and supporting innovation.

Moving to the “**Promoting**” dimension, a notable category is “Bias Mitigation”. AI’s ability to mitigate cognitive biases and cognitive fixation on prior ideas is identified as a significant benefit. It is viewed as a means to reduce barriers in idea generation and stimulate user creativity. This aspect is appreciated as a valuable opportunity for AI in promoting creative thinking and problem-solving.

AI’s role in stimulating creativity is another key element in the “Promoting” dimension. Various methods, such as presenting visual stimuli and generating stimulus ideas, are discussed as ways AI can inspire and enhance creative thinking. Conversational agents and language models like ChatGPT are mentioned as valuable sources of inspiration and ideas.

The third category within the “Promoting” dimension is “Process Support (P3)”, which addresses AI’s role in supporting the creative process by providing targeted guidance, communication facilitation, and comprehensive moderation. AI’s ability to guide users toward novel ideas and enhance the efficiency and effectiveness of ideation efforts is highlighted.

Finally, the "**Generating**" dimension encompasses two value propositions: "Combination (G1)" and "Generation (G2)". AI's capacity to combine existing ideas to form novel ones is discussed, emphasizing the potential of AI in enhancing creative thinking through idea synthesis. Additionally, AI is recognized for its ability to independently generate new ideas, speeding up the idea generation process and providing a diverse range of novel ideas.

Already some real-world examples showcase AI's effectiveness in generating ideas, such as automatically generating fragrance formulas, performing various tasks like idea generation, and continuously producing ideas when prompted (Raisch & Krakowski, 2021, p. 196).

Thus, regarding those value propositions, the role of AI in idea generation in its multiplicity is thoroughly explored, encompassing various benefits and applications. These findings highlight the extensive potential of AI in enhancing the creative process and supporting users and innovators in generating valuable and innovative ideas. Nevertheless, the role of the human being cannot be ignored and many of the value prepositions emphasize the use in support of the human being.

4.3 Thematic Synthesis of Limitations

Similar to the synthesis of AI applications for idea generation, a thematic synthesis was employed to identify and analyze limitations to AI in the context of ideation. The articles were scrutinized for evidence of constraints and challenges associated with AI's role in idea generation, which were then distilled into value propositions and subsequently organized into broader dimensions. Among the fifteen articles included in the review, limitations of AI in idea generation were identified in nine publications. These limitations were encapsulated in eleven value propositions within a coding framework, and these value propositions were further categorized into three overarching dimensions. An overview of these value propositions and the higher-level themes is presented in Table 3.

4.3.1 Implementation

The first dimension, "Implementation", comprises value propositions related to the practical challenges of applying AI in innovation management. These include "Application", "Accessibility" and "Technology Readiness."

- Under the "Application" value proposition, it is noted that AI-based innovation management does not lend itself to universal application. Instead, tailored approaches are required to address specific innovation challenges, rejecting the

Table 3 Limitations of AI for idea generation

Dimensions	Value proposition		Reference
Implementation (I)	I1	Application	Füller et al., (2022, p. 2), Clegg et al., (2022, p. 47), Raisch and Krakowski (2021, p. 198), Dwivedi et al., (2023, p. 39), Gimpel et al., (2023, p. 84), and Johannsen et al., (2021, p. 234)
	I2	Accessibility	Johannsen et al., (2021, p. 235)
	I3	Technology Readiness	Haefner et al., (2021, p. 6) and Johannsen et al., (2021, p. 234)
Capabilities ©	C1	Automation	Haefner et al., (2021, p. 8)
	C2	Exploration	Haefner et al., (2021, pp. 5, 6)
	C3	Creativity	Dkhil et al., (2022, p. 628)
	C4	Autonomy	Haefner et al., (2021, p. 6) and Raisch and Krakowski (2022, p. 198)
	C5	Human Interaction	Dwivedi et al., (2023, p. 26) and Gimpel et al., (2023, p. 97)
Quality (Q)	Q1	Reliability	Clegg et al., (2022, p. 43), Raisch and Krakowski (2021, p. 204), Dwivedi et al., (2023, p. 6, 16, 26), and Bouschery et al., (2023, p. 144)
	Q2	Security	Füller et al., (2022, p. 15), Dwivedi et al., (2023, p. 26)
	Q3	Training Data	Füller et al., (2022, p. 16), Bouschery et al., (2023, p. 147), and Dwivedi et al., (2023, p. 26)

Source Own presentation

one-size-fits-all approach. This highlights the need for adaptive and flexible AI systems that can cater to unique contexts and requirements"

- "Accessibility" is another dimension where challenges are evident. Unstable internet connections are identified as a hindrance to the accessibility of AI, emphasizing the dependency on robust and stable infrastructure. This limitation brings attention to the digital divide, which could restrict the reach and effectiveness of AI in innovation management.

- The "Technology Readiness" value proposition points out that the technological capabilities of AI systems remain relatively limited, with few systems meeting the desired level of readiness. The gap between the theoretical potential of AI and its practical usability in real-world scenarios is underscored. The maturity of natural language processing mechanisms is also deemed insufficient for human-like conversations with chatbots, highlighting the preference for human communication partners.

4.3.2 Capabilities

Moving to the second dimension, "Capabilities", various value propositions shed light on AI's limitations in performing specific functions or achieving desired outcomes. These include "Automation", "Exploration", "Creativity", "Autonomy" and "Human Interaction."

- Concerning "Automation", AI solutions aim to automate workflows, but it is recognized that an entire set of tasks cannot always be fully automated. This implies the need for human involvement and oversight in processes that are too complex or nuanced for AI to handle independently.
- In the domain of "Exploration", AI systems are noted to have limited ability to explore problem spaces, a crucial function often required in innovation management. The inability of AI to explore uncharted territories and acquire new knowledge presents a limitation in innovation contexts.
- The "Creativity" value proposition highlights that AI struggles to emulate human creativity, a central aspect of innovation management. Given the importance of creativity in innovation, this limitation is of particular significance.
- "Autonomy" refers to AI systems' capacity to operate independently. These systems often struggle to navigate solution spaces independently, lacking self-awareness and purposefulness. As a result, human involvement in specifying goals remains essential in innovation management.
- Under the "Human Interaction" value proposition, issues may arise in human–computer interaction. AI, such as ChatGPT, may struggle to understand certain nuances or contexts, and ethical and cultural factors may be challenging to grasp. These limitations point to potential shortcomings in AI's ability to fully mimic human interactions.

4.3.3 Quality

The third and final dimension, "Quality", includes value propositions like "Reliability", "Data Security" and "Training Data."

- The "Reliability" value proposition raises concerns about the trustworthiness of AI systems and the quality of their results. It is noted that the quality and context of AI-generated ideas should be rigorously tested, as AI can introduce statistical biases and limitations. Understanding the results of AI, particularly those generated by pattern-based methods, can be challenging, emphasizing the need for human validation“

- “Data Security” is another critical dimension, where issues related to privacy, security, and potential misuse of data are highlighted. These concerns underscore the importance of addressing data security when using AI systems in innovation management.
- The “Training Data” value proposition underscores the significance of the data used to train AI systems. Insufficient labeled training data and data quality issues can hinder AI’s effectiveness. Bias in training data can potentially harm language models. High-quality, representative datasets are deemed essential for optimal AI performance.

Summing up the findings reveal a wide range of potential challenges that need to be considered for the effective use of AI for idea generation. These limitations include practical implementation issues, capability constraints and concerns about the quality and reliability of AI systems. Addressing these limitations is essential if the full potential of AI in innovation management is to be realized.

5 Conclusion

This research delved into the role of Artificial Intelligence (AI) for generating ideas, a pivotal aspect of the innovating process. By conducting a systematic literature review of 15 selected articles, it becomes evident that AI holds immense potential to support idea generation, offering numerous applications but also acknowledging certain limitations.

The review highlights the capabilities of AI systems not only to generate ideas independently but even more to assist in enabling human capabilities by fostering creativity, processual support, and data processing. However, the research uncovers also substantial challenges linked to AI implementation in idea generation. Issues concerning data quality, biases, and the opacity of AI systems may act as potential barriers to successful integration. Therefore, the aim should be to offer transparency regarding AI’s current landscape, enabling informed decision-making and mitigating potential disadvantages.

The reviewed articles underscore the significant potential for AI to generate autonomously and through combination but even more to enhance human innovators in the ideation process by various applications. This synergy between human abilities and artificial intelligence can form an even more valuable instance that can be referred to as a “hybrid intelligence”. Since AI is capable to complement human capabilities rather than replacing them. And still, if AI independently generates ideas, the importance of human validation is emphasized nevertheless, as suggested by Dwivedi et al. (2023).

Thus, this research shows that AI, with its multiple capabilities, can support ideation in many ways by forming a symbiotic entity with human users to transform the ideation process in innovation management and unlock new potential. However, consideration of the limitations and the correct and thoughtful use of AI are essential for success.

Given the dynamic nature of AI development, this research serves as a snapshot of the evolving landscape. It points towards numerous opportunities for further research on AI's role in the innovation process and the interaction between AI and human innovators.

References

Bouschery, S. G., Blazevic, V., & Piller, F. T. (2023). Augmenting human innovation teams with artificial intelligence: Exploring transformer based language models. *Journal of Product Innovation Management, 40*(2), 129–153.

Clegg, M., Hofstetter, R., Blohm, I., & Bravin, M. (2022). Human-machine creativity: How AI can influence human creativity in open innovation. *Marketing Review St. Gallen, 6*, 40–47.

Dkhil, A., Dammak, H., Mouatassim, M., & Gardoni, M. (2022). A new approach to ideation based on linkography combined with graph theory. *International Journal on Interactive Design and Manufacturing, 16*(2), 627–642.

Du Preez, N., & Louw, L. (2008). A framework for managing the innovating process. In *PICMET '08—2008 Portland International Conference on Management of Engineering & Technology* (pp. 546–558).

Dwivedi, Y. K., Kshetri, N., Hughes, L., Slade, E. L., Jeyaraj, A., Kar, A. K., et al. (2023). So what if ChatGPT wrote it?" Multidisciplinary perspectives on opportunities, challenges and implications of generative conversational AI for research, practice and policy. *International Journal of Information Management, 71*, 102642.

Füller, J., Hutter, K., Wahl, J., Bilgram, V., & Tekic, Z. (2022). How AI revolutionizes innovation management—Perceptions and implementation preferences of AI-based innovators. *Technological Forecasting and Social Change, 178*, 121598.

Garbuio, M., & Lin, N. (2021). Innovative idea generation in problem finding: Abductive reasoning, cognitive im-pediments, and the promise of artificial intelligence. *Journal of Product Innovation Management, 38*(6), 701–725.

Gimpel, H., Graf-Seyfried, V., Laubacher, R., & Meindl, O. (2023). Towards artificial intelligence augmenting facilitation: AI affordances in macro-task crowdsourcing. *Group Decision and Negotiation, 32*(1), 75–124.

Haddaway, N. R., Page, M. J., Pritchard, C. C., & McGuinness, L. A. (2022). PRISMA2020: An R package and Shiny app for producing PRISMA 2020-compliant flow diagrams, with interactivity for optimised digital transparency and Open Synthesis. *Campbell Systematic Reviews, 18*, e1230. https://doi.org/10.1002/cl2.1230

Haefner, N., Wincent, J., Parida, V., & Gassmann, O. (2021). Artificial intelligence and innovation management: A review, framework, and research agenda. *Technological Forecasting and Social Change, 162*, 120392.

Hong, Q. N., Pluye, P., Fabregues, S., Bartlett, G., Boardman, F., Cargo, M., et al. (2018). *Mixed methods appraisal tool (MMAT)*. McGill University.

Johannsen, F., Schaller, D., & Klus, M. F. (2021). Propositions of chatbots to support innovation management process. *Information Systems & e-Business Management, 19*(1), 205–246.

Margherita, A., Elia, G., & Petti, C. (2022). What is quality in research? Building a framework of design, process and impact attributes and evaluation perspectives. *MDPI, 14*(5), 3034.

Mariani, M. M., Machado, I., & Nambisan, S. (2023). Types of innovation and artificial intelligence: A systematic quantitative literature review and research agenda. *Journal of Business Research, 155*(B), 113364.

Mhlanga, D. (2023). The value of Open AI and Chat GPT for the current learning environments and the potential future uses. *SSRN, 09*(05), 2023.

MIT-IBM Watson AI Lab. (n.d.). Research. Retrieved May 11, 2023, from https://mitibmwatsonailab.mit.edu/research

Page, M. J., Moher, D., Bossuyt, P. M., Boutron, I., Hoffman, T. C., Mulrow, C. D. et al. (2021). PRISMA 2020 explanation and elaboration: updated guidance and exemplars for reporting systematic review. *The British Medical Journal, 372*(160).

Poser, M., Küstermann, G. C., Tavanapour, N., & Bittner, E. A. C. (2022). Design and evaluation of a conversational agent for facilitating idea generation in organizational innovation processes. *Information Systems Frontiers, 24*(3), 771–796.

PwC. (2022). PwC 2022 AI business survey. Retrieved July 10, 2023, from https://www.pwc.com/us/en/tech-effect/ai-analytics/ai-business-survey.html

Raisch, S., & Krakowski, S. (2021). Artificial intelligence and management: The automation-augmentation paradox. *Academy of Management Review, 46*(1), 192–210.

Shea, B. J., Reeves, B. C., Wells, G., Thuku, M., Hamel, C., Moran, J., et al. (2017). AMSTAR 2: A critical appraisal tool for systematic reviews that include randomized or non-randomised studies of healthcare interventions, or both. *The British Medical Journal, 358*, j4008.

Templier, M., & Paré, G. (2018). A framework for guiding and evaluating literature reviews. *Communications of the Association for Information Systems, 37*(6), 113–137.

Thomas, J., & Harden, A. (2008). Methods for the thematic synthesis of qualitative research in the systematic reviews. *BMC Medical Research Methodology, 8*, 45.

Verganti, R., Vendraminelli, L., & Iansiti, M. (2020). Innovation and design in the age of artificial intelligence. *Journal of Product Innovation Management, 37*(3), 221–227.

Wahl, J., Hutter, K., & Füller, J. (2022). How AI-supported searches through other perspectives affect ideation outcomes. *International Journal of Innovation Management, 26*(9), 2240028.

Zhao, T., Yang, J., Zhang, H., & Siu, K. W. M. (2019). Creative idea generation method based on deep learning technology. *International Journal of Technology and Design Education, 31*(2), 421–440.

A Reference Model for Organizing Responsibilities in the Smart Factory

Manuel Etzkorn, Christian Tuschner, Felix Krauss, and Harald von Korflesch

Abstract Digitalization is conquering the factory floor and causing two different types of technology to interlock: existing operating technology (OT) is being joined by an ever-growing amount of information technology (IT). This creates new assets and services whose organizational management can no longer be adequately handled by applying analogue production theory. Therefore, there is a need for a framework that supports companies in shaping their organization according to the requirements of the (digitalized) smart factory. In order to close this research gap, this paper develops a framework in the form of an organizational reference model for the management of assets and services in the smart factory. For this purpose, the inductive reference modeling method according to Fettke (2014) is applied. The developed reference model shows a matrix of services, to which the responsible functions of the company are assigned. Key insights of the reference model are the central role for IT in the smart factory, while services relating to the production process are still run by OT functions. From the reference model can be derived, that it is not the classic IT function that reaches into the OT area but that there are new functions for digital operational technologies that overlap into the classic IT domain. As practical implication, this paper provides suggestions to organize responsibilities for smart factories. The created reference model can help companies to create their own organizational model or it can serve as a template for revising their own organization. For further research, this paper structures assets, services and functions in the context of the smart factory in a summarized presentation.

M. Etzkorn (✉) · C. Tuschner · F. Krauss · H. von Korflesch
University of Koblenz, Koblenz, Germany
e-mail: etzkorn@uni-koblenz.de

C. Tuschner
e-mail: ctuschner@uni-koblenz.de

F. Krauss
e-mail: fkrauss@uni-koblenz.de

H. von Korflesch
e-mail: harald.vonkorflesch@uni-koblenz.de

R. C. Geibel and S. Machavariani (eds.), *Digital Management to Shape the Future*,
Springer Proceedings in Business and Economics,
https://doi.org/10.1007/978-3-031-66517-2_15

Keywords Smart factory · Industry 4.0 · Reference modeling · Responsibilities

1 Introduction

The era of the fourth industrial revolution, commonly referred to as **Industry 4.0** (I4.0), represents a transformative phase in manufacturing, characterized by the combination of advanced technologies like artificial intelligence, the Internet of Things (IoT), Big Data, and Cloud Computing (Miloradov et al., 2022; Okeme et al., 2021). I4.0 aspires to establish a heightened level of efficiency and intelligence in manufacturing via the introduction of new technological possibilities for automation on cyber-physical systems (CPS) and especially on cyber-physical production systems (CPPS) (Shilenge & Telukdarie, 2022; Zhou et al., 2015). This shift represents a widespread infiltration of Information Technology (IT) into conventional manufacturing settings, profoundly reshaping the traditional factory environment (Miloradov et al., 2022; Okeme et al., 2021). Central to this transformation is the emergence of the "Smart Factory", a main aspect of I4.0, wherein equipment and machinery are interconnected through software, facilitating intelligent communication and autonomous processes (Cagliano et al., 2019; Okeme et al.,2021).

A notable characteristic of this evolution is the resulting **concurrent existence of Information Technology (IT) and Operational Technology (OT)** in the Smart Factory (Lautenschlaeger et al., 2021). While OT traditionally managed physical and analog operational technology, digitalization has integrated IT technologies and IT assets into the production environment (Adesemowo et al., 2016; The & Kuusk, 2021). This raises the question of whether the traditional IT function should still oversee IT assets and services that reach into the OT setting. Simultaneously, the role that traditional OT functions should play in the Smart Factory remains ambiguous, given their lack of technical expertise in managing IT assets and services (Seo & Evans, 2021). As the barriers between IT and OT functions hinder effective and efficient collaboration, the conventional organizational model of factories needs reconsideration concerning the management of IT and OT. This leads to the question about how responsibilities in the form of functions for assets and services in the Smart Factory need to be conceptualized (Ehie & Chilton, 2020; García de Soto et al., 2022).

As delineated by Adolphs et al. (2016) and Amadi-Echendu et al. (2021), an **asset** is a tangible or intangible entity bearing significance to an organization. Tao and Qi (2017) proffer an exhaustive taxonomy, cataloging assets into two principal classes: Manufacturing Resources & Capabilities and Manufacturing Big Data. The antecedent includes tangible and intangible resources tied to the production conduit, inclusive of: Material, Equipment, Robots, Products, MES (Manufacturing Execution System), ERP (Enterprise Resource Planning), CRM (Customer Relationship Management), and CAD (Computer-aided Design). The latter, Manufacturing Big Data, refers to data inputs and outputs from different phases of the production path: Production Data, Equipment Data, Users Data, Products Data, MRO Data (Maintenance, Repair, and Operations), and Supply Chain Data.

Beyond assets, **services** also occupy an essential niche in production (Adolphs et al., 2016; Tao & Qi, 2017). The expansion of IT in the manufacturing realm has underscored the prominence of services (Bauer et al., 2017; Schuh et al., 2019; Tao & Qi, 2017). Adolphs et al. (2016) and Usländer and Epple (2015) understand services as autonomous functionalities offered by an entity or facility that provide access to certain capabilities through predefined interfaces, always following to set constraints and policies. Tao and Qi (2017) highlight a direct connection between factory assets and their related services. They segregate these services into assorted categories, notably: Production, Product, Business Process, and Information services (Tao & Qi, 2017). Nested within these categories, they designate specific services, such as "Design Services" under the "Production" service category. Other services within Production include Simulation, Resources, Machining, Maintenance (of production assets), and Testing. The "Product" service category comprises the distinct services of Experience and Maintenance (of products). The "Business Process" category envelops specific services like Security Operations and Financial, while the logistics service is allocated in between the "Product" category and the "Business Process" category. The "Information" services category is divided into specific services such as Data, Model, Algorithm, and Knowledge. This categorization gives insights for the comprehension of services executable within a smart factory.

Recognizing the aforementioned complexities and driven by the necessity to offer actionable insights, this research endeavors to answer the following research question: **How can an effective and efficient allocation of responsibilities, also referred to as functions, for assets and services in the Smart Factory be achieved?**

This research question is investigated using the method of inductive reference modeling (see Chapter 2). The existing model understanding of I4.0 is foremost general and standards-driven, which can be seen in widespread models such as the "Reference Architecture Model Industrie 4.0" (RAMI4.0; DIN SPEC 91345:2016-04) or the ANSI/ISA-95 (The & Kuusk, 2021). Both models are more technically oriented and consist of several layers. The layers concerning the assets are each far distant from the layers concerning the services and functions, which means that the interrelationships between these aspects are not sufficiently apparent. With inductive reference modeling, an innovative bottom-up approach, we build a bridge between these layers and add specific insights on the organizational view.

The results of this research work are of importance for both research and practice. They contribute to a better understanding of the impact of digitalization on organizational structures and responsibilities in industry, especially in the smart factory, and provide practical guidelines for companies to efficiently adapt their operations to the requirements of the digital transformation. Thus, this work makes a valuable contribution to current research and to addressing the challenges associated with the integration of IT and OT in the smart factory.

In the following Chapter 2, the methodology of this paper based on inductive reference modeling (Fettke, 2014) is explained in detail. Chapter 3 presents and discusses the results. Chapter 4 summarizes the main findings of this thesis, discusses limitations, and highlights implications for further research.

2 Methodology

This paper applies the method of **reference modeling**, which addresses the creation of reference models. Reference models are generalized models that can be used in specific application domains (in this case: the smart factory) in two different ways. First, reference models can be used to help develop individual models. Reference models contain generalizable elements of the application domain under consideration. By reusing these elements, individual models of organizational structures (which applies to this paper) or processes in the respective application domain can be created with less effort. Second, they are a tool for analyzing and improving existing individual models. The reference model serves as a comparative model that condenses best-practice examples of organizational structures or processes in its elements, and thus serves as a template. Since organizational structures and processes presented in reference models do not have to be developed from scratch, reference models can save time and thus costs (Becker & Meise, 2005, p. 127; Schütte, 1998).

In order to build a new organizational model we used a five step approach (see Fig. 1) based on the method of inductive reference modeling according to Fettke (2014), which offers guidelines for the development of reusable reference models. Compared to other reference modeling approaches, the distinctive feature in Fettke's approach is that the essential data collection is based on individual company models, which we also relied on for this paper. This allows the perspective of practice to be taken into account not only in terms of content but also regarding how companies create and understand models. Furthermore, the taxonomy by Tao and Qi (2017) was used to provide an initial structure.

As first action for **step 1 (Initiation)**, an initial review of sources was conducted. Three aspects derived from the research question were relevant for the model: assets, services and functions. For the assets and services, data sources from research were available, specifically from the work of Tao and Qi (2017). The functions and their

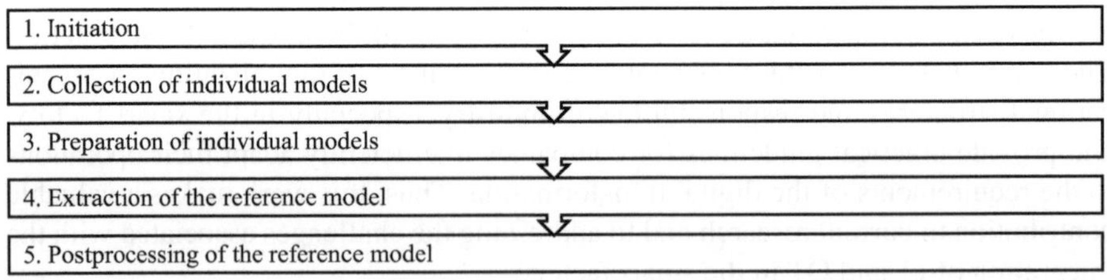

Fig. 1 Research design of this study based on inductive reference modeling according to Fettke (2014)

assignment to assets and services were going to be derived from the used individual models. Furthermore, step 1 demands the definition of requirements to develop a practical solution for which we defined five requirements in three different priorities (from "A" (high) to "C" (low)):

1. The model is intended to provide an overview of the relevant assets of the Smart Factory (priority 'A').
2. The model is intended to provide an overview of the relevant services of the Smart Factory (priority 'A').
3. Functions must be clearly assigned to each asset and service (priority 'A').
4. All functions involved in the processes and value creation in digitalized production must be mapped (priority 'B').
5. The categorization of assets and services should be expanded or modified if required in the modeling process (priority 'C').

Additionally, step 1 demands to specify modeling conventions. Since there are three relevant aspects (assets, services, and functions) that are interconnected, a matrix with two axes (assets, services) to be filled with the assigned functions was chosen as the basic convention for the model (see Fig. 2).

Step 2 (collection of individual models) requires a class definition of the companies under consideration, which are manufacturing companies in discrete (producing distinct items) and process manufacturing (producing material in volumes or weights). In addition, specific companies must be selected under consideration of their relevance, the researchers' access to these companies, and the feasible effort to collect or build up individual models. Five suitable companies were selected as part of this study (see Table 1). To establish the necessary relevance, two international process manufacturing companies, two international discrete manufacturing companies and one small/medium company was chosen. Because of strict secrecy guidelines gaining access was challenging, so that only companies with which the researchers have professional or private contacts could be included. Taking into account that the individual models were expected to have a high scope and high representativity, five individual models were seen as sufficient for this study.

The goal of **step 3 (preparation of individual models)** is to create homogeneous individual models and model synsets (synonym lists). To create homogeneous individual models, the individual models are anonymized and transferred to the matrix described in step 1. To achieve homogeneity of the individual models, model synsets

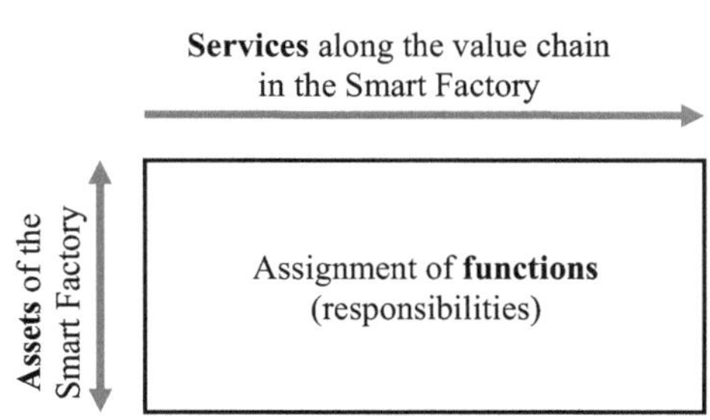

Fig. 2 Grand scheme of the matrix

Table 1 The selected companies for the reference modeling process

#	Type	Sector	No. of employees	Turnover
C1	Process manufacturing	Building Material	40.000	12.5 bn. €
C2	Process manufacturing	Chemicals	33.000	15.5 bn. €
C3	Discrete manufacturing	Automation Technology	31.000	6.2 bn. €
C4	Discrete manufacturing	Automotive	673.000	250.0 bn. €
C5	Discrete manufacturing	Automotive	900	200.0 bn. €

for the functions to be assigned to assets and services were created. For example, all functions of the companies dealing with maintenance, repair and servicing of machinery and equipment are grouped under the umbrella term "Maintenance & Field Service". For **step 4 (extraction of the reference model)**, similar parts of the different individual models have to be grouped into clusters. These clusters already result from the transfer of the individual models into the matrix, so that no additional action is necessary here. Every assigned function to the same asset and service is seen as one occurrence of a specific cluster. Then the number of all clusters were counted. Furthermore, threshold values must be defined to decide which content is to be included in the reference model. The abstraction value α was set to 0.4 which resulted to the inclusion of clusters, if they were found in at least two of the five individual models. Single occurrences of clusters were not included. The configuration value β was set to zero so that all five models were considered. Step 4 resulted in a raw reference model in the used matrix format. **Step 5 (postprocessing of the reference model)** involves the meaningful connection of model parts, the addition of deductively developed partial models and manual additions. Because the usage of the chosen matrix format already resulted in a readable and well-connected reference model in step 4, there were no further actions taken in step 5.

3 Results and Discussion

This chapter presents the findings of the study. First, the functions identified in the individual models are shown. Second, the assigned functions to the services and production assets of the smart factory are presented in the reference model in matrix format. Last, the results are discussed in the context of the research question and existing scientific literature.

The following list of functions with short explanations could be identified in the considered individual models:

- **Corporate Business**: Various areas of responsibility such as strategic planning, business development, finance, controlling, and investor relations.
- **Corporate IT**: Provision, implementation, and maintenance of IT infrastructure, applications, and IT services.

- **Data & Analytics**: Responsible for data collection, management, analysis, and interpretation.
- **Digitalization**: Digitalization of business processes and models.
- **Finance/Administration**: Financial activities, including accounting, taxes, financial planning, budgeting, and reporting; administrative tasks such as human resources, facility management, and general administrative duties.
- **Infrastructure**: Management, maintenance, and support of infrastructure components in the production environment, including IT systems, as well as physical infrastructure like buildings, power supply, and production facilities.
- **Logistics**: Procurement, production, distribution, and disposal logistics.
- **Maintenance & Field Service**: Maintenance and servicing of machinery, equipment, and other technical devices.
- **Marketing, Sales & Services**: Planning, implementation, and control of marketing, sales, and customer service strategies.
- **OT/Cyber Security**: Security and protection of operational technologies (OT) and associated systems, processes, and data from cyberattacks and other threats.
- **(Smart) Operations**: Utilizing intelligent technologies and automation to increase efficiency and productivity in operational processes.
- **Plants & Engineering**: Planning, development, implementation, and optimization of manufacturing and production facilities.
- **Strategy**: Definition and review of the company's strategy, development of business ideas and models, market and competition analysis, risk management.
- **Supply Chain Management**: Coordination and optimization of all activities along the supply chain.

The listed functions group departments or other organizational units of the companies under consideration, as explained in step 3 of the methodology (see Chapter 2). The functions "logistics", "infrastructure", and "digitalization" were detected in the modeling process but were not included in the reference model, because there was no double or greater occurrence of clusters containing these functions.

The final reference model (matrix of responsibilities for assets and services in the smart factory) is vertically split into two parts (see Tables 2 and 3) along the services. In relation to Requirement 5 (see step 1 of the methodology), the following subcategories were formed in the area of assets. The assets inside the category of "Manufacturing Resources and Capabilities" were split into two subcategories: Tangible Assets (including Material, Equipment, Robots, and Products) and Enterprise Software Systems (including MES, ERP, CRM, and CAD). In the category of "Manufacturing Big Data ", the subcategory "Production Data" (including Production Data, Equipment Data, and MRO Data) was established. The reason for this is that some of the individual models considered were not as detailed as the initial structure in terms of assets, or there were no differences in the responsibilities for the now grouped single assets. In the case of the services, no adjustment to the categorization was necessary and the division according to Tao and Qi (2017) could be retained.

The following paragraphs describe the results of the reference model in the order of the columns (services or service categories). For the service category "**Production**

Table 2 Reference model (matrix of responsibilities for assets and services in the smart factory), part 1/2

			Smart Factory Services				
		Service Category	Production Process	Product		Business Process	
Asset Category	Asset Sub-Category	Service	Design, Simulation, Resources, Machining, Maintenance, Testing	Experience, Maintenance	Logistics	Security Operations	Financial
Production Assets	Manufacturing Resources and Capabilites	Tangible Assets (Material, Equipment, Robots, Products)	Plants & Engineering; Maintenance & Field Service	Marketing, Sales & Services	Supply Chain Mgmt.	(Smart) Operations; OT/Cyber Security	Corporate Business; Finance / Administration
Production Assets	Manufacturing Resources and Capabilites	Enterprise Software Systems (MES, ERP, CRM, CAD)	-	-	-	Strategy; Corporate IT	Corporate Business; Finance / Administration
Production Assets	Manufacturing Big Data	Supply Chain Data	-	-	-	OT/Cyber Security	Corporate Business; Finance / Administration
Production Assets	Manufacturing Big Data	Production Data (Data of Production, Equipment, MRO)	-	-	-	OT/Cyber Security	Corporate Business; Finance / Administration
Production Assets	Manufacturing Big Data	Products Data	-	Marketing, Sales & Services	-	OT/Cyber Security; Corporate IT	Corporate Business; Finance / Administration
Production Assets	Manufacturing Big Data	Users Data	-	-	-	Corporate IT	Corporate Business; Finance / Administration

Process” in combination with the asset subcategory “Tangible Assets” the functions “Plants & Engineering” and “Maintenance & Field Service” could be assigned (see Table 2). Further allocations were not possible. In the case of the “**Product**” service category in combination with both the asset subcategory “Tangible Assets” and the asset “Products Data” the function “Marketing, Sales & Services” was mapped. In the connection of the “**Logistics**” service to “Tangible Assets” the function “Supply Chain Management” could be added. For the column of the service “**Security Operations**” all fields of the table could be filled. For “Tangible Assets” the functions “(Smart) Operations” and “OT/Cyber Security” were assigned. The related functions to “Enterprise Software Systems” are “Strategy” and “Corporate IT”. To the following asset “Supply Chain Data” and the asset subcategory “Production Data”, the function “OT/Cyber Security” was allocated. The “OT/Cyber Security” and “Corporate IT” functions have been assigned to “Products Data”, while the “Corporate

Table 3 Reference model (matrix of responsibilities for assets and services in the smart factory), part 2/2

Asset Category	Asset Category	Asset Subcategory / Service Category / Service	Smart Factory Services			
		Service Category	Information			
		Service	Data	Model	Algorithm	Knowledge
Production Assets	Manufacturing Resources and Capabilities	Tangible Assets (Material, Equipment, Robots, Products)	-	-	-	-
		Enterprise Software Systems (MES, ERP, CRM, CAD)	Corporate IT; (Smart) Operations	(Smart) Operations	(Smart) Operations	(Smart) Operations
	Manufacturing Big Data	Supply Chain Data	Corporate IT; (Smart) Operations	Corporate IT; (Smart) Operations	Corporate IT; (Smart) Operations	Corporate IT; (Smart) Operations
		Production Data (Data of Production, Equipment, MRO)	Corporate IT; (Smart) Operations	Corporate IT; (Smart) Operations	Corporate IT; (Smart) Operations	(Smart) Operations
		Products Data	Corporate IT; Data & Analytics	Corporate IT; Data & Analytics	Corporate IT; Data & Analytics	Corporate IT; (Smart) Operations
		Users Data	Corporate IT	Corporate IT; Data & Analytics	Corporate IT; Data & Analytics	Corporate IT; (Smart) Operations

IT" function was mapped to "Users Data". To all combinations regarding the service "**Financial**", the functions "Corporate Business" and "Finance / Administration" were assigned.

For the service category "**Information**" all fields except the row of "Tangible Assets" could be filled (see table 3). In case of the combinations of the service "**Data**" with "Enterprise Software Systems", "Supply Chain Data", and "Production Data" the functions "Corporate IT " and "(Smart) Operations " were assigned. The "Corporate IT" and "Data & Analytics" functions have been assigned to "Products Data", while the "Corporate IT" function was mapped to "Users Data". To the following "**Model**" **and** "**Algorithm**" services, the function "(Smart) Operations " was allocated to the assets (or asset categories) of "Enterprise Software Systems", "Supply Chain Data", and "Production Data". Additionally, the function "Corporate IT" was mapped to "Supply Chain Data", and "Production Data". The responsible functions for the combinations with the assets "Products Data" and "Users Data" are "Corporate IT" and "Data & Analytics". The assignments to the service "**Knowledge**" are the same as to "Model" and "Algorithm", except that in the assignment to the asset subcategory "Production Date" the function "Corporate IT" is omitted.

The following paragraphs discuss the results of the reference model in the order of the columns (service categories). In the column of the "**Production Process**" only one assignment could be made. This is because the individual models showed a narrow understanding of the production process, which is primarily concerned with tangible assets and operational technology. Thus, "Plants & Engineering" and "Maintenance & Field Service", are assigned. In the "**Product**" service category, it seems logical that the "Marketing, Sales & Services" function has been assigned. This function serves as a contact for customers and obtains its data from production and product data. For the "**Logistics**" service, the function "supply chain management" is responsible for factors of production in the production process, which physically takes place in the form of or with the help of tangible assets. An assignment in connection with the asset "Supply Chain Data" seemed obvious, but could not be confirmed by the individual models. In the area of "**Security Operations**", it is initially apparent that OT-related functions ("(Smart) Operations" and "OT/Cyber Security") are assigned to the tangible assets. To enterprise software systems, the reference model shows an allocation of the more administrative and IT-related functions "Strategy" and "Corporate IT". For the asset category "Manufacturing Big Data ", both IT and OT functions are assigned across the services. The security of supply chain, production, equipment, and MRO Data is associated with the OT ("OT/Cyber Security"). The responsibility for the security of products data can be in the area of OT as well as of the Corporate IT, while the security of users data is a responsibility to the Corporate IT. For the "**Financial**" service, there were no insights found apart from the obvious assignment of the content related functions "Corporate Business" and "Finance / Administration" to all assets. For the service category of "**Information**", there were no assignments regarding the tangible assets. Possible interpretations are that the information relating to tangible assets is also provided within the asset category of "Manufacturing Big Data" or that the information services are seen as support services with no direct connection to the tangible assets as core of the production. Underlining the argument of information services as support services, all the assignments with regard to information services contain the functions which can be located in IT and administration ("Corporate IT," "(Smart) Operations," and "Data & Analytics") and no functions of operational technology.

In the overall impression, it can be stated that IT is playing a central role in the organization of the smart factory, while services relating to the production process are still run by OT functions. The occurrence of the function "OT/Cyber Security" and its role in the "Security Operations" service is remarkable. It can be derived, that the topic of cyber security might no longer be subordinate to classic IT and that it is not the classic IT, that reaches into the OT area, but that there are new functions for digital operational technologies that overlap into the classic IT domain.

Compared to the layer models mentioned in Chapter 1, a new perspective has been developed. In the exemplary case of RAMI4.0, a direct reference between the Asset Layer and Functional Layer would not be permissible. The intermediary layers (Integration, Communication, and Information) have to be modeled alongside according the RAMI4.0 conventions (Adolphs et al., 2016). In the reference model of this paper, the intermediary layers are abstracted (Integration, Communication) or integrated as services (Information). This results in technical-level duplications (e.g., information originating from or needed for the production process being part in "Production Process" and "Information" service categories), but it provides a comprehensive perspective from an organizational standpoint.

4 Conclusion

In summary, we used the method of inductive reference modeling (Fettke, 2014) to build a reference model, which shows a potential organization of responsibilities for assets and services in the smart factory and thereby answers this paper's research question ("How can an effective and efficient allocation of responsibilities, also referred to as functions, for assets and services in the Smart Factory be achieved?"). The contents of the reference model are derived from the individual organizational models of five companies and the framework for "*New IT driven service-oriented smart manufacturing*" according to Tao and Qi (2017).

The main findings of this study are the representation of the relationship between assets, services and functions, a list of functions, and the assignment of functions to assets and services in the smart factory. From the reference model can be derived, that it is not the classic IT function that reaches into the OT area but that there are new functions for digital operational technologies that overlap into the classic IT domain. Additionally, we showed how the promising method of inductive reference modeling can be used in the context of the smart factory.

As practical implication, this paper provides suggestions to organize responsibilities for smart factories. The created reference model can help companies to create their own organizational models for responsibilities in the smart factory or it can serve as a template for revising their own organization. For further research, this paper structures assets, services and functions in the context of the smart factory in a summarized presentation.

A limitation of this study is the number of individual models used. Even if the considered company models have a certain relevance, it should be examined whether the evaluation of a larger number of individual models would lead to different results. In addition, it might be useful to further examine the results through an interview study. On the one hand, this would enable an evaluation of the reference model and, on the other hand, help to better understand and interpret the results.

References

Adesemowo, A. K., von Solms, R., & Botha, R. A. (2016). ITAOFIR: IT asset ontology for information risk in knowledge economy and beyond. In *Global security, safety and sustainability—the security challenges of the connected world: 11th international conference, ICGS3 2017, London, UK, January 18–20, 2017, Proceedings 11* (pp. 173–187). Springer International Publishing.

Adolphs, P., Berlik, S., Dorst, W., Friedrich, J., Gericke, C., Hankel, M., & Matzler, S. (2016). Reference architecture model Industrie 4.0 DIN SPEC 91345: 2016-04. DIN, Technical Report.

Amadi-Echendu, J., Ramlal, R., & Englebrecht, F. (2021). Servitization and the Management of Engineered Assets. In *14th WCEAM Proceedings*. Springer International Publishing.

Bauer, D., Stock, D., & Bauernhansl, T. (2017). Movement towards service-orientation and app-orientation in manufacturing IT. *Procedia CIRP, 62*, 199–204.

Becker, J., & Meise, V. (2005). *Strategie und Ordnungsrahmen* (pp. 105–154). Springer.

Cagliano, R., Canterino, F., Longoni, A., & Bartezzaghi, E. (2019). The interplay between smart manufacturing technologies and work organization: The role of technological complexity. *International Journal of Operations & Production Management, 39*(6/7/8), 913–934.

Ehie, I. C., & Chilton, M. A. (2020). Understanding the influence of IT/OT convergence on the adoption of Internet of Things (IoT) in manufacturing organizations: An empirical investigation. *Computers in Industry, 115*, 103166.

Fettke, P. (2014). Eine Methode zur induktiven Entwicklung von Referenzmodellen. In *Multikonferenz Wirtschaftsinformatik* (pp. 1034–1047).

García de Soto, B., Agustí-Juan, I., Joss, S., & Hunhevicz, J. (2022). Implications of Construction 4.0 to the workforce and organizational structures. *International Journal of Construction Management, 22*(2), 205–217.

Lautenschlaeger, W., Frick, F., Christodoulopoulos, K., & Henke, T. (2021). A scalable factory backbone for multiple independent time-sensitive networks. *Journal of Systems Architecture, 119*, 102277.

Miloradov, M., Rakic, S., Lalic, D. C., Savkovic, M., Softic, S., & Marjanovic, U. (2022, September). Digital technologies as an essential part of smart factories and their impact on productivity. In *IFIP international conference on advances in production management systems* (pp. 179–187). Springer Nature.

Okeme, P. A., Skakun, A. D., & Muzalevskii, A. R. (2021). Transformation of factory to smart factory. In *2021 IEEE conference of Russian young researchers in electrical and electronic engineering (ElConRus)* (pp. 1499–1503). IEEE. https://doi.org/10.1109/ElConRus51938.2021.9396278

Schuh, G., Frank, J., Jussen, P., Rix, C., & Harland, T. (2019, June). Monetizing Industry 4.0: Design principles for subscription business in the manufacturing industry. In *2019 IEEE international conference on engineering, technology and innovation (ICE/ITMC)* (pp. 1–9). IEEE.

Schütte, R. (1998). *Grundsätze ordnungsmäßiger Referenzmodellierung: Konstruktion konfigurations- und anpassungsorientierter Modelle.* https://doi.org/10.1007/978-3-663-10233-5.

Seo, W. J., & Evans, N. (2021). Internet of things adoption challenges in enterprise asset management organisations. In *14th WCEAM proceedings* (pp. 175–186). Springer International Publishing.

Shilenge, M. C., & Telukdarie, A. (2022). Optimization of operational und information technology integration towards Industry 4.0. In *2022 IEEE 31st international symposium on industrial electronics (ISIE)* (pp. 1076–1081). IEEE. https://doi.org/10.1109/ISIE51582.2022.9831605.

Tao, F., & Qi, Q. (2017). New IT driven service-oriented smart manufacturing: Framework and characteristics. *IEEE Transactions on Systems, Man, and Cybernetics: Systems, 49*(1), 81–91.

The, Y. L., & Kuusk, A. G. (2021). Aligning IIoT and ISA-95 to improve asset management in process industries. In *14th WCEAM proceedings* (pp. 153–163). Springer International Publishing.

Usländer, T., & Epple, U. (2015). Reference model of Industrie 4.0 service architectures: Basic concepts and approach. *at-Automatisierungstechnik, 63*(10), 858–866.

Zhou, K., Liu, T., & Zhou, L. (2015). Industry 4.0: Towards future industrial opportunities and challenges. In *2015 12th International conference on fuzzy systems and knowledge discovery (FSKD)* (pp. 2147–2152). IEEE.

Digitalization in Accounting

Charles Richard Baker

Abstract This paper focuses on digitalization in accounting. Many aspects of accounting can be transformed through digitalization, among these are: tax return preparation, confirmation of receivables, investigation of outliers in populations of transactions through data visualization, and preparation of audit reports using AI and Chat GPT. In addition, accountants can facilitate the digital transformation of strategic plans and business models in order to make them more efficient and effective. This paper reviews the theoretical background of digitalization in business organizations, as well as the rationale for increasing digitalization in accounting and the potential areas for increased digitization in accounting. The paper also summarizes some essential technologies useful for digitalization and reviews experiences with digitalization of several large accounting firms.

Keywords Digitalization · Accounting and auditing · Data visualization · Data analytics

1 Introduction

Since the advent of computer technology in World War II, the work of accountants has evolved in concert with advances in Information Technology (IT). Two technological advancements have had a particular effect on organizations. The first was the emergence of computerized information systems (Granlund & Mouritsen, 2003). Introduced as early as the 1950s, computerized information systems enabled accountants to record large volumes of data in a more detailed manner than manual systems and produce better analyses of data for decision-making. The second technological advance arrived with the introduction of the World Wide Web (Internet) and Integrated Information Systems (IIS) (Porter & Heppelmann, 2014). IIS are essentially computer systems that support management control over business processes, but

C. R. Baker (✉)
Adelphi University, Garden City, NY, USA
e-mail: Baker3@Adelphi.edu

R. C. Geibel and S. Machavariani (eds.), *Digital Management to Shape the Future*, Springer Proceedings in Business and Economics,
https://doi.org/10.1007/978-3-031-66517-2_16

which are generally based on traditional accounting methods and techniques. In the late 1990s and early 2000s, enterprise resource planning (ERP) systems were introduced. ERP systems allow accountants to provide information for decision-making throughout the organization. As a result, a third phase of technological advancement has now come into existence. This third phase has been referred to as "digitalization" (Karimi & Walter, 2015).

2 Theoretical Basis of Digitalization in Organizations

IIS, ERP and digitalization can be considered part of IT, because IT is typically defined as a bundle of physical and/or social factors packaged into a recognizable form, such as hardware and software. From a technological viewpoint, digitalization emerged from several technological advancements, including IIS and ERP. At the same time, while IIS is considered to be IT (i.e., software), digitalization represents IT in a broader sense (i.e., technological artefacts bundled with socio-technical properties). Hence, distinctions can be made between IIS and digitalization from a technological point of view. More importantly, a distinction can be made from an accounting perspective. Digital technologies transform and expand the types of data generated and used by accountants (Arnaboldi et al., 2017).

Digitalization influences accounting practices in several ways. First, digitalization causes the boundaries of accounting to be increasingly fluid. Second, digitalization is driving new forms of power relations in organizations. Third, digitalization raises issues related to the production of knowledge for decision-making. These three observations highlight key questions for future research: How does digitalization affect the boundaries of accountants' work and the accounting profession itself? How will digitalization affect the relative power of various organizational actors in organizations and who will determine how digitalization is adopted and implemented? Finally, how does digitalization affect the production of knowledge relevant for decision-making?

The term, "Digitalization" is often used interchangeably with other similar terms, such as digitization or digital transformation. However, a distinction should be made between digitalization and these similar terms. Digitization refers to the technical process of encoding information into a digital form, which makes the digitized content programmable (Hylving & Schultze, 2013). As such, digitization represents a lesser degree of organizational change than digitalization. In contrast, digital transformation entails major organizational changes and, consequently, requires alterations in both strategy and the business model (Bharadwaj et al., 2013). Digitalization lies between digitization and digital transformation. Therefore, digitalization involves more than a mere technical process (e.g., digitization), but it does not necessarily entail a reconfiguration of strategy or transformation of the business model (e.g., digital transformation). Nevertheless, digitalization often requires changing the underlying assumptions related to the design and use of digital technologies (Thorseng & Grisot, 2017).

2.1 Key Definitions

"**Digital Initiative**" is the process of introducing digital projects into an organization. From an accounting perspective, a digital initiative means introducing the use of a new technology and new processes to perform a given activity or set of activities.

"**Digitization**" is the process of changing from analog to digital form. In accounting, this could mean using optical character recognition (OCR) to turn a paper document into a digital document. It could also involve moving from a paper document to gathering information from a user on a web page, so that the information can go directly to the digital application.

"**Digitalization**" is the use of digital technologies to change a business model. Digitalization is the process of moving to a digital business. For accounting, this refers to creating digital approaches to accounting practices. For example, rather than having a manual operation where people search for information about activities of clients, there could be a continuous monitoring system that searches through a database of information and summarizes that information for the users of the system.

"**Digital Transformation**" is the process of exploiting digital technologies to create a new business model. Digital transformation provides the ability to monitor and manage the new model. The new business model may be integrated with existing business models, but digital transformation may also require building new processes or reengineering existing processes (O'Leary, 2022).

3 Rationale for Increased Digitalization in Accounting

There are many reasons why accountants adopt digital technologies. First, there is often a need to meet deadlines in accounting tasks. By using computer technology, the speed and quality of the accounting information can be enhanced. The time needed for preparation of reports can be reduced and information may be made available in real time. If accounting processes are automated, accountants can spend more time with clients and thereby increase the quality of their services. Herbert et al. (2016) found that digitalization is used to eliminate or minimize routine and repetitive tasks, and thereby enables accountants to focus on more creative, non-routine and non-structured tasks that require more thought and creative skills. This change can affect the activities of experienced accountants. If data is cloud-based and readily available, clients may be willing to change accounting advisors more quickly than in the past if they become dissatisfied with the services they receive. Nevertheless, digitalization cannot perform the accountant's most valuable functions, which are interpreting and analyzing financial information. Despite the capabilities of advanced technologies and the influence of these technologies on auditors and audit processes, the need for human accountants will not necessarily diminish. The key is that basic services can be delivered more efficiently, allowing accountants to have more time to address their client's needs. While, accountants may focus primarily on the traditional task of moving form data entry, to recordkeeping to financial reports, financial managers are increasingly using structured data, unstructured data, and predictive analytics to access large databases related to customer information, financial trends and industry information to make forecasts. Accounting professionals will need to respond to technological changes so that they can become more effective. Digitalization implies a different philosophy in the way in which companies are managing and conducting their businesses, processes and activities. According to Mancini et al.(2016), keywords that characterize the philosophy of digital technology are ubiquity, openness and sharing. In other words, data and information become more freely available, and the flow of information is without restrictions among organizations. The availability of comprehensive data about the business in real time may have a significant impact on the way companies prepare their strategic plans. Data that are available to managers may be more accurate, so that companies' strategic plans can be more resilient in changing business environments.

4 Potential Areas for Digitalization in Accounting

At the heart of digitalization in accounting is cloud technology. By relying on the cloud to run operations, professional accountants can:

- Streamline repetitive processes and automate work flows
- Have a central hub for all data
- Reduce time wasted, and reduce lower costs
- Improve transparency and accountability with clients
- Ensure that even with high volumes of data, relevant insights are produced

Digitalization eliminates the need for laborious, time-consuming tasks. By taking over the repetitive parts of the process, it frees up time so that accountants can then focus on strategic tasks that require experience and creativity. Key benefits of digital technology for accounting are:

1. A central repository for documents with access control and collaboration.
2. Reduced data entry time. Data can be entered in one document and automatically updated in all connected places.
3. Work is preserved automatically to the cloud in real-time. This means documents can be recovered easily even if work is disrupted.
4. AI can enable accountants to spot patterns and trends in financial data to enable more informed decision-making.
5. By taking over manual work, technology ensures that even with limited staff, a firm does not feel overwhelmed with work.

The following aspects of digitalization in accounting are becoming more prevalent.

4.1 Continuous Auditing and Monitoring

Continuous auditing involves programmed modules imbedded in an organization's Accounting Information System that evaluate transactions as they occur through the year. Routine transactions are captured and tested in automated routines. If transactions do not pass the test to be categorized as routine transactions, they are copied to an exception file to be evaluated by external auditors at year-end. Examples of these exactions are invoice totals that are too high or too low for what has been sold or payroll cash disbursements, which do not correspond to an employee. Continuous monitoring provides the opportunity to digitalize a number of similar processes. One approach from such a system is to monitor continuously text sources, both internally and externally, for a range of different types of information. In so doing, these systems search for different types of information, such as information about competitors, information about customers and clients, information about management and other sources.

4.2 Data Mining

Data mining tools are able to handle increasing volumes and varieties of data. These tools can quickly diagnose errors in accounting data. Data mining is also used to improve and defend estimations, assumptions, decisions, and assertion. Data mining is the systematic practice of looking for issues or patterns occurring in data fields. Data mining allows a better understanding of data behavior and expectations about data values. Accounting may mine their data of find systems delays or errors in order to identify where new policies, controls, or technologies can improve operations. Some leading data-mining vendors include Apteryx, SAS, and Microsoft mySQL.

4.3 Smart Contracts

A business contract is created whenever two parties, agree on the consideration that one party will provide to the other party in exchange for goods or services. Contacts can range from simple exchanges to complex agreements with many stipulations. Contract review is important for proper accounting, such as revenue recognition or lease contracts. Historically, contract contents were not standardized, which meant that both parties had to conduct a detailed review of the contract to ensure proper accounting. A specific application of a smart contact is a secure shared online digital ocntrac. Smart contract are used in healthcare, trading, lending, real estate, insurance, legal services, warranties, employment, and gaming contracts.

4.4 Block Chain

Block chain allow businesses to access the same information in real-time from different sources. Many businesses are utilizing this delivery method to secure their sensitive accounting data and speed-up complex processes. Considering block chain only to be a technology for cryptocurrency is not accurate. Along with uninterrupted security and transparency, block chain can replace traditional ways of handling auditing, compliance and reconciliation tasks. Companies using block chain want to use it to ensure data integrity, process transactions and manage customer and supplier relations.

4.5 Big Data

Big data involves extremely large datasets that have particular storage challenges and generally need to be analyzed using computational methods. In accounting, the most significant impact of the development of big data is the impact on data management. Six under-researched areas of big data in accounting and finance are privacy and security, data visualization and predictive analytics, data management and data quality. Increased research in these areas will lead to improvements in industry practices, and more opportunities for cross-disciplinary research. Big data and data analytics will affect accounting in various ways; for example by influencing how business is conducted and how financial statements are prepared and audited. Big data can have a significant impact on the quality of decision-making process, because the data are comprehensive and the information is better understood. Availability of comprehensive data through digital solutions increases the effectiveness and efficiency of accountants. Big data can reduce the time for reporting because modern technologies provide real time updates. With analytic skills and tools, professionals can effectively analyze data and get insights that will change the way business decisions are made.

4.6 Robotic Process Automation

Robotic process automation (RPA) is a set of software technologies that record a specific order of human keystrokes and mouse activity steps within or across digital applications. One save or recorded, these routines can be repeated by simply re-running the tool. RPA tools are used for stable processes where the stages of the process do not change over time, such as when financial analysts download the closing stock prices of the same set of companies every day.

4.7 *Artificial Intelligence (AI)*

O'Leary (2022) has examined an AI application developed by Ernst & Young where the system uses AI to read contracts. That system is "ontology driven" (e.g., O'Leary, 2000). The system first digitizes written contracts using optical character recognition. Then using the digital version, the system is designed to find certain terms in the contract while a human confirms which of the identified terms was appropriate, and then the system captures the location of the terms in a spread sheet. In another example of using AI for digitalization of a process, developed an AI-based "end-to-end" invoice processing system using multiple steps to process invoices. This system has successfully processed 80,000 invoices automatically with low or no manual intervention. AI is also embedded in transformational approaches such as development of autonomic supply chains (O'Leary, 2008).

4.8 *Big Data Lake*

A data lake is a centralized repository that allows organizations to store all of their data at any scale, without having to structure the data, as in a data warehouse. Accordingly, data lakes can be seen as replacing or supplementing data warehouses in digital initiative projects. This can lead to a hybrid ecosystem, with both on premises and cloud computing, in which a data lake is used to include all the organization's data to create an enterprise view of that data and facilitate a culture of data analytics. A data lake can provide partners outside the firm access to their information to facilitate further digital transformation. For example, auditors could be granted access to the lake for a range of auditing tasks and continuous auditing, without disrupting accounting processes. Clients could be granted access to the portion of the lake that captures their purchases. Supply chain partners could be granted access to the portions that are related to goods movement through the supply chain.

4.9 *Digital Ecosystem*

Digital ecosystems consist of interconnected sets of services, typically aimed at controlling customer interfaces and customer interaction points such as advertising, messaging and search. Ecosystems are not a technology, per se, but instead involve interlinked strategies. Many of these emerging systems are for electronic commerce, but some of these ecosystems are for internal use of information (O'Leary, 2012). Some companies, such as Apple, Microsoft, and Alphabet can be considered ecosystems. Creating or extending the capabilities of an ecosystem leads to breaking out of traditional capabilities and including new capabilities. As a result, using ecosystems typically requires firms to think of ecosystem partners differently, sometimes including those with additional capabilities. Ecosystems could be used in a number of settings. For example, auditors could provide a platform for client interaction or supply chains could provide a platform for connections across the supply chain.

4.10 Internet of Things

The Internet of things (IOT) is a technology that can be an important part of digitization, digitalization or digital transformation of a range of processes, including electronic commerce and the supply chain. The strength of the IOT is that it can allow firms to monitor environments that previously they could not monitor because they lacked access to information. The IOT puts product information into a digital format. Using the IOT, firms can track products as they move through the supply chain, potentially tracking inventory as it moves around the world from supplier to buyer.

4.11 Additional Technologies that are Becoming Important for Digitalization in Accounting

Three additional technologies are important for digitization in accounting. The first is Alteryx. Alteryx has the ability to clean up large amounts of data from Excel and other types of data files. It also has the ability to manipulate data and convert it to usable form. Alteryx is relatively straightforward to use because it has a good user interface. However, it is not readily available. Large public accounting firms are acquiring Alteryx and employing it in their practice.

The next technology is UIpath. UIpath is process automation tool. This tool facilitates robotic processes in accounting. UIpath has the ability to automate various business processes. It can open files and manipulate the process. A typical application would be opening up a file, manipulating the data, saving the data, and then uploading that data to a shared database.

The final technology is Tableau. Tableau has been acquired by Salesforce. Tableau is a visualization tool, and it creates dashboards from data. The reason this tool is important is that many executives do not working with numbers. They want their data to be visualized. Many accounting firms are now preparing Tableau visualizations when they provides deliverables to their clients.

5 Some Examples of Digitalization in Accounting Firms

5.1 PwC

PriceWaterhouseCoopers (PwC) has created a division, which focuses on advising clients how to produce digital experiences for customers, clients, and employees. They believe that upskilling is a key factor driving the digital transformation of companies. They also believe that digital upskilling is fundamentally about culture. PwC focuses on building "digital fitness", which equips their employees with a broad base of knowledge across a variety of domains—such as data analytics, AI and automation, block chain, and design thinking. This digital upskilling strategy is a core business priority for the firm. They develop digital fitness through digitally enabled learning—including podcasts, immersive skill building, multimedia content, and quizzes via mobile platforms. They also have a Digital Fitness app, which provides employees with an assessment of their digital skills, and guides them to the tools and learning resources they need to fill gaps and make improvements. They also enable employees to accelerate their skills by offering a "career pivot" to become "Digital Accelerators". Accelerators learn a variety of coding languages and apply their skills across their client base. Almost a year was invested in creating a learning experience that brought Accelerators together for immersive training, followed by a personalized development path. To ensure the time needed to achieve learning, the investment included reductions in billable hours of Accelerators. They focused on client work while applying their new skills for at least two years. Freeing up time for them to learn, collaborate, and execute was a vital part of the program. The Accelerators use robotic process/desktop automation to improve processes that had been manually intensive. This could take tasks down from 1,000 + hours to just minutes, creating capacity for staff and their clients to focus on higher-value matters. Another key is building community among Accelerators and empowering them to organize in ways that amplify their successes. Staying connected, working together, and sharing knowledge that can elevate the entire organization is essential. That sense of connection is tech-enabled. The social element of the program encourages accelerated learning through shared learning among peers. The benefits of digitization can come "out of the lab". Automation of traditionally manual tasks are available for use by many people across the firm.

1. **Digital upskilling is a business and a people priority.** It is important that managers at all levels recognize development and upskilling as a business priority.
2. **Tech-enabled learning cannot happen without the right investments, assets, and processes in place.** Employees should be empowered with not only digital tools and resources, but also, the time to apply that learning. The acquisition of new skills needs to be recognized.
3. **Focus on building a growth mindset culture.** Commit to leaving nobody behind, as long as they choose not to be left behind. Being committed to lifelong learning is necessary in a digital and data-driven world. Organizationally enabled

learning is an implicit "contract" between the business and the learner/employee, who must be willing to opt in to what is available.

5.2 Deloitte

This section describes a survey of its clients conducted in 2023 by Deloitte with respect Digital Transformation. Digital transformation is perceived as an important investment. Executives surveyed by Deloitte ranked modernizing digital infrastructure as high in potential benefits and relatively low in terms of the difficulties of achieving it. The outcomes the executives expect from their digital transformation efforts include boosting efficiency, improving offerings, and creating new products and services. Reducing costs, although important, ranked fourth (see figure). This wave of future digital transformation efforts will likely look different from those of the past few years. As tools powered by artificial intelligence (AI) are incorporated into more enterprise, software and business processes, digital transformation is expected to evolve beyond infrastructure modernization. "It used to just be—how do you get to the cloud? Now it is how do I use AI and machine learning to make proactive decisions? How do I use generative [AI] in my workforce and automate all the things that I was doing manually? How do I use data to break down silos and create streamlined processes that give me more transparency and visibility into the business? The consensus seems to be that increasing automation is sensible and leaders are looking to AI to contain costs, reduce errors, and automate processes, all of which can increase efficiency. AI is catalyst for digital transformation; the focus is on AI-driven solutions, real-time solutions, real-time decision-making, and conversational chat bots. From an automation perspective, AI and machine learning are a large investment area directed towards 'How do we internally save money and time, or doing way more with fewer people?' Digital transformation often continues to mean infrastructure modernization, better data management, and software upgrades. The benefits of these transformation efforts include achieving efficiency, improving existing products, and reducing costs. Companies are focused on these goals. However, it is also important to focus on value. Digital transformation should be across the board. It is not only related to technology. It is also about how to deliver value to customers. Moving to the cloud does not mean that this is digital transformation. Overall, there is a need for a business transformation as well as IT transformation. As AI becomes an integral part of digital transformation, the important questions are: Are we just reacting to the market, or taking a longer-term, holistic approach to our AI initiatives? Can we define and articulate the value that we are trying to achieve with our AI implementations?

5.3 BDO

BDO USA wanted to build customized applications for its tax data to use internally with its own clients and sell to external organizations. At the time, the company's different departments were using different data management and analytics platforms for preparing and analyzing data and developing analytics applications but had not standardized operations on one platform. BDO had to do repetitive, time-consuming data preparation tasks manually. In 2019, BDO USA acquired TAXPE, a firm whose tools automate aspects of the income tax reporting process for large firms. That acquisition served as an impetus for BDO USA to search for a platform that could enable more automation. The BDO team narrowed their choice down to Alteryx and the Microsoft Power Platform. Ultimately, the low-code/no-code focus of the Alteryx APA led BDO USA to choose that vendor. In the nearly two years since it first began using digital automation capabilities from Alteryx, BDO USA has gained efficiencies that have led to cost savings and developed applications that it now sells to third parties. Alteryx is a data and analytics vendor founded in 1997 and based in Irvine, Calif., whose platform is designed to automate much of the data preparation process. Alteryx began focusing on automation in 2020. It formed a partnership with robotic process automation vendor UIPath in 2021 to further its automation capabilities. Alteryx has been transitioning its platform to the cloud, releasing its first cloud-native capabilities in February 2022,

BDO began a pilot program with Alteryx in 2020 and fully deployed Alteryx in September 2022. One example of a routine task BDO USA targeted for automation was filing K-1 tax forms, which involves uploading of data, data entry and a slew of calculations. In the nearly two years since BDO USA first began using Alteryx on a trial basis, the firm has accomplished what it hoped for. By automating what were previously manual tasks, the firm has saved about 100,000 work hours, Fuller said. Alteryx has essentially taken over BDO USA's data management, letting the firm transition its focus away from mundane accounting tasks and make technology that leads to efficiency and a new focus. Those technological terms include a strong development operations program and a focus on enabling agile decision-making. In addition to increasing efficiency, BDO USA has used Alteryx to build applications it is now selling to third parties. The firm is beginning to train what will become a group of Alteryx champions. Those employees will then become analytics and automation leaders within their departments and train others.

6 Conclusion

This paper has focused on digitalization in accounting. Many aspects of accounting have been transformed through digitalization. Some of these have been discussed in prior sections of this paper. In addition, as can be seen from the examples of digitalization experiences of several large public accounting firms, accountants can facilitate the digital transformation of business models to make them more efficient and effective. This paper has reviewed the theoretical background of digitalization in business organizations, as well as the rationale for increasing digitalization in accounting and the potential areas for increased digitization. The paper has also summarized some key technologies for digitalization and reviewed experiences with digitalization among several large accounting firms. Because digitalization is an ongoing topic, future research may concentrate on tracing and explaining emerging trends in digitization.

References

Arnaboldi, M., Azzone, G., & Sidorova, Y. (2017). Governing social media: The emergence of hybridised boundary objects. *Accounting, Auditing & Accountability Journal, 30*(4).

Bharadwaj, A., El Sawy, O. A., Pavlou, P. A., & Venkatraman, N. (2013). Digital business strategy: Toward a next generation of insights. *MIS Quarterly, 37*(2), 471–482.

Granlund, M., & Mouritsen, J. (2003). Special section on management control and new information technologies. *European Accounting Review, 12*(1), 77–83.

Herbert, I., Dhayalan, A., & Scott, A. (2016). The future of professional work: will you be replaced, or will you be sitting next to a robot? *Management Services Journal,* 22–27.

Hylving, L., & Schultze, U. (2013, January). Evolving the modular layered architecture in digital innovation: The case of the car's instrument cluster. *ICIS 2013 Proceedings, 2,* 1525–1541.

Karimi, J., & Walter, Z. (2015). The role of dynamic capabilities in responding to digital disruption: A factor-based study of the newspaper industry. *Journal of Management Information Systems, 32*(1), 39–81.

Mancini, D., Lamboglia, R., Castellano, N. G., & Corsi, K. (2017). Trends of digital innovation applied to accounting information and management control systems. In K. Corsi, N. G. Castellano, R. Lamboglia, & D. Mancini (Eds.), *Reshaping accounting and management control systems—New opportunities from business information systems* (pp. 1–19).

O'Leary, D. E. (2000). Different firms, different ontologies, and no one best ontology. *IEEE Intelligent Systems and Their Applications, 15*(5), 72–78.

O'Leary, D. E. (2008). Supporting decisions in real-time enterprises: Autonomic supply chain systems. *Information Systems and e-Business Management, 6*(3), 239–255. https://doi.org/10.1007/s10257-008-0086-0

O'Leary, D. E. (2012). The virtual close and continuous monitoring at Cisco. *Journal of Emerging Technologies in Accounting, 9*(1), 111–126.

O'Leary, D. (2022). Digitization, digitalization and digital transformation in accounting, electronic commerce and supply chains. Working Paper, University of Southern California.

Porter, M. E., & Heppelmann, J. E. (2014, November). How smart, connected products are transforming companies. *Harvard Business Review,* 92.

Thorseng, A. A., & Grisot, M. (2017). Digitalization as institutional work: A case of designing a tool for changing diabetes care. *Information Technology & People, 30*(1), 227–243.

AI Platform of Enterprise Financial Stability Analytics

Tea Munjishvili, David Sikharulidze, Teona Shugliashvili, Shota Shaburishvili, and Leila kadagishvili

Abstract This paper introduces an AI platform designed for analyzing the financial stability of enterprises, with a specific focus on cultivating optimal decision-making capabilities. The platform enables users to construct diagnostic models utilizing logistical regression, deep learning neural networks (NN), and predicate rules. Moreover, users can develop predictive models for diverse processes using regression systems and neural network models and apply these models in real-world scenarios. This paper discusses a simulation-based mathematical model for evaluating the financial stability of small businesses. The model is implemented using FinSim, a software package developed by the authors and previously described in Munjishvili et al., (2023). The goal of the platform's general model is to achieve the following objectives: (1) develop a specific economic-mathematical model for assessing the financial stability of the enterprise and predicting bankruptcy, which can be applied in the real activity of the given enterprise; (2) learn and apply the new technology for developing an economic-mathematical model of financial stability assessment and bankruptcy forecasting for each enterprise in the study, and (3) develop organizational and technical measures for ensuring financially sustainable operations of an enterprise based on modeling the arguments included in the model of the real enterprise. In this article we apply the models to the real small-size enterprises' financial statements data, which in line of the Georgian law of accounting belong to

T. Munjishvili (✉) · S. Shaburishvili · L. kadagishvili
Ivane javakhishvili Tbilisi State University, Tbilisi, Georgia
e-mail: tea.munjishvili@tsu.ge

S. Shaburishvili
e-mail: shota.shaburishvili@tsu.ge

L. kadagishvili
e-mail: Leila.kadagishvili@tsu.ge

D. Sikharulidze
East European University, Tbilisi, Georgia
e-mail: d.sikharulidze@eeu.edu.ge

T. Shugliashvili
Ludwig-Maximilians-Universität München, Munich, Germany

R. C. Geibel and S. Machavariani (eds.), *Digital Management to Shape the Future*,
Springer Proceedings in Business and Economics,
https://doi.org/10.1007/978-3-031-66517-2_17

IV category. Using the available statistical data of three years, we carry out financial stability diagnostics of six real enterprises from IV category, namely: Nika 95 LLC, Sefo LLC, Offices LLC, Commerce LLC, Friendship LLC and Pharmakon LLC. The study finds that even with limited three-years data, the simulations predict bankruptcy.

Keywords FinSim · Small-Business · Financial Stability · Bankruptcy prediction · Simulation

1 Introduction

Before 2019, small and medium-sized businesses in Georgia weren't required to submit financial statements, leading to a lack of long-term data on business bankruptcies. However, with FinSim, users can create an economic-mathematical model of a firm (denoted as S_i) to assess financial stability and predict bankruptcy. This model can be developed either by an "analyst" with special rights or by a "student". The key advantage of "analyst" mode is that the "analyst" can modify data and edit calculated coefficients in the database. FinSim is a multilingual software supporting Georgian, English, and other languages. FinSim draws on the experience gained from Cyber1 and Cyber2 systems, previously developed and implemented in educational settings. FinSim is accessible at www.kiber3.tsu.ge.

FinSim is utilized in various contexts: (1) In enterprise management processes. (2) to educate specialists in higher educational institutions within countries sharing a common legal environment, including Georgia. (3) for training the specialists working in management fields such as economists, financiers, and others. (4) By investors to accurately determine the optimal investment size. (5) During the formation of the state budget, FinSim is used for tasks such as determining planned tax revenues and other related activities.

Six real companies of the IVth category were selected for 3-year factual analysis: Nika 95 LLC, Sefo LLC, Offices LLC, Commerce LLC, Friendship LLC, Pharmakon LLC. Utilizing statistical data from a span of only three years, it becomes apparent that simulation emerges as a viable method for predicting bankruptcy. Through modeling, we can ascertain the optimal trajectory for business development, which can then serve as a benchmark for future strategies.

The evaluation of the financial sustainability and bankruptcy forecast of enterprises in FinSim employs three distinct financial analysis models: the Altman Model (Altman Z-score) for non-industrial enterprises, referred to as Altman3, as well as the Springeit and Tafler models. The breakdown below illustrates that Altman3 utilizes 7 indicators, whereas the Springeit and Tafler models each incorporate 6 indicators. Notably, 4 out of the 6 indicators from Altman3 are integrated into these models (Table 1).

Special attention should be given to specific variables such as **total assets** (Arg1)**,** short-term liabilities (Arg6), long-term liabilities (Arg7). Specifically, it's crucial to

Table 1 Analyst's Table based on the financial statement of Nika 95 LLC

Bankruptcy Models and Model variables	Argument	Years		
		2019	2020	2021
Altman's model for non-manufacturing companies				
Total assets	Arg1	215,796	216,622	220,313
Working (operating) capital	Arg2	1756	4510	16,136
Retained Earnings / (Accumulated Losses)	Arg3	0	2199	682
Earnings before interest and taxes (EBIT)	Arg4	0	67,683	12,799
Own capital (share capital in case of a JSC)	Arg5	212,402	212,402	212,402
Short-term liabilities	Arg6	1928	0	7229
Long-term liabilities	Arg7	262	2021	0
Springgate model				
Income from realization	Arg4		70,375	22,813
Earnings Before Taxes (EBT)	Arg5		67,683	12,799
Taffler's model				
Income from realization	Arg3		70,375	22,813
profit from sales	Arg4		67,683	12,799

ensure that Arg1 is not equal to zero (Arg1 < > 0), and simultaneously, both Arg6 and Arg7 are not equal to zero (Arg6 < > 0, Arg7 < > 0). However, it is possible for scenarios where Arg6 equals zero while Arg7 does not, or vice versa, as these variables are divided in the formula for calculating the Altman Z-score. The table provided contains the actual data for a particular enterprise.

Modeling results of five types of registers are obtained:

- Registers of all the enterprises and models by years
- Registers of selected enterprises and models by years
- Registers of all the models of the selected enterprise by years
- Registers of the models developed by the analyst
- Single-variable modeling register.

2 Analysis

To analyze the model developed for a specific i-enterprise, we need to examine the effect of changing the value of each coefficient (∀b_i) when the value of the corresponding argument (∀Arg_i) changes by Δ digits. This analysis helps us understand how changes in the input variables affect the model's output or prediction.

When data, even for just one year, is inputted into FinSim, after the analyst selects a model, a field "Argument change bit" appears on the web page where the change rate of the argument can be entered. Upon entering the value of the argument change and clicking the modeling button, a table will be generated below. This table displays

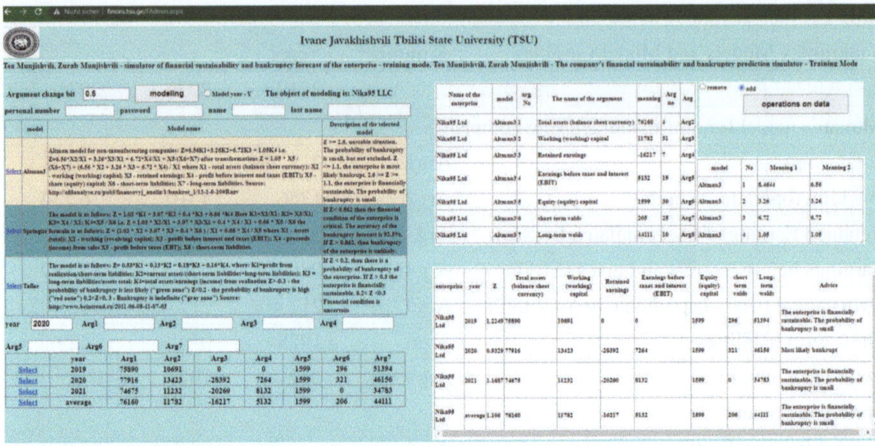

Fig. 1 The values of ∀Arg_i arguments when changed by Δ digit in **Altman Model** (*Source* Screen shoot own program www.kiber3.tsu.ge)

the position of any coefficient included in the model when the value of each argument (∀Arg_i) changes by Δ digits.

Figure 1 represents the scenario where the analyst selects the Altman model and evaluates the financial stability of Nika95 LLC under changed arguments by 0.5 bit. On the tables on the right-hand side, the results are displayed. On the below table on the right-hand side, we see that the Nika95 LLC is most likely bankrupt in 2020 under the 0.5-bit change of the arguments. Figure 2 displays the Kiber3.tsu.ge when the analyst has chosen Tafler (2a) and Springeit (2b) Models. To export this data to the client's computer in Excel format, the user can click on a line in the list (as shown in Fig. 3). Please note that the program is currently under reconstruction to add support for a mobile app.

Figure 3 displays the impact of the change in the value of the argument included in the model on the financial stability of the enterprise, while the values of the coefficients of the model are calculated based on the average values of the arguments. It is interesting to develop an economic-mathematical model of the enterprise's financial sustainability and forecasting with the values of the arguments of a specific year and based on it to study the impact of the change in the value of the argument included in the model on the financial sustainability of the enterprise. For this purpose, after selecting the line with identification information of the analyst and model name, the subsequent steps are required:

- select the Modeling Y Year tab.
- select the row in the table with the values of the year and the arguments.

Upon completing the selections as described above, a model will be generated using the values of the arguments from the chosen year. The result will be displayed on the table located on the right-hand side of Fig. 3.

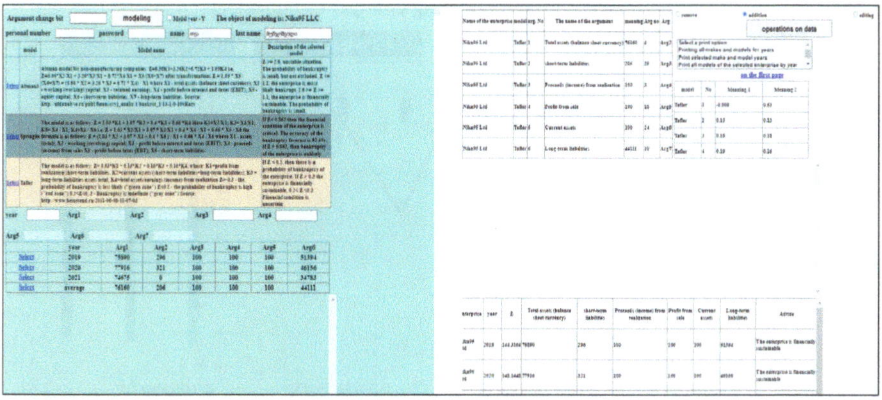

a: Tafler model

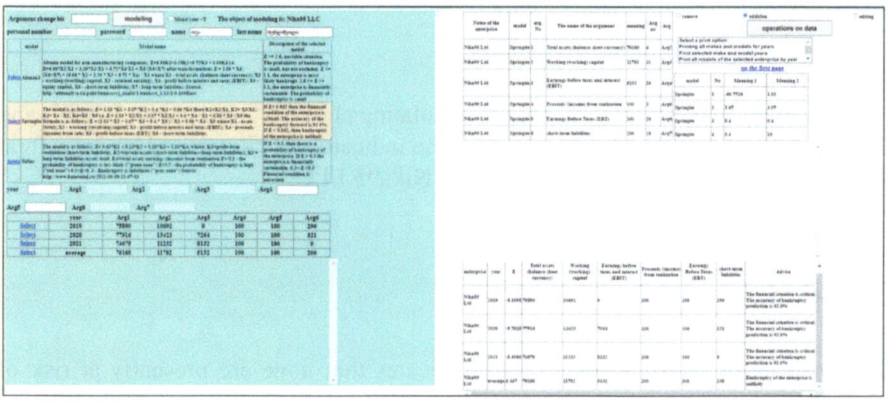

b: Springeit Model

Fig. 2 The values of ∀Arg_i arguments when changed by Δ digit in **Tafler** and **Springeit Models** (*Source* Screenshot own program www.kiber3.tsu.ge)

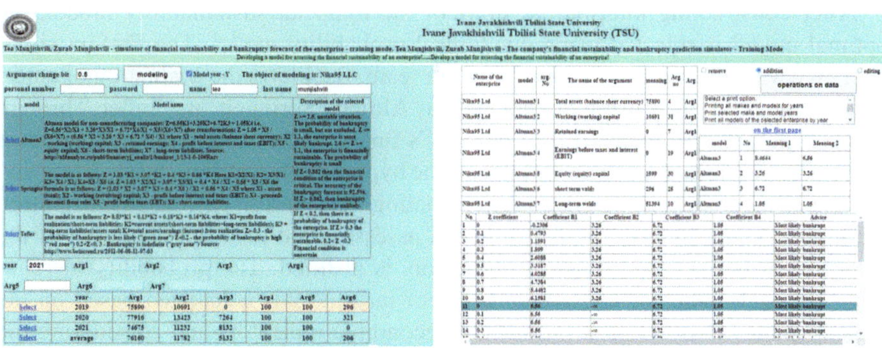

Fig. 3 Single-variable modeling (*Source* Own program www.kiber3.tsu.ge)

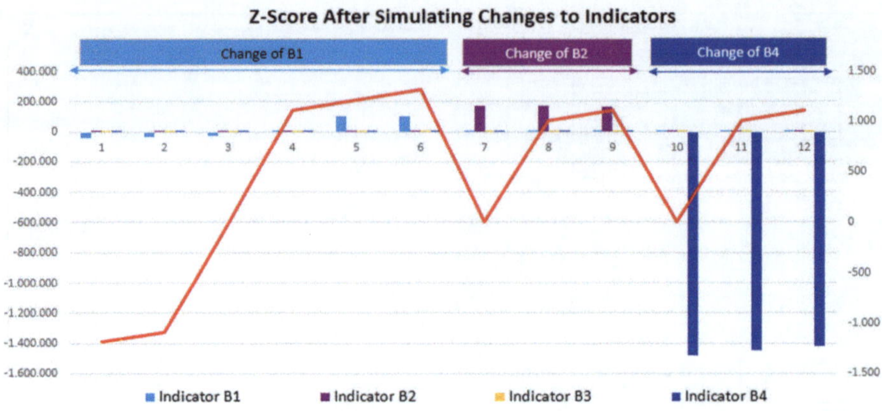

Fig. 4 Z score dynamics in response to single indicator change (*Source* Own web site www.kib er3.tsu.ge)

Figure 4 illustrates the Z-score after simulating changes to indicators B1, B2, and B4. As observed on Fig. 4, the change in the indicator B2 (Retained Earnings/Total Assets) has the most significant impact on Nika95 LLC.

3 Results

The analysis of six small enterprises indicates that none are presently at risk of bankruptcy. However, it's evident that their financial sustainability is susceptible to rapid fluctuations. There exists an opportunity for these enterprises to bolster their operations and explore additional business ventures by enhancing their financial indicators. The results of the bankruptcy forecasting are presented in Fig. 5.

After constructing multiple versions of the financial sustainability model, the optimal model is selected using our logical-probability model. The FinSim simulator (www.kiber3.tsu.ge) developed by our team, facilitates the evaluation of enterprise financial stability using models such as Altman, Springeit, and Tafler. Through these models, assessments of the company's financial sustainability are conducted using both single and multiple variables. The hypotheses regarding the structure and content of the indicator integrated for evaluating the enterprise's financial condition are tested using FinSim. The feasibility of assessing the financial condition of the enterprise using selected financial indicators is justified. The probability of reliability for each indicator and combination of indicators is calculated based on the logical connections between the selected economic indicators and considering the potential financial conditions of the enterprise. The process involves both calculating the impact share of each individual indicator and combination of indicators on the financial condition of the enterprise, as well as modeling the influence of

Model	Enterprise	Year	Z	Total Assets	Short-term Liabilities	Returns from sale	Profit from realization	Working (Current) Assets	Long-term Liabilities	Bankruptcy Forecast
Altman3	Nika95 LLC	avarage	1.11	76160	11782	-16217	5132	1599	206	The enterprise is financially sustainable
Altman3	Offices LLC	avarage	1.16	217577	7467	960	26827	212402	3052	The enterprise is financially sustainable
Altman3	Sefo LLC	avarage	1.11	96874	15541	8895	6558	9700	1233	The enterprise is financially sustainable
Altman3	Commerce LCC	avarage	1.19	1997	-1525	25	6367	0	1972	The enterprise is financially sustainable
Altman3	Friendship LLC	avarage	1.1	32891	6199	2857	1483	0	34	The enterprise is financially sustainable
Altman3	Pharmacon LLC	avarage	-1.44	318312	146	-140529	0	0	4735	Most likely bankrupt
Springate	Nika95 LLC	avarage	5.45	76160	11782	5132	100	100	206	Enterprise Bankruptcy Less Likely
Springate	Offices LLC	avarage	-359	217577	7467	26827	31063	26829	3052	Financial situation is critical. The accuracy of the bankruptcy forecast is 92.5%
Springeit	Sefo LLC	avarage	-0.5	96874	15541	6558	12780	6558	1233	Financial situation is critical. The accuracy of the bankruptcy forecast is 92.5%
Springeit	Commerce LCC	avarage	-1	1997	-1525	6367	65817	6367	1972	Financial situation is critical. The accuracy of the bankruptcy forecast is 92.5%
Springeit	Friendship LLC	avarage	-24.7	32891	6199	1483	2400	1483	34	Financial situation is critical. The accuracy of the bankruptcy forecast is 92.5%
Springeit	Pharmacon LLC	avarage	0	318312	146	0	79308	41934	4735	Enterprise Bankruptcy Less Likely
Tafler	Nika95 LLC	avarage	0.0008	76160	206	100	100	100	44111	There is a probability of bankruptcy
Tafler	Offices LLC	avarage	641	217577	3052	31063	26827	100	761	There is a probability of bankruptcy
Tafler	Sefo LLC	avarage		96874	1233	12780	12780	100	0	The enterprise is financially sustainable
Tafler	Commerce LCC	avarage	0	1997	1972	65817	6367	100	0	The enterprise is financially sustainable
Tafler	Friendship LLC	avarage	0	32891	34	2400	2400	100	0	The enterprise is financially sustainable
Tafler	Pharmacon LLC	avarage	0.08	318312	4735	79308	79308	100	143383	There is a probability of bankruptcy

Fig. 5 Final Results—Bankruptcy Forecasts (*Source* Own presentation)

each indicator and determining the specific contribution of combinations of indicators to the future financial condition of the enterprise. The financial development strategies of the enterprise are formulated based on the insights gained from the modeling process. The risk of financial unsustainability of the enterprise is calculated. Using the modeling results, the optimal version of enterprise development is identified, which can subsequently serve as a benchmark for monitoring the financial sustainability of the company. Based on the actual financial data, an assessment of the enterprise's financial sustainability is conducted, including forecasting the likelihood of bankruptcy.

In addition to the aforementioned findings of the research, the AI platform simulations enabled us to recognize significant issues, particularly the presence of gaps in the law, specifically the absence of requirements for financial reporting and the assessment of financial stability among small, IV category enterprises. The following deficiencies within the legal framework pertaining to small enterprises were brought to light:

- The research unveiled the absence of a minimum threshold defining which enterprises qualify as micro-enterprises, exempting them from the obligation to publish financial reports. This threshold holds particular significance, especially considering the tax exemption granted to micro-entrepreneurial individuals under the Tax Code of Georgia, allowing them to be exempt from taxes on income up to 30,000 GEL.
- The absence of an exemption for previously halted or inactive firms from the requirement to submit comprehensive reports.

4 Conclusion

This article examined the financial stability and made bankruptcy predictions of six real small-sized companies by utilizing an AI-powered learning platform and a simulation method.

The study presents several noteworthy aspects: (1) It employs mathematical methods, models, and algorithms for evaluating the financial stability of enterprises, including Altman's model, Olson's model, and the "scoring" method; (2) It explores the advantages and practical challenges associated with bankruptcy prediction models; (3) The study highlights that employing bankruptcy prediction models without adjustments may not yield accurate results, particularly in countries transitioning to a market economy like Georgia. In such contexts, where statistical data for small and medium-sized businesses are limited (only three years available), the efficacy of these models is compromised. Therefore, using bankruptcy prediction models for financial analysis in Georgian enterprises may not be appropriate. (4) It demonstrates that, among the financial sustainability and bankruptcy prediction models available, it is appropriate for a given small business to select a specific model that will differ from the standard model by the coefficient indicators.

The logical-probability model is chosen over other mathematical models due to its suitability for assessing the financial stability of an enterprise, especially in situations where data availability is limited. A forecast is generated assuming the continuation of the current trends in the enterprise's development. Modeling and corresponding conclusions are drawn based on the processing of data from the following small enterprises: Nika 95, Sefo LLC, Offices LLC, Commerce LLC, Megobroba LLC, and Farmakoni LLC. Teaching theoretical concepts regarding enterprise financial stability and bankruptcy forecasting, as well as developing decision-making skills, is facilitated through an electronic manual created using the programmed teaching method. This manual is accessible on the website Kiber3.tsu.ge.

References

Barak M., & Bedianashvili G. (2021). Systematic Inventive Thinking (SIT): A method for innovative problem solving and new product development. *Proceedings on Engineering Sciences*,*3*(1),111–122. https://pdfs.semanticscholar.org/553a/22497758657c0d953a6cd930fb743abae4fe.pdf

Bundesärztekammer. (2021). Ergebnisse der Ärztestatistik zum 31.12.2021. https://www.bundesaerztekammer.de/baek/ueber-uns/aerztestatistik/aerztestatistik-2021

Bundesministerium für Bildung und Forschung, Bundesministerium für Gesundheit, and Bundesministerium für Wirtschaft und Energie. (2020). Daten helfen heilen. Innovationsinitiative „Daten für Gesundheit": Roadmap für eine bessere Patientenversorgung durch Gesundheitsforschung und Digitalisierung. https://www.bundesgesundheitsministerium.de/fileadmin/Dateien/5_Publikationen/Gesundheit/Berichte/Roadmap_Innovationsinitiative_Daten_fuer_Gesundheit_barrierefrei.pdf (Accessed: 11 October 2022).

Bundesministerium für Gesundheit. (2022): Digitalisierung im Gesundheitswesen. https://www.bundesgesundheitsministerium.de/themen/digitalisierung/digitalisierung-im-gesundheitswesen.html (Accessed: 11 October 2022).

Gematik. (2022). E-Rezept: Das e-Rezept für Deutschland. https://www.das-e-rezept-fuer-deutschland.de

German Trade and Invest. (2022). HealthCare Market. https://www.gtai.de/en/invest/industries/healthcare/healthcare-market-65626

ITA - International Trade Administration. (2022). Germany - Country Commercial Guide. Health-Care and Medical Technology. https://www.trade.gov/country-commercial-guides/germany-healthcare-and-medical-technology

Kassenärztliche Bundesvereinigung (2022). Telemedizin. https://www.kbv.de/html/telemedizin.php

MarketsandMarkets. (2021). HealthCare IT Market - Global Forecast to 2026. Report Broschure with sample pages. Report Code: Hit 2005. https://www.marketsandmarkets.com/Market-Reports/healthcare-it-252.html?gclid=Cj0KCQjw48OaBhDWARIsAMd966DmFMogsnJm4S1 TWFOBTwGm9zOMOBMP5maA63JmF3BBvRnjgtqIjC4aAizqEALw_wcB

Munjishvili, T. (2015). *The system of discovery and estimation of knowledge "Cyber2"*. Scholar's Press, Saarbrucken HRB 18918.Published on:108

Munjishvili, T. (2019). The computer simulator-a modern training method of objects of an economic profile. International Journal of Advanced Trends in Computer Science and Engineering, 50-55. https://www.pjfas.jfas.info/index.php/jfas/article/view/4031

Munjishvili T. (2021). Application of fuzzy time series forecasting approach for predicting an enterprise net income level. E3S Web of Conferences 280, 02007, 1-7. https://www.e3s-conferences.org/articles/e3sconf/abs/2021/56/e3sconf_icsf2021_02007/e3sconf_icsf2021_02007.html

Munjishvili, T., Sigua, Z., & Shugliashvili, T. (2023). Digital Transformation in Education Self-study System "Cyber3s". In *Digital Management in Covid-19 Pandemic and Post-Pandemic Times: Proceedings of the International Scientific-Practical Conference (ISPC 2021)* (pp. 193–204). Springer International Publishing.

Statistisches Bundesamt. (2022). Gesundheitsausgaben 2020: Finanzierungsanteil der staatlichen Transfers und Zuschüsse auf 15,7 % gestiegen. Pressemitteilung Nr. 255 vom 21. Juni 2022. https://www.destatis.de/DE/Themen/Gesellschaft-Umwelt/Gesundheit/Gesundheitsausgaben/_inhalt.html

Transitioning into Hybrid Work Models: An Analysis of Performance Success Factors

Luisa M. Schönig and Richard C. Geibel

Abstract This paper examines the implementation of hybrid work models and elaborates on performance success factors that facilitate them. New and especially hybrid working models that combine physical and virtual work have become increasingly relevant in recent years. These working models offer a huge number of advantages for employers and employees. These benefits include, for example, increased flexibility, mobility, and cost savings. However, implementing these working models also brings challenges, such as adapting the corporate culture or implementing technologies and policies, as well as overstraining employees. The newly gained insights and specifications are used to develop a guideline that companies can use to implement and review the establishment of hybrid working models in a structured manner.

Keywords New Work · Hybrid Work · Digitalization · Flexible Working Models · Success Factors

1 Introduction

The world is undergoing global changes. Digitalization has fundamentally changed communication. New technologies, global connectivity, and social developments drive the transformation. For corporations, this also means a change in the way they operate and how employees work. Real-time communication is available and has shifted from a one-way exchange of information to a two-way interaction. Digitalization offers companies new opportunities to integrate modern systems and to connect with suppliers and customers. Moreover, companies' processes are becoming more transparent, and the need to keep up with progress is growing to remain competitive.

L. M. Schönig (✉)
Antwerpes AG, Cologne, Germany
e-mail: luisaschoenig@icloud.com

R. C. Geibel
E-Commerce Institut and IU International University, Cologne, Germany
e-mail: geibel@ecommerceinstitut.de; richardgeibel@iu.org

R. C. Geibel and S. Machavariani (eds.), *Digital Management to Shape the Future*, Springer Proceedings in Business and Economics,
https://doi.org/10.1007/978-3-031-66517-2_18

The intangible needs of employees are of great importance for a smooth workflow (Franken & Franken, 2020). Especially since the outbreak of the Corona pandemic, flexible working models have been increasingly integrated into the daily work of many companies and are becoming continuously substantial (Sonnenberg, 2021). This article addresses the issue of how the introduction of hybrid working models, affects companies, management and employees, and aims to identify success factors that lead to a target-oriented implementation in the company's everyday life and thus to improvements in the workplace.

2 Theory

Various models are emerging in which classic office work at the corporate location is taking a back seat, and so called New Working models, such as hybrid work, home office, or remote working, are becoming the new normal. These forms of organization differ enormously from the old norm and simultaneously pose new challenges to employees and managers. Strict hierarchies are to be dismantled, and freedom and individual responsibility are to be created. The aim is to give incentives for employees that increase their productivity and encourage them to develop their creativity. Individual self-realization is gaining importance (Helmold, 2021). For modern working approaches to be integrated meaningfully and efficiently into everyday work, it is crucial to involve suitable managers who can drive the change. In doing so, the concept moves away from traditional, highly hierarchical methods, where the manager acts as a controlling and directive authority, towards a freer leadership approach that is more like facilitation. Properly applied, the concept can be a win- win situation for both employees and companies. It provides employees with more creative freedom and increases the company's productivity.

Moreover, it enhances the company's attractiveness as an employer and attracts new, suitable employees. For this reason, every company needs to address this issue. Which concept of work can be integrated depends strongly on the respective company (New Work: Konzept & Beispiele Der Neuen Arbeitsformen, 2020). The advantages ofthe hybrid workplace system speak for the concept. These are mainly expressed in the concession of flexibility and autonomy to employees. This can positively influence the increase in productivity, loyalty, and creativity of employees. There is also the opportunity to reduce costs by restructuring and, if necessary, downsizing the office environment and the associated expenses for rent, furnishings, and technology. Travel costs for business trips can also be minimized or even dropped entirely. Reducing the distances traveled to work also positively impacts the environment. But fear of lost productivity is one reason employers struggle with the implementation. Proper measurement and monitoring to ensure that employees are performing at their best are in the interest of many leaders. Nevertheless, this collides with the aspect of trust that employees expect. Employee productivity, by definition, is the average work performance of an employee. Productivity measures the value, profit, and level of adequately performed tasks. Efficiency describes the effort the employee puts into his or her tasks. Efficiency is measured by the individual employee's effort into his or her work. Hybrid work generally aims to increase employee productivity while reducing personnel costs. This means that employees can concentrate better on their tasks if their needs are supported, and their work is as pleasant as possible. Eliminating disruptive factors such as commuting or office distractions increases their satisfaction, which is said to impact motivation positively. This increases productivity and leads to greater organizational efficiency. In addition, the system can have a positive impact on the work-life balance of individuals (Khan et al., 2021). However, on the other hand, it can also lead to isolation, frustration, stress, and overwork. For this reason, individual treatment of employees and their circumstances is essential.

3 Research Method

This paper aims to determine the effects of integrating new forms of work, especially hybrid models, on companies, managers, and employees and what performance success factors lead to work improvement. In addition, it is to be worked out how these can be integrated into the company's everyday work and how they can be measured and evaluated. "The virus has broken through cultural and technological barriers that prevented remote work in the past, setting in motion a structural shift in where work takes place, at least for some people" (Lund et al., 2020). The current economic and social situation as well as other external factors such as digitalization and the corona pandemic and their effects are included in the evaluation.

The work explores the following question: What key performance success factors contribute to the successful implementation of hybrid working models? In order to direct the implementation of hybrid work and to answer the research question, hypotheses are developed, presented and tested through qualitative research in the form of interviews. These refer to elements classified as crucial during the literature.

Hypothesis 1: Hybrid forms of work will prevail.

The home office, the company office, and any other place can become the new workplace, which employees also demand. This hypothesis aims to find out whether there is acceptance and a desire for hybrid forms of work on the part of employees. The relevance and the possibility of integrating hybrid forms of work into everyday company life are given and proven by the literature research. Nevertheless, acceptance by employees is a high-risk factor, which is why hybrid models can fail. The investigation of this hypothesis should help compare the literature research's tendency that hybrid working is gaining relevance with reality and develop a forecast for the future.

Hypothesis 2: Hybrid work models enable companies to increase employee productivity.

This hypothesis explores why strictly implementing hybrid working models is an essential and value-adding step for companies. According to the literature, by using hybrid work, companies can increase the productivity of their employees. In turn, it can reduce costs, provide better access to talent on a global scale and increase the competitiveness of companies. The combination of face-to-face and remote working provides the opportunity to reap the benefits of those working models. However, the assumption must be made that employees' productivity in the home office does not change or changes positively but is not reduced. For this reason, the hypothesis is of great importance for the study.

Hypothesis 3: Hybrid work models increase employee satisfaction as they allow for greater flexibility and autonomy.

This has an impact on loyalty to the company. This hypothesis addresses the elaboration that hybrid work models increase employee flexibility and autonomy. This impacts the work-life balance and, in the best case, leads to a higher level of employee satisfaction. Employees experience a better, more positive work atmosphere and feel valued. This, in turn, has a positive effect on the attitude towards the company, which is expressed in an increased loyalty of the employees towards the firm.

Hypothesis 4: The culture of trust within the company can be negatively affected because it is more difficult to monitor and measure the reliability and productivity of the individual employees.

This hypothesis examines the extent to which monitoring and flexible working, and thus the interests of employers and employees, collide. The distance makes it more difficult for managers to stay informed about what their employees complete in remote work or the home office. There is also a risk that employees feel overlooked. This can harm trust between employees.

Hypothesis 5: Corporate culture needs to be adapted to hybrid models.

Especially the role of managers and leaders is changing because communication is increasingly virtual, so new skills are necessary. It is evident from the literature that corporate culture has to adapt with the introduction of hybrid working concepts. New forms of communication must be introduced and exemplified. In addition, it is possible to integrate new technologies and tools for smooth collaboration, which is why it is advisable to include them in processes. Also the role of the leader has changed significantly due to the virtual world of work. Today's leaders must create an environment for their employees that meets the needs of both face-to-face and remote teams. Cohesion and trust must be created. Especially communication among each other has to be promoted, as the digital space, respectively the local separation, creates space for misunderstandings and distance can develop. In addition, a working environment must be created for each employee to receive all the necessary resources and support to work productively. Whether the role of the leader is really changing extensively, and what important competencies are necessary, will be examined with the help of this hypothesis.

Hypothesis 6: Hybrid work is not suitable for everyone.

According to the literature, the concept of hybrid work is not suitable for all employees. Especially the position of women as employees in a hybrid model is seen as particularly difficult in the literature. The merging of private and business life blurs the barriers, which can have a negative impact on mothers in particular in the form of stress and excessive workloads. Whether this is really a problematic development and how it can be addressed will be elaborated with the help of this hypothesis.

4 The Evaluation

The hypotheses developed were tested for their correctness by means of a qualitative analysis. This provides a comprehensive answer to the research question. In order to facilitate this, interviews were conducted with four persons, including three women and one man, aged between 25 and 62. After an evaluation of the qualitative method applied, the hypotheses were tested. The research question is answered and success factors for the implementation of hybrid working models are worked out. Performance success factors are to be elaborated. In addition, KPIs are formed to measure specific elements of the transformation. Finally, a catalog of recommendations is developed that supports the success of the integration.

Hypothesis 1: Hybrid forms of work will prevail.

All respondents clearly confirm this hypothesis. All participants report that hybrid work has been an integral part of their everyday working lives within their company since the outbreak of the Corona pandemic at the latest. In addition, they all state that overall hybrid work is a positive development, although they also mention disadvantages such as excessive demands, stress, and poorer communication. Moreover, the respondents classify as a decisive factor that the offer needs to be a comprehensive option for everyone in the corporate. In addition, it is emphasized that the choice of whether and to what extent this is then used is of equal value, as individual conditions such as the personal way of working and living conditions such as space and family have a decisive influence on this. Nevertheless, whether hybrid work will prevail and become an integral part of working life can be answered with a clear yes. However, this raises the question of what impact this will have or what primary conditions need to be created.

Hypothesis 2: Hybrid work models enable companies to increase employee productivity.

All but one of the interviewees stated that their productivity increases because, for example, they can concentrate better in the home office. Because they no longer have to travel to work, they save much time, which can be used for work. Nevertheless, it gets clear from the evaluation that hybrid working significantly impacts the interviewees' work- life balance, which is also confirmed by the literature. The impact of well-being improves as flexibility is improved. Moreover, arrangements can be made quickly and virtually, and working from home provides tranquility. However, it is also clear that negative feelings can arise for precisely this reason.

Communication, primarily, is described as a decisive factor affecting productivity. The relationships between the employees and the team can suffer considerably due to enormous reductions, as all respondents confirm. This risk is also underlined in the literature. In addition, the interviewees are increasingly concerned about surveillance or being overlooked.

One of the interviewees, in particular, complains about feeling like a worker bee and tells of her lack of energy, which harms her productivity in the home office. Also, one respondent stated that he felt that people who are not technically skilled and have language problems are at risk of being unable to keep up, which negatively impacts productivity. This ties in with the point of prerequisites. A crucial factor is that employees must be provided with the necessary virtual and physical resources. This includes software and hardware but also training and extra support. An advantage of the expanded range of work models is that a larger pool of talent and potential employees can be recruited. This underlines the potential increase in productivity through teams, as new experts can provide crucial new input. However, besides the great advantage, all respondents see a significant problem in the involvement of these new employees and the induction process. They note that the induction process is significantly hampered and complicated due to the distance and reduced personal contact. This underlines the need to develop a new basis of structures and forms of communication. Furthermore, it becomes evident that the basic foundation also lies in providing necessary equipment, training with these, and support.

Hypothesis 3: Hybrid work models increase employee satisfaction as they allow for greater flexibility and autonomy.

This has an impact on loyalty to the company. The hypothesis underpins the critical elements of why hybrid working is beneficial. It creates flexibility and autonomy. This has the potential to drastically increase satisfaction and comfort for employees, as they are less bound and can adjust their working day according to their individual needs. They describe this as a benefit that positively affects the feeling toward the employer and, thus, loyalty. The synergy is also confirmed in the literature. All respondents stated that this is a massive advantage for them and that it has a positive impact on their work-life balance. However, they also emphasized the disadvantages that can result from this.

Due to the integration of the daily work routine into the private environment, there is a substantial danger that the boundaries become blurred. The respondents also state that they check their e-mails more often after work. Two also say they worry about not feeling properly seen and valued. These various factors can significantly increase stress levels and dissatisfaction. Among other reasons, these factors can lead to negative emotions such as feeling overwhelmed and overworked, as well as a lack of organization and energy. Even though only one of the interviewees sees severe problems for certain groups of people mixing everyday life and work, this is an essential factor, as also described in the literature. Especially for working mothers, there is a risk of overloading themselves with household duties, childcare, and work, which increases stress. For all groups of employees, these factors can lead to a loss of loyalty due to the previously mentioned negative feelings and have a damaging effect on teams and loyalty to the employer.

Hypothesis 4: The culture of trust within the company can be negatively affected because it is more difficult to monitor and measure the reliability and productivity of the individual employees.

The fear of control mechanisms has a significant negative influence. The interviewees state that they have no such measures in place, but this can lead to a conflict with the need for managers to have control and knowledge of their employees' working practices. Literature confirms this point as well and classifies it as a hurdle. For this reason, making personal contact, inquiries and agreements are essential. This gives employees the feeling of precise tasks and information and allows the employer to gain knowledge about work performance. In this way, the employees' worries about being overlooked can also be reduced, in contrast to people who are more often present in the office, which one interviewee perceives as a significant disadvantage. Personal enquiry and obtaining feedback are decisive factors here.

Hypothesis 5: Corporate culture needs to be adapted to hybrid models.

Especially the role of managers and leaders is changing because communication is increasingly virtual, so new skills are necessary. Both literature research and the qualitative evaluation confirm that a change in corporate culture is necessary to implement hybrid work. In particular, the balance between face-to-face and remote working is an essential factor that must be considered to promote communication between remote teams and collaboration. Nevertheless, all respondents confirm that the personal aspect also needs to be actively promoted. As far as the job allows, a level playing field must be created for all organizational stakeholders to ensure fairness and avoid confusion. Especially the introduction of a proactive communication strategy and its integration into the corporate culture must be thoroughly thought through. Employees also value appreciation, as they emphasized in the survey. Regular feedback meetings are conducive to this. Managers increasingly need to take on the role of facilitators, which is crucial in promoting team communication. This can be achieved through further team-building measures, both virtual and face-to-face. The second component, the personal aspect, is particularly emphasized by the interviewees and should be addressed by managers. In addition, the manager must be responsive to individuals and their needs. According to the qualitative evaluation, feedback conversations and simple inquiries about well-being have a noticeable influence. Furthermore, it is the manager's task to exemplify the hybrid work concept and to act as a role model. Nevertheless, one interviewee stated that she had the feeling that the managers were less accessible. This must be avoided for a seamless communication and to maintain the role of moderator and motivator.

Hypothesis 6: Hybrid work is not suitable for everyone.

According to the literature, hybrid work is only suitable for some employees. Differences can arise in job profiles' differences. The respondents widely confirm this factor. Furthermore, the position of women as employees in a hybrid model is seen in the literature as particularly difficult. The fusion of private and professional life blurs the boundaries. For mothers, in particular, this can mean that they overburden themselves, as they do work and childcare together and overtax themselves with work. The interviewees confirm the possibility that employees are overlooked, but they clearly emphasize that this is not a question of gender or age. They consider it a general danger that managers must avoid. The aspect that mothers overload themselves in the home office, on the other hand, is instead confirmed. One interviewee clearly emphasizes this point. This leads to the conclusion that it is the employer's task to consider the employees' circumstances and respond to them. For one thing, getting feedback and offering support to the employees is essential. For example, it supports organizing work and managing the home office. Encouraging a healthy balance between work and private life is an essential factor; here, too, communication is the critical factor. Another group that needs special attention is new employees joining the company. Due to the distance, there is a danger that new team members will need to be sufficiently familiarized and that the connection to the team will become more complex. Managers must also pay special attention to this.

5 Performance Success Factors

Based on the results of the literature research and the hypotheses, as well as the verification and supplementation by the qualitative evaluations, the following section identifies and elaborates on central performance success factors that are decisive for the successful and sustainable implementation of hybrid working models. These are the result of the research question. A concise guideline will be created in the following, which lists the necessary elaborated factors for a successful implementation in the company's business routine. In addition, the effects of the respective factor and the implementation process are worked out. In addition, KPIs are determined, which help to measure the success of the implementation (Fig. 1).

Factor 1: Create a New Basis: New Structures and Rules for Hybrid Working.

This describes the need to create clear rules between mobile and stationary work in order to create a synergy. Agreements within the team and with managers are necessary to ensure conflict-free cooperation. Comprehensive regulations are important that apply to all employees. Transparency is crucial and the working systems must be elaborated. To this end, technical operations must be revised and courageous workers must be introduced to them. Communication is a particularly important factor here; clear agreements with managers and among colleagues as well as coordinated time management are indispensable. Equality is a particularly important factor here. The legal framework also needs to be revised. Clear rules especially require clarification of who is allowed to work hybrid. In the best case, all employees are given the possibility and the choice, but there are, as elaborated, occupational groups for whom the option is difficult or impossible. However, this must be addressed to ensure trust and fairness. The framework for how often this can be done and who decides must also be

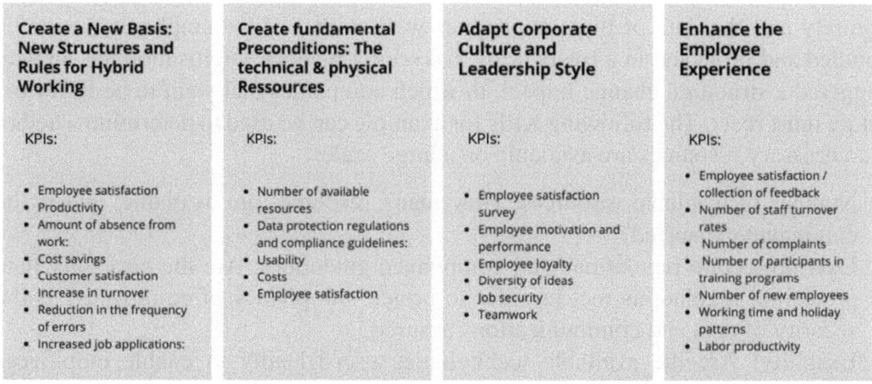

Fig. 1 Guideline for performance success factors (*Source* Illustration by the author)

defined. Areas of responsibility must be clearly identified, and operational systems need to be integrated. Legal regulations and agreements on available resources, such as office furniture, must also be defined and communicated.

The following KPIs are exemplary recommended to measure whether a new basis has been successfully introduced in the framework of hybrid working models:

- Employee satisfaction: What is the attitude of the employees towards the new model?
- Productivity: How has productivity changed compared to before the introduction?
- Amount of absence from work: Is there any downtime due to the new implementations?
- Cost savings: Were cost savings achieved? Where are the costs high compared to before the implementation?

Factor 2: Create Fundamental Preconditions: The Technical & Physical Resources.

The necessary basis for mobile and hybrid working is the technical infrastructure. Functioning video conferences, smooth communication, efficient hardware, access and data security—all of these are necessary basic requirements for hybrid working. More radical changes were driven by the lockdown and the Corona pandemic, what during this phase might have been accepted and tolerated as teething problems, now needs to be professionalized. This is particularly important to ensure cooperation between mobile teams, but also the combination of mobile and stationary staff. In addition to the technical equipment, a targeted implementation with an agenda, logging as well as a guided moderation and a fixed time management is particularly important. The tools and communication channels used must be uniformly introduced and standardized to enable seamless collaboration. In addition, there is the need for extensive training of the employees. Another factor that must be taken into account in the technical infrastructure is the security of the data. Processes must function securely and the data of the company, as well as that of the employees, must be handled and protected in a trustworthy and secure manner. Digitisation has already triggered a structural change impact, to which companies that want to be fit for the future must react. The following KPIs for example can be used to determine whether the necessary resources are available on a large scale:

- Number of available resources: How many resources are available, and is the contingent exhausted?
- Data protection regulations and compliance guidelines: Are the necessary data protection regulations met in order to protect the privacy of employees? Is the security of data and communications ensured?
- Usability: Are the available technologies user-friendly to enable employees to work effectively? Are assistance and support services, as well as training, frequently used?

Factor 3: Adapt Corporate Culture and Leadership Style

A very decisive success factor for the successful implementation of hybrid working models is the corporate culture and leadership. Hierarchies are abolished or redefined. The boundaries between private and professional experience are blurring and the boundaries between physical offices and virtual workplaces are disappearing. This is leading to distance, but the need for communication, togetherness and connection is becoming more important. For this reason, managers have to guide work processes in a controlled manner and act as role models; leading at a distance is a particularly great challenge. This balance between flexibility, but also structure and leadership, is a major hurdle for leaders who manage teams that are dispersed, even in different time zones. Leadership has to be reoriented, as the means of control that have proven themselves in the traditional office environment are no longer effective and require equivalents in the virtual environment. On the other hand, this also provides new scope for change to break old patterns and promote creativity. Another outcome that can result from hybrid work is the feeling of being overlooked by employees. A cultural change must be exemplified and not counteracted by managers. No matter how well hybrid working models are integrated, face-to-face exchange is made difficult, which is why it is particularly relevant to create meetings in the virtual space and to promote cohesion. Personal contact plays a particularly important role here, which is why empathy is so important. In the past, employees complained about excessive demands and frustration, which must also be responded to. The model is characterized by personal responsibility and flexibility of the employees, which is why a culture of trust as well as transparency must be promoted. The dilemma between control and loss of control must also be addressed. The following KPIs are recommended for monitoring and measuring the corporate culture and leadership style:

- Employee satisfaction survey: How satisfied are employees with the corporate culture and leadership style?

- Employee motivation and performance: Are employees motivated by the company culture and leadership style?
- Employee loyalty: How loyal are the employees, or do many employees leave the company for no other reason?
- Diversity of ideas: Are more ideas and innovations generated by the corporate culture and management style?
- Teamwork: How well do the company culture and leadership style influence and support teamwork?

Factor 4: Enhance the Employee Experience

Employees as well as managers need to be equipped with new skills. These span a wide range of areas and go far beyond technical skills. Drivers that can lead to success are openness and curiosity, and personal responsibility is becoming a core competence that employees must be encouraged to develop. For this, it is advantageous if different team members bring their respective competences together and thus new synergies can be created. In this context, working hours and a reduction of always-on demand expectations must also be reduced in order not to increase the stress level of the employees. This requires clear communication skills and a realistic assessment of capacities. The concept of the employee experience is also becoming more and more important. While companies have always measured and improved the customer experience, they must now also work on improving it internally. Internal touch points must be consciously created. The field of recruiting in particular has received an enormous boost from the possibility of hybrid work. The impact on personnel development and talent management in particular can receive an enormously positive boost through the implementation of hybrid working models, but also requires a reorientation. On the one hand, it is now possible to integrate employees who are far away into processes in real time and thus to integrate them as equal participants in projects. On the other hand, there are also difficulties, especially with onboarding and induction into the team. Newcomers to the profession need special support, as personal contact is more difficult. However, there are also tools and possibilities that can be used for this, but this requires a conscious decision on the part of the managers who have to lead and initiate this. Important occasions for employee experience, such as the introduction to the team, need to be rethought in order not to lose the bond with the company and with each other. Getting to know each other and the mutual exchange and learning from each other that goes with it must be taken into account. Extensive offers are necessary for this, and the help of external advisors and experts can be very helpful here. To measure the employer experience, it is advisable to use KPIs such as:

- Employee satisfaction/ collection of feedback
- Number of staff turnover rates
- Number of complaints
- Number of participants in training programs
- Number of new employees hired

6 Conclusion

This article aimed to define performance success factors for implementing hybrid working models. Hybrid work is more than a trend in the modern world. The mixed form of the home office, remote working, and present work in the office will develop into a central component of New Work. Successful integration into everyday business life creates the opportunity to react to the changing requirements of the labor market and establish a personal workplace that meets both the needs of the employees and the company's requirements. The acceptance that work no longer has to take place only in one place, and the demand of employees for this offer will continue to increase. The availability of hybrid, or remote, work also allows for expanding the talent pool, which companies can access across national borders. This promotes diversity and creates the opportunity to expand expertise within the company. In order to achieve the company's goals, it is advisable to offer hybrid working models to be competitive and an attractive employer in the future.

A planned strategy is essential, and particular attention should be paid to performance success factors such as the provision of necessary resources, the adaptation of the corporate culture and leadership style, the development of the employer experience, and the establishment of new structures. These need to be reviewed regularly and work processes should be adjusted where necessary. Flexibility is, therefore, also an enormously important factor here. For this, it is advisable to consider the implementation as a process and to stay up to date with new trends and technological developments. Companies that stick rigidly to the old office concepts are running the danger of becoming outdated. The employee will continue to be the focus of the world of work, which is why the needs of the individual must be taken into account in the creation of work processes. It is essential to create a culture of trust and cooperation in which everyone is seen and can address their problems. Particular attention should be paid to groups for whom working from a home office carries higher risks.

It is also essential to comply with laws and regulations, especially data protection and occupational safety. By overcoming these challenges, companies can effectively take advantage of the modern labour market and create a more efficient, productive, and less stressful working environment for themselves and their employees. Costs can also be reduced, and the company's productivity and competitiveness can be increased. For a successful implementation, it is advisable to use an implementation guide such as the one developed in this paper. How the respective factors are implemented depends on the company and the employees. Furthermore, it is not a sequence of steps but a process that takes place simultaneously. It must be continuously advanced, revised, and measured. This is where the use of KPIs helps. If used correctly, implementing hybrid working practices can bring significant benefits such as flexibility, time savings, a culture of trust and loyalty, an increase in productivity, and a better work-life balance. This makes the company competitive as an attractive employer and increases its productivity.

References

Franken, R., & Franken, S. (2020). Wissen, Lernen und Innovation im digitalen Unternehmen. In *Springer eBooks*.https://doi.org/10.1007/978-3-658-30178-1

Helmold, M. (2021). New work, transformational and virtual leadership. In *Management for professionals*.https://doi.org/10.1007/978-3-030-63315-8

Khan, M. B. A., Kuofie, M. H., & Suman, S. (2021). *Future opportunities for technology management education*. Information Science Reference.

Lund, S., Madgavkar, A., Manyika, J. & Smit, S. (2020, 23. November). *What's next for remote work: an analysis of 2000 tasks, 800 jobs, and nine countries*. McKinsey & Company. https://www.mckinsey.com/featured-insights/future-of-work/whats-next%20for-remote-work-an-analysis-of-2000-tasks-800-jobs-and-nine-countries

New Work: Konzept & Beispiele der neuen Arbeitsformen. (2020). https://www.avantgarde-experts.de/de/magazin/new-work/

Sonnenberg, P. (2021, Juni 13). Wie die Corona-Pandemie die Arbeitswelt verändert. *tagesschau.de*. https://www.tagesschau.de/wirtschaft/verbraucher/pandemie-und-arbeitswelt-101.html

The Importance of Digital Management for Small and Medium-Sized Wine Producing Companies in Georgia

Mariam Tvaradze

Abstract Digital management is a crucial and transformative concept that plays an important role in shaping the future of business, industry and society as a whole. In the conditions of rapid technological advancement, it is important for organizations to adopt digital management in order to increase the level of competitiveness and easily adapt to the ever-changing environment. One of the main focuses of digital management is the use of innovative technologies to optimize processes and improve overall efficiency.

The purpose of the study: This article explores the pivotal role of digital management in shaping the success and sustainability of such enterprises within the picturesque landscapes of Georgia. As the wine industry continues to evolve, the adoption of digital management practices emerges as a critical factor for optimizing processes, enhancing quality, expanding market reach, and making informed decisions. By delving into the challenges faced by these companies, we illuminate how limited resources and competition with larger entities necessitate innovative approaches. The benefits of embracing digital management encompass efficient data collection and analysis, streamlined inventory control, heightened quality assurance, targeted marketing, and improved decision-making.

Furthermore, we address the barriers to adoption and provide insights into overcoming them. Anticipating future trends, we discuss the implications of cutting-edge technologies and stress the need for adaptation to remain competitive.

Research methodology: 50 small and medium-sized wine producing companies (in Georgia) participated in the mentioned research. Qualitative research in the form of in-depth interviews and quantitative research were used. In the last part of the study, the received information is summarized and presented in the form of a conclusion.

In conclusion, this article underscores the imperative for small and medium-sized wine producing companies in Georgia to harness the power of digital management, ultimately fortifying their position in the dynamic landscape of the wine industry.

M. Tvaradze (✉)
East European University, GeorgiaTbilisi
e-mail: mariammtvaradze@gmail.com

R. C. Geibel and S. Machavariani (eds.), *Digital Management to Shape the Future*, Springer Proceedings in Business and Economics,
https://doi.org/10.1007/978-3-031-66517-2_19

Keywords Digital management in Georgia · Small and medium size companies · Georgian wine making companies · Transformation problems

1 Introduction

The wine industry is one of the most important industries in the world. It develops gradually. Recently, a new force has emerged that is shaping a new model of wine production and development - this is digital management. It is of special importance for small and medium-sized wine producing companies in Georgia. As the global market.

becomes increasingly interconnected and technology-oriented, digital management remains an indispensable strategy for the development of Georgian wine-producing enterprises.

The development of the Georgian wine industry and growth of wine producing companies have redefined the dynamics of the industry.

In the stages of development, small and medium-sized wine producing companies face various challenges: scarce resources, limited access to advanced technologies and struggle in a competitive market. However, in these challenges there are various opportunities such as digital management, through which it is possible to solve the problems existing in the modern wine industry, using world practices and so on. In this article, we will delve into the possibilities of digital management and its impact on the wine industry in Georgia. We identify the benefits of digital management, the potential degree of transformation, identify barriers that hinder processes and discuss future trends, as well as forecasts that promise to shape the trajectory of wine production. Based on the above, the role and importance of digital management for small and medium-sized wine producing companies in Georgia will be emphasized. As we traverse this path of exploration, it becomes evident that the integration of digital tools into every facet of wine production and distribution has the power to redefine the status quo, allowing these companies to not only survive but also thrive in a highly competitive and evolving landscape. The journey towards embracing digital management is not solely about adapting to technology but about embracing innovation as a cornerstone of progress. With a firm understanding of the transformative potential of digital management, let us embark on a journey that uncovers the importance of this integration for the small and medium-sized wine producing companies in Georgia.

2 Digital Management in the Wine Industry in Georgia

Due to digital innovations, most industries around the world are undergoing profound transformation, so the wine sector is no exception. Digital management involves the integration of technology into various aspects of business operations. This paradigm shift is especially relevant for small and medium-sized wine producing companies, which represent an important economic sector of Georgia. The concept of digital management includes several aspects: digital management in the wine industry at its core involves the use of technological tools to simplify and optimize processes, strengthen decision-making and create seamless synergy between the various stages of wine production and distribution. From vineyard management to marketing and distribution, Digital management offers a comprehensive solution to the challenges that have long plagued the wine industry, especially in the context of Georgia's growing trend. Technological progress in Georgia's wine industry: Georgia's wine industry has experienced remarkable growth in recent years, attracting attention for its unique winemaking traditions and diverse grape varieties. Small and medium-sized wine producers in the region play an important role in preserving these traditions. Due to the fact that Georgia holds a specific niche in the world market, the integration of digital management practices will have a decisive role in the development of the mentioned field. Vineyard Management and Agriculture: One of the fundamental aspects of wine production lies in vineyard management. Through digital management, wine producers will be able to get real-time data about their vineyards, which will help make accurate decisions. Sensor technology, drones and satellite imagery allow monitoring of soil conditions, weather patterns and grape health. Such insights help to optimize irrigation, prevent disease and improve the quality of the grapes, which in turn ensures the best results. Winemaking processes and quality assurance: Digital management systems can revolutionize winemaking processes. Temperature and humidity sensors combined with data analytics allow winemakers to closely monitor and control fermentation and aging conditions. As a result, we will get improved processes and a quality product. Moreover, digital traceability systems enhance quality assurance by tracking every step of the manufacturing process, ensuring compliance with standards and regulations. Marketing, Distribution and Consumer Engagement: In the digital age, effective marketing and distribution strategies are important for wine producers in Georgia to reach wider markets. Digital platforms, social media and e-commerce allow direct contact with the customer, eliminating intermediaries and allowing targeted promotions to be planned. In addition, digital tools help manage inventory, reduce excess inventory or shortages, and improve distribution logistics.

Georgia's wine industry continues to develop, the integration of digital management practices is emerging, as a basis for the success of small and medium-sized wine producing companies. New technology offers unprecedented opportunities to improve processes, improve quality and expand market access.

2.1 Challenges Faced by Small and Medium-sized Wine Producers in Georgia

Although the prospects for integrating digital management in the activities of small and medium-sized wine producers in Georgia are promising, the enterprises also face some challenges. The unique characteristics of the wine industry, together with the specific context of Georgia's wine development, represent a set of obstacles that these companies must overcome in order to fully exploit the advantages of technology-oriented strategies. (1) Limited resources and budget restrictions: challenges and difficulties can be considered that: small and medium-sized wine producers often work with limited financial resources compared to larger competitors, the upfront costs of implementing digital management systems, such as sensor networks, data analytics software, and training costs. In addition, allocating funds for technological investments and making the mentioned decision is a certain difficulty for managers. (2) Technical expertise and training: Adopting digital management requires a certain level of technical expertise to effectively implement and maintain the technology. Small wine companies may not have in-house IT departments or staff with the skills to manage these systems. An additional challenge is the need for specialized training or the hiring of external experts. (3) Resistance to change and tradition: The wine industry is steeped in tradition, often spanning generations. The introduction of digital tools and data-driven approaches may be resisted due to the traditional nature of winemaking. Convincing stakeholders of the benefits of digital management can be associated with difficulties. (4) Scalability and Customization: Using digital technologies, it is possible to increase the scale of production, but whether this comes with a decrease in quality and efficiency is debatable. In addition, the diverse nature of wine production means that any digital solution must be adaptable and configurable to different production methods and grape varieties. (5) Connectivity and infrastructure: Digital management relies heavily on consistent and robust connectivity, which can be difficult to achieve in regions with many vineyards. Due to the terrain of Georgia, providing a reliable Internet connection for data transfer and remote monitoring can become a problem. (6) Data security and privacy: Small and medium-sized wine producers may not have the resources to implement robust cyber security measures, leaving them potentially vulnerable to breaches that could harm business operations and consumer confidence. (7) Competition with large enterprises: Competing with large wine producers in terms of market visibility, distribution networks and financial influence is a big challenge for small enterprises. The resources that larger companies can invest in digital management can create a significant competitive advantage for smaller players facing these challenges.

2.2 The Benefits of Digital Management for Wine Producers

In light of the challenges faced by small and medium-sized wine producers in Georgia, the integration of digital management systems brings many benefits that can change their operations and competitive position. By using technology, these enterprises can not only cope with their challenges, but also gain new opportunities for growth, quality improvement and market expansion. (1) Data-driven decision making: Digital management systems allow wine producers to collect and analyze vast amounts of data on vineyard conditions, production processes and consumer preferences. This data-driven approach enhances informed decision-making, which allows manufacturers to adjust strategies based on accurate real-time insights. For example, data on weather patterns and soil conditions can inform irrigation and planting decisions, resulting in improved grape quality and yield. (2) Enhanced Quality Control: Maintaining consistent quality is paramount in the wine industry. Digital instrumentation facilitates tight quality control by monitoring and adjusting critical parameters such as temperature, humidity, and fermentation rate. This ensures that the final product meets the desired standards and retains its unique characteristics. (3) Effective inventory management: digital management systems improve inventory management, by providing real-time visibility into demand and distribution networks, costs can be optimized. (4) Targeted Marketing and Consumer Engagement: In an era where consumer preferences and purchasing behaviors are closely tied to digital platforms, wine producers in Georgia can use technology to directly engage with their audience. Social media, online platforms and e-commerce websites enable targeted marketing campaigns, increase brand visibility and help gain loyal customers. (5) Simplified distribution channels: by using digital channels, it is possible to establish a direct connection with consumers, which reduces additional costs such as intermediaries and etc. (6) Optimization of resources: Efficient allocation of resources is a key issue for small wine producers. Digital management systems optimize the use of resources in the use of water, energy and other resources exactly where they are needed. This not only reduces operational costs but also promotes sustainable development (7) Traceability and Compliance: Traceability, a growing concern for both consumers and regulators, is enhanced by digital management systems. Producers can trace the movement of grapes from the vineyard to the bottle, ensuring compliance with quality standards and transparency for the consumer about the origin of the wine. (8) Strategic growth and adaptation: digital management provides wine producers with data on market trends, on consumer preferences and industry developments. Enterprises with this information can strategically adapt to changing conditions, explore new markets, and develop innovative products. The benefits of digital management systems for small and medium-sized wine producers in Georgia go beyond operational efficiency. They allow these enterprises not only to survive, but also to develop and take over the world market.

3 Research Results

Up to 50 small and medium wine producing companies and family farms participated in the research.

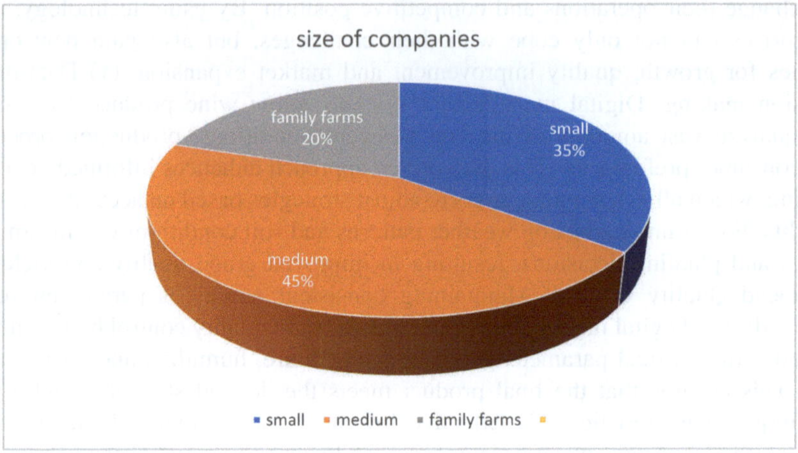

It is important to note the geographical location of the surveyed companies:

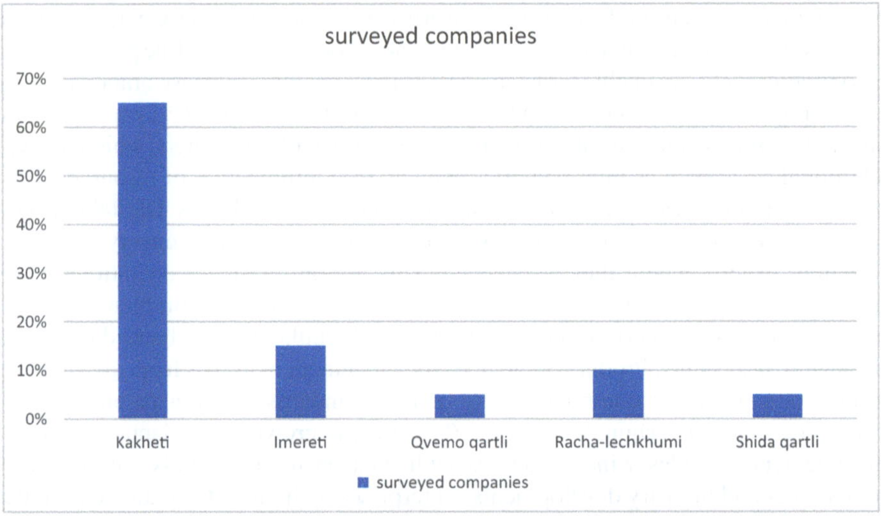

Based on the received information, we can draw the following conclusion:

In the main case, the following challenges are encountered in the process of wine production, which are related to maintaining consistent quality in a diverse assortment of grape varieties. Their limited resources make it difficult to monitor the unique conditions of each vineyard and to tailor winemaking processes individually. Most of the companies face problems in planning marketing campaigns, they cannot go beyond the borders of the country and they cannot get in touch with the customers of the international market. Some have adopted a comprehensive digital management system that involves installing weather and soil sensors in their vineyards. These sensors collected data on temperature, humidity, soil moisture, and more. They linked this data to winemaking software that allowed real-time monitoring of fermentation and aging conditions in their cellars. They have also created online platforms to plan marketing campaigns in the international market. As a result of the above changes, companies were able to optimize irrigation and nutrient supply, resulting in healthier vines and improved grape quality. With the use of digital technologies, they were able to optimize costs, constantly control the processes, which ultimately yielded results. And online platforms have connected companies to international markets and therefore potential customers.

The surveyed companies identified several main problems:

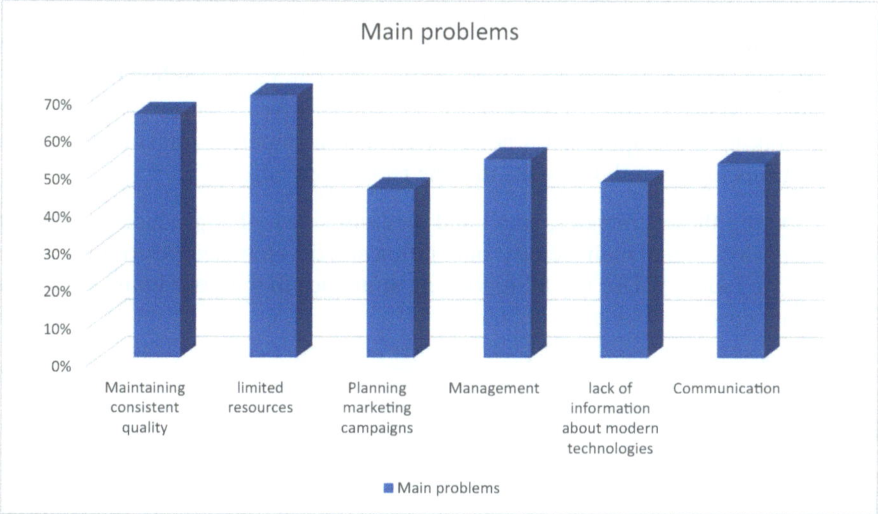

It is also worth noting the experience of several medium-sized wineries, Their main findings are related to resource management and inventory control. Several of them implemented a digital management system that incorporated IoT devices for real-time monitoring of water and energy consumption. This allowed them to identify inefficiencies, resulting in improved resource utilization. They also introduced a digital inventory management system that used analytics to forecast demand and adjust production accordingly. To stand out, they launched an Augmented Reality (AR) app that provided a complete virtual tour of their vineyards and winemaking processes. As a result, adoption of digital resource management has resulted in significant cost savings and reduced environmental impact.

Their inventory management system reduced waste and inventory, increased overall operational efficiency. The AR app provided a unique and interactive way for consumers to connect with the brand, which led to the promotion of their winery and increased peer-to-peer sales worldwide.

Companies use different strategies in digital transformation to avoid certain types of problems and challenges, for example:

1. Addressing cost constraints: it is considered that digital management is more of an investment than an expense.
2. Overcoming technical expertise gaps: training and development of priority personnel.
3. Managing resistance to change: foster a culture of openness and incremental change.
4. Scalability and Customization Challenges: Scalability and customization will be prioritized when choosing digital solutions.
5. Improvement of connectivity and infrastructure.
6. Ensuring data security and privacy.
7. Dealing with competition from larger enterprises: Strategy: Use your unique selling points. emphasizes authenticity, The personal touch and connection to the local community that small wineries can offer. Use digital marketing strategies to tell your brand story and engage with customers on a deeper level.
8. Change Management: Develop a comprehensive change management plan. Taking these approaches not only ensures a smoother transition, but also maximizes the potential benefits that the technology offers.

By adopting these strategies, small and medium-sized wine producers can meet the challenges of digital management integration and develop their positioning in the modern wine industry. Use digital marketing strategies to tell your brand story and engage with customers on a deeper level.

4 Conclusion

Georgia, as the homeland of wine, is passing through important stages in the development of the wine sector. The combination of tradition and innovation, symbolized by the adoption of digital management strategies, is the key to their sustainable growth and success in the modern wine industry. Amidst the challenges of limited resources, gaps in technical expertise, and resistance to change, these enterprises have demonstrated their resilience by recognizing the importance of technology-driven solutions. The benefits of digital management are vast and varied: from data-driven decision-making and quality improvement to effective inventory control and direct customer engagement. Through case studies, we witnessed how wine companies overcame obstacles, they have used technology to transform their operations and achieve positive results.

Forecasting the future highlights important trends such as IoT, AI, blockchain and others. An era of digital transformation is dawning, offering the promise of optimized vineyard management, enhanced quality control and deeper customer connections. These trends represent not only opportunities for small and medium-sized wine producers, but also a strategic advantage to strengthen their position in a competitive market. In a world where authenticity and sustainability resonate with consumers, digital management serves as a catalyst for these enterprises to showcase their unique stories, commitment to quality, and adherence to ethical practices. e-commerce platforms, Through smart packaging and blockchain-enabled traceability, they can foster a connection with consumers that transcends borders. The importance of small and medium wine production companies in Georgia in terms of digital management is unequivocal. By adopting innovations, these enterprises can not only cope with the complexities of the modern wine industry, but also develop on a global scale. As the heritage of winemaking meets the potential of technology, the journey of these winemakers becomes a testament to the harmonious coexistence of tradition and progress.

References

10 Tech Innovations That Are Changing The Wine Industry | Cult Wines (wineinvestment.com). https://www.wineinvestment.com/learn/magazine/2021/06/10-tech-innovations-that-are-changing-the-wine-industry/

14182 (wine.gov.ge). https://wine.gov.ge/En/Files/Download/14182

G&T: Georgian wine industry entering a new era – Investor.ge. https://www.investor.ge/2021/10/18/gt-georgian-wine-industry-entering-a-new-era/

General Strategies Of Georgian Winemaking Companies' Management In The Conditions Of Integrated Development (researchgate.net). https://www.researchgate.net/publication/305538459_GENERAL_STRATEGIES_OF_GEORGIAN_WINEMAKING_COMPANIES'_MANAGEMENT_IN_THE_CONDITIONS_OF_INTEGRATED_DEVELOPMENT

http://www.georgianwine.gov.ge/

https://wine.gov.ge/

Investing in innovation: Georgia's digital development journey - ITU Hub. https://www.itu.int/hub/2021/11/investing-in-innovation-georgias-digital-development-journey/

Revealing the challenges facing Georgia's wine industry from a natural winemaker perspective using Q-methodology | Emerald Insight. https://www.emerald.com/insight/content/doi/https://doi.org/10.1108/IJWBR-06-2021-0036/full/html

Saladze, A. (2018). *Untamed. 8000 vintages of Georgian wine*. Sulakauri Publishing.

Svanidze, A., & Costa-Font, M. (2023). Revealing the challenges facing Georgia's wine industry from a natural winemaker perspective using Q-methodology. *International Journal of Wine Business Research, 35*(1), 89–120.

The Biggest Technology Trends In Wine And Winemaking (forbes.com). https://www.forbes.com/sites/bernardmarr/2022/05/18/the-biggest-technology-trends-in-wine-and-winemaking/?sh=5aa2a1834e46

The Cultural Factor of Digital Entrepreneurship in the Context of Economic Growth

Givi Bedianashvili

Abstract This paper explores the importance of using the culture factor in terms of the impact of digital entrepreneurship development on economic growth in modern conditions. In this regard, first, the entrepreneurial ecosystem should be considered as a systemic concept of digital ecosystem interactions, which implies certain changes in the cultural component of digital entrepreneurship itself. The current stage of globalization is characterized by a number of specific aspects of post-industrial development, of which, in our opinion, is the most important is the actualization of the formation of a knowledge-based economy. It is must noting that globalization, related to the growth of uncertainty, leads to the addition of dimensions with a global perspective to the knowledge economy, such as resource-technological, informational, communicative, socio-psychological, and institutional structures. It should be noted too that in the process of formation of the knowledge economy, the innovative aspect of entrepreneurial activity acquires special importance in terms of all business subjects. The effectiveness of the entire innovation process depends on the effective functioning of knowledge-based entrepreneurship, which in turn determines the need for the development and implementation of an innovative entrepreneurship policy by the state. In parallel with the creation of the digital ecosystem within the framework of the innovative entrepreneurial policy, the formation of the institutional component, its systematic modernization in dynamics, the mutual compatibility and synchronization of general formal institutions, and business culture as an informal institution necessary consider.

Keywords Digital entrepreneurship · Economic growth · Culture

G. Bedianashvili (✉)
Ivane Javakhishvili Tbilisi State University, Tbilisi, Georgia
e-mail: givi.bedianashvili@tsu.ge

R. C. Geibel and S. Machavariani (eds.), *Digital Management to Shape the Future*, Springer Proceedings in Business and Economics,
https://doi.org/10.1007/978-3-031-66517-2_20

1 Introduction

Entrepreneurial activity has always been the main factor of socio-economic development of any country in the world. This is especially evident when considering the problem of economic growth, when the effectiveness of the functioning of the entrepreneurial sphere within the country uniquely determines the rates of economic growth, as well as the state of the social sphere and the well-being of people. It should be noted that in modern conditions, against the background of the high importance of the formation of a knowledge-based economy, the innovative aspect of entrepreneurial activity is gaining special relevance in terms of all business entities (Bedianashvili et al, 2021). The effectiveness of the entire innovation process depends on the effective functioning of knowledge-based entrepreneurship (Bedianasvili, 2017, 2018). Undoubtedly, a special role is assigned to digitization and the understanding of the corresponding new entrepreneurial paradigm and business models in this process.

When considering the problems of economic growth in the conditions of digitization of entrepreneurial activity, economy, and society, it is important to reveal and consider the features of modern globalization. On the other hand, in terms of the impact of digital entrepreneurship development on economic growth, the careful use of the culture factor is of great importance.

2 Methodology, Research Methods and Data Sources

System analysis, synthesis and modeling methods were used in the research. The methods of induction, deduction, qualitative, quantitative, comparison, statistical analysis, benchmarking were also used in the research process. The actual analysis included the processing of the literature surrounding the problem, the search for statistical data, the sorting of the data found, and the quantitative analysis, as well as the consideration of expert opinions within the research. The sources of statistical data were the materials of the International Monetary Fund (IMF), World Bank (WB), United Nations (UN) and other international organizations, as well as the National Statistical Office of Georgia.

3 Entrepreneurship and Economic Growth: A Retrospective and Modern Concept

If we analyze historically the dynamics of the scientific economical idea and the modern conceptions of the phenomenon of entrepreneurial activity (Acs, 2006; Baumol, 1990; Bedianashvili, 2017; Beugelsdijk, 2017; Blaug, 1989; Bojnec & Ferto,2012; Drucker, 1993; Erkomaishvili, 2016; Hofstede, 2011; McClelland, 1987;

Schumpeter, 1942, 2012; Simon, 1967; Veblen, 1904; World Economic Forum, 2013) distinctly can noticeable the main of the modern concept of entrepreneurial model.

For example, the famous contemporary researcher of entrepreneurship V. Baumol points out the great importance of the institutional factor in entrepreneurial business (Baumol, 1990). He mentions that entrepreneurship is the ability of the individual to invent and obtain the new means for the growth of his well-being, power, and prestige. He says that the realization of above-mentioned ability is not always directed to creating the additional public product. The rules of economic activity define the direction of entrepreneurial ability and this direction can be productive, non-productive, or destructive. As Baumol says, according to the "rules of the game", the entrepreneur takes decision how to get the income: by implementing the innovation, by setting up an enterprise and to accomplish his business legally or not, avoid paying taxes or set up illegal business.

J. Say notes that the entrepreneur implements the coordination of the product factors (land, capital and labor). To his opinion the entrepreneurial ability is the fourth factor that complements the effectiveness of the manufacture, and in the society, there is always some kind of demand on entrepreneurial business. As it is known, entrepreneurial ability was discussed as a specific factor only in the XX century, and only afterwards the concept of human capital of the entrepreneur appeared in science (Blaug, 1989).

T. Veblen points out that the motivation of entrepreneurial business is to get profit; the source of high profit is the instability in the market and the entrepreneurs always try to create such instability (Veblen, 1904).

The interesting view was by I. Schumpeter. In his opinion the entrepreneur is a smallholder person who implements innovations in his business; The innovations lead us to losing balance, to blowing up business activities and as a Result the economic growth is obtained. To his mind it is not necessary for the entrepreneur to be the owner, the main thing for him is to have ability to implement and use the innovations in his farming business practice, thereto the entrepreneur can't be always the generator of new ideas and innovations, his main task is to use novelties and to get profit with the help of using these novelties (Schumpeter, 1942).

And we consider interesting M. Allais's point of view about entrepreneur business according to which the entrepreneurs can get the universal welfare only in the existence of rival environment that is formed by the social institutions. As the author notes, the state can make laws of institutional limits and change them, but it must be done according to the effectiveness of the economy of market. And exactly this determines the blooming and the dying of the cultures and civilizations (Allais, 1988).

Among the modern researchers we must mark out the famous theoretician of management and innovational economics P. Drucker He gave the entrepreneurial phenomenon the new conceptual view, according to which the results of entrepreneurs' creative business are reflected not only on economics but on the entire society. As the author notes, in the society of informational era those entrepreneurs who will feel the tendencies of changes in the business and will adapt operatively to these changes will be survived. And those entrepreneurs will become the leaders who

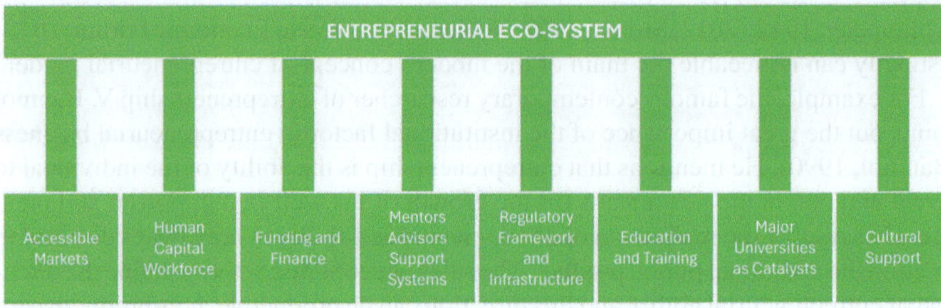

Fig. 1 Model of entrepreneurial ecosystems (*Source* Own Presentation based on World Economic Forum [2013])

will be able to generate changes in their business. To P. Drucker's mind the informational society will require transformations not only in the economic field, but above-mentioned society will transform the system of education principally and will activate the non-commercial organizations. Intellectuals who will be able to generate new ideas will be required on the labor market. And those specialists who will be able to implement these ideas will be required as well. Thereto the development of education system is expected to develop towards two directions: (1) preparing the specialists with the knowledge of wide ideology and creative skills and habits; (2) preparing narrow specialists with the profound knowledge of proper profiles (Drucker, 1993).

Modern concepts of entrepreneurial activity focus on the model of the entrepreneurial ecosystem and the allocation of relevant components (see, for example, World Economic Forum, 2013—Fig. 1; Acs et al., 2018a—Fig. 2; Stam &Van de Ven, 2021—Fig. 3).

The modern entrepreneurial ecosystem is a complex dynamic socio-economic system, and it is in this context that it is appropriate to determine its relationship with the digital ecosystem, taking into account the peculiarities of digital entrepreneurship.

4 Digital Entrepreneurship, Modern Globalization, and Culture

Various theoretical and applied studies are devoted to the study of culture problems in entrepreneurial activity (see, for example, Beugelsdijk, 2007; Beugelsdijk et al., 2014; Gherkenashvili, 2023). There are also interesting studies devoted to the use of digital technologies in entrepreneurship, including economic growth issues (Acs, 2006; Acs et al., 2018b; Acs et al., 2023; Bedianashvili & Maglakelidze, 2021; Bedianashvili et al, 2021; Bedianashvili et al, 2022; Bouberka et al, 2023; Didero et al, 2008; Edler &Fagerberg, 2017; Lafuente, 2023; Munjishvili et al, 2023; Nambisan, 2017; Nambisan et al, 2019; Sepashvili, 2021; Song, 2019; Spigel & Harrison, 2018;

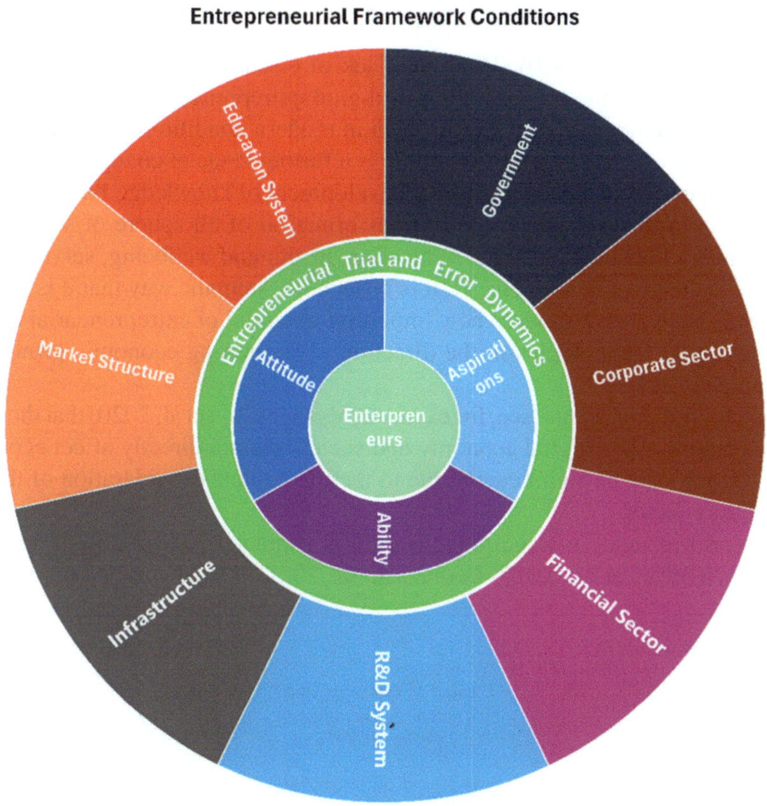

Fig. 2 Configuration of the entrepreneurial ecosystem (*Source* Own Presentation based on Acs et al. [2018a])

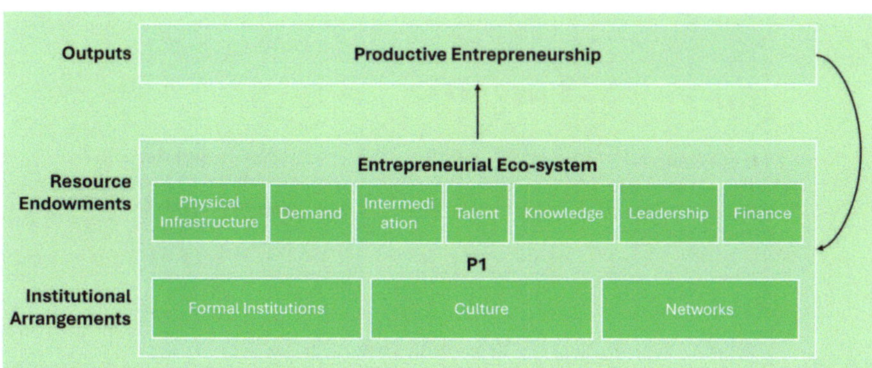

Fig. 3 Elements and outputs of the entrepreneurial ecosystem (*Source* Own Presentation based on Stam &Van de Ven [2021])

Szerb et al., 2022; Stam & Ven, 2021; Tokmazashvili, 2023; Vyshnevskyi et al, 2020; Zhylinska et al., 2020). There is a lack of research on the characteristics of the manifestation of the culture factor in digital entrepreneurship, which does not correspond to the relevance of this problem in modern conditions.

The concept of digital entrepreneurship is a further stage of change in the format of entrepreneurship in the context of the development of knowledge-based economy and business in the process of digital transformation of all sphere of society sach as economy and business, industry, education, health and wellbeing, service sector, social life, state governance (Fig. 4). It is in such a systematic way that it is possible to gradually activate the modern new important potential of entrepreneurial activity based on digital technologies in the direction of promoting economic growth and development.

Separate studies show us (see, for example, Vyshnevskyi et al, 2020) that the levels of development of the digital economy and society cannot directly affect economic growth, which may be significantly due to the incomplete consideration of the role of the culture factor.

The world in modern stage globalization is characterized by a high degree of uncertainty (Baker et al., 2016; Bedianashvili, 2021). Under these conditions, the

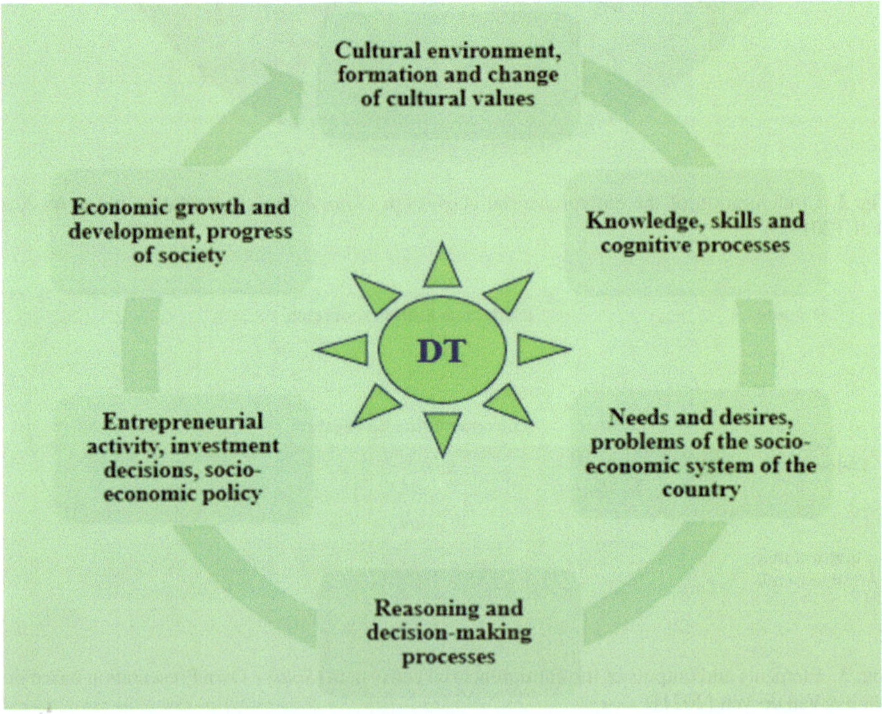

Fig. 4 Entrepreneurial activity, economic growth and development in the context of changes in cultural values of society and digital transformation (DT) (*Source* Compiled by the author)

most important for any state is to ensure the sustainability of the functioning of the socio-economic system of its country (Bedianashvili, 2023).

In this regard, the systems presentation of the culture as important factor of the economic growth of country and entrepreneurial activity. This is especially important in conditions of modern confrontational (about confrontational globalization see Papava, 2022).

One of the first and recognized approaches in the modeling and quantitative measurement of culture and values was developed by G. Hofstede. In the Hofstede model (Hofstede, 2011; Hofstede Insights, 2022), quantitatively measurable separate blocks of culture are allocated, which systemic represent community values in unity. In the recent version of this model the following six blocks and the corresponding index are represented: PDI—Power distance index—It reflects the willingness of human beings to adopt the hierarchical structure of power in society and institutions and its unequal distribution; Individualism (IDV—Individualism vs. Collectivism) represents the choice of people (preferential attributes of society) between activities of independence and interdependence (prioritizing the interests of relevant groups); Unacceptance of uncertainty(avoidance, uncertainty avoidance, UAI—Uncertainty avoidance index) shows the level of tolerance(uncertainty) of the individual and society as a whole towards uncertain (Indefinable) situations. Masculinity (Femininity, MAS—Masculinity vs. Femininity) is an assessment of individuals and society as a whole according to such properties as Purposefulness, advancement of interests, rigor, and focus on success. Long-term orientation (short-term orientation. LTO—Long-term orientation vs. short-term orientation) is an indication of how people and society are focused on the long-term, strategically pragmatic future, as opposed to traditional short-term (operational) orientation. IVR—indicator Indulgence, which indicates the level of restraint and forgiveness—the lower the index is, the greater the impact on society, people's behavior, traditions, and norms, and vice versa, the great value of the indicator points to a relatively high level of personal impulsive behavior.

It is clear, in conditions of high uncertainty, the cultural factor is of decisive importance for economic growth, as well as for the progressive development of entrepreneurial and innovative activities. The Studies and a comparative analysis show that the transformation of cultural values, such as the strengthening of long-term orientation(pragmatism), reduction of power distance, and development of individualism qualities, is most important for Georgia (Bedianashvili, 2020).

For digital entrepreneurship, the cultural factor has special importance directly in the process of digital transformation, which is the process of changing business models, operational processes and customer interactions using digital technologies. Given that an organization's culture includes the values, beliefs, norms, and behaviors of individuals, it can have a profound impact on an organization's ability to adapt to digital change. It is clear that an open, innovative and adaptable corporate culture can enable successful digital transformation. It is clear that effective digital transformation can increase productivity, reduce costs and create new opportunities for economic growth.

Successful digital transformation requires changes in corporate culture. However, it is important that workers and management are ready for change, willing to learn and develop new skills, and open to innovation. Organizational culture can certainly be a key factor in the success or failure of digital transformation.

Digital entrepreneurship drives the development of digital ecosystems, including startups, incubators, accelerators, venture capitalists and other participants that facilitate the creation and development of new entrepreneurial activities forms.

Digitization and digital transformation can contribute to economic growth. This creates new opportunities for entrepreneurship, innovation, and job creation, improving service quality, reducing costs, and increasing the competitiveness of companies, which overall contributes to economic growth in the country.

Digital entrepreneurship often leads to the emergence of new markets and industries such as online commerce, fintech, digital services and many others. These new markets create jobs, stimulate investment and as a result contribute to economic growth and development.

5 Conclusion

Digital entrepreneurship is the result of a long-term historical period of conception and development of entrepreneurship as an activity, conditioned by the process of modern industrialization and features of globalization.

For the progressive use of the culture factor in digital entrepreneurship, in the context of economic growth, there is a need for interrelated and systematic consideration of the mentioned problems.

The process of digital entrepreneurship and digital transformation without considering the institutional provision and cultural features cannot give us the basis for the effective impact of digital technologies and digital transformation on economic growth.

Digital transformation implies certain changes in work forms, internal processes, and relationships, and it may become necessary to transform and redefine values, norms, and expectations within the company. Organizational culture must be adaptable and able to adapt to these changes, support new initiatives and encourage innovation.

In the conditions of digital economy and entrepreneurship, considering the features of the stage of confrontational globalization, it is important to develop cultural values gradually and adequately in the process of digital transformation.

Globalization and digital transformation are also driving cultural diversity, which can affect how companies engage with different cultures as part of their digital transformation strategy.

In the conditions of rapidly changing technologies and markets in the digital environment, it is of great importance to form and develop a culture of adaptability and flexibility, which will allow entrepreneurs to quickly respond to changes and effectively innovate their business.

References

Acs, Z. J. (2006). How is entrepreneurship good for economic growth? *Innovations: Technology, GovernanCe, Globalization, 1*(1), 97–107.
Acs, Z. J., Szerb, L., & Lloyd, A. (2018a). *Global Enterpreneurship Index*. GEDI.
Acs, Z. J., Estrin, S., Mickiewicz, T., & Szerb, L. (2018b). Entrepreneurship, institutional economics, and economic growth: An ecosystem perspective. *Small Business Economics, 51*(2), 501–514.
Acs, Z.J., Lafuente, E., & Szerb, L. (2023). Introduction: Entrepreneurial ecosystems. In Z. J. Acs, E. Lafuente, L. Szerb (Eds.), *The Entrepreneurial Ecosystem.* Palgrave Studies in Entrepreneurship and Society. Palgrave Macmillan. https://doi.org/10.1007/978-3-031-25931-9_1
Allais M. (1988). an outline of my main contributions to economic science. https://www.nobelprize.org/nobel_prizes/economic-sciences/laureates/1988/allais-lecture.pdf
Baker, S. R., Bloom, N., & Davis S. J. (2016, November). Measuring Economic Policy Uncertainty. *The Quarterly Journal of Economics, 131*(4), 1593–1636, https://doi.org/10.1093/qje/qjw024
Baumol, W. J. (1990). Enterpreneurship: Productive, unproductive and destructive. *Journal of Political Economy, 98*(5), 893–920.
Bedianashvili, G., Bichia, Q., & Natsvlishvili, E. (2021). Development of entrepreneurial activity, labor market and modern challenges of higher education. *Globalization and Business, 12*, 21–31. (In Georgian). https://doi.org/10.35945/gb.2021.12.002
Bedianashvili, G., Zhosan, H., & Lavrenko, S. (2022). Modern digitalization trends of Georgia and Ukraine. *Scientific Papers Series Management, Economic Engineering in Agriculture and Rural Development., 20*(3), 57–74.
Bedianashvili, G. (2017). Formation of knowledge economy and innovative entrepreneurial policy: Institutional aspects. *Globalization and Business., 3*, 10–16.
Bedianashvili, G. (2018). Knowledge economy, entrepreneurial activity and culture factor in modern conditions of globalization: Challenges for Georgia. *Globalization and Business., 5*, 32–37.
Bedianashvili G., & Maglakelidze A. (2021). The digital economy and business in the conditions of pandemic. Conference Proceedings: *"Social Sciences for Regional Development 2020". Part III. Issues of Economics* (pp. 26–36). Daugavpils University.
Bedianashvili, G. (2021). Macroeconomic and Cultural Determinants of the COVID-19 pandemic crisis. *Bulletin of the Georgian National Academy of Sciences., 15*(2), 191–197.
Bedianashvili, G. (2023). Macrosystemic challenges of uncertainty under the conditions of confrontational globalization. *Bulletin of the Georgian National Academy of Sciences, 17*(2), 174–179.
Bedianashvili, G. (2020). *Culture as an institution in economics and business: Macroeconomic system approach.* Universal. (In Georgian).
Beugelsdijk, S. (2007). Entrepreneurial culture, regional innovativeness and economic growth. *Journal of Evolutionary Economics, 17*(1), 187–210.
Beugelsdijk, S., Slangen, A., Maseland, R., & Onrust, M. (2014). The impact of home–host cultural distance on foreign affiliate sales: The moderating role of cultural variation within host countries. *Journal of Business Research, 67*(8), 1638–1646.
Blaug, M. (1989). *Great economists since Keynes: An introduction to the lives and works of one hundred modern economists.*
Bojnec, S., & Ferto, I. (2012). Broadband availability and economic growth. *Industrial Management and Data Systems, 112*(9), 1292–1306. https://doi.org/10.1108/02635571211278938
Bouberka, M., Fadel, S., & Derrar, H. (2023). Digitalization and the Information Society in Algeria: Digital transformation actors and key variables. Econometrics. Ekonometria. *Advances in Applied Data Analysis, 27*(2), 21–44.
Didero, M., Gareis, K., Marques, P., & Ratzke, M. (2008). Differences in innovation culture across Europe. Transformative Use of ICT in EU Regions. Transform, Germany.
Drucker, P. F. (1993). *Innovation and entrepreneurship: Practice and principles.* Harper Collins Publishers Inc.

Edler, J., & Fagerberg, J. (2017). Innovation policy: What, why, and how. *Oxford Review of Economic Policy, 33*(1), 2–23.

Erkomaishvili, G. (2016). Small entrepreneurship supporting policy in Georgia. *World Academy of Science, Engineering and Technology International Journal of Economics and Management Engineering, 10*(5), 1409–1412.

Gherkenashvili T. (2023). Pathway for elaborating model of culture of innovation and creativity at Universities as Prerequisite for their performance. In R. C. Geibel & S. Machavariani (Eds.), *Digital Management in Covid-19 Pandemic and Post-Pandemic Times* (pp. 179–191). Springer Proceedings in Business and Economics. https://doi.org/10.1007/978-3-031-20148-6_17

Hofstede Insights (2022, January 17). National Culture. https://hi.hofstede-insights.com/national-culture

Hofstede, G. (2011). Dimensionalizing cultures: The Hofstede model in context. *Online Readings in Psychology and Culture, 2*(1). https://doi.org/10.9707/2307-0919.1014

Lafuente, E. (2023). World Technology Frontier: Directed technical change and the relevance of the entrepreneurial ecosystem. In Z. J. Acs, E. Lafuente, & L. Szerb (Eds.), *The Entrepreneurial Ecosystem. Palgrave Studies in Entrepreneurship and Society*. Palgrave Macmillan, Cham. https://doi.org/10.1007/978-3-031-25931-9_3

McClelland David, C. (1987). *Human motivation.* Boston University.

Munjishvili, T., Sigua, Z., & Shugliashvili, T. (2023). Digital Transformation in Education_Self-study System "Cyber3s". In R. C. Geibel & S. Machavariani (Eds.), *Digital Management in Covid-19 Pandemic and Post-Pandemic Times* (pp. 193–204). Springer Proceedings in Business and Economics. https://doi.org/10.1007/978-3-031-20148-6_18

Nambisan, S. (2017). Digital entrepreneurship: Toward a digital technology perspective of entrepreneurship. *Entrepreneurship Theory and Practice, 41*(6), 1029–1055.

Nambisan, S., Wright, M., & Feldman, M. (2019). The digital transformation of innovation and entrepreneurship: Progress, challenges and key themes. *Research Policy, 48*(8), 103809.

Papava, V. (2022, May 23). Pandemic, war and economic sanctions: From turbulent to confrontational globalization. *Eurasia Review*. https://www.eurasiareview.com/23052022-pandemic-war-and-economic-sanctions-from-turbulent-to-confrontational-globalization-oped/?fbclid=IwAR1zLFJs1kUFJWgp6qRXRWhLOy2OWnWjwIVUjMwjphnjqs0OKoUQSi12Z4I

Sepashvili, E. (2021). Focusing on digitalization: Core for national economic policies to compete globally. *Globalization and Business, 12*, 13–20.

Schumpeter, J. A. (2012). *The theory of economic development (An inquiry into profits, capital, credit, interest, and the business cycle).* Transaction Publishers.

Schumpeter, J. (1942). *Capitalism, socialism, and democracy* (1st ed.). Harper and Brothers.

Simon Herbert, A. (1967). Theories of decision-making in economics and behavioral science. *Journal: Organizational Decision Making,* 201–222. Prentice Hall, New-Jersey.

Song, A. K. (2019). The digital entrepreneurial ecosystem—A critique and reconfguration. *Small Business Economics, 53*, 569–590.

Spigel, B., & Harrison, R. (2018). Toward a process theory of entrepreneurial ecosystems. *Strategic Entrepreneurship Journal, 12*(1), 151–168.

Szerb, L., Somogyine Komlosi, E., Acs, Z. J., Lafuente, E., & Song, A. K. (2022). The digital platform economy index: Country rankings and clustering. In The *Digital Platform Economy Index 2020.* Springer Briefs in Economics. Springer. https://doi.org/10.1007/978-3-030-89651-5_4

Stam, E., & van de Ven, A. (2021). Entrepreneurial ecosystem elements. *Small Business Economics* (in press).https://doi.org/10.1007/s11187-019-00270-6

Tokmazashvili, M. (2023). Barriers to digital business and challenges of social innovations in Georgia. In R. C. Geibel & S. Machavariani (Eds.), *Digital Management in Covid-19 Pandemic and Post-Pandemic Times* (pp. 3–11). Springer Proceedings in Business and Economics. https://doi.org/10.1007/978-3-031-20148-6_1

Veblen, T. (1904). Theory of Business Enterprise. http://www.businessbuildersbanquet.com/software/veblen2.pdf

Vyshnevskyi, O., Stashkevych, I., Shubna, O., & Barkova S. (2020). Economic growth in the conditions of digitalization in the EU countries. *Studies of Applied Economic, 38*(4), 1–9. https://doi.org/10.25115/eea.v38i3%20(1).4041

World Economic Forum. (2013). Entrepreneurial ecosystems around the globe and company growth dynamics. In Report summary for the annual meeting of the new champions 2013.

Zhylinska, O., Bazhenova, O., Zatonatska, T., Dluhopolskyi, O., Bedianashvili, G., & Chornodid, I. (2020). Innovation processes and economic growth in the context of European integration. *Scientific Papers of the University of Pardubice, Series D: Faculty of Economics and Administration, 28*(3), 1–12.

Digital Marketing and Corporate Social Responsibility: Strategies for Brand Building and Stakeholder Engagement

Elene Dundua

Abstract In recent years, the digital landscape has undergone a remarkable transformation, ushering in new opportunities for corporations to engage in socially responsible initiatives while simultaneously advancing their marketing objectives. This research paper investigates the role of digital marketing in promoting Corporate Social Responsibility (CSR) campaigns, building brand reputation, and fostering meaningful engagement with stakeholders.

The study adopts a mixed-method approach, incorporating qualitative and quantitative analysis and primary data gathered from surveys and interviews with marketing professionals and CSR experts. The research analyzes how companies across diverse sectors leverage digital marketing tools and social media platforms to advance their CSR efforts while simultaneously reinforcing their brand reputation.

Firstly, the paper explores the use of digital marketing strategies to amplify the reach and impact of CSR initiatives. It delves into how companies maximizing engagement and encouraging positive actions towards social causes.

Secondly, the research highlights the role of social media as a powerful channel for fostering brand-consumer relationships and dialogue. Companies are increasingly employing social media platforms to encourage user-generated content, by doing so, organizations are better able to build trust, authenticity, and transparency in their CSR communication.

The findings indicate that the strategic integration of digital marketing into CSR campaigns enables companies to reach a broader audience, establish stronger brand reputations, and foster deeper connections with stakeholders. However, the success of such initiatives depends on a balanced approach that combines genuine social impact with transparent and responsible communication.

In conclusion, this research provides valuable insights for marketing professionals, CSR practitioners, and business leaders seeking to harness the potential of digital marketing for social good. By understanding the dynamics of digital platforms and aligning marketing strategies with authentic CSR efforts, corporations

E. Dundua (✉)
International Black Sea University, Tbilisi, Georgia
e-mail: edundua@ibsu.edu.ge

R. C. Geibel and S. Machavariani (eds.), *Digital Management to Shape the Future*, Springer Proceedings in Business and Economics,
https://doi.org/10.1007/978-3-031-66517-2_21

can effectively contribute to positive social change while strengthening their brand presence and reputation in the digital age.

Keywords Digital Marketing · Corporate Social Responsibility (CSR) · Social Media · Brand Reputation · Stakeholder Engagement

1 Introduction

Corporate social responsibility encompasses the diverse societal activities undertaken by an organization to enhance alignment between the social expectations of a company and the behavior of its stakeholders. In response, various researchers have demonstrated that a positive relationship exists between an organization's CSR engagement and its economic performance and social performance. Effective communication is a major concern for businesses in the modern era, it can enhance how consumers evaluate and perceive an organization, ultimately influencing their decisions, opinions, and trust in the company. Corporations often integrate CSR strategies into their branding framework for building and creating a strong brand. Prior researchers have acknowledged CSR as a fundamental catalyst for cultivating resilient brand identities and concluded that CSR leads to brand authenticity, positive brand relations, perceived quality and building strong brand equity.

Digital marketing has resulted in boosting trust in consumers (Wind, 2002) before making any purchase consumers first collects information of the same. Digital marketing creates a base which is considers a paramount for the business thus providing satisfaction. Organizations adopt specific strategies and use marketing channels to communicate with different types of stakeholders. Stakeholders possess their distinctive modes of communication and may exhibit preferences for specific channels over others. In the digital context, organizations have the capacity to leverage a multitude of digital media platforms to engage with precise target audiences. It is quite recent that researchers have acknowledged the importance of social media to improve word of mouth in an online context. In this light, this research investigates the rationale for using the digital media for marketing purposes and for corporate communications with stakeholders. Digital marketing can increase consumer awareness of a product or a service through various digital channels such as social media, search engines and email marketing (Kannan, 2017).The objective of this study is to examine the role of CSR communication on social media on stakeholders' engagement, encourage companies to reach a broader audience, establish stronger brand reputations, and foster deeper connections with stakeholders.

2 Theory

2.1 CSR Communication and Stakeholder Engagement

The European Union (EU) promotes Corporate Social Responsibility through policy frameworks, reporting requirements, financial support, and collaboration with stakeholders. Its emphasis on sustainable finance aligns with broader social and environmental objectives. Unfortunately, in Georgia, CSR is not widely embraced or integrated into business practices. This lack of adoption can vary, influenced by factors such as cultural norms, regulatory environments, and awareness. Efforts to promote CSR continue to be essential to address this disparity.

There is a multitude of internal and external factors that act as barriers to the adoption of CSR initiatives. Understanding these obstacles is essential for organizations seeking to navigate and overcome challenges in their CSR efforts.

The engagement strategy is based on dialogue with stakeholders in a symmetrical two-way communication, thus activating an iterative process of mutual interpretation and information exchange. Thus, companies not only influence, but are themselves influenced by stakeholders. Businesses in the recent era have comprehended the importance of being engaged in CSR dialogues and efforts as a way to socialize with the stakeholders, including consumers (Perelygina et al., 2019). It is well-established in the literature that through their engagement in CSR, organizations do not merely expect better stakeholder's attitude (consumers in this case) but build strong stakeholder–business relationships (Abitbol & Lee, 2017).

Businesses have been increasingly depending upon digital platforms to communicate their CSR activities, especially through interpersonal networking websites on social media. (Perelygina et al., 2019)This shift from conventional media to social media platforms has been acknowledged after realizing the fact that the consumers' involvement might be enhanced using virtual platforms because virtual platforms are flexible and interactive in comparison to conventional media (Duffett, 2017) Numerous scholars argue that the interactive potential of social media can enhance the effectiveness of CSR communication with stakeholders, including consumers. Hence, social media platforms have become valuable tools for organizations to communicate their CSR involvement through these digital channels. Moreover, organizations that actively engage in CSR tend to establish a more prominent online presence, reflected in metrics such as a higher number of followers, when compared to those with less involvement in CSR.

2.2 Digital Marketing and Brand Reputation

According to (Lawal, 2017) 's research, social transparency has a significant impact on brand development. Digital marketing allows brand to establish stronger and more transparent relationship by providing tailored experiences (Kumar, 2019). Contemporary research emphasizes the significant relationship between digital marketing and CSR in elevating brand reputation social media platforms provide opportunities for organizations to communicate their CSR initiatives, receive feedback, and thereby enhance their reputation among stakeholders. Researchers highlight the potential of social media for fostering stakeholder dialogue. They emphasize the significance of using digital marketing strategies such as storytelling, interactive content, and user-generated content to engage stakeholders in CSR discussions. This engagement is seen as instrumental in promoting CSR campaigns effectively. The development of new technologies, including social media and review sites, allow companies to improve their performance and to enhance their communications (Westerman, 2014).These innovations have an effect on the communications' choices of companies or entrepreneurs and their strategic decision-making processes (Cohen, 2017).

2.3 Communicating CSR on Social Networks

Social media is often considered one of the most important components of digital marketing (Al-Hawary, 2021).

The evolution of social media has demonstrated substantial advancement in facilitating effective consumer engagement, contributing significantly to brand establishment and the promotion of sustainable consumption practices. Consumers expect brands to connect with them more on an emotional level than just selling their products and services.

Marketers tend to prioritize consumer engagement when they aim to establish enduring connections with their customers, leading to increased focus on this aspect, many online users have subscribed to different social media networks, for different reasons. According to Zhao and Chen (2022), consumers tend to develop a more psychological bond when they are satisfied with the brand and its involvement in marketing. Consumers attain perceived advantages and satisfaction through their participation in social media interactions.

Corporate communication strategy is a significant outcome of an organization's strategic thinking process. New digital technologies can help companies to interact with online users and leverage their image and reputation among several types of stakeholders. Chief marketing officers may face difficulties and risks in managing the opportunities associated with the new challenges of digital transformation, their main goal is to achieve a competitive advantage by improve their corporate image and reputation through their digital presence. The latest technological developments have transformed the corporate communication landscape and have led to significant changes in the industry. Hence, the communication professionals need to possess adequate digital and language skills to prepare and disseminate relevant content online. They can use digital media channels, including emails, corporate websites, blogs and social media.

3 Research Method

In this study, a comprehensive research approach was adopted, incorporating both qualitative and quantitative methodologies. quantitative method allows to report results in an unbiased, objective manner, in contrast to the qualitative method, which allows to study the attitudes, behaviors, performance, and motivation of participants (Creswell, 2005).The survey questionnaire was provided to 20 selected companies, it was distributed among a random sampling of industrial and nonindustrial not-for-profit and for-profit corporations in Tbilisi, Georgia. Data collected were limited to email surveys because these instruments provided the researcher the best opportunity to obtain a random sample. It allows equal opportunity for individuals to be selected from the population (West, 2008). Email surveys allow one to collect data from large sample populations at minimum cost and allow participants to respond at their own convenience (West, 2008).

Differing from the quantitative approach, qualitative research takes an interpretative stance, focusing on subjectivity rather than objectivity. It is especially well-suited for researchers explore, describe, explain and deeply understand underexplored issues within specific local contexts. For this study, the semi-structured interview method was selected due to clarify research question. This method enables participants openly and effectively articulate their thoughts and perspectives.

Data were thus collected through in-depth semi-structured interviews which was carried out with 5 mid-level managers from Small and Medium-Sized companies actively involved in CSR initiatives, representing a variety of sectors. Participants were selected by specific criteria, such as their affiliation with a department related to CSR (e.g., CSR, HR, or marketing departments) to express their actual experiences and shape perceptions of other companies' CSR commitment in the Georgian context as a developing country.

The analysis performed using the above discussed approach is shown in the next section.

3.1 Results and Discussion

At first, the respondents highlighted aspects of CSR that are widely recognized for their potential to shape and enhance a company's brand reputation. However, it's essential to consider that the impact can vary depending on the specific context and industry in which a company operates. Demonstrating ethical behavior, such as fair labor practices, transparency, and responsible sourcing, can significantly enhance a company's brand reputation.

Key points raised by the interviewers included the highlighting of consumers and stakeholders being more likely to trust and support a company that conducts its business with integrity. Commitment to environmental sustainability, including reducing carbon emissions, minimizing waste, and using eco-friendly materials, can have a

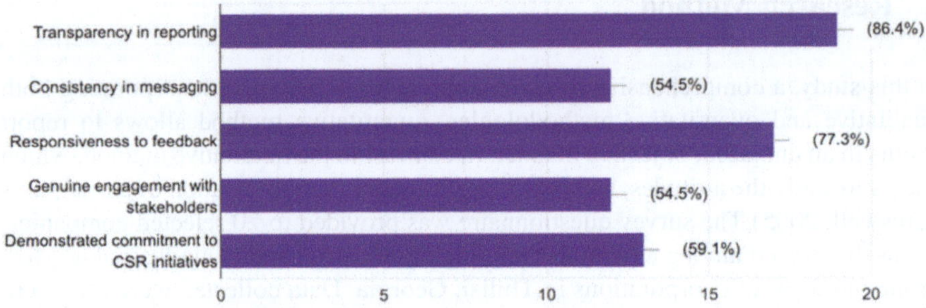

Fig. 1 Key elements for building trust and authenticity in company CSR communication on social media *source* Own graphic based on primary research findings

substantial positive influence on a company's brand reputation. This is especially important in a world increasingly focused on environmental issues. Companies that engage in philanthropic activities, support community initiatives, and give back to society often enjoy a better brand reputation. This demonstrates a commitment to social well-being and community development.

respondents induced key elements contribute to building trust and authenticity in a company's CSR communication on social media by including arguments, openly sharing information about CSR initiatives, progress, and challenges fosters trust. Transparency enables stakeholders to see the company's commitment to making a positive impact, as well as Consistency, in messaging and actions is vital. Companies should align their CSR communication with their actual practices to demonstrate authenticity over time. Actively engaging with stakeholders through social media, listening to their feedback, and responding constructively can help build trust. It shows a genuine commitment to dialogue and improvement. These elements help create a genuine and trustworthy image for the company's CSR efforts, reinforcing authenticity in its communication (Fig. 1).

The perception among Georgian consumers is that local companies prioritize profit over considerations for customers and other stakeholders. To build trust and ensure long-term profitability and survival, it is crucial for companies to shift towards a more customer- and stakeholder-oriented approach. Demonstrating genuine interest in the well-being of customers, stakeholders, and society at large is seen as a necessary element for sustained success in the long run. This shift not only aligns with evolving consumer expectations but also contributes to a positive corporate image, fostering trust and loyalty among stakeholders, which are essential for the enduring success of any business.

Organizations implementing digital marketing and social media for CSR often face challenges to effectively incorporate CSR initiatives into a digital marketing strategy, a company should align these efforts with core values, set clear objectives, be transparent, create engaging content, foster two-way communication, use data for measurement, leverage user-generated content, collaborate, involve employees, maintain consistency, be prepared for crises, and provide reporting with third-party verification. This approach helps create a positive impact on society and enhances the company's brand image authentically.

The vast majority of respondents believed that, for the benefits and opportunities it could bring, all companies should implement CSR strategies in social media. However, it is important to emphasize that ethical considerations and potential risks associated with digital marketing and social media in CSR promotion should not be ignored.

In discussions during the interviews it was highlighted that Companies need to prioritize transparency, authenticity, data privacy, and responsiveness to effectively mitigate these concerns and maintain trust with their stakeholders. There are indeed ethical considerations and potential risks associated with the use of digital marketing and social media in CSR promotion. One primary ethical concern is the risk of "greenwashing," where a company exaggerates or misrepresents its CSR efforts to appear more socially responsible than it actually is. This can mislead consumers and erode trust. To mitigate this risk, companies must ensure transparency and honesty in their CSR communication. They should align their CSR initiatives with their core values and ensure that their actions match their words. Independent verification or adherence to recognized CSR standards can add credibility. Another significant concern is data privacy. Collecting and using personal data for CSR initiatives through digital marketing must respect individuals' privacy rights. Companies must follow data protection regulations, obtain consent when necessary, and be transparent about how data will be used for CSR purposes. Furthermore, there is the risk of backlash on social media. Negative feedback or criticism can be amplified on these platforms, potentially damaging a company's reputation. Mitigation involves actively listening to feedback, responding thoughtfully, and demonstrating a commitment to improvement. Companies should also be prepared for crisis management to address any negative publicity effectively.

Most respondents find digital marketing useful for raising consumer awareness, but sometimes the information is not convincing. Consumers prefer advertising to be informative rather than persuasive, helping them make informed decisions. Therefore, companies should adjust communication strategies to provide more informative content through persuasive advertising. Respondents also seek increased transparency about the social responsibility efforts of Georgian companies and improvements in their quality.

For the effective communication it is important to choose digital marketing channels based on the target audience, objectives, and content type. For a broad reach, consider platforms like Facebook or Instagram. For B2B, use LinkedIn. Customization and data analytics are key to effective CSR communication.

Data and analytics can assess the impact and effectiveness of digital marketing efforts for CSR by tracking engagement metrics, website traffic, social shares, and sentiment analysis. They provide actionable insights to refine strategies and demonstrate the ROI of CSR initiatives (Fig. 2).

The survey results reveal that Facebook and Influencer Marketing are considered the most effective digital marketing channels for promoting CSR campaigns, with percentages of 87 and 60.9%, respectively. This underscores the dominance of social

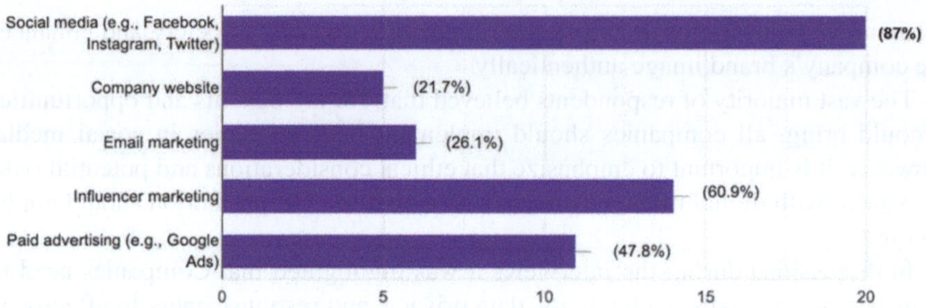

Fig. 2 Social media platform usage preferences
source Own graphic based on primary research findings

media, especially Facebook, in driving engagement and awareness for CSR initiatives in Georgia.

While the Company Website scored at 21.7%, it indicates that maintaining a dedicated CSR section on the company's site is still seen as valuable, albeit not as prominent as more dynamic channels like social media.

Email Marketing, with a percentage of 26.1%, suggests that direct communication through email plays a moderate role in CSR campaign promotion. This may indicate that while not as dominant as social media, email marketing still holds significance for targeted communication.

Paid Advertising, such as Google Ads, scored at 47.8%, reflecting its effectiveness but also suggesting that, while impactful, paid promotions are perceived as slightly less influential than organic methods like social media and influencer partnerships.

Interviewees openly shared their ideas about social media that it is effective instrument for CSR communication, it help organizations to build better corporate image and provide more transparent information to stakeholders. In conclusion, a comprehensive CSR promotion strategy should heavily leverage Facebook and Influencer Marketing, supplementing them with a well-maintained Company Website. Email marketing and paid advertising play supporting roles, with their effectiveness depending on the specific campaign goals and target audience preferences (Fig. 3).

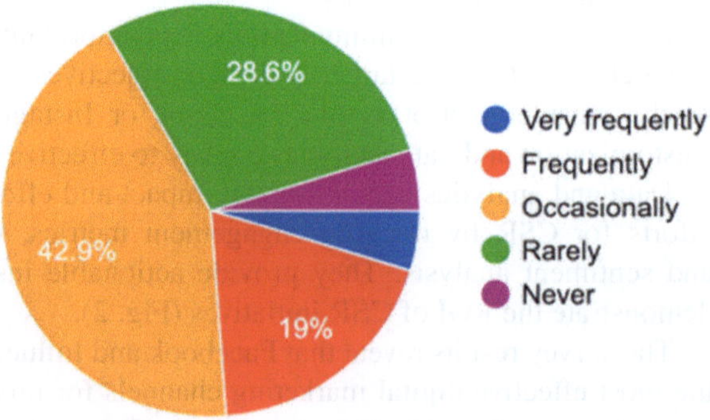

Fig. 3 Frequency of engagement with companies on social media for CSR initiatives or social responsibility efforts *source* Own graphic based on primary research findings

Fig. 4 The significance of CSR aspects on company brand reputation *source* Own graphic based on primary research findings

The data indicates diverse levels of engagement with companies on social media platforms regarding their CSR initiatives. A notable 19% of respondents reported frequent engagement, 42.9% engage occasionally, and 28.6% engage rarely. This suggests a range of interest and interaction, with occasional engagement being the most prevalent, followed by frequent and rare engagement. The findings underscore the varied ways in which stakeholders interact with CSR content on social media.

The research analysis emphasizes the importance for Georgian companies to transparently share their reports on marketing-related social responsibility activities with the public. This finding reiterates the consumer demand for increased information about companies' social responsibility efforts. Therefore, companies must fulfill this consumer demand to succeed in the market by effectively leveraging their goodwill (Fig. 4).

According to the survey responses, stakeholders perceive ethical business practices, social responsibility, and employee well-being as the most impactful aspects of CSR on a company's brand reputation. These findings suggest a strong emphasis on responsible business conduct and a positive contribution to societal well-being. Environmental sustainability, while still significant, garnered slightly lower recognition, and philanthropic efforts were perceived as having a comparatively lesser impact on brand reputation. Companies may find value in prioritizing ethical practices and social responsibility to enhance their overall brand image. The advantage of social media over conventional communication tools in this regard is that it can take on board number of stakeholders at the same time and provide cost and time efficient medium of communication.

The reputation and social responsibility of a company play a crucial role in product purchasing decisions. Companies can influence this consumer segment through effective marketing tools. By engaging in targeted marketing activities, companies can enhance consumers' perception of their social responsibility, thereby attracting more customers. This, in turn, is expected to positively impact the success of the companies and contribute to their financial performance (Fig. 5).

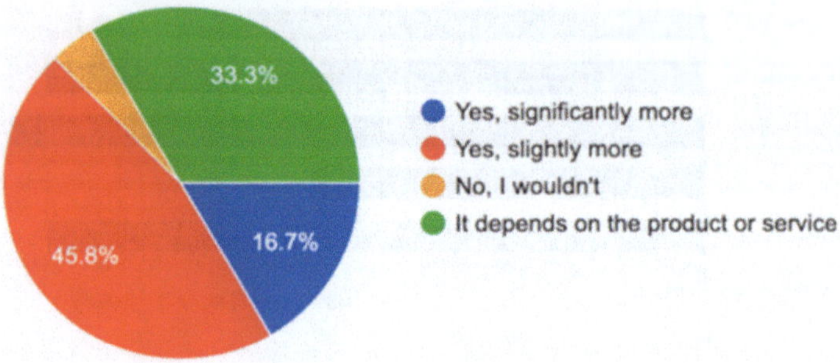

Fig. 5 Consumer willingness to pay premium for products/services from companies with strong CSR efforts and reputation *source* Own graphic based on primary research findings

It is crucial aspect to explore is how CSR communication via social media impacts stakeholder behavior. When probing customers about their inclination to purchase products from companies that communicate their CSR activities on social media.

Ethical reputation is a significant factor for consumers when making purchasing decisions. Notably, respondents who are informed about corporate social responsibility express a greater willingness to pay more for products from socially responsible companies compared to those unfamiliar with CSR. This conclusion suggests that companies should prioritize communication about social responsibility to cultivate a more loyal customer base (Fig. 6).

The analysis of responses indicates a clear positive association between CSR engagement and favorable perceptions, with 77.3% of respondents viewing CSR-involved companies more favorably. While 9.1% hold equal and less favorable views, and 4.5% see no difference, the overall trend underscores the strategic importance of CSR in shaping positive public perceptions and consumer preferences. Businesses can leverage this by emphasizing and transparently communicating their CSR initiatives to align with evolving consumer expectations (Fig. 7).

Respondents show diverse behaviors in sharing CSR content on social media: 34.6% do so frequently, another 34.6% occasionally, 15.4% have not shared, and 15.4% are unsure. The findings highlight a significant interest in CSR content sharing,

Fig. 6 Consumer perception of companies engaged in CSR activities vs. non-engaged companies *source* Own graphic based on primary research findings

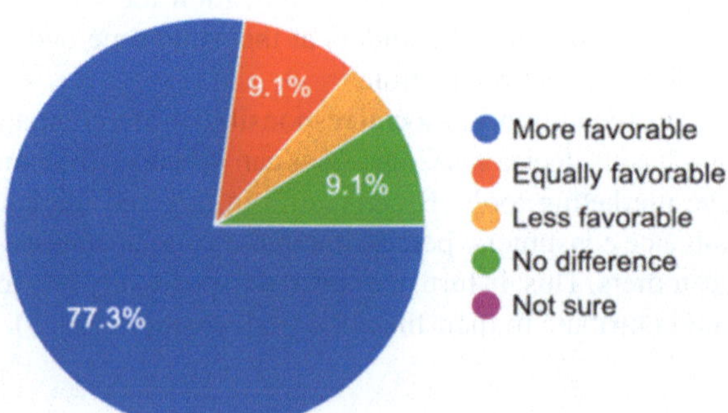

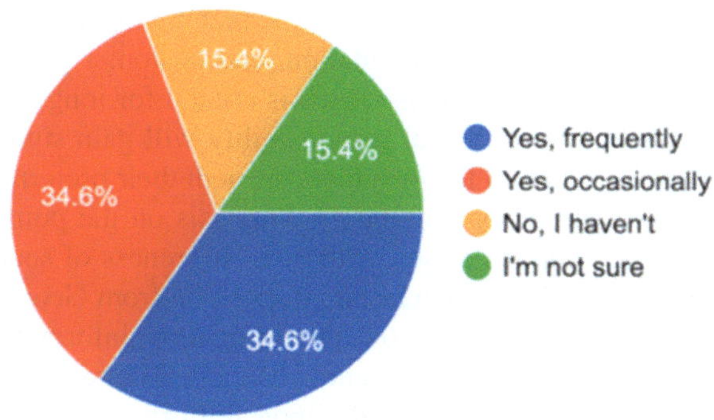

Fig. 7 Consumer engagement: Sharing or reposting CSR content on personal social media profiles *source* Own graphic based on primary research findings

but a notable portion is either less engaged or uncertain about their involvement. Understanding the motivations behind these behaviors is essential for companies aiming to optimize their CSR communication strategies.

Here it is important the examine, the demographic profile of respondents who says that they never reposted CSR content. The detailed analysis of demographic profile of such respondents may provide interesting information. They might be older people, or people with less access to computer and internet facilities, who use hardly use social media (Fig. 8).

Opinions on companies' effectiveness in engaging stakeholders through digital marketing and social media for CSR are diverse. This mixed response suggests that there is room for improvement in companies' digital marketing and social media strategies related to CSR, with a significant portion acknowledging their effectiveness but a notable minority expressing dissatisfaction. Further analysis and understanding of specific factors contributing to these opinions could guide companies in enhancing their CSR communication through digital channels.

Interviewees who were aware of social responsibility efforts by Georgian companies mainly remembered specific events rather than the companies themselves. This shows that consumers are genuinely interested in social responsibility and pay attention to the activities of Georgian companies.

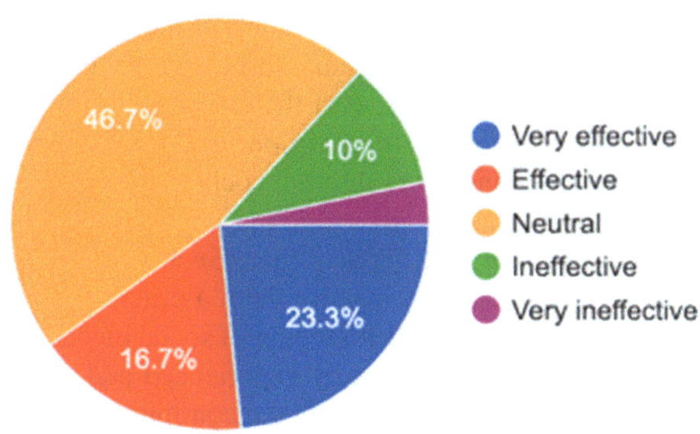

Fig. 8 Effectiveness of companies in stakeholder engagement through digital marketing and social media in CSR context *source* Own graphic based on primary research findings

For companies, this indicates that taking social responsibility measures can improve their image, reputation, and customer goodwill. It also allows for effective product advertising, which is crucial for long-term effectiveness, success, and competitiveness. Social responsibility will gain significance if companies provide more information to consumers through their preferred communication channels.

The interviews featured an emphasis on the point that the Georgian consumer expresses dissatisfaction with their awareness of social responsibility in the social space and calls for increased information from Georgian companies. Consequently, companies should prioritize providing more information about their social responsibility activities through digital channels. The research reveals insufficient available information about the social responsibility of marketing. This inadequacy stems from a lack of consumer awareness on social responsibility and, concurrently, a scarcity of such activities undertaken by companies. To address this, companies are encouraged to engage in more social responsibility-related activities to enhance customer satisfaction. Moreover, there is a need for more informative communication with consumers through preferred information sources. Among these, personal experiences and social networks are highlighted, underscoring the significance of personal trust. Notably, consumers also express a desire for information about companies' social responsibility via the Internet. This research suggests that companies should not only increase their social responsibility activities but also prioritize communication through preferred channels to bridge the awareness gap and meet consumer expectations.

4 Conclusions, Limitations and Further Research

The lack of awareness and a clear vision of Corporate Social Responsibility can be a significant hindrance to its adoption. Many companies perceive CSR as a costly burden and remain fixated on short-term financial gains, often driven by a cost-per-share mentality. This means that there is a lack of awareness and ignorance of its importance, as well as confusion and misunderstanding about its role in decision-making the absence of programs could further contribute to this lack of clarity, which, in turn, may impede the integration of CSR into corporate strategies and practices.

Social media marketing should be considered as a means of gaining a competitive advantage, irrespective of the company's size, number of clients, or marketing budget. Any company focusing on the consumer market should integrate communication with consumers through social media into its marketing policy. The adoption of social media marketing, and its potential advantages businesses, especially in the promotion of CSR activities. Such initiatives directly impact the awareness of a brand's reliability, making them a crucial consideration in effective corporate strategy. A thorough understanding of social media marketing methodology is necessary, it should be overseen by experienced and qualified personnel in this field, to implement strategy accordingly the continuous monitoring of current developments in social media marketing is essential.

CSR offers companies a range of benefits. By showing dedication to social and environmental causes, companies can boost their brand reputation, stand out in the market, and foster loyalty among customers. Engaging in CSR activities also makes companies more attractive to job seekers and helps retain current employees by creating a positive work environment. Additionally, being perceived as socially responsible enhances customer relationships and loyalty. Beyond these advantages, CSR opens up new business opportunities, including partnerships with like-minded organizations and access to new customer segments. In essence, CSR is a comprehensive strategy that strengthens brand, employee satisfaction, customer relations, and creates new business possibilities.

This study represents an endeavor to assess the current state of the hyper-dynamic field of social media consumer engagement in sustainable consumption. Research explores the role of social media in attracting consumers to sustainable brands or products. I believe that this review will provide the scholarly community with a foundation to initiate and conduct relevant research in this emerging and vital area.

When discussing research limitations, it is essential to be transparent and honest about the study's shortcomings. These limitations can encompass factors such as sample size, data collection methods, time constraints, or access to resources. Acknowledging these limitations is crucial for maintaining the study's credibility and highlights areas where future research can improve or expand upon the findings.

In conclusion, the study on 'Analyzing the use of digital marketing strategies and social media for promoting CSR campaigns, building brand reputation, and engaging with stakeholders' underscores the growing significance of digital platforms in the context of CSR. Through a comprehensive examination of current practices, the study reveals that organizations are increasingly employing digital marketing strategies and social media to convey their CSR initiatives, foster brand reputation, and build meaningful connections with stakeholders.

However, this research also acknowledges certain limitations. It is essential to recognize that the effectiveness of these strategies can vary greatly across industries and regions, and their impact on brand reputation may differ among different companies. Furthermore, the study acknowledges that the ethical considerations and potential pitfalls associated with the use of digital marketing for CSR demand continuous attention and mitigation.

To advance this field of study, future research should delve deeper into the specific strategies and tactics that yield the most favorable outcomes for organizations. Additionally, it is imperative to explore the long-term effects of digital CSR communication on brand reputation and financial performance. In the evolving landscape of digital marketing and social media, continuous research is required to adapt and refine strategies to ensure they remain both effective and ethically sound.

Bibliography

Abitbol, A., & Lee, S. (2017). Messages on CSR-dedicated Facebook pages: What works and what doesn't. *The Public Relations Review, 43*, 796–808.

Al-Hawary, S. I. (2021). Does mobile marketing affect customer loyalty in UK? *International Journal of Business Excellence, 23*(2), 226–250.

Cohen, B. A. (2017). The generative potential of emerging technology to support startups and new ecosystems. *Business Horizon, 60*(6), 741–745.

Creswell, J. W. (2005). *Educational research: Planning, conducting, and evaluating quantitative and qualitative research* (2nd ed.). Pearson Prentice-Hall.

Duffett, R. (2017). Influence of social media marketing communications on young consumers' attitudes. *Young Consumers, 18*, 19–39.

Kannan, P. (2017). Digital Marketing: A framework, review and research agenda. *International Journal of Research in Marketing, 34*, 22–45.

Kumar. (2019). Study growth of digital marketing in Indian scenario. *Parmana Research Journal, 9*(1), 388–394.

Lawal, E. M. (2017). The significance of corporate social disclosure for high-tech manufacturing companies: Focus on employee and community aspects of sustainable development. *Corporate Social Responsibility and Environmental Management, 24*(4), 295–311.

Perelygina, M., Lam, W., & Kucukusta, D. (2019). CSR communication strategies and stakeholder engagement of upscale hotels in social media. *International Journal of Contemporary Hospitality Management, 31*, 2129–2148.

Preston, D. (1995). The stakeholder theory of the corporation: Concepts, evidence, and implications. *The Academy of Management, 20*(1), 67.

West, B. T. (2008). Statistical and methodological issues in the analysis of complex sample survey data: Practical guidance for trauma researchers. *Journal of Traumatic Stress, 21*(5), 440–447.

Westerman, G. B. (2014). The nine elements of digital transformation. *MIT Sloan Management Review, 55*(3), 1–6.

Wind, J. (2002). Digital marketing. *Symphonya. Emerging Issues in Management,1*, 43–54.

Zhao, X., & Chen, R. (2022). How brand-stakeholder dialogue drives brand-hosted community engagement on social media: A mixed-methods approach. . *Computers in Human Behavior, 131*(4), 107208.

The New Law of Georgia on E-commerce—Opportunities and Challenges

Zviad Gabisonia

Abstract On June 13, 2023, the Parliament of Georgia adopted the Law on E-commerce. With the adoption of this law, in my opinion, two of the most important issues were laid—Georgia was placed in the legislative framework of the e-commerce market for the first time, and a new subfield of technology law was born in the Georgian law—e-commerce law.

1 Introduction

On June 13, 2023, the Parliament of Georgia adopted the Law on E-commerce. With the adoption of this law, in my opinion, two of the most important issues were laid—Georgia was placed in the legislative framework of the e-commerce market for the first time, and a new subfield of technology law was born in the Georgian law—e-commerce law.

In this article, I will try to discuss the main essence and principles of both issues.

E-commerce is known to refer to the purchase and sale of goods, services, or information over the Internet or through other electronic networks. It involves the online exchange of goods and services between businesses, customers, or both. E-commerce is any type of business process where interaction between entities is carried out electronically.

There is no unified opinion on the date of e-commerce formation, however, the version is the most popular version according to which the transaction of selling marijuana among students from Stanford University's Artificial Intelligence Laboratory and the University of Massachusetts University of Technology in 1971 or 1972 was the first act of e-commerce.

If we reject this comic fact, the creation date of the first e-commerce system will be extended to 1979, when the famous inventor, innovator, and entrepreneur, Michael Oldrich, created his online store. In the following years, several similar products were

Z. Gabisonia (✉)
Business and Technology University, Tbilisi, Georgia
e-mail: zviad.gabisonia@btu.edu.ge

R. C. Geibel and S. Machavariani (eds.), *Digital Management to Shape the Future*, Springer Proceedings in Business and Economics,
https://doi.org/10.1007/978-3-031-66517-2_22

released on the market, however, the real boom of such systems is directly related to the creation of the World Wide Web and the first mass web browser Netscape Navigator, which made e-commerce available to inexperienced users in information technology.

In 1995, Jeff Bezos launched the portal amazon.com and Pierre Omidyar ebay.com. Alibaba.com was launched in 1999, and in the same year, the volume of the e-commerce market reached USD 150 billion. At first glance, e-commerce was a direction that could not be threatened by stable growth, but in 2000, the "dot-coms" bubble broke out and thousands of companies working in this direction went bankrupt. Only the strengths that have survived since then go through stable growth and make astronomical profits. Today's e-commerce market is much more attractive than at the end of the last century, and reasonable participation in it will no doubt benefit both experienced businessmen and startups.[1]

2 The Notion of E-commerce and the Scope of Action

According to Article 1 of the Law of Georgia on E-commerce of 13 June 2023 (hereinafter referred to as the "Law"), "E-commerce implies the provision of services to the information community". E-commerce consists of three closely related parts: business entities (participants), processes, and networks (through which participants connect and implement processes). E-commerce in general allows its participants to implement the following capabilities:

- Sellers—submit goods and services to the Internet network, receive online, and process customer orders;
- Buyers—get acquainted with catalogs of various goods and services and make an order through standard internet browsers.

A similar approach is provided for by Article 2(d) of the Law, which in the concept of a service recipient includes a natural or legal person who uses the services of the information community for professional or other purposes (including for the search or access thereof) of information, and a natural person acting for personal purposes, outside of his/her business activities or entrepreneurial or professional activities.

The most widely used e-commerce technology is EDI (Electronic Data Interchange)—electronic data exchange. EDI is a method of consistent transactions and processing them in interactive mode. According to some analytics companies, U.S. companies alone make 500 billion worth of purchases annually. One of the main aspects of EDI work is choosing the path through which information is transmitted from one place to another or directly or through additional service networks of VAN

[1] See Z. Gabisonia. Some issues of legal regulation of e-commerce. Georgian-German Journal of Comparative Law, N6/2020, pp. 111–123. 42–43, http://lawjournal.ge/6-2020/ (last viewing date 09.08.2023).

(Value Added Network). A VAN is an intermediary that stores information in the email box until it is requested by one of the parties.

The scope of e-commerce action is distributed in the distribution of transactions between business customers and the state and the distribution of rights and obligations. Accordingly, several main directions are separated: (a) B2B (Business to Business)—(business-business) In this case, the two companies make a business transaction through the Internet. The main objective of B2B is to increase the efficiency of interactions between companies in the market.

a. B2B (Business to Business)

   In this case, the two companies make a business transaction through the Internet. The main objective of B2B is to increase the efficiency of interactions between companies in the market. A) B2B (Business to Business)—(Business to Business) In this case, two companies make a business transaction through the Internet. The main objective of B2B is to increase the efficiency of interactions between companies in the market.

   There are the following types of B2B:

   1. Corporate website. It is intended for interaction with the company's partners and clients and contains information about the company, personnel, leadership, products;
   2. Online store designed for a product key. Can be posted on a corporate website. It allows you to place orders, make electronic payments, and deliver the goods to the client;
   3. Information website of a separate field. Intended for placement of information on individual fields, companies included in them, market status indicators, and sectoral standards;
   4. E-shopping grounds. Intended for the implementation of the direct "online" activities of specialists, company key, and supply services.
   5. Brokerage websites that act as intermediaries between buyers and sellers.

b. B2C (Business to Consumer)

   In this case, the company directly sells its products and services to customers. The main objective of B2C is to ensure transparency of the company's activities and facilitate its interaction with its clients.

   The most popular form of B2C is electronic stores. The most famous representative of e-commerce B2C is the world giant Amazon ("Amazon") (www.amazon.com).

   B2C is the most common and popular type of e-commerce.

c. C2C (Consumer to Consumer)

   In this case, one customer directly sells his product to another customer. The most famous representative is the company "Ibe" ("eBay") (www.ebay.com).

d. C2B (Consumer to Business)

   In this case, the customer means the price for the goods or services provided by the company. The most famous representative was the company Priceline (www.priceline.com).

Recently, new directions appeared, of which it is worth mentioning:

e. B2G (Business to Government)

This includes all electronic transactions between companies and government organizations. For example, in the United States, information on public procurement is published on the Internet, and companies can send their business proposals electronically.

f. G2B (Government to Business)

Includes providing information to business organizations by state government and local self-government through state and municipal internet portals.

g. G2C (Government to Consumer)—and C2G (Consumer to Government)

Refers to the organization of interactions between government bodies and citizens. On the one hand, this is the range of services provided by state and municipal internet portals (collection of taxes, registration of vehicles, provision of information to the population, etc.). On the other hand, it is a system of feedback to the population (information on the reaction of the population to the actions of the government through the Internet, conducting sociological surveys, and election referendums).[2]

3 Law of Georgia on E-commerce

It should be noted that before the adoption of the law, there was no legislation regulating the services (e-commerce) process of the Information Society in Georgia. At the same time, there was no regulation of any kind that would prohibit the imposition of general monitoring obligations on "interim service providers" and would take into account the determination of their rights and obligations, as well as the system of appeal for the removal of illegal information available on the Internet, the grounds for the origin of the obligation to remove the removal and the legal grounds for exemption from this obligation. In addition, there was no legislation regulating the obligation to protect the rights of service recipients in the e-commerce process and to provide the service provider with minimal information, which reduced trust in service providers and increased risks for service recipients.

In addition, in the process of e-commerce, the protection of the rights of service recipients and the obligation to provide information by service providers, as well as to place the electronic contract in the process of service/e-commerce of the information community in a certain legislative framework, is necessary for the development of e-commerce to encourage service recipients to take effective steps towards protecting the rights of service recipients, more actively To benefit from e-commerce services, especially when the COVID-19 pandemic in 2019–2021 once again demonstrated the importance of using e-services.

The Law of Georgia on E-commerce regulates the activities related to the services of the e-commerce/information community, the responsibility of the persons

---

[2] Z. Gabisonia. Internet Law and Artificial Intelligence, Tb. 2022, p. 13. 221-223.

providing these services, as well as the concept of an electronic contract for this Law and the procedure and conditions for signing it. The principles of the activities of the service provider and recipient of the information community, their rights, and obligations shall be determined.

It should be noted that the rights and obligations determined by law do not apply to areas that fall within the scope of special regulation, including the protection of the interests of a party in court and its representation; Issues provided for by the Tax Code of Georgia and the Customs Code of Georgia; Registration of immovable property rights in the Public Registry; the registration of the right for which a special form is established by the legislation of Georgia; Notary activities; A holder of a permit to organize gambling businesses, including gambling and/or profitable games (except for the holder of a permit to arrange a promotional lottery, if a permit to organize a promotional lottery is not issued to the organizer of gambling and/or profitable games) and to the holder of a permit to provide gambling and/or winning games; TV and radio broadcasting services; Voice telephone (including telegraph, telefax and telex) services; The exchange of information between persons by e-mail or other, similar, individual communication that is not related to their commercial activities; Regulation area of the National Bank of Georgia; Activities carried out by an administrative body within the scope of its public legal authority. In addition, the legislation regarding the provision of electronic communication services establishes a special regulation in the field of electronic communications. In particular, the Law of Georgia on Electronic Communications and the normative acts issued by the Georgian National Communications Commission based on it shall establish specific obligations related to the provision of electronic communication services. For example, Article 8 of the Law of Georgia on Electronic Communications regulates the issues of secrecy of information transmitted by the user, Article 5 of the Regulations on the Provision of Services in the Field of Electronic Communications approved by Resolution No. 3 of 17 March 2006 of the Georgian National Communications Commission defines the obligation to provide relevant information to customers, Article 12 of the same Regulations With this in mind, the draft law will not apply to relations related to the provision of electronic communication services and are regulated by special legislation.

The said exceptional provision of the law shall not apply to the rights and obligations of electronic communication service providers as interim service providers, which shall be determined by Articles 11–14 of the Law.

The definitions of the terms given in the law are important, they offer completely new definitions for the Georgian legislative space, and it should be noted that these definitions are used only for this Law and may be otherwise understood for other legislation. For example, the services of the information community are—by electronic means and based on the individual request of the service recipient, to provide services remotely in exchange for remuneration. Subsequent sub-paragraphs disrupt the importance of all four components to make the law easy for interested parties. It should be borne in mind that if we do not have all four components of this in this case, we are not dealing with e-commerce and therefore the issue goes beyond the scope of regulation of this Law.

In the development of the law, the European expert provided examples of the definition of the information community, according to which: transportation services will be considered as services of the information community when the service recipient orders the service through the application and does not have contact with the service provider at the time of the implementation of this order. Such is the case with a taxi service when the application is called, the location and destination are indicated, the payment is made electronically, and the driver is not involved in the whole process, he only provides offline services, and the services of the information community are provided independently of him/her with the satisfaction of all four components.[3]

Also, the services of the information community are any transactions made without physical presence by electronic devices, remotely, upon the individual request of the recipient and in exchange for compensation. It shall not be considered as a service of the information community, for example, to perform a medical procedure/operation using electronic means when the patient is the accompanying person of the service provider; Introduction to the electronic catalog in the company's office or store with a consultant; Booking a plane ticket in the travel agency's office regardless of the use of a computer or other electronic device; Electronic video game in a gambling club when the service recipient is physically present; Also, the services of the information community are not services provided by electronic devices through data processing. For example: removal of money from an ATM or purchase of a train ticket from a special device, transactions made from the same enrollment machines (PayBox); Parking or highway access vehicles; any kind of services received by voice phone, as well as direct marketing; And services that are not provided based on individual request, such as TV broadcasting and radio broadcasting, as well as teletext, it is worth noting that call-to-call audiovisual media services belong to the services of the information community.

In the definition section of the terms, it is important to include the definition of "service recipient". The law divided this notion into two subsections. A recipient of services defined by Article 2(d.a) of the Law is a natural or legal person who receives the services of the information community for professional, official, or other purposes, and the recipient of the service provided by Article 2(d.b) is a person who also falls under the definition of the service recipient, but in a narrower sense, that is, the recipient of the service provided for by sub-paragraph (d.b) is a natural person who acts only from his/her interest. Depending on the e-commerce process. The separation of these two categories of service recipients from each other has become necessary to the extent that, according to the law, persons who are not persons provided for by Article 2(d.b) may apply different rules.

It is important to clarify in the law that e-commerce/information community services are not a licensing activity and it is not necessary to obtain any specific license or permit and/or authorization to start such activity. This definition shall not apply to the provision of products or services through the services of the e-commerce/information community for which the licensing regime is established by the law of

[3] See Explanatory card on the draft law of Georgia "On E-commerce", https://parliament.ge/legislation/25495 (last viewing date 11.08.2023).

Georgia, in such case a person receives a license or permit or authorizes the basic activity from which this Law does not exempt him/her.

Article 5 of the Law serves to protect the rights of service recipients, to the extent that it establishes certain obligations for the delivery of services to the information community in compliance with certain types of requirements for the provision of commercial messages. The second paragraph specifies that the requirements of the Law of Georgia on Personal Data Protection shall apply to unwanted commercial messages sent for direct marketing purposes.

From a legal point of view, Article 7 of the Law is important, which explains that unless otherwise provided for by law, the norms established for the signing of a contract under the Civil Code shall apply to the electronic agreement.

The concept of an electronic contract is an innovation for the Georgian legislative space, the definition of terms provides its definition, and paragraph 2 of the seventh article also specifies that in the case of the need to sign an electronic contract, the norms provided for by the Law of Georgia on Electronic Documents and Electronic Trust Services shall apply for electronic signature.

According to the law, an electronic agreement is an agreement concluded by electronic means for this Law; Accordingly, the rules established by the Civil Code apply to it concerning the terms of conclusion and execution of the contract. The electronic contract is verified by a trusted qualified electronic signature.

However, one important point should be noted here. The point is that in modern e-commerce, especially on well-known trading platforms (Amazon, Alibaba, eBay, Taobao, etc.), the concept of electronic contracts is perceived differently. An electronic contract is concluded on modern e-commerce platforms once the user registers on the platform and agrees to a consumer agreement. Accordingly, such consent does not require any credible qualified signature on the part of the consumer and is limited to the entry of user data and the consumer contribution through electronic action.

Therefore, I think that the reference of the law in this section to a qualified signature, on the one hand, is due to scrupulous observance of the requirements of the legislation (since other types of testimony are still not recognized by our legislation), and on the other hand, I think that once the law is enacted in practice, it will clearly show us the less practicality of this requirement and the need for legislators to certify an electronic contract with other simpler technologies. Requires the user to make any kind of trusted qualified signature and is limited to entering user data and consumer contributions through electronic action.

The next issue related to the electronic agreement is the contents of this agreement. The point is that e-commerce no longer uses standardized electronic contract forms and regulates these issues in a completely different way. As I mentioned above, it would be good if further development of e-commerce legislation introduces concepts such as "consumer agreement", which is more complex in its content than "electronic contract" and at the same time, the existence of industrious electronic agreements will not be necessary to grant the legal force of concluding an e-commerce transaction. Such definitions will make it more difficult to produce such disputes in court.

4 The Birth of the Georgian "E-commerce Law"

As we touch on the doctrinal issues of e-commerce law, it is important to explain that e-commerce law is one of the important fields of modern technology law. The industry has begun to evolve with the development of Internet consumer and trading platforms, and today covers issues such as domains, electronic agreements, digital signatures, and other issues.[4]

The main challenge of e-commerce law is that e-commerce exclusions and transactions are subject to the country's internal state law. Consequently, this leads to the main problem of regulation of electronic law—the absence of jurisdiction frameworks.

Common legal problems related to e-commerce include the following issues:

Concluding a contract. Common legal problems related to e-commerce include the following issues: concluding a contract. In e-commerce, contracts are regulated by domestic law or by the law of the country elected by an electronic agreement by the parties.[5]

Customer protection. E-commerce businesses are often connected to consumers, and many countries have consumer rights laws to protect consumer rights in online transactions. This may include disclosure requests, privacy protections, and the right to cancel purchases. In this regard, the Law on the Protection of Consumer Rights which is important in Georgia of March 29, 2022, is important.[6]

Intellectual Property Protection. In e-commerce law, special attention is paid to intellectual property law issues such as the protection of trademarks and trademarks, brands, patent rights to inventions, etc.

Data protection and privacy. E-commerce platforms process user data and must comply with data protection and privacy laws to protect users' personal information. In this regard, the new Law on Personal Data Protection adopted by the Parliament of Georgia on June 14, 2023, is important.

It is important to note that the legal landscape of e-commerce is constantly evolving. The main reason for this is that the rapid development of technology pushes the legislator to the need for new, more modern regulation, and this process is more like an endless marathon—technologies are much ahead of their legal regulatory capabilities.

---

[4] On e-commerce law issues, see Z. Gabisonia. Internet Law and Artificial Intelligence, Tb. 2022, p. 13. 217-333.

[5] See Z. Gabisonia. "Norms of Private International Law and Reservations in Consumer Agreements", German Journal of Comparative Law, N7/2020, pp. 10-11. 21-32 http://lawjournal.ge/2063-2/ (last viewing date 17.08.2023).

[6] See https://www.matsne.gov.ge/ka/document/view/5420598?publication=1 (last viewing date 19.08.2023).

5 The Principles of E-commerce Envisaged by the Association Agreement Between Georgia and the European Union

As it is known, between Georgia and the European Union, or rather, on the one hand, between Georgia, and on the other hand, the European Union and the European Atomic Energy Community and their member states adopted the Association Agreement (hereinafter referred to as the "Association Agreement"[7] or "DCFTA").

This agreement was preceded by long-standing negotiations between Georgia and the EU. In particular, preparations for the DCFTA negotiations began in 2009. The process of preparing for the commencement of negotiations to obtain a free trade agreement was based on the visit of the Commission services' fact-finding trade mission to Tbilisi on 13–14 October 2008. After the visit, in March 2009, the European Commission presented to the Government of Georgia recommendations on reforms to be implemented in various areas (EU Commission's Recommendations Regarding Georgia's Preparedness for the DCFTA Negotiations). According to the recommendations, the European Commission has allocated four priority areas to start negotiations: technical barriers in trade, sanitation, and phytosanitary measures (food safety), intellectual property rights, and competition.[8]

Part 6 of Chapter IV of the Association Agreement (Establishment, Service Trade, and E-commerce) is fully devoted to e-commerce issues. In particular, Article 127 (Goals and Principles) specifies that:

1. The parties recognize that e-commerce increases trade opportunities in many sectors, agreeing to promote the development of e-commerce, especially in matters arising from e-commerce by the provisions of this chapter.
2. The parties agree that the development of e-commerce should be compatible with international data protection standards to ensure the trust of e-commerce users.
3. The parties agree that electronic transactions should be treated as provision of services under paragraph 3 of this chapter (delivery of services outside the boundaries), which may not be the subject of a customs fee.

The Association Agreement obliges the parties to conduct dialogue with each other on the issues of e-commerce regulation. In particular, Article 128 (Cooperation on E-commerce) states that "(1) The parties shall conduct a dialogue on the regulation issues arising from e-commerce, which includes the following issues:

a. the recognition of certificates of electronic signatures issued to the public and the simplification of certification services outside the borders;

---

[7] See official texts of the agreement in Georgian: https://matsne.gov.ge/document/view/2496959?publication=0&fbclid=IwAR1XRk25y6RenzKTtCsp3P7FD

PQk9hPjw3CibyqWjz4xyPrHuEkUfpJMKeo; In English: https://eur-lex.europa.eu/legal-content/en/TXT/PDF/?uri=CELEX:22014A0830(02)fbclid=IwAR0tUVA1ziX7ZRT4dazE3fGE5vD3mZY9z UN-AG2wDR9oZ1dkYYnHL-00eL4 (last viewing date 23.08.2023).

[8] http://www.dcfta.gov.ge/ge/agreement (last viewing date 25.08.2023).

b. the responsibility of intermediary service providers for the transfer or storage of information;
c. the relation to arbitrary access to e-commerce communications;
d. consumer protection within the framework of e-commerce;
e. other issues related to the development of e-commerce.

(2) Cooperation may take the form of an exchange of information on the relevant legislation of the parties and its implementation on these issues.

Particularly interesting is the second paragraph of Chapter 6 of Chapter IV of the Association Agreement (Establishment, Service Trade, and E-commerce), which regulates the issues of "Intermediary Service Provider Responsibility". According to Article 129, "(1) The parties recognize that the services of intermediaries can be used by third parties for unlawful actions and intermediary service providers must be ensured to take measures specified in this subsection. (2) For Article 130 of this Agreement, a 'service provider' means a provider of transfer, routing, or connections for digital online communications, between two or multiple points defined by the user, with the data chosen by the user, without modifying the content. For Articles 131 and 132 of this Agreement, "Service Provider" means a provider or a means operator for online services or access to the network.

According to the agreement, if the services of the information community consist of information transmitted by the service recipient to the communication network, or the provision of access to the communication network, each party shall ensure that the service provider is not responsible for the transmitted information provided that the supplier:

a. does not initiate the transfer;
b. does not select the recipient of the transferred information;
c. does not select or alter the information transmitted (Art. 130, p. 1).

The transfer and availability of the information referred to in the first paragraph includes automatic, intermediate, and short-term storage of the transmitted information for the period necessary to carry out the transfer to the communication network provided that the information is not stored for longer than a reasonable period required for transmission (Art. 130, p. 2). This article shall not affect the ability of the court or administrative bodies to require the service provider by the legal system of the parties to terminate or prevent the violation (Art. 130, p. 3).

The development of the law was led by the obligation of the Interim Service Providers (ISPs) under the Deep and Comprehensive Free Trade Area Agreement with the European Union, the determination of their rights and obligations by the legislation of Georgia, and the actual situation in the country under which intermediate service providers are not protected from the obligation of general monitoring, which may at any moment be the absence of legislative regulation. They were put on a very heavy burden in the conditions. The following three articles of the Association Agreement are devoted to the issues of the responsibility of the intermediary service provider ("caching"[9] and "hosting"[10]) (Art. 131 and 132) and the absence of general monitoring obligation 11 (Art. 133). We will have a separate discussion on these issues below, so we will not stop here.

References

Gabisonia, Z. (2022). *Internet Law and Artificial Intelligence*, Tb.

Gabisonia, Z. (2020). Some issues of legal regulation of e-commerce. *Georgian-German Journal of Comparative Law, 6*, 111–123. 42–43, http://lawjournal.ge/6-2020/ (last viewing date 09.08.2023);

Gabisonia, Z. (2020). Norms of private international law and reservations in consumer agreements. *German Journal of Comparative Law, 7*, 10–11. 21–32. http://lawjournal.ge/2063-2/ (last viewing date 17.08.2023)

Explanatory card on the draft law of Georgia "On E-Commerce", https://parliament.ge/legislation/25495 (last viewing date 11.08.2023)

https://www.matsne.gov.ge/ka/document/view/5420598?publication=1 (last viewing date 19.08.2023)

http://www.dcfta.gov.ge/ge/agreement (last viewing date 25.08.2023).

[9] **Article 131. Responsibility of intermediary service providers: "Caching".**

1. If the services of the information community include the information provided by the service recipient in the communication network, each party shall ensure that the service providers are not responsible for automatic, intermediate and short-term storage of information if it is due only to one reason that the information provided to them at the request of other recipients of the service is effectively provided that:

a. the supplier does not change the information;

b. the supplier fulfills the conditions for access to information;

c. the supplier fulfills the information update rules that are widespread and used in production;

d. the supplier does not interfere with the legal use of technologies that are widely distributed and used in production to obtain data on the use of information; and.

e. The supplier shall take operational measures to delete the information stored by the supplier or terminate access to the information after it becomes known[23] that the information was removed from the network from the source of transmission or that access to it was terminated, or the court or administrative body requested the deletion or termination of access.

This article shall not affect the ability of a court or an administrative body to require a service provider to terminate or prevent violations by the legislation of the parties. See https://matsne.gov.ge/document/view/2496959?publication=0fbclid=IwAR1XRk25y6 RenzKTt Csp3P7FD PQk9hPjw3CibyqWjz4xyPrHuEkUfpJMKeo.

[10] **Article 132. Responsibility of intermediary service providers: "Hosting".**

1. If the services of the information community include the retention of the information provided by the service recipient, each party shall ensure that the service provider is not responsible for the information stored at the request of the service recipient on the condition that:

a. the supplier is not aware of the non-conundrum activity or information and is not informed of the facts or circumstances from which the service provider is not aware of the facts or circumstances from which Unlawful activity or information becomes clear; or.

b. if such information is received, the supplier acts operationally to delete or terminate access to the information;

Digitalization of Georgia's Banking Sector

Natia Kakhniashvili

Abstract Innovations and technologies in the XXI century and every industry is developing rapidly. In the wake of world globalization, new trends are spreading faster and it has become easier to spread information and exchange data. In fact, we find innovation intensively in technology, science and the financial sector in the financial sector, the innovations offered by companies are important, this is especially visible when it comes to online payments and managing financial operations. The Open Banking system has already been launched in Georgia, and thanks to it, the financial sector has moved to a completely new stage. Open banking is a unique, innovative experience for consumers in Georgia, and involves both sharing and access to information available in all banks. Within the framework of the open banking system, it becomes easier for users to carry out financial operations and transactions, as it makes the online payment system more flexible and allows businesses to save time and appear more professional and modern. It is important to communicate correctly with brands using modern technologies. In addition, such an innovative method helps startups that have just appeared on the market, and allows them to gain access to the financial data of customers even before the implementation of open banking regulations, and thus to improve their services and digital products. For startups, this means a lot of support and benefits. However, entering the digital world comes with its own set of challenges. This requires constant observation of new trends, updated services and strategies—online marketing, site optimization, speed and fluency. In order for the customer to be able to communicate with the business online without any restrictions and purchase a specific product or service from it, at least a proper payment system and banking services are required.

Keywords Financial sector · Bank · Innovations · Technologies · Digitalization

---

N. Kakhniashvili (✉)
Tbilisi State University, Tbilisi, Georgia
e-mail: Natia.kakhniashvili@tsu.ge

R. C. Geibel and S. Machavariani (eds.), *Digital Management to Shape the Future*,
Springer Proceedings in Business and Economics,
https://doi.org/10.1007/978-3-031-66517-2_23

1 Introduction

In the modern period, the banking sector is crucial, particularly to national economies. Since innovative products lower costs and create a stronger relationship with clients, banks are working to advance technology and stay up to date with emerging trends. The actions made by banks during the COVID-19 epidemic, which were aided by cutting-edge technologies, provide evidence for this claim (Gult & Taggart, 2020).

A wide range of services, including electronic financial transfers, ATMs and point-of-sale terminals, online and mobile banking, are provided by banks to their clientele. Cutting-edge technology enables the banking industry to consistently and excellently offer sophisticated services to a range of segments.

The goal of the study is to examine and evaluate contemporary banking technology and products, as well as to talk about how the Georgian financial system has adapted and introduced them. It is crucial to understand the effects that the use of digital, smart services has on the outcomes of the business's operations, as well as the primary obstacles and potential solutions. The purpose of the study is to determine the strong and weak areas, as well as the relevance of innovations launched globally for Georgian commercial banks. The relevance of the topic is determined by the relatively effective efforts that Georgia has made recently in terms of developing and implementing fintech and AI-related solutions.

1.1 Methodology

The research approach employs a combination of research methods. The work is based on qualitative research, for which summaries of published studies of investment companies, financial statements of auditing companies, and articles from Georgian and international journals about financial and supervisory technologies, artificial intelligence, data science, and digital services are provided.

New ideas are developed and generated in direct relation to digital technology. Regarding the banking sector, innovation is driving its growth. Its primary objectives are to raise the standard of banking services, expand the range of banking products, fortify delivery methods, boost long-term effectiveness, and raise the stability of the company. Given the aforementioned justifications, it is evident how crucial innovation is to the functioning of commercial banks. The following objective components emphasize the necessity of financial innovation.

Product differentiation is necessary in the context of global competition, and one of the keys to banks' success is their ability to introduce innovation in order to attain this goal. Banks now have higher standards for this procedure as a result. When a foreign bank intends to invest in the global financial market as a result of financial globalization, the banking system needs to be competitive in the stock market. Financial innovation is becoming more and more evident as the public's interest in financial services and products increases along with the emergence of a financial culture. (As of 2022, G. Tsutskiridze).

The experience of developed nations makes it evident that innovations are multi-faceted and can be grouped according to several criteria, such as the extent to which technological components have changed, the possibility for innovation, the caliber of the invention's introduction, and many more. For instance, China has a big market for financial technology. China has been successful in this regard primarily because a sizable portion of the populace uses technology regularly. The graphic displays the Internet user growth dynamics between 2008 and 2018. The user base is growing annually. This is a stimulus for the Chinese market to create the latest innovative services and products. It should also be noted that China is one of the leaders in the field of Internet payments. There is a trend of declining cash and more and more people are getting involved in mobile payments. Since 2014, more Chinese people have accessed the internet via mobile devices than computers. The number of mobile internet users in China increased steadily over the previous decade.China's internet population grew by 11 million in June 2023 compared to December 2022. Over one billion people had access to the internet in the country, resulting in a fast-growing mobile app market (https://www.statista.com/statistics/265140/number-of-internet-users-in-china/).

Because of globalization and technological advancement, businesses must embrace new technologies to become more efficient. These technologies are the outcome of scientific research and knowledge. It matters how the bank puts its ideas into practice and what tools it employs to make these ideas a reality.

Georgia now boasts a robust and successful competitive environment, mostly because of the appropriate legislation and adaptable National Bank regulatory procedures. The services and completed projects of Georgian fintech and AI startups should be taken into account.

Optio.Ai—Financial organizations can classify consumer transactions into distinct groups using a cloud-based solution. The startup's primary clientele includes fintech firms, people, banks, and other financial institutions. The World Bank collaborated with the Innovation and Technology Agency of Georgia to provide 100,000 GEL in startup funding. The company's product line is separated into four primary categories:

1. Optio Discovery—a platform that provides categorization and sorting of financial transactions.
2. Conversational Banking—a chatbot that provides remote services to representatives of financial institutions.
3. Optio Insight—study, analysis, and segmentation of consumers' spending behavior.
4. NLP—services related to natural language processing.

Optio.AI collaborates with the banking industry in Georgia. The company's services are used by three commercial banks. A prime example of a fintech company and commercial bank working together is the bot that Terra Bank is showcasing, Terra Botin, which was developed in conjunction with Optio.Ai. Certain financial services could be accessed remotely by Tera Bank customers. This was Georgia's first significant fintech company-commercial bank collaboration. Following that, the business began collaborating with other banks to implement fintech solutions.The company automates bank processes using machine learning and artificial intelligence tools. Since 2020, Optio.Ai has been cooperating with Bazisbank and introducing innovative approaches related to artificial intelligence. http://www.optio.ai (2023).

Pulsar.Ai The artificial intelligence-based services provided by are available to users. NLP is one of their key specialties. Natural language processing, voice message recognition, and text conversion (Speech to Text, Text to Speech Visual Recognition, and Verification) are among the services offered by the company. They also make chatbots, which are highly useful in today's Georgian financial industry. The business unveiled a platform where users may register and then design a bot that suits their requirements. The first business to develop a Georgian-language bot was Pulsar Ai. They developed the T bot, which was recognized internationally, for TBC Bank.

Quickcash.Ai is a fintech business based in Georgia that is developing a platform for alternative lending. Through the utilization of data from multiple different sources, the system they developed assesses each user's creditworthiness individually. Due to their lack of extensive and informative databases, Georgian microfinance institutions can greatly benefit from the aforementioned platform. The business now collaborates with a few financial institutions in Georgia and intends to expand globally. In addition, to test the algorithm, the company itself started lending to small and medium-sized companies. The process is fully automated and the customer is contacted only at the final stage when the contract is signed. https://qcash.ge (2023).

Plug and Pay—The business develops and oversees the payment networks required for online shopping. E-commerce has grown significantly in importance in the modern day as more and more individuals have access to the Internet. Large, medium, and small businesses, as well as individuals who sell their handcrafted goods, employ remote channels for product sales. In these conditions, it became very important to have a smooth, simple payment system. Plug and Pay system is used by the leading commercial banks of Georgia. https://plugandpay.ge (2023).

Raisin provides clients with a remote, entirely digital service. Electronic means are used for document dissemination of any kind. Customers can obtain European bank products through the company's platform without having to go far from their homes. The following is the work schedule:

1. The user opens an account on raisin.com, the company identifies the user by scanning the ID card and transferring the minimum amount to Raisin's account.
2. Then, the user selects a deposit product from one of the partner banks in Raisin's online banking system and fills out the online form.
3. After the expiration of the contractual period, the partner bank credits the invested amount and interest benefits.

In recent years, many fintech and artificial intelligence companies have been established in Georgia, and it is worth noting that their development rate is quite high.

For instance, the first-ever appearance of Neo Bank—Space in Georgia occurred in 2018. This is one of TBC Bank's creative endeavors. Space is a bank that offers every kind of service online. The user can always have a bank branch with him by installing a mobile application on any smartphone running the iOS or Android operating systems. It is not possible to create an account, add multiple bank cards, utilize the Space app as a digital wallet, or handle money round-the-clock for the user. Additionally, commission-free instantaneous money transfers between cards from other banks are possible.

The application was downloaded by over 600,000 people within a year of its release, with approximately 160,000 of those users creating accounts. This is the first time that account opening for approval, user authentication, and verification are all completed electronically. The user provides consent to share specific categories of information throughout the registration process. Personal information is then scanned using a passport or ID card. The application requests a selfie from the user and uses the ID card or passport to confirm the person's identification. The user can remotely open an account and receive a space plastic card via courier after completing a few more steps. The application's primary benefit is that users of several banks may manage all of their accounts from one location. Additionally, the fact that Space has access to a vast information base and can accurately determine creditworthiness thanks to open banking makes it simpler to obtain a loan. The Space piggy banks give users the chance to take part in accumulation initiatives. Space continues to grow and actively collaborates with Visa, a big global corporation, making use of its knowledge centers.

As there aren't many comparable, totally digital banks in the area, Space intends to make use of the fact that TBC Bank got a banking license in Uzbekistan in 2020.

The majority of Georgia's commercial banks offer Internet and mobile banking, which helps Georgia's financial industry become more digital and provides customers with more convenience and speed.

1.2 Results

A growing trend of development in Georgian commercial banks functioning in the direction of fintech, AI, and data science characterizes the current situation. Most commercial banks work on one-off, standalone initiatives with Georgian fintech businesses and get ancillary, supporting services in return. Customers will eventually be able to obtain complete banking services remotely thanks to the introduction of fintech solutions and the development of digital services. The aforementioned advancement in the field of financial technology development has a favorable effect on the outcomes of bank operations. The advancement of financial technologies directly and favorably impacts a commercial bank's financial metrics.

The development of digital services hastened the expansion of the loan portfolio, as demonstrated by the case of Georgia's two biggest banks. In 2014, they began creating digital services. We looked at the portfolio's yearly growth before and after

2014 to assess the dynamics. As mentioned in the financial statements, the total portfolio growth was 16% in 2013 (compared to the prior year), 25% in 2014 (when they started actively implementing digital services, based on the responses), and 38% in 2016 (compared to the prior year). In 2017 and 2018, the growth rate remained high at 17 and 21%, respectively. Thus, we can conclude that the bank's financial metrics are positively impacted by the advancement of financial technologies and direct digital services. Commercial banks prefer to outsource the development of financial technology and digital services, and they consistently look to fintech and artificial intelligence firms for assistance. Their primary collaboration with fintech companies occurs when the company's internal development of a certain direction is linked to a broader resource. Also, a large number of banks decide specific cases according to the scope and nature of the project (which depends on many factors, for example, how many qualified personnel they have for the implementation of a specific project, whether it is worth switching personnel for the mentioned work, etc.).

2 Conclusions and Recommendations

The degree of integration between technology and money is becoming more and more significant for the current world, according to the research that has been done.

The development of fintech, artificial intelligence, data science, and digital services is crucial for any nation. The global investments committed toward fintech attest to the significance of the aforementioned challenges. Modern technological advancements are spreading quickly throughout many industries, posing significant difficulties in both positive and negative ways. The benefits of digital technologies include increased communication speed, widespread information availability, increased productivity at the expense of less time, increased business opportunities and Data security concerns, an increasing reliance on digital technology, manipulation of digital media, social distancing, and adverse environmental effects are some of the drawbacks of digital technologies. it's also important to note that because the Internet has supplanted traditional services, there is no longer a direct channel of communication between customers and banks. This has a negative effect on certain customers since they believe that Internet-based services are less dependable and riskier because digital transactions are very risky. decreased employment opportunities (Nozadze, 2023).

It is noteworthy how crucial government engagement is to the advancement of fintech and AI; more Georgian companies should be permitted to grow, and greater emphasis should be placed on marketing initiatives.

To reduce the risks associated with fintech, artificial intelligence, and process digitization in general—personal data insecurity and cyber fraud—suitable supervisory standards must be in place. Fintech companies and other financial sector participants will be required to adhere to these standards.

More informational meetings with industry professionals from Georgia and the world's top information technology-producing nations should be organized in collaboration with the private sector. In this sector, sharing expertise and experience is crucial.

The development of digital services has a direct beneficial association with the financial outcomes of the organization, as demonstrated by the research. It is crucial that the business accurately assesses the money invested in fintech and AI development and determines that the costs incurred will result in significantly greater returns in the future.

The important problem is the deficiency of qualified personnel in the technological field. Companies must think about the development of this direction and care about the improvement of their staff, by financing the various types of masterclasses and training.

The experience gained in the financial sector allows the representatives of the modern banking sector to create and offer customized products to the market. (Kakhniashvili, 2021).

Ultimately, by heeding the aforementioned advice, players in the banking industry, fintech startups, and the public sector will be able to grow and develop the digital services market in tandem while staying abreast of contemporary developments. Stronger competition will result from this, which will benefit the nation's economy.

References

Tsutskiridze, G. (2022). *Banking management lecture cycle.*

Nozadze, M. (2023). *Digital revolution and its consequences.* PMO.

https://www.statista.com/statistics/265140/number-of-internet-users-in-china2023/

http://www.optio.ai (2023).

https://qcash.ge (2023).

https://plugandpay.ge (2023).

https://www.nbg.gov.ge/index.php?m=742

Kakhniashvili, N. (2021). *Optimization of lending system in the conditions of global pandemic in Georgia, XXX*. International scientific and practical conference, social and economic aspects of education in modern society (pp. 3–5). Fields of Science: Social Science and Economics, Company—Scholarly Publisher RS Global Sp. z O.O.Warsaw.https://doi.org/10.31435/rsglobal_conf/25062021

Gult & Taggart. (2020). *The impact of Covid 19 on the economy of Georgia.* Tbilisi.

MIX
Papier aus verantwortungsvollen Quellen
Paper from responsible sources
FSC® C105338

If you have any concerns about our products,
you can contact us on
ProductSafety@springernature.com

In case Publisher is established outside the EU,
the EU authorized representative is:
Springer Nature Customer Service Center GmbH
Europaplatz 3, 69115 Heidelberg, Germany

Printed by Libri Plureos GmbH
in Hamburg, Germany